Brian Masters ... n
subjects as d ...
dukedoms in ...
Marie Corelli. His groundbreaking study of mass
murderer Dennis Nilsen, *Killing for Company*,
won the Crime Writers' Association Gold
Dagger for Non-Fiction in 1985, and has been
made into the ITV drama, *Des*. He is also highly
regarded for his journalism.

www.penguin.co.uk

By Brian Masters

True Crime

SHE MUST HAVE KNOWN:
THE TRIAL OF ROSEMARY WEST

KILLING FOR COMPANY:
THE CASE OF DENNIS NILSEN

THE SHRINE OF JEFFREY DAHMER

THE EVIL THAT MEN DO

ON MURDER

MOLIERE

SARTRE, A STUDY

SAINT-EXUPERY

RABELAIS

CAMUS, A STUDY

WYNARD HALL AND
THE LONDONDERRY FAMILY

DREAMS ABOUT H.M. THE QUEEN

THE DUKES: THE ORIGINS, ENOBLEMENT
AND HISTORY OF 26 FAMILIES

NOW BARABBAS WAS A ROTTER:
THE EXTRAORDINARY LIFE OF MARIE CORELLI

THE MISTRESSES OF CHARLES II

GEORGIANA, DUCHESS OF DEVONSHIRE

GREAT HOSTESSES

THE SWINGING SIXTIES

THE PASSION OF JOHN ASPINALL

MAHARANA – THE UDAIPUR DYNASTY

GARY

THE LIFE OF E.F. BENSON

VOLTAIRE'S TREATISE ON TOLERANCE
(Edited and Translated)

THUNDER IN THE AIR:
GREAT ACTORS IN GREAT ROLES

SECOND THOUGHTS

GETTING PERSONAL (AUTOBIOGRPAHY)

'SHE MUST HAVE KNOWN'

Brian Masters

CORGI BOOKS

TRANSWORLD PUBLISHERS
Penguin Random House, One Embassy Gardens,
8 Viaduct Gardens, London SW11 7BW
www.penguin.co.uk

Transworld is part of the Penguin Random House group of companies
whose addresses can be found at global.penguinrandomhouse.com

Penguin
Random House
UK

First published in Great Britain in 1996 by Doubleday
an imprint of Transworld Publishers
Corgi edition published 1997
Corgi edition reissued 2020

A CIP catalogue record for this book
is available from the British Library.

ISBN
9780552178341

Typeset in Sabon by Falcon Oast Graphic Art Ltd.
Printed and bound in Great Britain by Clays Ltd, Elcograf S.p.A.

The authorized representative in the EEA is Penguin Random House Ireland,
Morrison Chambers, 32 Nassau Street, Dublin D02 YH68

Penguin Random House is committed to a sustainable
future for our business, our readers and our planet. This book
is made from Forest Stewardship Council® certified paper.

For
Juan Melian Macias

Contents

Foreword

When Frederick West was arrested on 25 February 1994, it was for the murder of his daughter Heather. Nobody then had the smallest suspicion that the remains of other young women would be found beneath the house where he had lived for twenty-two years and in which his wife had raised a family of eight children. As the allegations and charges multiplied, they appeared to point to a familiar pattern of lust murder, wherein a man with inadequate sexual powers but inordinate sexual appetite translates his frustrations into the most squalid sadistic brutality, forcing himself upon girls who cannot find him wanting and will not offer resistance because they are either trussed, immobilized and silenced or they are dead. Later, Rosemary West was also charged with all but two of the murders for which her husband was awaiting trial, and I assumed the evidence would relate to her compliance or acquiescence in his activities, presumably under duress. But on 1 January 1995, Frederick West committed suicide in his cell at HM Prison Winson Green, Birmingham, thus cheating the judicial process and preventing justice ever being achieved on behalf of the girls whose families had been hurled, for a second time, into their appalling grief.

For several weeks, it seemed as if the charges against Rosemary West would be dropped, there being insufficient evidence to warrant a trial. It was generally thought that, as an alleged accomplice, she could not be held to account for crimes the main perpetrator of which was himself dead and untriable. But it was not to be. Not only was she indicted on ten of the twelve charges

Frederick West would have faced, but the Crown was proposing that she was, in some instances, far more than an accomplice in joint venture; she had murdered alone, in the absence of her husband.

This book attempts to examine and evaluate the evidence which brought Mrs West to trial. It does so without the assistance of Rosemary West herself, who has declined to co-operate, and is therefore solely the responsibility of the author and represents his view and nobody else's.

I have assumed some knowledge of the case on the part of the reader, and therefore the first chapter plunges without preamble into one of the charges of murder. Anyone entirely new to it will discover the other charges, the background and the history, as they emerge gradually from a consideration of the legal and psychological implications which are thrown up by Chapter One, and they are in any event visited more than once as different aspects call for separate analysis.

Brian Masters
Castries, 1996

I
Charmaine

There was one moment in the trial above all others which was almost intolerably heart-rending. A full-face enlarged photograph of Charmaine West was beamed on to a screen on the wall between the witness-box and the press benches. Of those who died, this was the only likeness we, in the body of the court, saw (the jury, of course, saw photographs of them all). She was a dark-haired, dark-eyed, happy little girl of eight years, with an endearing broad smile which revealed that her two upper front teeth had not yet descended, leaving an amusing wide gap, of which she appeared to be delightfully unconscious. It was a picture full of life and vigour, light-heartedness and hope.

David Whittaker, the odontologist from University College, Cardiff, then superimposed over this photograph another, transparent image of the skull which was found twenty-three years later and which prosecution and defence accepted was that of Charmaine. It fitted exactly, the line of the jaw following precisely the fleshy photograph which we could still see behind. And there were the two front teeth, high in the bone, waiting to descend and fill the gap.

The demonstration was of crucial importance, for it helped indicate when Charmaine might have died. And if we knew when she died, we might have a better idea who could have killed her.

Charmaine's mother was Catherine Costello ('Rena'), Frederick West's first wife. Her father was an unknown Asian bus-driver. Rena had been pregnant with her when she met Fred, who did not seem to mind, although one of his other children later said that both he and Rena had wanted to abort the baby, 'but Charmaine was born anyway in March 1963'.[1] Fred and Rena had married four months before, in November 1962, but he was not with his wife when she gave birth, at the Alexander Hospital in Glasgow, so she gave the baby the name Mary.[2] Fred had appeared in time for the christening, however, at St Mary's Roman Catholic Church on 6 September, and that is when the name Charmaine first appears – Charmaine Carol Mary West. Thereafter she was often known as 'Char'.

Her beginnings were not auspicious. She was not wanted and she was in the way. Rena had always been anxious to escape the restrictions and glumness of Glasgow, but she had expected something rather more exciting than what she got. She had worked as a street prostitute in Glasgow at the age of sixteen, and at eighteen was a bus conductress, which is how she had met Charmaine's father, but shortly afterwards went south into England and found a job as a waitress at a café in Ledbury. There she met a man from the neighbouring village of Much Marcle, Frederick West, twenty-one years old, short but handsome in a rather *louche* kind of way, with dark curly hair, full lips, a yellow-tooth smile, and a touch of the gypsy in him. He was blunt and candid, a farmyard animal really, smelling of the fields in which he had been reared and, like a farmyard animal, frank about the mechanics of sexual reproduction. He liked to touch and to fornicate whenever the opportunity presented, and if it did not, he would manufacture it. Though barely literate, he was a ceaseless chatterer, dreamer, boaster. He promised Rena the earth. What she did not know was that Frederick West had already disgraced himself in the village where he lived by forcing sex upon a thirteen-year-old girl, for which he had been arrested for rape at the age of eighteen. He had also been accused of incest with his sister. He was plausible, charming, but dangerous.

The newly-weds and baby Charmaine went to live in the Bridgeton area of Glasgow, at 25 Savoy Street. Fred took a job as an ice-cream man, selling directly from a van which he rented from Walls. He was already known as a tireless worker, out with the van at all hours of the day and night, but there were whispers amongst the neighbours about his night activities. He could not really be selling ice-cream in the small hours of the morning, yet he was often not home until much later. He spent a lot of time alone on a plot of land which he guarded jealously for no apparent reason. And when he did come home he would often behave abominably to Rena, screaming at her, beating her around the head, being 'rough' with her (a word which will occur again at a significant point in this narrative, and at the trial). He demanded sex constantly, and when she gave herself to him, congress was complete within seconds, making her feel squalid. Sometimes he hurt her with excessive pinching, and tried to tie her up. He was possessive towards her, and at the same time encouraged her to flirt. It was a baffling mixture. Fred was altogether an alarming man, but Rena loved him. She sought solace with neighbours and girlfriends, one of whom was to come to grief as a result of this connection. Meanwhile, she gave birth to Fred's daughter Anne Marie on 6 July 1964.

For most of her life this girl would be known as Anna-Marie, although she now (1996) calls herself Anne Marie. At the very beginning Rena called her Hannah, writing to Daisy West (Fred's mother) that 'Hannah does nothing but cry day and night',[3] but the name did not stick. We shall henceforth keep to the name Anne Marie.

From the first Fred doted on her, and she was to grow up in the sure knowledge she was her father's favourite. Her evidence of just how far this favour went would paralyse a courtroom into disbelief thirty-one years later, but for the moment it is important to recognize the implications for Charmaine, who was immediately regarded as a nuisance. While Fred would unleash his temper upon Rena and Charmaine, still an infant, dragging them out of bed for a beating if necessary, he would always find excuses for Anne Marie.[4]

The next few years are wildly peripatetic, and it is difficult to keep track of the family's movements. Fred left Scotland at the end of 1965 and returned to Herefordshire leaving Rena and the children behind. He said he would get settled first, then send for her. He wrote and told her he had got a job (which was true) and found a lovely house (which was not), and that he would drive up to Scotland to fetch her. By this time Rena had two friends – Isa Thompson and Anne McFall – young girls who wanted to go with her for a better life, and perhaps earn better money. In addition to which, Anne confided to people that she was somewhat infatuated with Fred.

As Fred's new job was trimming and skinning hides in an abattoir, the van in which he came to fetch the girls was filthy and smelly, though he did not seem to notice. He collected Rena, the girls and Isa. Anne McFall was to make her way down a few days later. The fabulous new home turned out to be a scruffy caravan on a campsite adjacent to Fred's home village of Much Marcle. There were hundreds of trailers on the site and the quality of life was basic. Isa and Anne earned money by baby-sitting in other caravans, while Rena was being pressured by Fred to work as a prostitute, an idea which excited him for reasons other than financial.

During 1966 Frederick West moved three times, to three different caravan sites, and on some occasions was alone with the children. Rena and Anne McFall kept returning to Scotland, for reasons one can only surmise, and Isa went back once and for all. Each time Rena left, Fred asked the child care authorities to look after Charmaine and Anne Marie, because he had to keep his job and earn a living, and could not cope with them at the same time. They were placed with foster-parents for a few weeks in the summer of 1966. There was never any question of removing the children for their own safety.

14

On the contrary, whenever child care officers visited the caravan the little girls, though scruffy and obviously very poor, appeared to greet him with real affection. With what can now be seen as painful irony, they reported that Frederick West was the one stable, caring factor in the children's lives.

In 1967 Rena decided to run away, taking the children with her. She devised a plot whereby men friends from Glasgow would motor down and retrieve them, without Fred's knowledge, but Anne spilled the beans and told him. Fred intervened, furiously declaring that he would not part with the children.[5] So Rena went off without them again, probably thinking they would be safe in the care of Anne who, by this time, was carrying Fred's child and expecting to settle down to a happy marriage with him once things had been sorted out with Rena. Fred's account of what happened was rather different. When in Glasgow, he had accidentally run over a little boy with his ice-cream van. 'This little lad got to like it,' he said, 'and he come every day and I bought him a bright coloured ball, about that big, about four- or five-inch ball, and I gave it him the day before . . . and in this cul-de-sac they had hedges which was about three foot high.' He backed his van to park and heard 'one almighty bang and I stopped there and then and it was on top of his head and it was his head that had made the bang'.[6] The little boy died, and West was not charged as there was no dispute that it had been accidental, but, he said, the boy's family were after him and persuaded Rena's gang, the Skulls, to pursue him. Anne McFall, whom he had seen crying by the kerbside one day and had befriended, warned him what was happening, and permitted him to escape. She saved his life, he said. The three men who drove down from Glasgow were out to get him, and he had to hide from Rena.

Apart from the accident with the little boy, none of this was true. West had met Anne because she was a friend of Rena's; she had subsequently become his mistress. They hoped her baby would be born on his birthday, 29 September. 'You know, I spent more time, every minute I could with her,' he said, 'and most of the time combing her hair, you know . . . I mean I'd never had a relationship like that before, not with one girl that wanted me and nobody else.'[7]

Twenty-seven years later, police dug up her body in Fingerpost Field, Kempley. Beside the skeleton was a foetus in the seventh month of gestation. The baby had been conceived at the very spot where its remains were found, where Fred and Anne used to sit and watch badgers.

At the end of that year Rena was back with Fred and they made the fateful move to the Lakehouse Caravan site at Bishop's Cleeve near Cheltenham. Fateful, because there was living in Bishop's Cleeve a family called Letts, with seven children – three boys and four girls. The youngest of the girls was called Rosemary.

Frederick West met Rosemary Letts at a bus-stop in Cheltenham in 1969. They were both waiting for the same bus to Bishop's Cleeve and he engaged in conversation with her. As his children were to suggest when they were adult, he probably 'stalked' her there.[8] She resisted his advances at first, as she had had unhappy experiences with men already, despite being only fifteen years old. We now know she had been spoilt by her schizophrenic and otherwise terrifying father whose sexual attentions she did not, perhaps, altogether resist. But she was intrigued. Fred told her he was looking after his two little girls, who needed a mother's care, a confession which excited her interest, for she had always been maternal even as a child, and liked nothing better than to look after her two younger brothers.

Rena left again in October. The children were placed in care at their father's request, but returned shortly afterwards, for the Social Services reported a 'young woman' looking after the children in a very satisfactory manner. Rosemary said that she was appalled by their condition and immediately cleaned them up, and that she couldn't bear the idea of their being taken away yet again. 'I felt sorry for them because their mother was not there,' she said. 'I wanted to look after them.'⁹ Before the end of the year Rena had returned, and Rosemary was back with her parents, who locked her in her room to keep her away from Fred. They said, after meeting him once, that they were alarmed she should fall into his clutches. Soon after her sixteenth birthday she was living in Fred's caravan. Rena had gone.

In July 1970 the young couple (not yet married) moved into a ground-floor one-bedroom flat at 25 Midland Road, Gloucester. In October Rosemary gave birth to her first child with Fred, a girl whom they called Heather. Two adults and three infants were now sharing two rooms. Much would be made of these cramped conditions as constituting a hardship for Rose, who was herself not yet seventeen, but there was never any indication that she could not cope. On the contrary, the children were always clean and tidy, well turned-out and decent. Rose herself was, according to neighbours, smartly dressed as far as it was possible to be on the unskilled earnings of Fred, who turned over his entire pay-packet to her. Rose's mother noticed how the children had improved since the caravan days with their father.

She also noticed, however, that Fred continued to be gentle to the point of abject forgiveness with Anne Marie, and to be harsh with Charmaine. 'Fred cared more for Anne Marie than for Charmaine,' she said. 'Charmaine was a lovely, happy little girl, and Rose always seemed to make them look nice.'¹⁰ Neighbours agreed, and Anne Marie herself corroborated that Charmaine was frequently chastised, though more by Rosemary than by Fred. Rosemary used to smack her, she said, but she resolutely refused to cry, whereas she, Anne Marie, would burst into tears at the smallest provocation. This, of course, was because she had learnt, as children quickly do, that tears would bring Daddy to the rescue, whereas Charmaine had long ago realized that tears would get her nowhere. She knew, with that solid intuition which is a child's salvation, that her dad was her enemy, and nothing Rosemary could do would make amends for that truth. Besides, she didn't belong to Rosemary, and she would not oblige her by doing as she was told.

Charmaine started to say that she wanted to go and live with her real mother. There was never any dispute about this. It has been reported by Mrs Tyler (Rosemary's sister), Mrs Giles (the upstairs neighbour at 25 Midland Road), Anne Marie West, and Rosemary herself. It became common knowledge within the family that Charmaine was unhappy and that it would be much better for everyone concerned if a way could be found for her to live with Rena. 'I was perfectly willing to keep Char on,' said Rosemary, 'but if it was best for her to be with her mother, then I understood. She was resisting me, not eating, running away.'' Charmaine's best friend was Tracey, the daughter of Mrs Giles who lived upstairs. She retained a vivid memory of seeing Charmaine standing on a chair with her hands tied behind her back and Rosemary poised with a wooden spoon as if about to hit her. Char was treated in hospital in March for a puncture wound to her ankle. Yet Mrs Giles, who knew both Rosemary and Fred very well and was often chatting with Rosemary in her kitchen, frankly declared that she had never seen Rosemary hit the children.

In November 1970 Frederick West was imprisoned for dishonesty, and Rosemary had perforce to look after the three little girls by herself. A letter she wrote to him at this time was to be held against her by the prosecutors. In it, she said that she thought Char liked to be handled 'rough' – 'but, darling, why should I be the one to have to do it?' 'How rough is "rough", Mrs West?' was the tendentious question Brian Leveson QC posed for the Crown. Nobody thought to point out that the very fact she should make such a remark to her imprisoned husband indicated that, in normal circumstances, he had been the one to handle Charmaine in this way, and that now he was no longer there, she was not at all sure how she could take his place. She would surely not have had cause to plead why should she be the one to exact harsh discipline, had she been used to it and did not mind it.

Various dates in the summer of 1971 are at the core of the prosecution's case that Rosemary West murdered Charmaine. The photograph of the little girl displayed to such pitiful effect in court was taken on 29 April 1971. It had been posed for a house-to-house photographer seeking business, and Anne Marie was in the original, sitting beside her. Frederick West was certainly in prison at this time, which means Rosemary happily arranged for the girls to sit, and was proud of them and their appearance; in a household fraught with misery and grim reality she would not have welcomed the intrusion at all. There is a record that Rosemary took Anne Marie and Charmaine to visit Fred in prison on 7 May. Charmaine again appears on a school photograph at the beginning of June. School documents indicate that she had left by the end of term, 31 July, but are not specific about the last date of her actual attendance. Fred was released from prison on 24 June; at least, that is the date he stated in letters that he was looking forward to coming home. There is no actual documentary proof, however, that he was in custody fully up to that date. Rosemary had applied to visit with two children, aged seven and eight, on 15 June, and in the following week he was on a pre-release course. He may well have been let out immediately afterwards.

David Whittaker's dental examination of Charmaine's skull led him to conclude that it was only two to three months further advanced in development from the 29 April photograph, which would suggest she died between the end of June and the end of July. (To be scrupulous, he also said that death could have occurred almost immediately after the photograph, but that in his opinion a distance of 'not more probably than two to three months' was most likely; in any event we know that death did not occur immediately, because Charmaine was alive on 7 May, the beginning of June, and almost certainly 15 June.) The reason it is possible to be unusually precise is that there is continual eruption and movement within the gums at this age, thus permitting accurate measurement. Another odontologist, John Ritchie, who studied Whittaker's report, gave his opinion in a written statement that 'a lapse of at least four months, *and more probably six*, after 29 April 1971 prior to death is therefore indicated' [author's italics].[12] This places the child's death between the end of August and the end of October 1971. This second statement was not given in evidence, so the jury had only Whittaker's estimate to guide them, but even with that, it should have been obvious that there was a huge weight of probability, only just short of certainty, that the little girl died when Frederick was back at home. Added to which, they already knew that he had murdered Anne McFall four years earlier (this was one murder to which he did not confess, yet had, perversely, accurately shown police where to dig for her remains). They also learnt that he had possibly been responsible for another unsolved murder, unrelated to his domestic life, which I shall consider later.

Despite all this, the prosecution claimed that Rosemary killed Charmaine in a fit of anger in that tiny flat (in front of the other two children, one wonders?), dumped the body in the coal cellar (some traces of coal were found with her remains), and waited for Fred to come out of prison so he could dispose of the body. As counsel was to put it, 'Her wish to be rid of Charmaine had been granted.' This was the sheerest speculation, in opposition to the evidence rather than arising from it, and yet it was sufficiently persuasive, taken in tandem with the character of the defendant as presented before the court, for them to find her guilty as charged. She was, by the way, seventeen years old at the time of this murder, still a girl herself (the next-door neighbour testified she had assumed she was about fourteen), and not quite ten years older than Charmaine.

'It is impossible to date exactly when Charmaine vanished,' said Mr Leveson during his opening statement at the trial.[13] The Crown had therefore to discover ways of making it more possible, and their only help in this regard was the memory of Mrs Giles, the neighbour upstairs. Shirley Giles had moved away from Midland Road in January 1971, and had promised her daughter Tracey she would return for a visit so that the two friends could bid farewell to one another. She did so, only to discover Charmaine had already left, much to her daughter's dismay. Precisely when this visit took place was to prove a very awkward problem, for Mrs Giles maintained that she saw a little model caravan, made by Fred in prison out of matchsticks, and was so impressed that she wrote to him and asked him to make one for her. The letter is extant, though, infuriatingly, undated. Still, the fact that it exists shows that Fred received it, and if he received it, he must have been in prison at the time. It was a friendly communication. 'Dear Fred,' she wrote, 'I loved the caravan you made, it's really lovely. Please do one for me. Ron [her husband] says he will gladly pay for it.' Now, if Charmaine had already left, and Fred was still in custody, then the case against Rosemary looks, circumstantially at least, rather stronger. But the letter makes no mention of Charmaine at all, which is odd, if her departure had caused such surprise and distress. The lack of reference to her would seem to indicate rather that everything was normal at home and that nothing special regarding Char merited specific comment.

The problem remains, Mrs Giles was deeply confused about the date of this visit, not altogether surprisingly, as she was asked to recall a memory nearly a quarter of a century old. She gave three different versions, two in contradictory statements, and one in court. Richard Ferguson QC for the defence was keen to demonstrate that she had changed the date of the visit from September to March because the police had subtly requested that she do so, in order to concur with their theory. He reminded her that Rosemary had lent her Heather's baby clothes for her third daughter Claire who was born in August 1971. He also tore from Tracey, Mrs Giles' daughter, that she had been holding on to a pram, which could only have been used for Claire, and would again point to a date in September, long after Fred's release from custody. Yet Mrs Giles felt sure Rosemary was looking forward to his coming home. The caravan and the letter implied his continued imprisonment. The only reasonable explanation is that more than one visit took place (they were, after all, good friends, and Mrs Giles had not moved very far away), and it was at a later one that Charmaine's departure caused such unhappiness to little Tracey. Rosemary had more than once taken her family to visit the Gileses at their new home in Cinderford, but stopped doing so when Fred came out of prison, which would point to the necessity of Mrs Giles making the journey to Gloucester. The fact that Fred was not there at the time should cause no surprise, for he had to go out to work. Mrs Giles, though, could only recall one visit. So much turned upon evanescent uncertainties dredged up from dim and distant recollection.

Rosemary's own version of what happened is as follows. Charmaine grew more and more vocal in her demands to live with her real mother, whereas Anne Marie 'was quite settled. She wanted to stay with her dad, and she made that quite clear.' She admitted she was finding it a burden to deal with Char when she was disruptive, but 'I had nobody else to discipline the children. It was my job.' On one of her visits to Fred in prison Rose discussed with him Char's yearning to be back with Rena, and he agreed it might be a good idea.

He said he would 'sort it out' – a depressingly familiar phrase in this story and one that rings true, for Fred had his own way of sorting things out.

When he returned home, he told her that he had contacted Rena and that she had agreed to come to the house and pick Charmaine up. 'He advised me that I would be better off if I was not around, as his wife [Fred had not divorced Rena] would not be too pleased that I was looking after her children. I was too young to have anything to do with decisions like that. It was their past life.' Rena duly came, and Rosemary walked past her in the hall, without a word, to go to her mother's house in Bishop's Cleeve. 'I came back late in the evening, and Char had gone. Fred told me Rena had taken her back to Scotland. I was very happy about it', for the girl's sake, she said, as much as her own.[14]

It is worth pausing at this point to reconsider the evidence of Mrs Giles, who testified that plans had been made for Charmaine to return to her mother, which was why her daughter Tracey was so anxious to see her once more before she left. So the departure was a known impending event, not a surprise out of the blue. The Crown did not say as much, but their case implied that the murder was premeditated, that somehow Fred and Rose had discussed it, that she was to announce the girl was about to leave, but that she should kill her instead and Fred would tidy up when he got home. None of the other evidence supports this notion, which is at any rate inherently ridiculous. It is far more consonant with common sense that Fred said he would deal with the matter, that he did, and that he told Rosemary the girl had gone according to plan. There was no reason why Rosemary should disbelieve him.

Anne Marie, who was seven at the time, confirmed that Char had always wanted to be with her mum, adding that she had announced to her one day that her mum was going to come back for her and take her away. Even she knew of the plan in advance, and Char had herself been told of it. It was her father, she said, who told her that Char had left, and she felt 'that my sister would be happy now'. She did not say that her father was still in prison at the time, although the Crown attempted to elicit this information. In her original statement, read out at the committal proceedings in Dursley, she had not said that he was. It was perhaps a detail too precise to expect a little girl to recall.

Let us look a little closer at the correspondence between Fred and Rosemary during the former's imprisonment in early 1971. 'You can bring Char and Anna [Anne Marie] as it is an open prison,' Fred wrote. 'Please bring them with you darling.' The letters are full of endearments addressed to Rosemary and to the girls. 'You are my precious diamond never to be lost or hurt,' he told her. 'A star fell from Heaven right into my arms.' 'Give Heather a big cuddle, the biggest one you can . . . I know you have a hard life without me.' Rosemary made sure the girls wrote to him and enclosed their letters with her own. 'Thank Anna and Char for their letters,' he replied. She also sent photographs of them (probably the very ones taken on 29 April) which he put on his cell wall. With a mixture of affection and lust, Fred looked forward to his release when he would have fifty-two weeks in bed with her, and produce two sons ('I hope we don't have all girls'). There was mention between them of the son they anticipated, whom they had already decided would be called Stephen. 'The honour of having our son is yours, or there will be *no* son for me,' he wrote.

Rosemary was noticeably more domestic than lustful in her correspondence. While he appeared to count the days to their next session in bed, she was playing houses. 'When I get married I want to bring our girls to a home,' she wrote, 'one we can call our own . . . I've got a sewing-machine, I can do all the curtains and covers and so on.' She said how much she missed their tiffs and subsequent reconciliations when he would send a note to the kitchen with 'TEA' written on it, the passport to peace. She also mused upon how odd it was that anyone should care so much for her, not yet realizing, perhaps, the price she would have to pay.

Anne Marie gave her cause for concern, because she doted on her father so much that taking her to prison upset her when it was time to leave. 'It's not her fault you're inside,' she wrote, showing that she was able to place herself in Anne Marie's position and feel her chagrin. She was yet more perceptive. 'How is it you only know Anna's date of birth and not Char's and Heather's?' she asked in a moment of irritation. 'If you ask me your whole life is Anna.' And with words which would later assume real significance, she foresaw potential disaster: 'Remember darling you can't fall in love with your own daughter, nor spend the rest of your life with her. She's got to grow up and go away and be married just like the rest of us. I reckon that when you come home and there's something wrong that *she* don't like, you'll chuck me out.' This is a letter which identifies the insecurity of a young mother and presages the intensity of jealousy which would grow between her and Fred's pet. It seemed to bother her far more than the intransigence of Char, in whose position she also seemed able to place herself in order to comprehend it.

So what of the references to Charmaine in this correspondence? The 'rough' letter reads in part as follows:

> I think Charmaine likes to be handled rough but darling why do I have to be the one to do it? I would keep her for her own sake if it wasn't for the rest of the children. You can see Char coming out in Anna now and I hate it.

Fred wrote on 9 April, 'Now about Char, yes or no. I say yes but it is up to you darling, and then we can have our SON.' A month later he wrote, 'You say yes to Char. That's good. I will see to it when I get out but don't tell

25

her for you know what she's like, and you can have our son as soon as I come out.'[15] To claim that this means they are discussing whether or not to murder the little girl is, I submit, preposterous. Char is getting difficult, and is unhappy. She wants to go to her mother. Rosemary says she will 'keep her for her own sake', which means 'be a mother to her', not 'allow her to go on living', and when Fred says 'don't tell her for you know what she is like', he does not mean 'don't tell her that we're going to kill her', but 'don't tell her we're letting her go to her mum or she'll get impatient and even more awkward'. Besides, it was an easy matter for Fred to arrange – 'I will see to it when I get out.' Rena was a loyal writer of letters and he would know where to find her.

Fred explained that they wanted to avoid Rena so they could keep Charmaine with them. 'Rose come to me and say that Rena had been for Charmaine,' he said, 'and that what Rose said in her letter was whether she was gonna let Rena have her or not or whether we were going to dive off a bit quick before she come back . . . what I said to her was if Rena took Charmaine would it be all right with her, and for a while she didn't want to know, and then I said to her we will have a son of our own . . . what I didn't want her to do was to tell Charmaine so Charmaine goes and tells Rena that we move and Rena is sat there waiting for us.'[16] According to this version, they were prevented from moving anyway, because their gas and electricity had been cut off due to non-payment of bills.

Rosemary West's account, that Rena had collected her daughter after arrangements had been made by Fred, did not vary at any time. Her mother, her sister, her brother all corroborated the fact (her brother did not give evidence, but proffered his account in an interview with the press). Mrs Giles' first statement confirmed that Rosemary was waiting for Char's mother to turn up. Under lengthy interrogation by police in 1992, at the time of her arrest on other charges which were subsequently dropped, she said the same, and during the murder investigation of 1994. There was little here to foster serious doubts.

Frederick West's account, not given until twenty-three years later, was graphic and blunt. He said he took Rena and Char out of the house, either in his van or her Vauxhall car – he was vague and contradictory about this – and went with Rena to a pub where he proceeded to make her drunk. Charmaine, meanwhile, fell asleep in the back of the car, because she too had been given something to drink. He took Rena to a field, strangled her and buried her; he recalled the ground was hard, which pointed to high summer, probably July or August. Then he went back to the car where he found Char still sound asleep. 'I'd forgotten all about it,' he told police. 'There was Charmaine in the back of the car and I thought shit what am I going to do now. So anyway I strangled her while she was sleeping cos there's no way I could have touched her any other way and wrapped her up in the back and drove back to Midland Road.' He took the car into a big garage by the side of the house, of which he had the use, and from which he could gain entry to a big basement at the back, 'and I put her in there'. Years later, after he had moved to Cromwell Street, the landlord of Midland Road asked him to do some work on an extension. This was, he said, a perfect opportunity to rebury his stepdaughter's remains further down in the core. The police asked where they would find her body. 'You won't,' he said. 'Not without taking the building down, cos she's in the footings.' He added that he was worried about Rosemary finding out, because 'what's she gonna say?'[17] In a later gloss he added that he had made love to Rena before murdering her. He also said that Char's skeleton had been dug out by a bulldozer during the building work and taken away in a skip.[18]

The voice is authentically that of an addictive killer entirely indifferent to the emotional content of what he is saying, indeed incapable of understanding that there is an emotional content, although he may recognize that

27

other people do have such scruples and is able, when the occasion demands, to simulate them. Here, however, his only emotion is for himself – fear that his wife may learn what he has done.

The police were reluctant to credit the story, on the grounds that it would have been far simpler to murder Charmaine in the same field as Rena and bury her there. Why take the risk of discovery by bringing the body back to Midland Road? This is sensible, in a logical man with sequential thought, but it takes no account of the nature of a repetitive murderer whose central characteristic, as I hope to show, is a catastrophic lack of impulse control. It is perfectly in keeping with such a person's operative manner that he would act first and think afterwards. With Charmaine's body in the car, it would not have occurred to him to do anything but drive back home and deal with the matter there. He said after killing Rena he had cleaned himself up in a cattle-tank at the edge of the field and burnt her clothes; so he was all ready to go home when he spotted Charmaine and remembered he would have to see to her as well.

When Rena's remains were dug up, there was found with them a little red boomerang, obviously a child's toy. There was also a length of metal tube. The first clue, which Mr Ferguson would call in his final speech to the jury, that 'little silent boomerang', might well indicate that Rena and Charmaine were killed on the same day, that Charmaine's toy was hurled into her mother's grave. It is not conclusive, but it is difficult to imagine a different explanation for its presence. The second clue is yet more sinister.

As the trial will later demonstrate, it was Frederick West's belief that little girls should be 'broken in' by their fathers, and he would use metal objects to penetrate them before he attempted to do so himself, for, like many a sexual obsessive, he did not value his own abilities very highly. It is possible that he assaulted

Charmaine that day and her mother interfered and was killed for her pains. This would imply that Charmaine witnessed her mother's death and dismemberment. Now that Frederick West is dead, we shall never know whether his own bald account of what happened might need elaboration, but I would only ask the reader to bear this in mind as further truths relating to this man's behaviour are revealed.

There is also the matter of the 'signature'. Repetitive killers always operate in the same way, which makes it easier for investigators to identify them, or at least to determine that disparate murders were committed by the same man. Sometimes the signature lies in the sheer ferocity of the attack. Jack the Ripper was so-called because he eviscerated his victims – literally ripped out their intestines and placed them above the corpse's shoulder. His twentieth-century counterpart the Yorkshire Ripper (Peter Sutcliffe) similarly tore his prey apart with such savagery that some police officers could not bear to look upon the result. Jeffrey Dahmer in Milwaukee bored holes in the skulls of the young men he murdered with an automatic drill, then boiled them dry and kept them as souvenirs. He also liked to place his head on a man's stomach to listen to the music of the bowels. John Christie kept the pubic hairs of the women he killed in a matchbox. Rapists can often be identified by the manner in which they leave their semen, or the degree of comfort they paradoxically allow their victims. All fetishists are singled out from the crowd by the particular fixation which distorts their emotional or lustful responses to stimuli which would leave other people unmoved, and one may have a fetish (for blond hair, for pointed feet, for plastic raincoats, even for doughnuts) without ever harbouring murderous impulses. But just as these fetishes serve to distinguish their carriers from the rest, as their 'signature', so too is the murderer's signature, by way of his treatment of the victim either before or after death, a form of identity card.

Frederick West was no exception.

The remains of Charmaine were recovered from under the back kitchen at 25 Midland Road, beneath a layer of concrete, on 5 May 1994. Mr West had told excavators where to dig. When the pathologist Professor Bernard Knight came to examine the bones, he noticed that two thigh-bones were sticking up vertically, separate and at some distance from the main body, which appeared to be slumped in a sitting position. He was at a loss to explain how these bones could have moved through soil displacement after burial, and one was bound to wonder if their position indicated dismemberment. Furthermore, both of Charmaine's kneecaps were missing, and of a total possible seventy-six finger and toe joints, forty-seven were missing. They were simply not there, and must have been removed. The body had been naked when placed in the earth.

On 11 April Professor Knight had likewise attended the excavation of Rena West's remains at Letterbox Field. It was clear that dismemberment had taken place at the thighs and at the neck, and once again, thirty-five of the expected seventy-six toe- and finger-joints were missing. Rena's bones had been jumbled up in a horrid mess, deeply insulting to the reverence one normally feels for mortal remains, and mingled with them were the piece of metal tubing and the child's boomerang, lodged at the base of the skull.

Anne McFall's remains were found at Fingerpost Field on 7 June 1994, at a spot indicated by Frederick West. Her legs had been removed at the hip. She had been decapitated. Thirty-six of her finger- and toe-bones had gone, as had her kneecaps. It is already possible to see emerging the characteristic, if rather macabre, 'signature' of this murderer, written in the routine dismemberment, the affectless, offensive burial, and the missing bones. While it has been noticed that kneecaps can become mobile in the grave area, once the tendons and ligaments which hold them in place have rotted away, they do not disappear altogether, except when the whole skeleton disappears, as eventually it must, perhaps after centuries. But it is normally the smallest and most fragile bones which will disappear first. The seven-month-old foetus that Anne McFall was carrying was still recoverable nearly thirty years later, despite the fact that its bones would have been extremely pliable, fragile and destructible. There is no reason why these tiny bones should survive while others, stronger and in better condition, should have disintegrated. It is simply not possible. The missing bones were removed.

Professor Knight told the court that fingers and toes were quite easy to remove, and that kneecaps did not present much difficulty, providing one had a sharp knife.

Yet another element of the killer's 'signature' was observable with the remains of Anne McFall, although its significance does not become clear until the later murders are set in comparison with it. Anne's wrists had been held by some kind of cord, like a dressing-gown cord, or rope. It was long and intertwined, and may have been used for purposes of restraint. It is not easy, let us say, to posit an alternative explanation. Remember, too, that she died in the late summer of 1967, when Rosemary Letts was a thirteen-year-old girl. Certainly the police recognized the 'signature' very early on. The fact that these and all subsequent victims were buried in a small hole, were dismembered and were naked, 'every single piece of information', said Detective Constable Harris, 'would indicate that one person must have had at least a part in all twelve', and Detective Constable Barnes added, 'The person that was responsible for Anne McFall is likely to be the person responsible for all of them.'[19] Detective Constable Morgan told West, 'There was a girl that even Rose had taken to, and that you wanted, yet you killed her because you'd got all worked up and you didn't know what you were doing half the time, do you remember you said that?', to which West replied, 'That's quite true.'[20]

Such clarity of view would dissipate when West committed suicide and could no longer be tried.

Frederick West was twenty-six, personable and charming, though not in any very subtle way. He did not seduce with wit, or generosity, or thoughtfulness and imagination, but rather bombarded with his flash, outgoing personality. One could not call it a technique, for that presupposes conscious attack; rather it was a habit. Fred had the habit of talking at his audience, an endless flow of talk, what is sometimes called the 'gift of the gab'. And like many a gabber, almost everything he said was untrue. He was a chronic, compulsive liar, a characteristic which, many years later, was to drive police officers frantic with frustration as they endeavoured to slice truth from fiction in his florid accounts. He lied to Rena. He lied to Anne McFall, telling her he had a mansion, or a thatched cottage for her, when all he could provide was a dirty, smelly cramped caravan. He lied to Mrs Letts with his story of owning hotels and the like. He lied to workmates with outrageous descriptions of road accidents he had witnessed. He lied to neighbours, his children, his employer, to whomever strolled into view. He would even approach strangers in the street and start telling them stories. This was not because West was deceitful in a properly wilful way, but because he was incapable of understanding that truth had an absolute meaning, independent of what he happened to be saying at any one time.

Akin to the man who suffers from Korsakov's Syndrome, Fred West could not prevent himself from making things up as he went along. The true Korsakovian is afflicted with a terrible disease which robs him of all identity and memory. He does not know who he is, and has no past, because he cannot remember further back than the beginning or the middle of the sentence he is engaged upon. He is obliged, condemned, to reinvent himself with every utterance, to create a personality and a past. One follows the other helter-skelter, none of them true, and none of them false either, in the sense of knowingly diverting from the truth, wittingly misleading the listener. He just doesn't know, and doesn't know what there is to know. I do not suggest that West was a Korsakovian, but his continuous myth-making and self-aggrandizement presented a sane parallel to one. Whereas the man with Korsakov's has a nervous disease, the man who invents in a seamless stream of conversation has a kind of personality disorder which, carefully examined, may be the prelude to something worse.

Fred West told tall stories, I suggest, because they were much more interesting than his own dreary life and his own paltry personality, and they were worth hearing. They tumbled over one another, Fred forgetting one as soon as he had embarked on the next. The reason for this compulsion was that he was gripped by a florid fantasy life which did more than merely compensate; it overwhelmed and suffocated dull, sweaty truth. And this is important because nearly all repetitive or addictive murderers, sometimes called 'serial killers', are fantasists of the most extreme kind, and murder erupts when they can no longer keep fantasy in its place as a story-teller. It is no surprise, then, that they are all chronic liars. Dozens of examples are available, but the most advanced was Kenneth Bianchi, one of a pair of lust murderers who terrorized Los Angeles in 1977 as the 'Hillside Stranglers'. At his trial Bianchi successfully bamboozled psychiatrists and (some) lawyers into thinking he had multiple personalities and suffered hallucinations. In fact, he was just very good at telling stories.

Fantasy may be benign, even helpful, and children learn to hone their imaginations by experimenting with it. Most adults hold on to fantasy of some kind or another in the safe knowledge that it is a mere game of the mind, an entertainment, and they tend to keep it very private. But West so lost his grip on reality that he believed what he was saying because he was saying it. This would be harmless enough if it were mere grandiosity, but West's fantasies were sexual, the most dangerous kind because they have to nudge at reality to keep themselves in trim, and may eventually cross the barrier into the real world where real people are swallowed up by them.

Fred West was a sexual obsessive. He thought about sex all day long, every day. Everyone agreed that his talk was ceaselessly smutty, that he wanted to know what people did sexually, when they last did it, and what they wanted to do next. He was fascinated by the sight of animals copulating, and could not resist touching, or 'groping', virtually every girl or woman who crossed his path. He fantasized that all women were nymphomaniacs, that they were 'begging for it', 'couldn't have enough of it', and, especially, couldn't have enough of him. When he engaged in sexual intercourse, kissing was not part of his repertoire; it was crude coupling, and over within minutes. His wife Rena said he was obsessed with sex, and Isa called him a weirdo. He was constantly unfaithful to Rena, because his drive to express his fantasies completely overwhelmed any sense of decorum or decency, and he assumed everyone else was like him. Later, he would fantasize that his wretched victims had enjoyed his attentions. While he and Rosemary were living at Midland Road, she went to hospital to give birth to her second daughter Mae, and came home earlier than expected, to find Fred in the bedroom of her next-door neighbour. When he came out of prison in 1971, he asked Rosemary what other men she had lain with, and was astonished by her assertion that she had been faithful. He told her that she should have as many men as she could, and made it clear she should do so because he wanted her to. Thus began a drama of corruption that was to endure all their married life, wherein she was made to prostitute herself in order that he might watch and listen. His sexual appetite was literally insatiable, incapable of being sated, and, it must be said, in time hers was to become so too.

West's satyriasis, fuelled by pornography, was paralleled

by a restlessness, a hyperactivity, which was abnormal. He could not sit still. Everyone called him a 'worka-holic', obsessively active. He was a man of the night, mysteriously out long after everyone else had retired to bed. In Scotland, when other ice-cream vans were brought back to the depot by eleven or twelve in the evening, his would be out until three or four the next morning. By contrast, his attention to personal hygiene was almost nil. He wore old clothes, had repellent eating habits, and stank of sweat and self-neglect. He was self-ish to a degree, wanting everything to serve his needs and desires of the moment. Everyone was answerable to him, and he required to have complete power over every house in which he lived. When he was thwarted, he could be ill-tempered, even brutal. His beatings of Rena were heard all over the caravan-site at Bishop's Cleeve.

West was a thief, again by obsession, out of compul-sion rather than need. He stole for pleasure, no matter what and no matter from whom. One of his brief prison sentences had been for petty theft, and in years to come he would filch from houses in which he worked as builder or decorator. He did not see why he should pay for anything if he could just as readily steal it, and would siphon petrol from other people's cars to avoid going to the petrol-station. He was known to steal bicycles not for gain, but for fun, and he would stare at the gutters in the road looking for things to pick up.

One further trait served to characterize this affable, gypsy-like line-spinner which assumed significance in the light of subsequent events. He was unduly fascinated by gadgets, things which would work, to the extent that they held far more interest for him than people who could feel. Necrophilic people – those who take delight in death and the deadness of things – are typically en-amoured of objects and how they function. They like to take them to pieces and put them together again, rig up contraptions, tinker with their cars. Biophilic persons, on the other hand, give time to life-enhancing purposes, such as looking after children, creating objects of comfort, making love rather than having sex. Jeffrey Dahmer might feel the body of an animal in his arms, but he was feeling the contours of its bones and was indifferent to the affection it might bestow. He later enjoyed dissecting their dead bodies, and would graduate to doing the same with human beings. Frederick West saw women as objects to be penetrated, receptacles for his lust. He went so far as to boast to somebody that he knew how to perform abortions, and had manufactured a gadget for the purpose. This may well have been another of his lies, but it was interesting that he should see the female vagina as an object which invited interference. The necrophile objectifies, petrifies, every manifestation of life.

At the age of eighteen Fred had suffered a severe accident on his motorbike and had lain unconscious for eight hours before he was discovered and taken to hospital, where he remained for a week. A severe head injury had left him in an almost catatonic state, and thereafter his brothers noticed a change in his personality, a shortness of temper and swing of mood which had not been detected before. There are scores of examples of serial killers who have suffered head injuries which damaged their pre-frontal lobes, where scientists suspect there resides the seat of inhibition, preventing violent responses to frustration or resistance. Perhaps West's descent into pathological killing can be traced in part to that accident. But his obsession with sex, which is its real source, was manifest before the accident.

This, then, was the man whom Rosemary Letts encountered at a bus-stop in Cheltenham and who was to dominate her life. Barely educated (a 1951 report had listed him as 'retarded'), rough, obsessive, violent and sexually rapacious, he was a perpetual pubescent, a man arrested at that moment of development when the world is unfathomable unless it exists for his pleasure, before that time when the glorious mutuality of human life is revealed. His very immaturity was a danger.

Rosemary herself was working in a bread shop and giving her mother £3 a week for her keep. She was sexually experienced, having lived for short periods with an older man, been twice raped by strangers in a park, and possibly molested by her mad father, a tyrant and a schizophrenic who terrified all her brothers and sisters but was not so harsh with Rosemary. Bill Letts ruled by fear, but his favourite Rosemary was spared his worst excesses. There is a parallel here, for Fred was said to be his mother's favourite, and may have been broken in by her when he was twelve years old. Indeed, it may well be that incest was such a common and unremarkable event that both Fred and Rosemary would have thought its avoidance rather odd. The possibility of incest as the central dynamic in this terrible story will be considered in a later chapter.

Rosemary was prettily, even prissily dressed, not just like the schoolgirl that she was, but the schoolgirl she had been a few years earlier. She seemed to want to look like a little girl in a frock and with white socks. She seemed reluctant to grow up, in fact. Her black hair hung in loose, long curls to beneath her shoulders, and her dark eyes shone enticingly from a glowing face. She was exactly the type to excite the paederastic Frederick West. Her mother said she was 'very babyish in her ways, still a child herself, really.'

Indeed, children had always been her greatest source of pleasure. She had spent her time with her younger brothers, Graham and Gordon, rather than with the four older siblings, because she manifestly enjoyed looking after them, taking them to the shops, giving them treats, 'playing mum' in fact. She used to stand Gordon in the kitchen sink to wash him. The maternal features of her character were discernible very early. It is not only she who affirms that what attracted her to Fred West was his two little girls. 'I loved them straight away,' she said. 'I felt sorry for them and wanted to look after them. It was his children that really interested me, I suppose, more

37

than him.' This was the only moment during her evidence that she smiled. Her mother said, 'I thought it was the children who attracted her. She adored small children. She never actually said that she loved him.'[21] The similarity of this testimony cannot but be genuine; the two women had not conferred or spoken to each other for about eight years.

She was better educated than he, in so far as she could read and write with ease, and was to read with pleasure in later life, whereas Fred rarely looked at a book. But she made no particular mark at school, was neither very good nor very bad. Her school reports tended, however, to the positive. Rosemary was 'a cheerful pleasant girl who deserves every encouragement', 'a keen, steady pupil, shows much promise', 'always co-operative and helpful, rather unsure of herself', 'finds school work difficult . . . *talks* far too much'. She shone only in needlework, and earned the nickname 'Dozy Rosie' from her brothers and sisters because she seemed to drift through the day in a dream, locked into permanent reverie, only coming to life when she was required to look after the youngsters. She once wore a dunce's cap and stood in the corner. A schoolfriend said, 'She was the kind of girl about whom you have to think hard to remember.'[22] This is precisely the cocktail of apparent infantile gormlessness and physical maturity which made her attractive to men and accounted for Fred's persistence (he had to invite her out three times before she accepted). She was exactly what he wanted.

Rosemary cleaned up the caravan for him, but later told her children she had been irritated to find different girls, some of whom she recognized from school, calling to see him.[23] Perhaps that was why she agreed to become intimate with him, in order to keep him. She could also look after the little girls without risk of losing them to somebody else. She had heard how often their mother deserted them, but not that Rena's frequent escapes had been from Fred's brutality. Or perhaps having a sexual encounter with this man was neither here nor there. But once he had started on his promises and pictures of future comfort and bliss, she was hooked. Her own family life had recently been broken by her mother's and younger brothers' escape from their father. Rosemary had gone with them to her older sister's house, and was then simply left there. 'I came back one day after work, and Mum and my brothers were not there. They'd moved on and abandoned me.' Her voice trembled as she said this. Though the volatile household had reassembled after a fashion since this episode, Rosemary no longer felt secure. She wanted to get out. Frederick West offered the opportunity.

All accounts concur that Bill and Daisy Letts were shocked at Rosemary's choice. They thought Fred was a ne'er-do-well, beneath what even their working-class standards required, and they forbade her to see him. She disobeyed, so they asked the Social Services to take her into care as being beyond their control. Perhaps they intuited that life with this man would end up in prostitution – he obviously had no values to which they could relate. When she turned sixteen in November 1969 she could be held no longer, so her parents threatened that if she continued to visit West, they would sever all contact with her.

It is then that the account becomes confused, for Rosemary claims she fell pregnant by Fred and told her parents before Christmas, whereupon they locked her in her room for two weeks and arranged for the baby to be aborted. An ambulance was even summoned, but Rosemary escaped to join Fred once and for all. But her first child Heather was not born until 17 October 1970, making it impossible that she was carrying her eleven months previously. Perhaps Heather was her second pregnancy, but in the absence of any evidence, we must assume she mixed up the months in her recollection, and that the court did not see fit to correct her.

Both the Wests separately recalled the day they started

39

life together. Rosemary said she had a tearful farewell with her little brothers Gordon and Graham, who had accompanied her to the bus-stop, and having met Fred, walked with him to a five-bar gate by a field, which she found romantic (she always, by the way, preferred country life, and years later cherished a vain hope they would one day leave Gloucester for good). Fred's recollection is as follows: 'We stood at that gate and something happened to us both, we crashed into each other and just locked so solid in each other's mind, it was just unreal I mean. Rose knew that something had happened at that gate and so did I but we weren't a hundred per cent sure what had gone on, and from that time we have absolutely been locked into each other.'[24]

The move to 25 Midland Road and the departure (as we now know, the death) of Charmaine took place in 1971. One of Rosemary's letters to Fred in prison that summer, dated 22 May 1971, stated, 'We've got a lot of things to do darling in the next couple of years. And we'll do it just loving each other.' She also told him that she wanted to hear everything there was to tell about his relationship with Rena. By now, it is clear, she was looking forward to a future. In the light of subsequent events, both these remarks have assumed a sinister echo. The first is meant to indicate that she and Fred were so besotted with one another that they would do everything henceforth together, as a team. As Mr Leveson would repeat often enough, they were 'in it together', and she was 'up to her neck in it'. Only when 'it' is known to be murder can the fairly innocent hope of happiness be misconstrued. If 'it' is simply, in Rosemary's view, a lifetime of being cherished and raising children, then the desire to do a lot in the next two years betokens adding to the family, getting on materially, moving house, establishing themselves properly, and is the sort of love-letter millions of young people exchange. As for the second wish, to know all about Rena, that has been interpreted as a macabre longing to be told how she was murdered,

40

whereas it could, and surely is, simply the desire of the lover to replace her predecessor by bringing her forth in conversation, thus precluding the former wife from having any hold over her man by means of shared and private memories. Again, anyone might demonstrate such curiosity.

Besides, Rena was probably still alive, if her supposed arrival to collect Charmaine took place in late summer that year.

The police challenged West with his assertion that he and Rose had been 'locked into' one another, which they thought might be interpreted as becoming accomplices in crime, to which he responded, 'We're not evilly locked together at all, I mean Rose might look a bit hard-faced and that but Rose is as soft as a kitten, and I mean I know that because I've lived with her for so long . . . I've been tempted over the years to tell Rose I must admit, but I never ever did, I always backed off it.'[25]

Frederick West and Rosemary Letts were finally married at Gloucester Register Office on 29 January 1972. He had been tinkering underneath a car half an hour earlier, and she had to beg him to take his overalls off for the ceremony. Apparently he found some money in the park on the way home, which paid for the marriage licence, and they celebrated with a drink at the pub. Within two days, he was suggesting she should sleep with other men. 'He nagged and nagged her to do it, so eventually she gave in . . . he used to grind her down, night after night.'[26] More than likely, her degradation as an available sexual encounter had probably started even before the marriage.

Their second daughter, Mae, was born on 1st June that year (she had been expected in May, hence the name May June West), and the landlord Mr Zygmunt proposed that the young family, now bursting out of the tiny flat, should move to a house he owned at Cromwell Street. It was much larger, with six rooms on three floors, a back garden with trees, and a dank, unused cellar. The water-table was so close to the foundations of the house that at high-tide the basements in the street flooded, and the windowless cellar at No 25 became as noisome as a cess-pit. The rest of the house was in a somewhat dilapidated condition. Fred was proud of his ability to turn his hand to anything, and would not regard the status of odd-job man to be inferior. On the contrary, he was too proud ever to ask a builder's assistance. Whatever had to be done to the house he would manage alone. Over the next years, there would be a constant sound of banging and sawing and nailing as Fred improved his new home.

In late summer Fred, Rosemary, Anne Marie, Heather and baby Mae moved in. Within months a young girl called Caroline Raine had joined them, ostensibly to help look after the baby for a wage of £3 a week, all-in. She didn't last long, however, and left. Towards the end of the year, in Tewkesbury, Caroline came across the Wests again as she was hitch-hiking home following a visit to her boyfriend. She accepted the lift they offered.

What then happened to Caroline, whose name today is Caroline Owens and to whom I shall refer as such, forms the base of the case against Rosemary West for the murder of seven young women who disappeared over the next few years and whose remains were eventually discovered under the basement or in the back yard. There being no evidence that Mrs West had anything to do with the deaths of these girls, victims of Frederick West, the evidence of her participation in an assault on Caroline Owens at the end of 1972 had to be introduced instead, and the jury invited to make a comparison. This is what lawyers call 'similar fact' evidence, which judges are usually reluctant to allow into the proceedings because it may confuse issues and risk convicting a defendant, not because he *is* guilty of the charge he faces, but because he *has been* guilty of other charges which he does not face.

This is what happened in the trial of Rosemary West.

We must first look at the principle of 'similar fact' evidence and see how and in what circumstances it may be introduced.

2

Similar Facts

It was Fred's idea to take in lodgers at 25 Cromwell Street. After all, there was room enough on the top floor and the revenue would be useful. Though they initially rented the house, they would soon negotiate a mortgage of £5,000 and Fred would need the extra money to pay it off. Rosemary did not like the idea. 'I didn't believe I was capable of taking on that sort of responsibility,' she said. Besides which, she was setting up home with her own family and naturally wanted the house to herself. But Fred dismissed her objections and, as usual, had his way.

The first lodgers were young men, barely out of adolescence, who wanted somewhere cheap and cheerful to live, where they would not have to provide exhaustive references and their loosely structured lifestyles would not be questioned. This was the era of caftans and beads, free love and flower power, centred on London but with ripples extending to provincial cities like Gloucester. Though they did not take much to the caftans in Gloucester, the philosophy of 'doing your own thing' with the help of LSD and marijuana held a strong enticement, and many of the first lodgers at Cromwell Street were much more keen on smoking dope than looking for work. Rosemary called them 'drop-outs'. Within a few months, there were six of them crowding into three spare rooms. 'They stripped the wallpaper', said Rosemary, 'and painted the walls in psychedelic colours, black and purple.'' She felt the home was intruded upon by these people, but Fred appeared to revel in it. He was often upstairs with them, though neither he nor Rosemary ever showed interest in drugs. They were, however, very interested in sex, and Fred would send Rosemary upstairs to go to bed with the boys while he listened, watched or simply imagined. She did as she was told, and was not altogether reluctant perhaps, despite the fact that she had a little girl, a toddler and a baby to look after. And she was still younger than the boys who lived upstairs.

Two of these, Ben Stanniland and Alan Davis, would eventually give evidence at the trial when they were on the verge of middle-age. Each testified that Mrs West crept into bed with him shortly after he moved in, and their recollections, though brief, helped to conjure a picture of free-and-easy life in an uncommonly tolerant and progressive household. It must have been intoxicating for young men whose libidos were never at rest, and they took advantage to bring girls back as often as they liked. Thus began the character of 25 Cromwell Street as a house to which, for one reason or another, many young girls found their way, or, to use Mr Stanniland's word, 'drifted'.

One of the first was Caroline Owens. She lived with her mother and stepfather in Cinderford, south of Gloucester, and used regularly to hitch-hike to Tewkesbury to visit her boyfriend, Tony Coates. In the autumn of 1972 she was seventeen years old, pretty and dark-haired. Thumbing for a lift back from Tewkesbury one evening, she was picked up by Mr and Mrs West in a small grey Ford Popular, and they offered to take her all the way to Cinderford, although the journey involved considerable extra mileage. Their inconsequential chat on the way was quickly manoeuvred on to personal matters, during which the Wests discovered that Caroline did not get on well with her stepfather and would quite like to leave home. They immediately suggested that she might come and live with them, free of charge, and in return for helping Rosemary look after the children she would be paid pocket-money of £3 a week. As she had always wanted to be a nanny, Caroline eagerly accepted the offer.

Quite properly, Mr and Mrs West went to visit Caroline's parents to reassure them she would be all right as part of their household, and they took the three little girls with them. She moved in without further ado, sharing a room with Anne Marie, then aged eight, and shortly thereafter she had sex with both Ben Stanniland and Alan Davis on the same night. She also took her boyfriend Tony to the house. There was something coarse about the atmosphere, however, which made her uncomfortable. Mr West talked about sex far too much – he seemed obsessed with the subject – and told her that Anne Marie had already lost her virginity as the result of an accident when the handlebar of her bicycle injured her. The truth, as we shall see, was much more sinister. Caroline also became aware that Mrs West was paying possibly too much attention to her, complimenting her on the niceness of her hair and walking into the bathroom when she was bathing. But it was Fred whom she recognized to be the malign influence in the house. 'He picked on Rose a bit,' she said. 'I tried to stick up for her, and he told me to mind my own business. I left because I didn't like Fred.'[2] Her residence at Cromwell Street had lasted one month.

On 6 December Caroline Owens was again hitch-hiking out of Tewkesbury when Fred and Rosemary West spotted her and offered her a lift. At least they were people she already knew. This time, however, the journey turned into something decidedly unpleasant. What precisely happened that night is open to some doubt. There are different accounts and interpretations based upon rusty memories. It is safe, therefore, to rely upon the only contemporary version that exists, which is a news item in the *Gloucester Citizen* dated 13 January 1973, with the headline 'City Pair Stripped and Assaulted Girl'. Caroline had made a complaint against Mr and Mrs West with the police, as a result of which the couple appeared before Gloucester City magistrates on charges of indecent assault and causing actual bodily harm and, on pleas of guilty, were both fined £25 on each count (a total of £100). 'We were asked by the prosecution not to put the girl in the stands,' said West, 'so we pleaded guilty.'³

According to the newspaper report, Fred drove the car that night into a dark lane near Mitcheldean, on the way to Cinderford, whereupon he and Rosemary began to undress Caroline. Fred then put some tape over her mouth before driving back to Cromwell Street, where he bundled her into the house and to their bedroom. Inspector William Kingscott, prosecuting, told the magistrates that Caroline was in fear of her life when Mr West produced a knife, but this was, in the event, used to remove the tape and no more. Mrs West made her a cup of tea. After that, her hands were tied behind her back and her mouth gagged again, this time with cotton wool. The Wests proceeded to behave indecently with her, then all three appeared to have fallen asleep. In the early hours of the morning, Caroline woke up and took a bath. Then she was tied up again and subjected to a renewed assault, followed by yet another cup of tea and the suggestion that she should return to live with them. (It later transpired that the children had said they missed her.) 'In desperation, she agreed,' said Inspector Kingscott. She left the house later in the afternoon of that day, bearing rope burns, bruises and grazes.

Appearing for the defence, Mr Conrad Sheward cast doubt on the allegation of a coercive element in the sexual encounter, despite the gagging and tying involved. 'It would have been very difficult if there had not been any passive co-operation,' he said. 'She made no attempt to call for assistance, the door was left unlocked throughout but she made no attempt to get away.' Mr Sheward made it clear that Caroline counted herself a friend of the Wests, whom she had continued to see since ceasing to be resident in the house (although he did not say how many times), and that she did not report the matter to the police until several days afterwards. The magistrates were evidently persuaded that Caroline was, to some extent at least, a party to what had occurred, as was reflected in the comparatively light fines they imposed and the lack of a custodial sentence. They could not have known that sexual licence at 25 Cromwell Street, involving tenants and visitors, was extravagant and rampant. The victim of the assault, however, did know this, because she had lived there and been part of it.

Caroline Owens did not appear in court. The details as reported in the press at the time were given by her in a written statement which has since been lost. It is therefore impossible to check it against her later version, given to the police, the *Sun* newspaper, and the court twenty-two years later. Snippets from Fred West's statement at the time had also been reported, to the effect that he had meant no harm and only produced a knife in order to cut away the tape from her mouth. (It is significant, by the way, that it was *he* who had applied the tape in the first place, not his wife.) Rosemary West's statement declared, 'I don't know why I did it. It just happened.'[4]

One other contemporary document exists. The police constable who arrested Mrs West on 9 December 1972, Kevin Price, came across his notebook in the attic of his home when he was about to move house. According to established custom, it would have been discarded long since. The notebook recorded that when Mrs West was accused, she said, 'Don't be fucking daft, what do you think I am?' And when PC Price said he would examine the car, she added, 'Please your bloody self.'[5] This at least demonstrated that Rosemary West used coarse language and lacked any innate respect towards police officers. It also showed she was not especially cunning, for in his search of the car the constable discovered a button from Caroline Owens' clothing. Thirdly, the outburst revealed that

Mrs West was prone to mendacity when cornered.

Following the arrest of Frederick West in February 1994, Caroline Owens was invited by police officers to reconstruct her statement of twenty-two years earlier, so she sat down to write out what she could remember. There were nine statements altogether, three of which (26 February 1994, 22 March 1994, 1 July 1994) were referred to in court. A fourth statement on 6 October 1994 was intended to clarify her relationship with the other lodgers, in other words to admit sexual contact. Between the first and second statements the involvement of the *Sun* newspaper and the nature of its interest in her forthcoming evidence was made manifest, and almost certainly helped to expand her memory; it was suggested in court that she withheld the most sensational page of her manuscript in order to extract a higher price from the editors.

Her testimony, delivered in a cool, considered manner which commanded belief, was graphic and repellent, involving a degree of gynaecological examination and sexual tampering. Mrs Owens averred that Rosemary West had initiated the attack, with fondling in the back of the car before they reached the house, and that Mr West had punched her on the mouth and knocked her out. Once they were at the house, 'what Mrs West did I had never come across before'. This involved cunnilingus amongst other things. Not only was Caroline seventeen at the time, but Rosemary was still only eighteen, almost her exact contemporary, and was pregnant with her third child. Mrs Owens further revealed that Fred had hit her several times between the legs with a leather belt, held behind his head and lashed down upon her with great force so that the buckle struck her, and that, when Rosemary had gone out of the room to make tea, Fred had raped her. She had not reported this in 1972 in order to avoid giving evidence, as the couple were going to plead guilty to other charges anyway. Besides, the intercourse was over in a matter of seconds and did not seem so important at the time.

She and Fred concurred that he got it over with quickly because he was afraid Rosemary would find out, another interesting illumination in view of subsequent allegations.

Rosemary West agreed, in her evidence, that she had fondled Caroline in the back of the car, because her husband had persuaded her that she was willing, although 'I didn't think she was that way inclined'. As soon as she showed resistance, she said, she stopped, and pleaded with Fred to stop as well. But Fred was evidently uncontrollable once his sexual curiosity had been aroused. Rose could remember little more of this incident, save that she knew Fred had got her into a great deal of trouble and she resolved never to let it happen again, because she had been 'terrified I would lose my family'. (This was, be it noted, Rosemary's first and only brush with the police at that point.) Apparently, it was she who had comforted Caroline when she had appeared upset, but even this she could not recall, when it would have been very much in her interest, on trial, to remember an act of kindness.

Frederick West in a separate interview confirmed this version of events. 'I was trying to get her on lesbian and see how she reacted,' he said. 'I mean it went wrong anyway . . . I would probably have took her back home and put her in bondage or something but I mean Rose just didn't want to know about it . . . that was the reason why the lady went home . . . it all ended when Rose backed off . . . once Rose touched her and she screamed then that was Rose finished . . . Rose had her untied as soon as we got in the house. And Rose sat on the bed with her for a long time talking to her.' As for the rape, he said, 'Well, she didn't do a lot about it, put it that way. I mean she could have screamed then and the whole house would have heard her.' (The size of the house, the number of its inhabitants, and the likelihood of concealing behaviour within those walls, was a matter which would receive a great deal of attention for other reasons, and it was interesting that the murderer himself should draw attention to it so early.) Later, 'Rose said what about some breakfast, so Rose went and got some breakfast for her and then her and Rose spent the rest of the day downstairs.'[6] Ben Stanniland, who had heard no cries for help, came across Caroline in the morning as she was busy hoovering the sitting-room, with Rosemary near by. She made no complaint. Later in the day, after she had left, he ran into her at the launderette. Again, she made no complaint, although Rosemary was no longer by her side and she could have spoken freely to a man roughly her own age who had been a friend and a lover. She agreed that she had played with the children in the hours she spent at the house before making her 'escape'.

Stanniland had observed no bruising on Caroline's face. Nor had her friend Doreen Bradley, to whom she first told the tale, before confessing to her mother. Nor did the doctors who examined her, despite the cruel infliction of blows with a buckle which drew no blood. She was given no medication. And in the weeks that followed, she was so little perturbed by the dangers of hitch-hiking that, as her own diary relates, she accepted rides from strangers on eight occasions.

The importance of Mrs Owens' story was not that it pointed to sexual assault, which had been admitted, but that it provided the Crown with a template or model on which to construct the final narratives of seven young women, about whose deaths nothing was known save what forensic evidence revealed in the state of their bones. They had all been restrained, tied or gagged in some way, and presumably tortured while so bound, and it was to be the Crown's case that, because Mrs West was present when Caroline had been assaulted, she must also have been present when those seven unfortunate girls met their ends. Crucial to this scenario was Mrs Owens' memory of a specific threat made by Frederick West (but missing from the 1973 report) that he would

51

let his black friends use her and then he would bury her under the paving-stones of Gloucester. But the reasoning which flowed from one fact to many guesses was not only flawed in several respects, but in the most central one, positively perverse.

Before arguing this point, which will involve an examination of what is meant by 'similar fact' evidence, there are grounds for suggesting that none of the evidence of assault against Caroline Owens, heard in 1973, should have been heard again to support charges against Rosemary West in 1995. It is a vital principle of the English system of justice that nobody should be prosecuted twice for the same offence. It is easy to see why. In a country less attached to freedom of the individual – under a totalitarian regime, for example – a determined government could harass one of its perceived enemies by repeated criminal prosecution until they 'got' him. In England, no-one would dream of attempting to prosecute a defendant for an offence for which he or she has already been tried, whether the result of that trial was acquittal or conviction. If such an attempt were made, the defence could enter a plea of *autrefois acquit* or *autrefois convict* which would effectively bar all proceedings on the count concerned. 'If the accused is charged with an offence which is identical in law and on the facts to one of which he has already been acquitted or convicted, then *autrefois* will bar any further proceedings on that charge.'[7] Even if the defence does not raise *autrefois*, the judge may do so on his own discretion and prevent evidence being heard.

The answer to which is, of course, that Mrs West was *not* charged a second time with indecent assault against Caroline Owens. This did not form one of the ten counts which she faced at her 1995 trial, and therefore she was not technically being tried for a crime in respect of which she had previously been convicted and fined. But a great deal of the evidence heard against her, occupying two days of intensive questioning and referred to repeatedly over a period of seven weeks by prosecution counsel Brian Leveson, was introduced *as if* she were being tried on that count, which did not figure in the indictment. The 1973 case was heard all over again, in detail, despite the fact that it was entirely irrelevant to any of the ten counts which Mrs West did face.

Even so, it was within the judge's powers of discretion to halt a line of prosecution if he felt that to allow it to continue would be unfair or oppressive to the accused in the light of previous proceedings. Mr Justice Mantell, trying Rosemary West in 1995, declined to exercise this power.

The purpose of the *autrefois* rule is to avoid double punishment. It was not avoided in the West case. In effect, once it was perceived that the total lack of evidence against the accused in respect of seven counts of murder would make it difficult for her to be punished for them, it would have to be arranged for her to be punished a second time for the assault against Caroline Owens, and much more severely than before. The one would stand in place of the others. To achieve this, the Crown would need to argue by analogy.

We have already seen that for the count relating to the death of Charmaine, the prosecution had to rely upon motive and opportunity as their main planks, both of which I have tried to show were inadequate with regard to Rosemary West, and tended rather to point towards Frederick West. The same arguments of motive and opportunity would be alleged later in the indictment with regard to the deaths of Shirley Ann Robinson and Heather West. It is with the seven counts in between that a different tactic had to be employed. These counts were murders as follows:

– Lynda Gough, 19, some time after 1 April 1973.
– Carol Cooper, 15, some time after 9 November 1973.
– Lucy Partington, 21, some time after 27 December 1973.

– Thérèse Siegenthaler, 21, some time after 13 April 1974.

– Shirley Hubbard, 15, some time after 13 November 1974.

– Juanita Mott, 18, some time after 10 April 1975.

– Alison Chambers, 17, some time after 1 August 1979.

Lynda Gough had briefly stayed at 25 Cromwell Street, and had been the lover of one of the boys resident on the top floor. She had therefore come into contact with Mrs West. As for the other six, there is no record that any one of them had ever been to Cromwell Street alive or that the defendant had ever met them. (A tenuous clue lies in a letter from Alison to her mother, claiming to be living with a family of five children and an older girl her own age, but the letter was posted hundreds of miles away in Northampton.) There was, in fact, no connection whatever between six of the victims and the accused, save that their skeletal remains were all found at the house where the accused had lived with her husband and family at the time of their disappearance, and where she continued to live. On the other hand, the seven sets of remains had much in common each with the others. The bones of these young women, silent for so many years, once discovered were suddenly ferociously eloquent. As Mr Leveson said in his opening address to the court, they told a story 'more terrible than words can express'.

They had all been decapitated and dismembered, their legs cut off at the hips, their jumbled pieces then thrown or stuffed into a vertical hole in the ground and covered over. That they were not bones at the time of interment, but recognizable as parts of once-living people, and were none the less pressed into the earth in this manner, defeats the imagination. (The soil surrounding the bones was discoloured by rotted flesh.) Only an utterly unreachable psychopath would have been capable of such action. They all bore evidence of having been bound in some way, for in their haphazard graves were found ropes and cords, instruments of constraint, some still trussed up as they had been at the moment of death. Their skulls were wrapped with sticky tape, of the kind used to seal parcels (and similar to that which Frederick West had applied to the mouth of Caroline Owens), sometimes passing under the chin and round the head several times. In one instance, there protruded from the tape, at the level of the nostril, a plastic tube, indicating that the girl had been kept alive and able to breathe but otherwise rendered immobile, mute and helpless.

In all cases, a number of bones were missing from the fingers and feet and both kneecaps had been removed, recalling the 'signature' of the murderer of Anne McFall and Rena West, who had been similarly disgraced in death and whose remains were found where Fred West indicated they would be. The remains of Charmaine fitted the same pattern, and had again been disinterred where Mr West pointed. Furthermore, it was he who showed police officers where to dig under the cellar for five of the victims, and beneath the extension in what had once been the garden for the other two. Mysteriously, one girl was lacking a shoulder-blade, a disturbing circumstance which has received no viable explanation.

Photographs of these remains, and expert evidence of their condition, constituted evidence in the trial. Evidence is any information that can be put before a jury to assist them in understanding the facts in issue; therefore it must go to prove or disprove something, or, in the words of Lord Simon of Glaisdale, 'make the matter which requires proof more or less probable'.[8]

The remains of these girls proved the place of their interment and their dismemberment before it. They also tended to prove great suffering before death. But they could not show how the girls died, nor precisely when, nor where, nor at whose hands. They offered no clue as to whether there had been a witness or witnesses to the murders. They were therefore circumstantial evidence, pointing not directly towards the accused, but to circumstances from which a jury might infer the guilt of the accused. Evidence is not less important because it is circumstantial, and it would be wrong ever to refer to a case as being founded 'only' on circumstantial evidence. But it is in the nature of circumstantial evidence that there must be a lot of it, because one circumstance would be insufficient to impugn a defendant against whom there is no direct evidence whatever. It is the cumulative effect of several circumstances that carries weight, when 'the whole taken together may create a conclusion of guilt with as much certainty as human affairs can require or admit of'.[9]

It falls to the judge, then, to decide whether circumstantial evidence can be admitted for consideration by the jury. Obviously, the location and state of the remains found at 25 Cromwell Street were admissible as facts, but their link to the defendant was so disputable that other circumstances had to be introduced by the Crown, circumstances which would normally not be admitted. These were evidence of previous convictions, mentioned above, which is excluded because juries would be so influenced by it as to pre-judge the defendant; and evidence as to propensity, which means the defendant's disposition and behaviour on other occasions. Both tend to give rise to a feeling rather than a conviction of fact (if she did *that* once, then she can do *this* now; or if she is *that* sort of person, she is quite capable of *this* kind of act), and therefore the rule which prohibits them is 'one of the most deeply rooted and jealously guarded principles of our common law'.[10]

But for the Crown's case against Rosemary West, it was essential that these normally inadmissible circumstances be allowed in order to depict a wider picture of life at Cromwell Street, what lawyers call the *res gestae*, or the whole story leading up to the crime and not just the story of the crime itself. Without these elements, they would have had no case against her at all and would, presumably, have had to drop charges.

The two elements – previous conviction and propensity – are interlocked, for they both illustrate what is called the 'character' of the defendant, one by direct evidence of fact, the other by allusion and inference. Character in a court of law does not mean personality, as it might mean to a novelist or a bartender, indicating generosity, humour, candour, deceit, infidelity, or anything of that sort. A defendant is of 'good' character if he or she has no previous convictions for a criminal offence, and of 'bad' character if there is a history of such convictions, or indeed only one. If reference is made in trial to a previous conviction, it is the judge's duty to point out that this evidence is of limited significance only, in so far as it is relevant to the defendant's credibility (in demonstrating 'bad' rather than 'good' character), and not at all relevant to the defendant's guilt. In other words, a previous conviction is evidence of 'character' (in the limited judicial sense), but no evidence whatever of character, in the wider sense of everyday use. It is evidence of fact only from which no inference whatever should be drawn. Therefore, in cross-examining a defendant, counsel for the prosecution may only make reference to the previous conviction in order to establish that it took place, and to alert the jury to what plea was made on that occasion. He must not ask questions designed to show that the previous conviction makes it more likely the defendant committed the offences now charged. Arguably, this is precisely what Mr Leveson did at the trial of Rosemary West. As he questioned her and listed the torments suffered by the seven girls, he paused at the end of each one, turned from the defendant to the jury, and said, 'Just like Caroline Owens.'

There is a further provision to protect against prejudice in section 4(1) of the Rehabilitation of Offenders Act 1974, which directs that 'once a conviction is spent the rehabilitated person shall be treated in law as a person who has not been convicted or charged with the offence'.[11] When the conviction resulted in a fine, as it did in Mrs West's case in 1973, then the conviction is regarded as 'spent' five years later, i.e., in 1978, after which time she is a person without previous convictions. Although this Act does not specifically apply to evidence given in criminal proceedings, the Lord Chief Justice made a direction in 1975 that no reference should be made by judge or counsel to a spent conviction 'unless the interests of justice so require'.

Mr Justice Mantell evidently did consider that the interests of justice were at stake, for the spent conviction of Rosemary West formed, with his sanction, the main prop of the case against her throughout the seven weeks of her trial. Even so, as a previous conviction on charges substantially different to those at issue now, it was still inadequate by itself. It had to be bolstered by the second circumstantial element – that which went to propensity. It was necessary to suggest that the behaviour of Rosemary West with regard to Caroline Owens (and also, as we shall see later, with regard to witnesses Anne Marie Davis, Miss A and Kathryn Halliday), *and not just her spent conviction*, indicated her involvement in the deaths of seven young women. And for this to succeed, the doctrine of 'similar fact' had to be brought into play.

Broadly speaking, 'similar fact' allows these prohibitions (against previous conviction and propensity) to be overturned if the evidence introduced by such means is so powerful in proving guilt that it outweighs the prejudice which it must necessarily create. It is for the prosecution to demonstrate before the judge, in the absence of the jury, that the similar fact evidence possesses this overweaning power, which must go far beyond showing that the defendant has a propensity to commit the kind of offence charged, and it must be *in support of other evidence*. 'It is, in short, evidence which renders other evidence more probable.'[12] If there is no evidence apart

58

from the similar facts, then these similar facts cannot be allowed. There was indisputably no evidence to connect Rosemary West with six of the seven girls, and only the most fragile to connect her with the seventh. And yet this evidence, which amounts to informed guesswork, was permitted to be heard.

The similar facts were: a) that Caroline Owens was abducted by Mr and Mrs West while hitch-hiking, and it was assumed that the dead girls had also been abducted while hitch-hiking; b) that Caroline Owens had sticky tape applied to her face, as did all the girls whose bound skulls were found at Cromwell Street; c) that Mrs West was sexually attracted to Caroline, and it is assumed the girls who died were the objects of her lust. I shall deal with the responses to these later.

It is worth looking at the rules which permit similar fact evidence, and which have exercised appeal courts down the years. The starting-point is a ruling made by Lord Chancellor Herschel in an appeal by Mr and Mrs Makin against the Attorney-General for New South Wales in 1893. The Makins had been found guilty of murdering an infant boy whom they had taken to nurse for an agreed sum. The similar fact evidence against them related to other infants fostered for payment in the same way and subsequently buried by the Makins in their garden. It should immediately be clear that this was a far stronger case of 'similarity' than that which applied in the Rosemary West case. The evidence against the Makins was not just similar, but identical; the evidence against Mrs West was conjecture. Even in that past instance, Lord Herschel said it would be unfair to allow this evidence except when it helped determine whether the act committed was accidental or designed, or 'to rebut a defence which would otherwise be open to the accused'.[13]

The implications of this ruling have been thrashed out in detail on many occasions since, the most notable being when defendant Derrick Boardman, a headmaster convicted of buggery with a pupil, appealed in 1974 on the grounds that his conduct with other pupils, the subject of different charges, was allowed in as 'similar fact'. Among the Law Lords who gave weighty opinions on the matter were Lord Justice Orr, Lord Hailsham of St Marylebone, Lord Morris of Borth-y-Gest, Lord Cross of Chelsea, Lord Wilberforce and Lord Salmon.

Lord Justice Orr said that there was a crucial difference between inferring guilt from similar facts and inferring guilt from a series of similar *allegations*, which is arguably what the Crown successfully did in prosecuting Mrs West.

Lord Morris of Borth-y-Gest quoted Viscount Simon's 1952 ruling that 'occurrences which merely tended to deepen suspicion do not go to prove guilt' and went on to emphasize the doctrine of 'striking similarity' and particular patterns. According to this, the fact that the defendant Boardman more than once requested a boy to sodomize him pointed to 'striking similarity', which is perhaps a trifle naïve, as there cannot be many different patterns in which such an offence can be committed. 'I do not know what this means,' said Lord Wilberforce. 'All sexual activity has some form or other and the varieties are not unlimited.' As for the approaches to the boys, he said, 'I do not myself find them particularly striking,' and that the standard of 'striking similarity' risked being set too low. (It was on this occasion that Lord Hailsham made the observation that if Boardman had worn a Red Indian head-dress on each occasion, it might have been more worthy of note.) By the same token, 'bondage' is hardly a special technique employed by a specific defendant, but a commonplace of thousands of individuals who derive pleasure from such activity.

Lord Hailsham was characteristically trenchant. 'Similar fact evidence or evidence of bad character is not admissible for the purpose of leading to the conclusion that a person, from his criminal conduct or character, is likely to have committed the offence for which he is being held . . . no number of similar offences can connect a particular person with a particular crime . . . when there is nothing to connect the accused with a particular crime except bad character or similar crimes committed in the past, the probative value of the evidence is nil and the evidence is rejected on that ground . . . what is *not* to be admitted is a chain of reasoning and not necessarily a state of facts.' Since the connection made by Mr Leveson between Mrs West's conviction of sexual assault on Caroline Owens and her supposed involvement with the murder of the seven girls was precisely a chain of reasoning, *and nothing more*, it is to be wondered what would have happened to the case against her had Lord Hailsham been presiding.[14]

Of special relevance to the present case was a reflection made by Lord Cross. If two boys were to make accusations of homosexual approaches made to them by the same man, he said, no doubt the ordinary man in the street would tend to think there was 'probably something in it'. 'But it is just this instinctive reaction of the ordinary man which the general rule is intended to counter and I think that one needs to find very striking peculiarities common to the two stories to justify the admission of one to support the other.'[15] Once her husband had committed suicide and she was left alone to face charges, the general view of Mrs West was that 'she must have known', that it was impossible for her to have remained in ignorance of what her husband had been doing and that, therefore, she 'must have' been a party to it. Prosecuting counsel Brian Leveson was not embarrassed to open his cross-examination of the defendant with a bold echo of precisely this 'ordinary man's view' which had been expressed in uninformed conversation up and down the land, fuelled by many newspapers whose concern with truth and justice was not immediately manifest. There can scarcely have been a more potent illustration of why similar fact evidence should be treated with the utmost caution, and allowed before the jury only when it is so striking as to be irresistible. When it merely encourages the easy notion that 'there must be something in it', then it does not serve justice, but bows meekly to prejudice.

Although the Boardman case still offers the most comprehensive consideration of 'similar fact' principles, many lawyers today regard it as too restrictive, compelling juniors to spend days trawling through statements in search of similarities sufficiently 'striking' to pass the test. They prefer to rely upon the more recent House of Lords ruling known simply as *D.P.P. v. P* (1991), which stated that what mattered was what the fact proved, not how striking it was. There was, said Lord Chancellor Mackay, 'an infinite variety of circumstances' in which these similar facts could be useful, and 'no single manner' of assessing their probative value. It must 'in each case be a question of degree' in weighing their relevance against the prejudice they create. Which places each and every trial judge back where he began.

In 1665 at Bury St Edmunds two widows, Amy Duny and Rose Callender, stood trial on thirteen counts of witchcraft. None of the people they had allegedly bewitched could give evidence, some because they were dead, others because they were mere infants, two because they were in too deep a state of bewitchment to attend court. Three children did turn up, but were struck dumb until the end of the trial, so their contribution was limited. There being no evidence connected with the charges which the defendants faced, the court had to make do with stories that the two women had caused pigs and geese to drop dead, chimneys to topple over, and fish to slide from boats back into the sea. They did not call it 'similar fact' evidence in those days, but on the strength of it the two 'witches' were hanged.[16]

As junior counsel for the defence, Sasha Wass put it during the committal proceedings at Dursley (necessary to determine whether Mrs West should face trial) that the examples of inference against Rosemary West were 'attractive at first blush', which was precisely why they needed to be scrutinized with the greatest attention. Not only were they unsustained by the evidence, they were contradicted by it, she said. 'The Crown must not be allowed to indulge in detective work by advancing a theory unsupported by the evidence.' Miss Wass went on to maintain that for similar facts to be significant, something more than mere similarity must obtain – they must have a strong degree of probative force, which is to say they must not only suggest a link, but go a long way towards proving it. They must go well beyond simple suspicion that 'there must be something in it'. Furthermore, even if there were a sustainable link between murder on the one hand and, on the other, sexual proclivity as demonstrated by the 'similar fact' assault upon Caroline Owens, then it would point to Frederick West and not to Rosemary West.

A case in 1986 demonstrated clearly enough how and when evidence of similar facts may assist the pursuit of justice. A defendant called Butler was accused of raping two women. He had picked them up, on separate occasions, at a bus-stop, driven them to a place where he had obliged them to perform various sexual acts, then raped them. The prosecution was permitted to call an ex-girlfriend of the defendant to offer similar fact evidence to the effect that she had performed identical sexual acts with him in identical circumstances. This was held to have strong probative value, as indeed it did.[17]

The end-product of the defendant's conduct, both in respect of the charges he faced, and in respect of the similar fact evidence offered by the girlfriend, was sexual intercourse. That is why the two were allowed to be linked. The end-product of the abduction of seven young women whose remains were found at Cromwell Street was death preceded by sexual torture of an unnameable kind, which we can only guess at because the forensic evidence permitted no certain conclusions, whereas the end-product of the assault on Caroline Owens was lesbian activity, bondage applied by Frederick West and a quick rape by him in Mrs West's absence; and, ultimately, release. If this assault points to anything with which it could be compared, it would be lesbian conduct with regard to the defendant, and rape preceded by threatening behaviour by her late husband. It could not point to murder, because at no time was Mrs Owens' life in danger, and if it did, it would point to murder by Mr West.

Prosecuting counsel claimed these similar facts also pointed to propensity on the part of Mrs West. I have already shown that propensity would be insufficient cause to allow them in any event, but supposing propensity were enough, what would it be propensity for? For lesbian activity, for acquiescence in coercive sex, for abundant sexual appetite, and, as the magistrates found in 1973, for indecent assault (the actual bodily harm was Fred's doing, as Mrs Owens confirmed). There is not the slightest hint, however, of a propensity for murder. Therefore the evidence was misleading and prejudicial in the extreme. Its only purpose was to make the defendant appear an unattractive character.

It cannot be stated too often that a cardinal principle of the English judicial system is that a defendant is not required to prove his innocence. Lord Chancellor Sankey put it succinctly in the House of Lords in 1935. 'While the prosecution must prove the guilt of the prisoner,' he said, 'there is no burden laid on the prisoner to prove his innocence and it is sufficient for him to raise a doubt as to his guilt.'[18] In the last chapter, I endeavoured to show that a very serious doubt was raised as to Rosemary West's guilt of the murder of her husband's stepdaughter Charmaine West. Right until the jury came into court to return their first verdict, I was convinced that an acquittal was inevitable in law, and required by justice, because there was the strongest possible likelihood that Frederick West, already with a history of murder as a way of 'sorting out' a problem, had been released from custody by the time Charmaine was killed, and because

Rosemary West, at that point, was a teenage girl with no history of harm-infliction whatever. As it turned out, this doubt was not sufficient for the jury at Winchester Crown Court.

When it came to the deaths of Miss Hubbard, Miss Siegenthaler, Miss Mott, Miss Chambers, Miss Cooper and Miss Partington, the doubt raised was even stronger, namely that the defendant had met none of them and therefore was not present when they died. (The case of Lynda Gough was slightly different, and will be considered below.) This was Mrs West's defence on those counts, and in law she was not required to prove it; 'the only burden that is laid upon the accused', said Lord Devlin, 'is to collect from the evidence enough material to make it possible for a reasonable jury to acquit.'[19] The onus was entirely upon the prosecution to disprove this defence, and the only way they had of so doing was to invite speculation and imagined dramas by introducing details of a previous offence which was not 'similar' but different, which was spent, and which ought not have been admissible as evidence.

Additional material against the defendant would come from a witness identified only as 'Miss A', whose testimony was unreliable, and from Anne Marie Davis, daughter of Frederick and stepdaughter of Rosemary, whose evidence, once again, was at times irrelevant. We shall see later that Anne Marie painted a damaging and pitiful portrait of life in Cromwell Street, a life in which she had suffered terrible degradation at the hands of the father she adored, from the age of eight to the age of fifteen. She would quite properly excite the anguished sympathy of all who heard her in court, yet her evidence would have nothing whatever to do with murder, and would be introduced, once more, under the 'similar fact' rule that its impact as proof far outweighed its undoubted impact in engendering prejudice against the defendant. This time, the proof would be of incest by her father with, on two occasions out of scores, the acquiescence and encouragement of her stepmother. It would also be proof of foul and dishonourable disregard for a little girl's inherent dignity. There would be indications that Mrs West had a short temper and disciplined her children severely. There would, however, be no evidence of murder with any probative value at all, let alone value sufficient to balance the large amount of prejudice it created. Anne Marie's contribution to the trial of her stepmother would consist entirely in denigration of character, with no similar fact at all. Yet it was allowed before the jury, with the anticipated devastating effect.

As for Miss A, whose identity is protected by court order, she would give evidence of having been present at Cromwell Street when two other teenage girls, both naked, were tied down, gagged and sexually abused with instruments, by Mr and Mrs West acting together. She would then allege that she was subjected to the same treatment before going home. This was introduced as 'similar fact' with potentially far more probative value than that which pertained to Caroline Owens, for it appeared to demonstrate sexual torture by two people with joint and identical purpose, and it could therefore be used to validate the otherwise purely hypothetical notion of what might have happened to the seven dismembered girls before they died.

Unfortunately, Miss A's testimony was suspect. Counsel for the defence would elicit from her various admissions. At the age of fourteen she had been infatuated with Mrs West's brother Graham Letts and had run away with him to lead a fully consensual sexual life. When this went awry, she made false claims to be pregnant by him, going so far as to send him pictures of a baby she said was his. She claimed not to have known that Mrs West was Graham's sister when she went to Cromwell Street, and since, in an earlier statement to the police, she had declared that she had never been to Cromwell Street, and was now stating the reverse, with a vivid account of what she alleged happened at the

66

house, it was easy to doubt everything she said. It later transpired that she had been there more than once, and each time voluntarily.

Medical records showed that she had fantasized over a number of years, with many imagined pregnancies – some within the same year – and repeated hallucinations of seeing people with other people's heads on their shoulders. She had attended clinics to be treated for gonorrhoea regularly over a long period, indicating an active sexual life, and had been examined by psychiatrists who suspected a schizophrenic condition. She had mentioned the ordeal at Cromwell Street to no-one for almost twenty years, until the arrest of Frederick West in 1994. When she gave a history of her background to a psychiatrist, she made no mention of Mr and Mrs West who had, supposedly, been responsible for one of the most harrowing moments of her life. She did, however, mention the fact that her father had raped her when she was young, and that she had suffered additional sexual abuse from her brother. There might be, as counsel put it, plenty of harsh experience upon which this 'unfortunate young woman' could draw in order to give spurious substance to her fantasies.

If the evidence of one was doubtful, and of the other irrelevant, there remained only the certainty of the 1973 conviction for assault upon Caroline Owens to serve as a model for the seven murders about which we knew virtually nothing. And yet the parallels between that event and what was at least discernible from the forensic evidence of human remains pointed away from Rosemary West in every regard. First and most obvious was the fact that Mrs Owens was alive, which implied that the one occasion on which we were sure that Mrs West participated with her husband in sexual assault, the victim survived, from which one might well draw the inference that she could not have been present on the other seven occasions. Secondly, the restraining tape which was applied to Mrs Owens was applied by Frederick

West, and removed by Rosemary West, from which one might again draw a reasonable inference that she was not there to stop her husband when he bound the heads of victims before killing them. (Another minor incident that I have not mentioned, but which is relevant here, was when Fred had put handcuffs on a next-door neighbour at Midland Road in 1970, and Rose had remonstrated with him, saying, 'Get them off her!' On the other hand, Miss A claimed that Rose was the one to apply the tape.) Thirdly, Mrs West and Caroline spent hours after the event which was the subject of complaint, talking, attending to the children, cleaning the house, with no apparent fear or threat. The only threat which had been uttered came from Fred, and that, it seems, had not been taken seriously at the time, as Fred's chatter was notoriously fanciful and Caroline had heard plenty of it when she had been living there for a month.

For all these reasons, the inadmissible similar fact of the assault upon Caroline Owens was, even when admitted, a fact which tended to point to Mrs West's innocence.

Of the seven girls interred at Cromwell Street, the only one known to have any connection at all with Rosemary West was the first to disappear, Lynda Gough. Her story appears to wrap together the gruesome details of death and dismemberment with the less remarkable circumstances of life in a loose and libertine household. Lynda was the eldest daughter of a Gloucester fireman and had worked as a seamstress of the Co-op. She chafed somewhat at home, because she resented her parents' interference in her life. It was by no means an unhappy home, but Lynda was a young woman who wanted to make her own way. 'She didn't always accept advice,' said her gentle and decent mother on the witness-stand, ruefully. 'She started to rebel, like a lot of teenagers. They think they're clever, but really they're only just beginning their lives.'[20] Lynda met Ben Stanniland at a café, and he took her back to his lodgings on the top floor of 25 Cromwell

Street. For the next six months, she was a frequent visitor and had regular sexual encounters not only with Ben but with other boys living there. It was already a house to which youngsters came and went in their droves, often several a day, the landlord and landlady downstairs apparently paying very little attention to them.

A former boyfriend of one of the female tenants, Shaun Boyle, said the house was 'well known as a place where drifters and drop-outs and teenagers who had been kicked out of home could look for bedsits. You'd never question it if someone moved on.'[21] Anne Marie concurred. 'Sometimes people would stay a few days and then go, it was the normal circumstances we lived in. No-one questioned whether people stayed or left.'[22]

Rosemary West testified that she recalled bumping into Lynda on the stairs one day, outside the bathroom, and noticed her old-fashioned spectacles and hair which hung down in front of her face. As far as Rosemary was concerned, she was just another of the visitors. But Mrs Gough says that a woman called at her house one evening to take Lynda out, and that this woman was short, fat, with dark hair, and older than Lynda. Could this have been Mrs West? She was dark, she was five months pregnant with her son Stephen, and she might have looked older. At nineteen, she was in fact seven months younger than Lynda.

On 19 April, Lynda left a note for her parents telling them not to worry about her, she had left home and found a flat in the centre of town. It is supposed that she moved in with the Wests, but nobody can confirm this, and even her boyfriends there remember her solely as a visitor. The suggestion that the Wests asked her to look after the younger children, in the way they had captured Caroline Owens, is mere conjecture, though she appears to have told one of the lodgers that that was her intention. Mr and Mrs Gough never saw their daughter again. They assumed she would be back soon, as she could not earn enough to maintain a flat by herself, and had taken none of their suitcases with her.

Two weeks later, Mrs Gough, increasingly worried, started her own enquiries, which led her to Cromwell Street. She knocked at a house, which was answered by a lady whom she recognized as the one who had called for Lynda some time earlier. Her husband was with her. They told her that Lynda had left and gone to Weston-super-Mare. 'There was not a great deal of conversation forthcoming,' said Mrs Gough, 'I got no feedback from them. I noticed the woman was wearing Lynda's slippers, and there was some of her clothes on the washing-line. She said Lynda had left them behind. I remember it flashed through my mind that she wouldn't have had enough luggage to take everything with her. We were feeling very hurt, almost abandoned if you like, that Lynda went off and didn't keep in touch, although she had promised she would.'

It would have been tactless to question this ageing and warm-hearted woman about the kind of slippers her daughter had been used to wearing, and whether they were noticeably different from any other kind. Where had they been bought? What pattern or colour were they? How many thousands of pairs like them were in circulation? Mr Ferguson asked none of these questions, nor did he ask Mrs West if she could recall the slippers she wore one day in April twenty-two years earlier, an impossible feat of memory if she were innocent of any crime with respect to Lynda Gough. It was such a chaotic, disorganized house, with so many transients occupying its space, that any number of items may have been discarded. On the other hand, Mr Ferguson did point out that it was not possible to see the washing-line, which hung between trees at the back of the house on the left, from the front-door in the side alley on the right. I have been there, and can confirm this myself.

The boys upstairs noticed Lynda's absence. How she became involved in the events which led to her death it is impossible to say. Fred gave an obscenely fantastic version in his confession to police, obviously made up on the spur of the moment in his relentlessly inventive fashion, which it would serve no purpose to repeat here. It is certain, however, that she fell into his clutches somehow and died at his hands somewhere, eventually to be the first victim buried at the house. The manner of her burial bears some scrutiny.

Behind the back wall of the house was an inspection pit, of the sort used to examine the underside of motorcars. There had once been a garage on the site. Lynda's naked body was buried in this pit, to be excavated years later after a bathroom had been built over it during one of Frederick West's many building extensions. The pit was the size of a grave, and could have taken a full-length body quite comfortably, without the need for dismemberment. Yet Lynda's body was dismembered, several fingers and toes and wrist-bones were taken away, some cervical vertebrae were removed, and some chest bones. Her head was separate, and the legs had been dislocated at the hips. The kneecaps were not there. All this points already to the 'signature' of the killer, and this signature now appears, for the first time, to be compulsive and obsessive, as in the manner of a necrophile. For if the body was dismembered when it did not need to be, then it was done so for pleasure and gratification, as a lonely, masturbatory task by a severely deranged individual.

Furthermore, with a pregnant wife and three children in the house, and up to six lodgers (the precise number in April 1973 is uncertain, but even a lesser total would have had many visitors), it would have been impossible to undertake such a lengthy and messy dismemberment, and savour it to the full, on those very premises without risking discovery. It is more than likely (but admittedly speculative, with no more probative value than the evidence I have been questioning above) that Fred took Lynda somewhere, violated, tortured and killed her, chopped up her remains, and brought them back in the dead of night for interment as his property, his souvenir, in the grounds of his own house. We shall see later the crucial element of control which underlies this obsession.

And what of Rosemary West? Did she lie about only seeing Lynda once, on the stairs? And if so, why? Did she habitually lie rather than enter into embarrassing dialogue? Did she resent intrusion? Was she an obdurate, foul-mouthed woman who lived perpetually on the edge of enmity, picking fights with anyone who challenged her, and putting on discarded slippers as a token of her right to do as she pleased in her own house? Or did she know perfectly well what had happened to Lynda?

It is time to look at life in Cromwell Street and the characters of Mr and Mrs West a little more closely.

3

At Home

There was nothing whatever unusual to distinguish 25 Cromwell Street from any other end-of-terrace house, except the extraordinary number of its inhabitants. A lodger complained in 1975 to Gloucester City Council that the place was dreadfully overcrowded, and other lodgers were rehoused by the Council in 1981 on the same grounds.[1] An awful lot of people 'must have known' what was going on there.

The front door, down a passage by the side, was not well lit in the 1970s, but in the gloom there always seemed to be a lot of young girls gathering by the door, even late at night, leaving, entering or simply waiting and smoking. The whole of Cromwell Street was given over to tiny flats and bedsitting-rooms, for an ever-changing population, but No 25 had the reputation of being the best bargain in Gloucester. Lodging there cost as little as £5 a week, cash, and no questions asked. The extensive police investigation of 1994 succeeded in tracing one hundred and fifty people who had lived in the house at one time or another, some for a night or two, others for a protracted sojourn.

One of the tenants of longest duration was Elizabeth Brewer, a friend of Shirley Robinson who was to disappear in 1978. She lived there for four years, and declared, 'I would say that some of my years in Cromwell Street were among the happiest of my life . . . if you were someone who'd been on the road, someone who was a bit lost, it could be like a security. Many of us wanted to belong to this, an extended family.'[2]

73

The front door was still decorated with its original blue, white and orange panes of glass, and on the frame were two bells. The door opened on to a hall with, opposite, another door on the right leading to the cellar, and a staircase on the left, the banister painted in pale green, which went up three flights, with a landing and two rooms on each storey. In view of what would later be said about the size of the house and the secret activities which occurred within it, the central position of the staircase holds some significance, for it was fairly wide, and the landings were of a generous size, so that sound would carry up to all parts of the house very effectively.

When I examined the building, it was of course a shell, and a rather ghostly one, with echoes on the walls to offer but faint suggestion of what had once been a crowded ménage. The ground-floor room on the left had originally been Mrs West's special room, in which she entertained customers, for the most part West Indian friends of her husband who were sent to her at his behest. Fred liked the idea of being able to make arrangements of this nature, and would offer his wife with generosity. There was a hidden spyhole in the door, at waist-level. The wallpaper was covered in pale pink flowers, and there was in addition a child's fresco of a vase with flowers. The room on the right had been the marital bedroom.

The staircase was hung with brown wallpaper and led to the first-floor front room, with a fairly innocent poster of an attractive girl, wearing little, on the back of the door. This had been the bar, complete with counter and inverted bottles with optics as in a pub. There remained a poster covering one entire wall opposite the fireplace, which represented a Caribbean scene with deep-blue sea and waves crashing against high rocks. This was presumably also meant to make West Indian guests feel at home, and was a later addition to the décor of the house. (This had originally been a bedroom for lodgers.) Wall lights hung either side of the fireplace. Opposite was a kitchen with a sink in the corner and tiled surround, a central ceiling fan, an original fireplace painted blue, and cheap wallpaper depicting Chianti bottles, glasses of wine and Swiss clocks. Next to this room was a bathroom. Up again, and two bedrooms on the top floor completed the accommodation, with fitted wardrobes and, in one, a vanity unit in the corner. On the top landing, more spacious than the others, there was a row of clothes-hooks. One floorboard very noticeably squeaked.

In later years, Fred built extensions on the ground floor which added a living-room, plus another kitchen and bathroom, and the other rooms in the original part of the house altered their purpose. Rosemary's special room moved to the top floor and was fitted out to contain spotlights and a draped four-poster bed. But the simple arrangement of six rooms on three floors would have been the house that the early lodgers knew, and only part of the extension was in place when Liz Brewer lived there. The cellar was closed off in her day. Fred later converted it to a bedroom for the children, and one may still see on the walls their scribbles in coloured crayons as well as the drawing of a heart, symbol of an adolescent crush, and cartoons of Mexican figures. When I was there, the floor was marked in five places to indicate where girls had been previously buried. The ceiling is so low that an adult cannot stand erect, and one of the beams, supporting the floor above, has two portions notched out of it, over which ropes could be thrown and tied.

Rosemary West gave birth to eight children, six of them during the twenty-two years that she lived here. With her stepdaughter Anne Marie, there were nine altogether, although Anne Marie left home before the last two were born. In addition, Rosemary looked after one of her husband's love-children for a period, a boy called Steven who had been conceived and born during Fred's Scottish period, when he had been married to Rena. Fred said that Rosemary burst into tears of pleasure the day

Steven called her 'Mum' for the first time. (Fred had two other illegitimate children in Scotland, he said, a boy called Gareth and a girl called Anne.[3]) One visitor marvelled so at the abundance of children that she thought Rosemary must have been running a nursery. According to Rosemary's brother, Graham Letts, she did indeed foster two children at one point, though not for very long.[4] She fell pregnant so regularly that her mother Daisy Letts was moved to express concern. 'I had a big family like you,' she wrote, 'mainly because in those days there was no way not to. Then when I had all the misery with Dad and the boys doing things wrong, I just wished they had never been born. Now, Rosie, when I see you having babies I just can't think of you going through all that, you were married quite young and had no outside life at all. I feel Fred should make sure you don't have more babies . . . it's because I love you dear that I can't take seeing you like you are. God Bless You.'[5] But Fred bluntly refused to wear a condom, and the contraceptive pill made Rosemary feel sick.

Oddly, there was not a great deal of noise and bustle and children's babble in the house, for they were disciplined quite sternly, and as soon as they were out of infancy they were given so many tasks to accomplish that they were always busy.

Both parents had inherited the habit from their own upbringing of requiring children to make themselves useful and share the burdens of running a house; they were never waited upon or spoilt in any way. They were each from very poor families and had learnt how to 'make do' from an early age. The habit was to render their own children's lives somewhat cheerless.

Frederick West had grown up on a farm where hard work was essential to survival. His father, Walter, was regularly in the fields before dawn to tend to the farmer's cows, and his large family were disciplined from an early age to pull their weight. The boys – Fred, John and Doug – had to chop wood and haul in coal for the fire first

76

thing in the morning, help milk the cows, pick hops and hunt rabbits, all as part of joint family undertaking with no slacking or whining permitted. They kept chickens and grew vegetables to support themselves, the one supplement to Walter's £6-per-week wage being a generous supply of fresh milk. Their own pig would be killed by the local slaughterman and provide the family with bacon for months on end, and they had a tiny orchard of their own as well. There was no lavatory, so the entire family made use of a bucket which was emptied into a sewage pit outside once a day. This attracted rats, which Daisy, Walter's wife, used to scare off with blasts from her husband's shotgun. It was a harsh life, devoid of treats, and the six children understood that if they wanted something special for themselves, they would have to earn the money to buy it. They would sometimes pick daffodils in the fields and sell them at the roadside.

Fred knew how to draw a lamb at the age of eleven, and in common with most farm-reared boys, handled his first gun at fourteen. There were five dogs on the farm – Lassie, Ben, Brandy, Whiskey and Lad – each with his own task. He described his mother Daisy as 'dominant': 'My mother knew exactly what was going on,' he said, 'you never kept nothing from my mother. You could tell her the biggest lie you ever thought up, Mother would just listen and then tell you the truth and that was it, finished.' His father was 'the most understanding person you'd ever meet. You could go to Dad and ask him anything. He was always calm. He was a massive man, mind, big man, tall, you know, massive hands on him but he wouldn't hurt a fly and he always understood you whenever we had problems . . . he was so placid it was unreal.'[6]

When he was fifteen Frederick West bicycled to Hereford for his first job, without telling his mother. It took him two days to get there, and he earned a few shillings, some of which he sheepishly gave her when he reappeared, covered in cement and builders' dust and full of apologies. It was also at fifteen that he had his first suit.

Rosemary's family was constantly on the move during her infancy, even living briefly in a big house in Chipping Campden which went with her father's job. Mostly, they lived in poor circumstances, scraping by on a small income and piling into two rooms. They lined up to bathe in a tin bath once a week. Life was not without its pleasures, however. A neighbouring old lady was generous with her tin of biscuits, always sparing a couple of digestives for the little girl. As she grew older, Rosemary helped a woman who lived in the flat underneath with her washing and ironing, being happiest pretending to be a housewife herself. She celebrated Guy Fawkes' Day every year with a guy in an old pram, and at Christmas her father dressed up as Santa Claus, as best he could. They had a dog called Ben who loved raw eggs and once stole a box from the village butcher who used to display them outside his shop. When the dog appeared with the box in his mouth, Daisy Letts told him to take it back immediately, which he promptly proceeded to do. The family was too poor to permit Rosemary to take part in school trips, except on one occasion when she travelled with a school party to London to hear the Vienna Boys' Choir. It was an experience that stayed with her.

Like the Wests, the Letts family upheld a similar ethic of work required from children. The girls had to clean rooms, iron clothes, look after the baby, do the shopping. Their mother, also called Daisy, was ferociously clean, scrubbing the outside lavatory four times a day and constantly patching old clothes because they were too poor to afford new ones. Their father, Bill, required them to sit in silence during meals and return to their chores like clockwork afterwards, punishing them for the slightest variation from the perfection he demanded. Rosemary had been brought up to believe that good discipline was the sign of a well-run household and the glue which bound a family together. Her father was obsessive about

78

order, requiring chairs to be in their correct position, knives and forks not to be clattered at table, children not to speak unless spoken to. His was an exaggeration of the principles of good manners and respect for elders, which would have been comic were it not for its potentially poisonous influence. His example was especially bad for Rose, whom he spared the most of his wrath, for she saw his conduct as worthy of emulation, but had not the intelligence or subtlety to appraise its likely effect. She had seen him throw precious food away, and break new eggs into the dustbin. Bill Letts was puritanical and regimented to a probably pathological degree, a circumstance which would have a bearing upon his daughter's developing personality. For the moment, it is sufficient to note that the habit of hard work was one that both Rosemary and Fred had known from their infancy.

It was a habit they unrelentingly imposed upon their own brood. The three eldest – Heather, Mae and Stephen – spent much of their spare time cleaning the house, scrubbing the kitchen floor, passing the vacuum-cleaner in other rooms, dusting and bleaching the toilet bowl. Rose would watch over them as they performed their chores and make them start all over again if they were incorrectly done. In addition, they were responsible for cleaning their bedrooms thoroughly and making their own beds. They mended plugs, washed and ironed, helped their father haul cement. And before they went to school, they would have to polish their shoes and look clean and smart. They were given bus money to get to and from school, but because they had no pocket money, the three of them walked the four miles as fast as they could to save it.[7]

Quite clearly, Mrs West thought it was part of her job as a mother to make her children learn self-sufficiency, instructing them from the age of eight upwards. She would brook no objections, both because she felt it was her duty to teach them how to fend for themselves, and because she harboured a deep resentment of disobedience in any measure. Her children Stephen and Mae relate one of her oft-repeated remarks in response to any expression of reluctance on their part when faced with a job to do: 'If you don't like it, you know where the door is,' she said. Another of her comments was 'If you're going to live here', that 'if' being a hideously loaded conditional which was calculated to sow insecurity in the hearts of the young.[8] This is obviously how it is now seen by Stephen and Mae, and how it is considered by observers who have since pored over the climate of life in that house to winkle out signs of malevolence.

The children have said they never had a proper Christmas, because they were allowed only to choose a cheap present from the Argos catalogue, yet there is another account of a Christmas complete with decorations and properly wrapped gifts, turkey and trimmings.[9] Rosemary regarded Christmas as the one day in the year which was exclusively hers, and she made the best of it. Her husband was indifferent, just as he never knew the birthdays of his children (apart from Mae June's, fixed eponymously), while she enjoyed making a fuss about a birthday. Some have claimed that the Wests never went to see their children perform at school, either on sports day or in amateur theatricals, yet there are stories of Rosemary at least turning up at school to offer support, and one major occasion when the children took part in a school fancy-dress competition. This was, admittedly, at a much later period (1989) and involved the younger children. Rosemary helped them prepare their costumes – one a clown, another as a cat, a third a pirate and the youngest a rabbit.[10] She had obviously mellowed since the days when she had run the house like an Army camp.

Both parents were consistent, however, in never offering to help their children with homework, or giving praise for good marks achieved at school. They simply did not consider that education mattered very much, because they never understood its purpose. But it might have helped had they understood how much children value encouragement and how much they need to please parents before all else.

All the West children were well fed, despite their relative poverty. Rosemary would take Fred's weekly wage, which he handed to her unopened, and return some to him for cigarettes. The rest she spent on food, preparing three set meals a day, every day, with a proper roast on Sunday, followed by her own home-made cakes. Even when money was scarce (for Fred was not always in work), she was able to rustle up bread and milk or bread and dripping, with a cup of Bovril. Sometimes on Saturday they all had fish and chips. They never went hungry. She also taught Anne Marie how to make jam and pastry; she became adept at Bakewell tarts in particular.

Rosemary was house-proud. While still at Midland Road and not yet eighteen she had been admired by her neighbour Mrs Agius for the whiteness of Heather's nappies, which she boiled in a bucket on the stove, and beamed with pride at the compliment. The mother of her son Stephen's girlfriend remembered that Rose was not at all pleased when he came in with muddy boots after she had cleaned the floor (which at least demonstrates she did not rely on her children to do *all* the housework).[11] She was hopelessly inept on the telephone, snatching it up when it rang as if it were inimical to her interests and barking 'What?' as a greeting. Equally, she slammed it down without a farewell. The same inherent hostility informed the shopping expeditions on which she usually took some of the children, who grew steadily more embarrassed as she snapped at assistants, thumped tables and kicked doors. It was as if she expected haughty treatment and was determined to neutralize it in advance.

For relaxation she turned to crochet or needlework, at which she was fairly accomplished. There were cushions in the bar-room upstairs, embroidered 'Mum' and 'Dad', and she shared knitting patterns with a neighbour who would give evidence against her at the trial. In prison she made baby clothes for her grandchildren and, when her son Stephen married, she sent him and his bride a cushion she had made in her cell.

Money was so scarce that the family was given a grant to pay for school uniforms, which Rosemary usually contrived to be too big, so that the children would grow into them and make them last longer. Uncle John West, Fred's brother, was a dustman, and he would on occasion salvage a pair of shoes which had been dumped and offer them for the children's use. (He also brought home second-hand toys from the same source.) Everybody agreed, however, that they never looked scruffy. All the West children were clean, tidy, well turned out, and a good deal better presented than some of their classmates. Even if they had to use washing-up liquid to clean their hair, there was no doubting their spotlessness. They were given free school dinners on the grounds of penury. Rosemary also had a practical sense, tying a bus-pass and winter gloves to school satchels so they would not be mislaid on board.[12]

'All the headteachers of schools attended by the West children recalled that the children seemed cared for and their attendance gave no cause for concern, and in some cases was singled out for praise,' affirms a report by the Gloucestershire Area Child Protection Committee. 'Every absence was covered by a parental explanation and no deliberate avoidance of PE [physical exercise] was ever detectable.'[13] This should be borne in mind when we turn to consider the allegations of extensive truancy by Anne Marie and her constant abstention from PE classes to evade sighting of her bruises. A social worker who visited 25 Cromwell Street in 1988 found the children to be 'well and not neglected'.

For a woman who undoubtedly adored babies, it was paradoxical that Rosemary West declined to feed her own at the breast. Perhaps she had learnt to associate breasts with sex. Also, she found it curiously awkward to express any affection for her children as soon as they grew out of nappies. We have already seen that, as a girl herself, she had lavished attention upon her younger brothers Graham and Gordon and that one of the main enticements which brought her into Fred West's caravan in the first place was concern for his two little girls, Charmaine and Anne Marie. She was a good mother to her first-born, Heather ('I loved her very, very, very much,' she was to say in court), and lavished attention upon the rest as they appeared. She was even contemplating trying for another baby when Fred was arrested in 1994. But she utterly lacked the patience which the care of a growing and exploring child demands, and seemed to consider their need to discover things for themselves as a personal affront. She smacked and reproached them too readily, revealing by this a glaring sign of her own lack of maturity, and in consequence was too hurt to tell them that she loved them; perhaps, in the full and proper sense of affection-with-respect, she never did. 'If Mum had said to me "I love you" before we went to sleep,' says son Stephen, 'I think I would have fainted. I'd have been sure she was on something.'[14] On the other hand, she did not like Stephen staying out late when he had to go to school the next morning, even when he was a young adolescent, and telephoned his girlfriend's house to make sure he came home in time for a good night's rest. The girl's mother went to see Rosemary about it, and they sat in the kitchen chatting about the unreliability and ingratitude of teenagers.[15]

With other people's children she was often more demonstrative, and one of them, who testified against her in court, said that she was a combination of young mother and big sister, somebody to whom one could tell one's troubles and from whom one could expect sympathy. This witness (Miss A) went several times to Cromwell Street and was always welcomed. But the fact that Mrs West was sexually attracted to young girls, and that this was the one who painted a horrid picture of sexual activity at the house (said by the defendant to have been invented) rendered her earlier praise somewhat less valuable. On the other hand, Mrs Margaretta Dix, a neighbour who lived opposite No 25 and had no axe to grind, would tell how the day she found her husband dead on the bathroom floor, following a heart attack, it was to the Wests that she turned for help. 'Fred did everything in his power to save my husband', she told the court, 'and Rose took me over to her house, tried to calm me down, offered me endless cups of tea and reassuring talk.'[16] Frederick West recalled this occasion himself: 'I mean that man practically died in my arms you know,' he said, telling the police that his wife saw as little of him as anyone, because there only had to be a knock at the door and he would be off helping someone out of a fix.[17]

Even Anne Marie, who detested her stepmother for complex interweaving reasons, felt able to mention certain acts of kindness.

The point about Rosemary West, and it is a fairly important one, was that she was not subtle. She was completely without pretensions or guile and would not have known how to be cunning. She said what she was thinking, never pausing to edit her words or make them more palatable, no matter who was there to hear her. Oaths sprinkled her vocabulary and irritation gave it an edge. It was as if she assumed everyone looked down on her for her poverty and (for many must have known) her prostitution, and she would rise to a bait even before it was dangled. If she clipped one of her children round the head in a public place, like a shop or the campsite where the family regularly spent their holidays at Barry Island near Cardiff, she would not worry that strangers might remonstrate with her, for she was ready for them, and gave out a silent message that she was not to be wrestled with. Mae said, 'No-one told her how to treat her kids. If they had tried Mum would have hung them out to dry.'[18] She did not bother to adapt her mood to the circumstances, and did not care where she was or whom she was with.

This is not to say that violence was essential to her disposition, only to her reactions. 'Rose wouldn't harm anybody,' said Fred. 'I mean Rose didn't have a violent nature at all. I mean she used to shout at the children and things like that, but like all mothers do.'[19] Tara was known as 'Moses', shortened eventually to 'Mo', and when her father called her DeMoses she returned with DeDad; she was scarcely ever scolded. Stephen was a perpetual worry, sticking screwdrivers into light-sockets, or holding his breath as long as he could for a dare.

Like many who smart under the notion they have a grievance against the world for treating them *de haut en bas*, Mrs West was steeped in cynicism. She told her stepdaughter Anne Marie that nobody ever gave you anything for nothing or liked you for what you were, only for what you could give them.[20] It was for this reason that she nursed a lifelong grudge against everyone in authority – be they social workers, bureaucrats, officials of any kind – whom she regarded as interferers and hustlers to be thwarted at all costs. Highest among them were police officers, self-important in their uniforms and with their posh jargon, whom she treated with undisguised scorn.

It must be remembered that neither Rosemary nor Fred belonged to meek law-abiding families. Both the West brothers and the Letts brothers had frequently been in trouble with the police, mostly for petty offences, and Fred was the champion of them all, with offences for theft, larceny, non-payment of fines, driving without insurance, driving without road tax, in addition to the more serious charge he had faced of rape before he met Rosemary, and they mount to a list to fill a whole page. According to his son Stephen, he might almost be said to have brought them up to be petty thieves, as they had accompanied him on many a filching expedition in their infancies. It was not surprising, then, that the one unifying force which would bring Rosemary striding to their defence, with as much aggression as a lioness protecting her cubs, was an enquiry from the police. A policeman was a natural enemy. What she perceived as his threatening posture brought out all her love for her kids at last, and on such occasions they felt cherished. Fred said of her, 'Don't get Rose wrong, Rose lives by the law properly, I mean although she doesn't like the law she will not have it broken you know.'[21]

Oddly, her own prostitution seems not to have attracted the attention of the police, unless it be, as some have suggested, because policemen were among her clients. Prostitution was a constant throughout the twenty-two years Rosemary West spent at Cromwell Street, a permanent ingredient in the weird cocktail of her life along with crochet, Sunday roast, clean children and motherhood. It began as a perverse way of pleasing her husband, who made it clear from the start that he was excited by the idea of his wife having overt sexual relations with other men. It accorded with his notion that sex should be a permanent daily feature of everyone's life, that men and women were always coupling like rabbits, and that any resistance to such a notion would be abnormal. Whenever he felt the urge for orgasmic release, he satisfied it immediately, with whomever was at hand, and returned to what he was doing before. A sexual encounter might be over within a couple of minutes, as long as it would take a more orthodox man to masturbate.

The crucial implication of this was that the female body existed for him as an aid to male masturbation, and that when he wanted more prolonged satisfaction, he had perforce to resort to esoteric practices, with disastrous consequences. As far as his relations with Rosemary were concerned, he made it clear that he would only be excited if she prostituted herself, just as his first wife Rena had done. Mrs West's voice trembled when she remembered how it began. 'He told me he wanted me to go with other men,' she told the court. 'He was always bringing the subject up, and giving me reasons why I should. He was very persuasive. He persuaded me to jump into bed with the boys upstairs, that was his idea, and he would use emotional blackmail if I argued. He said you're not doing enough for the marriage, you've got to play your part. He went on and on, it was an everyday thing.'[22]

Her daughter Mae's recollection concurred. 'If she didn't do what Dad asked he'd say she was a bad mother and wife and that good wives should always do what their husbands said.'[23] 'He nagged and nagged her to do it,' said Stephen, 'so eventually she gave in.' This suggests another facet of Frederick West's psyche which will need to be explored in the light of his crimes, and that is the overwhelming need to control and determine that what happens should accord with his needs and desires, whatever they may be. But for the moment it is enough to trace the sequence which led Rosemary West into using her sexual nature, the opposite of his in that she was not spent within seconds but could perform inventively for long periods, to satisfy her husband by proxy. The men she slept with were initially surrogates for the inadequate man to whom she was wed, surrogates designed to please him rather than her. (With him, she would have often to feign orgasm, she said.) Neither of them would ever admit as much, but Fred needed Rosemary to submit to better men than he. He would watch through a spy-hole, and expect a full verbal account afterwards. Later, he rigged wires and speakers over the house so that he could idly watch television while listening through ear-plugs to the sexual music of his wife's groans. Even the children could not disturb him when he was so engaged. Sex was the point and pleasure of his life.

There was an occasion when the Wests were invited to a wedding one Saturday. Rosemary looked forward to it, both because they rarely went anywhere together, and because her routine life was so predictable and (perhaps she felt) sordid. She made sure that earlier in the week she had sexual relations with all the regular partners assigned to her by Fred in order to keep Saturday free. Still, however, he insisted on dropping her off at another man's house, a new customer he had made arrangements with that day. She sat in the corridor of the house weeping.[24] Still more bizarrely, West always insisted that his wife submit to intercourse with him immediately following her return from an assignment to which he had sent her. He said this was because her previous encounter had made her wider to receive him, a remark which both betrayed and concealed the truth. It demonstrated that he demanded subservience from her; and it demonstrated also that he was inadequate without the fuel of fantasy.

Of course, it would be disingenuous to hold that Mrs West's prostitution was wholly and entirely designed as marriage therapy. She had not been a virgin when she met Fred, and there is evidence she was promiscuous even as a fifteen-year-old, or at least a promiscuous flirt with wandering hands and little resistance. Her prostitution developed over the years from easy availability, with no money exchanged (Fred once made his wife available to a friend in return for mending his car), to regular professional work for a fee. And she undeniably enjoyed it, if the little black book in which she recorded size of penis be any guide, but even this, it could be argued, was meant to titillate her husband; such would certainly meet his requirements. No embarrassment arising from Rosemary's prostitution has been recorded, and both parents were manifestly pleased when she gave birth to three half-caste children, Rosemary because she adored babies, Fred because they were visible proof that his wife was a fine sexual performer and breeder.

On the other hand, as the older children approached puberty with an awareness that their mother had sexual clients, both she and they were conscious of tensions within the family. They had never been taught shame, and were used to seeing their parents wander in and out of rooms naked or in underclothes (though Rosemary hardly ever wore knickers), yet shame was mysteriously what they felt when they knew their mother was 'entertaining'. One of the two bells by the front door was for clients, and the children habitually fell quieter than usual when that bell rang and their mother disappeared to her room, interrupting dinner if need be. And yet, even within this eccentric, almost bohemian atmosphere, Rosemary managed to show vestiges of maternal concern. She would leave the room where she was engaged with a lover, just to check the children were all right. And when she placed advertisements for her services, under the name 'Mandy', giving the telephone number at Cromwell Street, she warned Stephen that strangers might call and that he was, in that event, only to take a name and number and say that 'Mandy' would call back. 'She told me to put the phone down if they started talking dirty.'[25]

Fred had no such compunction, could scarcely find anything but sex to talk about, encouraged his children to think about it, and regarded prostitution as so befitting the role of a woman that he made his daughter Anne Marie available to his friends and Rosemary's clients as soon as her breasts started developing.

Several consequences of Mrs West's prostitution have a bearing on this story and the charges which she eventually faced. In the first place, there could be no secret about it in view of the fact that three of her children had black fathers, as neighbours cannot fail to have noticed. It was not an activity which she sought, therefore, to conceal or about which she dissembled. Her candour in this regard might be taken as one trait of character to be borne in mind. Secondly, those of her clients who have been traced confirm that conventional sexual intercourse was on offer, not deviant or aberrant sexual activity, an even more important circumstance to hold in view when considering the supposed manner in which seven girls died. Thirdly, Mr West frequently made bargains with men he worked with, or acquaintances of such men, that he would send his wife to spend the night with them, and there were many occasions when, once he was home, she left the house to return only the following morning. This is potentially very significant if one accepts that the disposal of dead bodies took place under cover of darkness, late at night. Fourthly, Mrs West seems to have found in her occasional lesbian encounters an antidote to the coercive nature of her dealings with men at her husband's behest; these were meetings she chose for herself and which might have more of tenderness in them than the selling of her body to be used. Finally, it will be seen that as her eldest daughter Heather grew into a sensitive age, she was appalled by Rosemary's promiscuity and shrank into a morose sullenness more serious than the general timidity of adolescence. She appears to have been shocked to discover that the father of two of her siblings was a man whose legitimate daughter she knew at school, and Rosemary herself testified that she suspected Heather turned against her because of the men. At any rate, it was this unhappiness which would settle Heather's determination to leave home and provoke a 'problem' which her father would have to 'sort out'.

In assessing the character of Rosemary West, it is essential, then, to weigh what part her sexual life played in the escalating turmoil of her children's psychological development (and, tangentially, to discern its irrelevance to her husband's spiralling descent into sadistic murder). Her other abiding fault, which also brought emotional confusion to the family, was her temper and predilection for discipline.

Hurled into the position of stepmother and mother when she was herself a mere girl, then abandoned to the task when Fred went to prison, she started to apply discipline at an age when she ought still to have been subject to it herself and free of adult responsibilities. So she slapped and shouted and threatened as best she could, conscious that such was her job, and conscious also that Fred approved of a strong arm. She wanted so very much to please him in these first two years ('It just

seems queer that anyone should think so much of me,'
she had written[26]), that she vowed to be as stern a mother
as he would wish. She appears to have treated all her
children with intermittent, and sometimes frightening,
harshness almost until they left home.

Some of the stories that have been related are familiar
enough, and not especially malign. When the children
were fussy with their food and picked at it indifferently,
she made them eat it even when it was cold; Stephen
recalls his sisters sitting there for three hours until they
obeyed. For the West children to cite such instances as
proof of cruelty smacks of too much cajoling and exaggeration by the newspapers that were paying them. By
the same token, Stephen, Mae and Heather were once
thrown outdoors in the rain as punishment for talking to
one another late at night from their separate beds; they
stayed outside for a quarter of an hour and got wet as
well as miserable.

On occasion Rosemary's anger is merely comic.
Standing in the kitchen and frustrated at being unable to
locate the dishcloth, she yelled 'dishcloth, dishcloth,
dishcloth' in frantic manner, causing all the kids to
scurry around hunting for it rather than let her reach
crisis point. For when she did, it was not funny at all.
There are stories of her lashing out with a rolling-pin and
hitting a child on the head with a breakfast bowl. Worse,
she scared her daughter Mae with the point of a knife,
nicking her flesh several times. By Mae's own admission,
the episode lasted only a few seconds, but as an illustration of loss of control it is alarming. She was capable of
smashing a knife suddenly down on the table, and the
kids had to make sure their fingers were out of the way.

Still worse are two events related by Stephen, then
picked up and repeated by other commentators on the
West case. In one, Stephen was called home from school
when his mother found out that he had stolen some
of the pornographic magazines she kept upstairs.
(According to Anne Marie he sold them to schoolfriends,

but according to Stephen himself it was Heather who had taken them, and he who paid the price.) When he came home, she made him strip, bend over the lavatory pan and hold his hands behind the pipe leading to it. She tied his hands together and thrashed him in what was severe and humiliating punishment for a twelve-year-old. This is the child whom she told the court she spoilt when he was little, because 'you know what mums are like with their boys'. He says she looked as if she was enjoying it, though one is bound to wonder how he could see what she looked like if his face was staring down at the toilet bowl.

His other account is very disturbing. Rosemary was once so angry with him that she placed her hands around his neck and lifted him off the ground, he says for fully five minutes. Five minutes is a very long time, and I doubt whether such a motion could be sustained so long, but however long it lasted, if it is true then it is the first small piece of evidence which could proclaim Rosemary West capable of murder. By itself, it is woefully insufficient for such a conclusion. It suggests, however, a response to frustration and inability to articulate which is typical of the short-tempered and is very dangerous.

It is against this background that one must set the statement by Fred that his wife did not have a violent nature and only scolded as all mothers do.

The evidence of Anne Marie West will be given due weight in the next chapter, but it must here be treated with caution. She, too, tells of humiliating treatment at the hands of her stepmother which involved beatings, kickings, stabbings and displays of unnatural glee, but her principal resentment is against the father she adored, for quite different reasons, and her attitude towards her stepmother had been, from the very moment Rosemary entered her life and fractured her closeness to her father, one of the deepest intolerance. She is said by others in the family to nurse such a fierce hatred for her stepmother as may never be assuaged, and her testimony, once more

92

kindled and possibly enlivened by the participation of a daily newspaper which published the account in book form, may have within it a vindictive element.

One example: Anne Marie told the court that her step-mother had scratched her breasts until they bled. The records indicate that she fainted at the swimming baths on her ninth birthday and was taken to the Gloucestershire Royal Hospital where she was examined by a consultant who noticed bruises and scratches on her chest. Mrs West was summoned and interviewed. She 'offered [unspecified] explanations for the marks and Anne Marie appeared to the doctor to be *a happy child who seemed fond of Rosemary West* [author's italics].'[27] Another record of the same incident shows that Anne Marie said her mother had been responsible for the injuries because she had been a naughty girl.[28] As we shall see, Anne Marie was more or less conditioned into believing she deserved all the indignities which were inflicted upon her, and this childish response rings true. We should also remember Frederick West's risible and insulting explanation for Anne Marie's loss of virginity at the age of eight (an accident with her bicycle). I do not suggest that Mrs West never scolded or indeed injured her step-daughter, only that such incidents were as nothing compared to the treatment meted out to her by her father, and that Rosemary's behaviour was exaggerated in hindsight to match hideous memories.

There are other indications that the West children suffered abuse, but not at the hands of their mother. Instances of gonorrhoea and thrush suggest sexual interference by Fred. Over a period of twenty years, thirty-one instances of West family children attending the Accident and Emergency departments of the local hospitals for domestic injuries have been recorded, which the health authorities maintain is not unusual for a family of eight over such a long span. However, when some of these injuries are scrutinized, they are shown to include a child with an injured finger caused by a sledgehammer

(Fred's injury to Stephen), and others relating to fingers, thumbs, toes, ankles and hands. Analogies with Mr West's apparent habit of removing toe and finger joints from the corpses of his victims prompt chilling and unwelcome reflections, and suggest that it was he who was most likely to have been responsible for these attacks, in blind obedience to some inner demon which itched with remembered visions.

There are also indications of Mrs West having behaved with exemplary kindness on other occasions. Stephen recalls that she stayed up all night with him to comfort him after a worry at school, and there is plenty of testimony that she was heard berating her husband for being too hard upon the children. Even Anne Marie allows that when once her father took her to watch through the spy-hole in the door of her mother's room when she had a client, and she found out, she was furious with him for having exposed the girl to such a thing. Mae writes, 'She did have eight kids and a husband like Dad, so it's not surprising she was so stressed'. She further states that the last time her mother struck her was when she was fifteen, since when 'she's been an absolutely brilliant mother'. Rose once confessed to her, 'I know I was nasty when I was younger but I had a lot of problems.'[29]

Those problems resided, for the most part, in the personality of Frederick West. We have already seen in Chapter One how he appeared in his twenties. Those same characteristics sharpened with age, and bear some repetition.

His was a personality composed of disparate elements connected by one subterranean theme, namely a complete and total absence of moral sense. He could not in justice be called immoral, because that would suppose a moral structure of which he was aware and which he had made a conscious decision to reject. Even amoral is hardly the accurate adjective, for amoralism implies a wish to replace the idea of moral structure with anarchy, and the amoralist must, therefore, be once again aware of the moral structures he determines to disregard. Frederick West was a primitive, like the Wild Boy of Aveyron who emerged from the forest untouched by cultural notions of right and wrong, alive only to immediate needs and satisfactions. He simply did not understand that there was a moral dimension to human behaviour, and any attempt to reason from a moral point of view would have met with incomprehension. This empty hole where the seat of conscience should reside is, by the way, the first characteristic of the serial killer.

Fred displayed his moral vacuity in a variety of ways. Most immediately visible was his extraordinary record for petty theft. From the age of twenty, when he appeared before Ledbury Magistrates' Court charged with stealing a watch-strap and two cigarette cases, for which he was fined £4, and throughout his adult life, he was constantly being punished for small-scale theft, nothing grand or impressive, just a tedious, unrepentant repetition of schoolboy pilfering. Given that there are records of about twenty appearances before the courts on such charges, there are almost certainly many other occasions on which he was not caught. It would never have occurred to him that he should not steal, still less that he merited a reprimand for so doing. When he was once fined £20 by the magistrates at Newent for stealing pieces of hardware from a building site where he was employed, he said that other workmen took things, so why shouldn't he?[30] The quasi-innocence of this response recalled his attitude when arrested for sexual intercourse with the thirteen-year-old girl, and he had been questioned about his habit of touching little girls in general. 'Well, doesn't everyone do it?' he said.

His son Stephen said, 'He stole anything he could get his hands on. He was an incredible thieving machine.' Mae agreed: 'He would see a pile of bricks or cement in the road and go back that night when it was dark and load them into his van. Practically the whole of our house extension was made from stolen goods, right down to the wooden support beams which held the roof up. He was quite open about it; he never liked to pay for anything. When he did repair jobs in people's houses, he'd leave a latch open on a window and later that night he'd steal objects he had liked the look of. Our house was full of ornaments which he'd claim he had been given by a satisfied customer. At one time we had seven video recorders, the same number of televisions, and loads of radio cassette players in the house. He loved hoarding.'

If Fred took his son Stephen to the park, it was not for fun, but to steal bicycles. 'He didn't need the stuff he stole, most of it was useless . . . Dad wouldn't even pay for bus or train tickets. Funnily enough, it wasn't really the money that made him do it, he gave his complete wage packet to Mum. He wouldn't spend a penny on himself, it was a compulsion.'[31] Anne Marie says that one of the reasons she was expected to pick up men was to recruit suitable accomplices to accompany her father on thieving trips.[32]

There are some interesting words which crop up in the above. Fred stole not to counter deprivation but in order to *hoard*, as the result of a *compulsion*. It is well established that the tendency to hoard implies what Freud called an 'anal-retentive' character, and moreover that this is closely allied to the urge to sadism. They are different aspects of the desire to control and retain possession. And they manifestly do not emerge from reasoned logic, but from untutored compulsion. Fred's stealing was straightforward, unadulterated, painfully simple impulse-satisfaction. So, indeed, would be his sadistic treatment of the girls he abducted. He stole for pleasure, not the pleasure of contemplation and reward (he would forget about the *object* of the theft almost immediately), but that pleasure which feeds the hunger for momentary thrill, the intense gratification of the self. Girls upon whom he worked his sadistic fantasies would also be objects in which he lost interest as soon as they were done with. He could not remember the names of most of them; he may well not have bothered to find out what they were called.

That he had the most florid fantasy life is attested by his total inability to tell the truth, except by accident, as we have already seen in Chapter One. An endless stream of fantasy and invention flowed from his lips, most of which nobody took seriously for an instant. Many witnesses would testify that they never believed a word he said, and since he was a very chatty man, accosting strangers in the street with his loquacity, there were rather a lot of words to disbelieve. His wife Rosemary was so used to his cock-and-bull stories that she paid no attention to them. Once again, he did not lie in order to undermine the moral value of truth-telling, but because he did not know how not to. Whatever he was saying was valid while he was saying it. He told his children that he died after the motorcycle accident when he was eighteen, and the cold of the mortician's slab had jerked him back to life. He boasted that he was a friend of the pop-singer Lulu and had travelled the world with her. He would tell the police he had had affairs with three nuns.[33] Was he lying, was he a fool, or was he mentally unbalanced? Howard Sounes is surely right to point out that Frederick West was 'for much of his life, and for much of each day of his life, profoundly deluded'.[34]

While this would be harmless were it confined to tales of shoulder-rubbing with the famous, it was mortally dangerous when the fantasies spilled over into real life and engulfed innocent girls in the process. It is highly likely that he believed girls derived pleasure from torture and rape, and that he thought they besieged him with their passionate desire to be pleasured by him. Then there are the incredible tales he poured out to Janet Leach, the unfortunate woman who pulled the wrong straw and found herself his one-and-only confidante throughout the period of his remand. She believed him, and embarrassed herself in the process, as we shall see when we come to examine the trial.

Telling lies would also prove to be far from harmless when it came to unravelling which of his lies his wife was prepared to accept, and how much she had taken on his habit. For instance, she gave many explanations for the disappearance of her daughter Heather in 1987, none of them true. The court would have to decide whether she was lying on her own account, or repeating lies she had heard from her husband and chose to accept. This was more problematic than it appears at first, for if she did accept the stories he told of having seen Heather after her disappearance, why should she be more gullible at that point, when she had long since learnt to listen with only half an ear? Mae says that her father had told them Heather had visited him in Birmingham while he was on bail in 1992, five years after she had last been seen, and that she would be home within a week. All nonsense, made up without thought or sequence, and on hearing it, Rosemary told him to shut up. The question is why, if she did not believe him then, she told police that she had believed other of his stories relating to Heather's well-being? The compulsive liar scatters moral confusion about him and lays waste the most honest attempt to understand.

He appears also to have been hyperactive and prone to repetition-compulsion, unable to sit still for long without rushing out to sweep the patio in a pre-ordained pattern, or tinker with the van to make sure it was in working order, or check on his tools. More anal character here, and, yet more sinister, a signal of necrophilic predilection, the absorption in things which were devoid of life in preference to creatures who pulsed with it. He was not overtly fond of his children and could never quite work out how many he had. He had no time for animals. (The two dogs arrived later, after he had been sent to Birmingham on bail – it was Rosemary who acquired them as companions.) Oddly enough, Frederick West's only known pets were tropical fish, cold-blooded and affectionless, a taste he shared with the Milwaukee necrophile Jeffrey Dahmer, who murdered seventeen young men and dismembered their corpses, but also cared for his fish-tank with remarkable devotion.

Fred displayed further small indications of a necrophilic character in his passion for gadgets and machines which worked according to rules which he could set and impose. Not only did he build and decorate all the extensions and modifications at 25 Cromwell Street himself, a fairly innocuous achievement one might think, and one he shares with thousands of other DIY enthusiasts, but he also engineered the purpose and personality of the house in his own image. It was a voyeur's house, and all the wiring and loudspeakers and drilling of peep-holes were not *only* designed to provide sexual excitement to a man whose libido produced disappointing results – whose own body, in fact, was not much use to him – but *also* and *especially* because he liked the things which recorded and objectified and petrified sex on tape or on film better than the experience of sex itself. It was the gadgets which gave him satisfaction, because they were objects he could control, whereas the live sexual act threatened a level of emotion which he could not understand and in which he lost control of what was happening and the effects he wished to engender. He was better at watching, recording and filming than at doing.

Hence the only sexual acts in which he was completely himself were those in which he was unchallenged master of events – the sadistic manipulation of girls' bodies. It was a solitary act also, because the girls were no more than objects to him and were not present as individuals in any way, and in my view it was the one act in which Rosemary could never share. Nobody could. Nobody in the world. She could never be allowed to find out.

His one skill was in making things, objects which could be put together and taken apart again, which did not resist his will or require *he* give *them* satisfaction.

Toy caravans, footstools, cabinets. He could draw, but he could not invest a drawing with life.

Fred was very keen in showing off his house and boasting of what he had done to it. He never once showed off his children. Even his wife was shown off only as an object for men's lust.

He also kept his own anger severely in control. Even as a schoolboy he had never been known to fight back when picked upon by another boy, relying instead on his brother John to stand up for him. He 'had a reputation for lacking bottle', said his daughter Anne Marie. The coward is often a man whose anger is so strong, so seething with power, that he keeps it rigidly under control, to be released only when he sees fit, on occasions where he can dictate how it should be used. It is a common-place of most habitual, repetitive killers that they seem to all observers to be mild men who would not hurt the proverbial fly, whose capacity for sadistic torture and murder it is inconceivable for his friends and acquaintances to imagine. Frequently, when such men are arrested, everyone assumes that the police have made a dreadful mistake. Fred West was certainly a wild card, a bit of a lad, telling tall stories and nicking things, but it is clear that nobody thought him a ruthless killer.

The person whose anger is released in a normal, regular way is the person it is safe to be with. The one who keeps it hidden from public view is dangerous. Fred so rarely lost his temper with his children that they remember the very few instances with clarity, as abnormal occurrences; most of the time he did not seem to notice they were there. People who knew him many years before in Scotland, when he was living with Rena, have vivid recollections of the one occasion he appeared to lose control, in a quarrel with John McLachlan, a rival for Rena's attention. Even then, he backed down very quickly. 'He couldn't tackle a man,' said McLachlan, 'but he was not slow in attacking women.'[35] And he preferred, on such occasions, there should be no witness.

He once told his son Stephen never to hit a woman because you did not know where it might lead. Perhaps he was trying to say something significant, but could only hint. Stephen also says that his father demanded, and received, respect within the house. Indeed, he looked up to him.[36]

Rosemary, on the other hand, lost her temper almost daily, and her shouting and yelling at the kids, her clipping them across the ear or behind the legs, even, dare one say, her striking them with a belt or a rolling-pin, denoted a person whose emotions showed, in the healthiest way, on the outside. Her temper may have been harsh, but it was not malign or poisonous, because it was frank. Serial killers are not made from such cloth.

The final and most outstanding ingredient in Frederick West's personality was the one which has already merited attention in these pages, and which seeped in and out of all the evidence heard at the trial of his wife, namely his pathological licentiousness. I say pathological because such a degree of lewdness in behaviour and language as he displayed went far beyond the ordinary joy in sexual allusion which infects every man's conduct at some time or another, and was almost certainly the result of mental disorder. Fred could not stop touching women. He would put his hand up his wife's skirt and then display his fingers to the children, inviting them to smell their mother. They learnt to get through their meal as quickly as possible so they could leave the room, as he was likely to grope Rosemary at the table, not furtively, but in such a bold manner that he wanted them to see and know what he was doing. Indifferent to the embarrassment of puberty, he would announce when one of his daughters was having a period with the remark, 'I see Harry Rags is riding in the two-thirty.'[37] He called Anne Marie 'Titless'. He would touch a neighbour's buttock on first acquaintance, and make remarks suggestive of sexual congress with her. He was happy to gaze with lubricious delight upon animals copulating, and his daily conversation was larded almost continuously with sexual reference. Workmates and neighbours tended to laugh at his obsession and ascribe it to yet another manifestation of his incorrigible myth-making. But it was not at all funny. It was the surface bubbling of a volcanic derangement which made life a hellish misery for his daughters, and, unsuspected by them or anyone else, brought several young women to a sordid and painful death.

'If Dad hadn't been abusing us, he would have been a really good dad,' said Mae.[38] 'Abusing' is Mae's safely formal word for systematic and repetitive rape by their father. Anne Marie was subjected to sexual intercourse with her father over a period of eight years. It was Heather's resistance to her father's attacks which probably contributed to her death. Mae resisted in more subtle ways and did not always succumb.

A habit of incest was the dynamic at the root of the West family's gross disorder. It polluted the air and discoloured the walls. And ultimately even that was not enough.

4

Anne Marie

A terrible hush enveloped No 3 court at Winchester
when Frederick West's daughter Anne Marie walked gin-
gerly into the witness-box after lunch on 18 October
1995. Those of us who had heard her statement read out
by junior prosecuting counsel Andrew Chubb at the
committal proceedings knew what to expect, but to the
jury it would all be new and understandably shocking.
Though her evidence had little to do with the murder
charges her stepmother faced, it would greatly assist the
Crown in making the defendant an object of hatred.
Essentially, however, Anne Marie's story threw a lurid
spotlight upon the hidden dynamic of life at Cromwell
Street, namely the concentrated power of Frederick
West's incestuous drive.

Anne Marie had always been in a classically vulnerable position. The only child of Fred and his first wife
Rena, with an older half-sister Charmaine who was
mysteriously treated as an intruder by her father, Anne
Marie's early years had been disastrously unstable. Rena
disappeared so frequently in order to escape Fred's
covert brutality, and reappeared with other young
women who were strangers to the little girls, that Anne
Marie could never form a clear impression in her mind
of who her mother was. Only the vaguest memory of her
survived into adulthood, and she never knew her surname. Time and again, the family was uprooted and dis-
persed, the little girls sent to various foster homes under
council care whenever Rena abandoned them. This was
always at Fred's request rather than on the intervention
of social workers, who reported, as we have seen, that he

appeared to be the one stable and caring influence in their lives. For Anne Marie he represented her only security and continuity, the tree to which she clung in a windswept world.

Moreover, he lavished attention on her at the expense of Charmaine, whom he openly derided, so that she felt from the beginning that she was special to him. 'I was very much a daddy's girl', she would tell the court, 'and when I was little I said that one day I would marry him.' To the police she said, 'I have always loved my dad. I would go so far as to say that I idolized him.'[1] Of course, she was not the only little girl to promise she would marry Daddy when she grew up, and it would be wrong to read too much into a fairly commonplace infantile ambition. Little boys who undertake to marry Mummy when Daddy dies usually equate dying with going away. But it would be fair to suppose that Anne Marie anticipated being with her father always, and that she would do anything for him.

When Rosemary entered the family life, Anne Marie was naturally resentful, and had to be told to call her 'Mum', which she resisted. She sought precious time alone with her father, and saw herself and him as allies against the newcomer. For her part, Rosemary said she and Anne Marie were able to get on well enough, except when Fred was around. At first she was 'just a little girl who needed looking after . . . the child I left home for'. But she soon detected that the daughter was using the father's loyalty to arm herself, and Rosemary lost all influence over her. 'I thought she would accept me as she got older, but obviously she never did,' she said. 'I tried to make rules, but was condemned for it. Fred said I had no right.' As for Fred, he never chastised his daughter. Anne Marie confessed, 'I used to look forward to a cuddle and a kiss when Dad came home.'

The reader will recall Rosemary's warning to Fred: 'Remember darling you can't fall in love with your own daughter. Nor spend the rest of your life with her.'

At the age of eight, Anne Marie lost her virginity to her father in the most grotesque and brutal manner. According to her testimony, Rosemary was present at the time and helped him do it. This she has denied. The details of the assault are extremely unpleasant, and anyone who wishes to mull over them may consult either the court records or, to a lesser extent, the account Anne Marie published, with the help of the *Daily Star*, in book form. Suffice it to say they represent one of the most deplorable violations of a child that I have ever had to read or listen to. There was another similar incident at a later date, in which Mrs West was also allegedly involved. Both she and Fred apparently told Anne Marie that what was happening was for her own good, that it would help her satisfy her husband when she grew up, and that she should be grateful to have such attentive parents. There was no reason that Anne Marie should not believe them, and she ascribed the pain and humiliation to her own stupidity.

The most important consequence of this first event was that, from that day for the next seven or eight years, Frederick West systematically and regularly subjected his daughter to sexual intercourse with him, without his wife's knowledge or approval. They had sex in the back of his van, on an old mattress. They had sex in fields and in old houses where Fred was working. They once had sex, with a grim nod to nostalgia, at their former home in 25 Midland Road, when Fred was engaged in redecoration there for the landlord. (Could this have been on the same occasion that he disinterred and reburied Charmaine's skeleton? There is no record of his having worked there twice.) Whenever Fred asked his daughter to accompany him on a job, she knew there was a likelihood he would want intercourse, and when the van stopped, she knew it was imminent. By the time she was twelve, she had been through this experience dozens of times, and was ready for different treatment, again with the squalid pleasures of her father in view. She was made available, along with his wife, to his West Indian friends, of whom there were about five regular visitors. This would occur once a week, on which occasions Rose was in the room. Anne Marie paid tribute to her stepmother's dubious concern. 'She was always making sure I was never hurt by any of the men,' she said.

The culmination of this long ordeal came when she was fifteen years old and her father made her pregnant. She told Rose that she felt something was wrong with her, because she could not stop bleeding and was in pain, and Rose took her to see the doctor. Neither of them knew the truth. The doctor sent Anne Marie straight to Gloucester Royal Hospital, where she was operated on for an ectopic pregnancy, so called when the embryo develops in the fallopian tube. Fred visited her there. 'The doctors think there might be something wrong inside,' he said. 'They are going to put you to sleep and have a little look.'[2] In an interview with the doctors, Fred gave the impression of being 'a caring and attentive parent concerned for his daughter's well-being.'[3] It was not until years later, after she had left home, that Anne Marie discovered what had happened to her.

Exactly when Fred transferred his attentions to his other daughters cannot be ascertained with precision. There is an eye-witness account of him lying on his back in the caravan with Charmaine, naked and aged about five, astride his crotch, but he appears to have allowed Heather and Mae to escape his lust until they approached puberty. 'Dad used to comment on our breast size or how they had grown a bit,' says Mae. 'He thought if he created his daughter he should be able to look at his creation and touch it. He said a father's right is to break his daughters in and it was his privilege to do it by the time we were sixteen . . . he'd say, "Your first baby should be your dad's".' Heather and Mae were united in protecting each other from their father's habitual lewdness. He would encourage them to walk in and out of the bathroom without a towel around them, which they naturally were very reluctant to do, and would bore holes in their bedroom door so that he could observe them undressing. There were many occasions when Fred would enter the bathroom and silently put his hand round the shower curtain to feel the body of one of his daughters. He said nothing, just touched his property. 'A groping sometimes lasted twenty minutes,' said Mae.[4] They went to bed fully clothed to undress beneath the sheets.

Fred saw no need to dissemble, as he felt there was nothing amiss in his attitude. He was heard to say to one of his younger daughters, 'It will be your turn next,' and was wont to point out, without provocation of any kind, that women were sitting on a goldmine, 'and if you don't lose your virginity young, then the older you get the more it will send you mental'.[5] It is quite possible he thought, in so far as cogitative thought was in the range of this severely limited man, that he was doing *good* by preparing his daughters for adulthood. Nothing in the account of his terrible assault upon Anne Marie when she was eight years old suggests for one minute that he thought his behaviour reprehensible. Both he and Rose gave her the impression she was making a great deal out of nothing with her ridiculous whimpering.

Fred was hardly more decorous in his attitude towards Stephen's approaching manhood, boasting about his prowess with Rose and predicting, amid laughter, 'You'll soon be ready to sleep with your mum.' Heather was the one who could not bear it. She grew more and more withdrawn and remote as she pondered her suffering alone, and would burst into tears at school when the contemplation of it overwhelmed her. She wanted to run away from home. 'The whole atmosphere was really making Heather miserable,' said her sister. She was desperately unhappy, and cowered when her father made one of his lewd remarks at her expense. When she told a schoolfriend that he came into her room at night and what then happened, she cried herself to a standstill. In the end, Heather was murdered, probably for making a fuss and resisting him.

In many respects Frederick West was typical of one common kind of incestuous father. In 1955 S.K. Weinberg studied 203 cases of incest and in his report divided the fathers into three categories. The first was the endogamic man who concentrates his sexual activities exclusively within the family and often chooses a daughter in memory of some idealized love, such as his mother or dead wife; this clearly does not apply to West. The second was the paedophilic man whose appetite is for young girls, some but not all of whom may be his own daughters – it is their condition which attracts, not their consanguinity. The third was the promiscuous man devoid of taboos and inhibitions. West was clearly an amalgam of Weinberg's second and third types.[6] They, like him, were sexually demanding, requiring quick release every day, and their wives generally complained that their love-making was empty of affection. It was agreed by everyone that West's love-making was rapid, functional and arid.

Another study by Lukianowicz pointed out that incestuous men tended to have sex with their wives as well as their daughters and that their demands were unusually persistent.[7] Various other papers on the subject reach conclusions which are manifestly not applicable to the West case, as that incest occurs when the father is faced with the psychological impact of a mid-life crisis,[8] or that the father has stable employment in a profession or is alcoholic. Some have found evidence of a background of deprivation in a chaotic family with poor parental example, which may well be relevant to West's child-hood, and the chronic inability to feel guilt seems to be a common factor in all cases. Typically also, the incest is regular rather than episodic and lasts for four or five years until the daughter leaves home to liberate herself. In a large family the father may well proceed from one daughter to the next, unless the eldest reveals what has been happening in order to protect her younger sisters.' Something very similar happened in the West household. Anne Marie submitted for seven years before effecting her escape by leaving home (she left home three times before and either returned or was brought back); Heather intended to do the same, and was assumed by the family to have been successful – perhaps she threatened disclosure with her sisters in mind, and that threat precipitated her death. And it was the actual revelation by a younger sister which finally led to enquiries being made.

The one analyst who has been most frank in his study of the problem is the Californian Professor of Psychiatry, Roland Summit. Anxious to escape from the tabulations and statistics which must occasionally appear to be a cold, emasculated substitute for the truth, Summit reminds his colleagues in the field of the one cardinal personality trait which all incestuous fathers must share, regardless of whatever special circumstances may mitigate it, which is a very sick selfishness. 'Molestation of a child is not a thoughtful gesture of caring', he writes, 'but a desperate, compulsive search for acceptance and submission. There is very little risk of discovery if the child is young enough and if there is an established relationship of authority and affection. Men who seek children as sexual partners discover quickly something that remains incredible to less impulsive adults: dependent children are helpless to resist or to complain.'[10]

It also often occurs that the habit of incest is inherited. If a boy grows up in a family wherein incest is accepted as an ordinary part of intra-family relations, he is more likely to repeat the pattern when he himself has a family. This is what Meiselman called the 'incestuous model' passed from one generation to the next.[11] Others have referred to such people being 'incest carriers', whose influence upon family life may extend to several generations. There is every possibility that Frederick West was exposed to the incest habit as a boy, and various family members are on record as saying that his father Walter took it for granted that it was his right to initiate his daughters into sexual experience; Fred's behaviour would then be a straight repetition of what he had learned at first hand. It is rumoured that Rosemary, too, suffered molestation at the hands of her father Bill. When the mother is the incest carrier, she will first of all signally fail to protect her own daughters from similar experiences, presumably because she thinks they are inevitable, and she will also, perhaps, vicariously enjoy what happens to her daughters in order to regain, in imagination, her own childhood, about which she has ambivalent feelings.[12] We recall that Rosemary was the favourite of her father, and that she continued to dress as a young girl well into adulthood. Moreover, it is highly pertinent to the current case that girls from incestuous families tend to choose husbands who are immature and untrustworthy, who they subconsciously know are likely to abuse their own daughters and ensure the continuation of the habit. It is already clear that Fred West was both immature and untrustworthy to a painful degree. Once the incest-taboo is broken and what was once 'unthinkable' becomes an event of quotidian banality, it is relatively easy for the transgression to recur in subsequent generations.[13] Indeed, incestuous fathers may well imagine that the very purpose of procreation is to provide a supply of nymphets for future use. With regard to this, we should pause to reflect that Fred West showed virtually no interest in his daughters except as sexual objects. That was what they were there for, as he frequently reminded them.

There are times when theorists go beyond what is logically persuasive in their desire to illustrate the mechanics of incest-inheritance, and suggest something merely fanciful, as in the contradictory notion that an incestuous father sees in his daughter a substitute for his first love, i.e., his mother.[14] But there is a more subtle variation on this theme, which may have a recognizable bearing on the West case. Starting with Freud, it suggests that the boy who has a severe fixation upon his mother is likely to become not only an incestuous father but, in time, a sadist and necrophile.

The mother-fixated man tends to be narcissistic. Given unconditional and frequently preferential love in infancy by a mother for whom he can do no wrong, he grows to regard himself as wonderful and special, without having to do or achieve anything to confirm this exalted status. He just is privileged, and will in adult life avoid any situation where he can be challenged or has to justify himself or risk attempting a task which he will fail to do as well as his distorted self-image demands. He continues to feel superior and special, but will seek only those situations which he can control, in order to avoid this specialness being exposed as sham and spurious. It is well attested by all West family members that Fred was his mother Daisy's blue-eyed boy, that he was singled out from among all her children for special cosseting and protection. He could do no wrong. He was always forgiven. He was cravenly admired in an overt manner which distinguished him at once from his siblings. He was, in a sense, prevented from growing up, learning his limitations and honing his qualities. Since adults do not abjectly admire as they should, the growing Fred eschewed them as sexual companions in favour of young girls who either would admire or could be made to accept without admiration, which he would supply for them. They would not question or challenge his superiority and narcissistic self-image, so it was safe to use them. When he tangled with a woman who had emerged from adolescence and had a mind of her own, as Rena had, he was so shocked that he lashed out and hit her, almost by way of silencing the blasphemy.

None of this is incompatible with West's need to have other men perform the sexual act with his wife because they would do it better than he. On the contrary, it was a device to protect the self-image, which would not have survived long had he been made to face reality in his own bed every day.

It is easy to see how this turn of mind can evolve into a passion for incest, as one's own daughters, so fragile and dependent, so habituated to obedience and admiration, would not puncture the self-image with intrusive, capsizing dissent. And if they did cry out in grief or pain, he could convince himself that it was for their own good and that they would be grateful. No argument or reason must be allowed to dilute this exquisite conviction. When he told his daughters that they needed a man to break them in, that no fool of a schoolboy would know how, and it should be their father to do it, he was not joking, not even exaggerating. He believed it, for in his mind he could not be bettered; had not his own mother always told him so? Anne Marie clearly fitted the bill and suffered in silence for seven years. Fred's self-admiration was intact.

One may also see how, one step further on in this chain, he could re-create the admiration with strangers, young girls whom he picked up casually and then rendered speechless by gagging and ultimately by murder. They could not be relied upon to acquiesce quite as easily as his own daughters had done. Had they been ready to, and behaved themselves, and accepted the gift he was ready to bestow upon them with his expertise, it may not have been necessary to silence them at all. If only they had behaved like his daughters! They, at least, knew what was what. There is some reason to wonder whether this is one of the reasons Caroline Owens survived, not only because she was the only one we know to have been seduced in Rose's presence, but because she did not make a fuss and resist.

Thus far, the theory is only my own, and does not therefore deserve the respect one might accord to a professional. But Erich Fromm has developed it further, with the suggestion that incestuousness which is truly malign evolves from a kind of autism in childhood.

According to this, the child is rendered so self-sufficient by his mother's love that he basks in it, without the need to move forward. He never learns to love his mother back, in fact, for she is only a bestower of love, and the little boy does not learn mutuality and the needs of others. 'These children never break out of the shell of their narcissism,' he writes. 'They never experience the mother as a love object; they never form any affective attachment to others, but, rather, look through them as if they were inanimate objects, and they often show a particular interest in mechanical things.' Jeffrey Dahmer is already clearly visible in this portrait. Might it also apply to Frederick West?

Fromm says that if an autistic or near-autistic infant has an incestuous fixation upon his mother, as West arguably did have, then the bond becomes malignant. He does not develop a sexual attraction towards Mother which, paradoxically, would be a properly healthy development ultimately leading to maturity, but sees her as symbolic, magnetic, absolutely necessary but immobile and petrified, almost as a thing. He does not escape this deadness, the quasi-death of autism, and spends his life looking to be re-united with it. 'There is no defence against Mother's destructiveness; her love cannot be earned, because it is unconditional; her hate cannot be averted, since there are no "reasons" for it, either. Her love is grace, her hate is curse, and neither is subject to the influence of their recipient.' This is perhaps another way of saying that the child's moral compass is rubbed out, annihilated. The end result of such malignant development is relationship to other people by destructive bonds and sadistic control.[15]

It would be perverse indeed to claim that Frederick West suffered from fully fledged autism. Such a garrulous and sociable man is in every outward respect the very reverse of autistic, and he bears no comparison in his social behaviour with the severely monosyllabic and smileless Jeffrey Dahmer. Yet there are enough clues in the smothering nature of Daisy's adoration, in Fred's unwillingness to explore relationships with anyone except to exploit them and squeeze admiration from them, and in his self-love and remarkable lack of affection, to sustain a connection between these and his mechanical, soul-less, selfish abuse of Anne Marie. Whether there is also a causal link leading on to sadism and murder is, perhaps, more debatable.

Two further considerations, less psychological than practical, may also be relevant to West's incestuous behaviour. One is that incest is statistically more common in large, overcrowded families than in a compact unit of, say, two parents and two children, living in spacious accommodation with bedrooms for each. In a severely overcrowded environment the father can sometimes 'slip into' an incestuous routine if only because the opportunity is pressed upon him at every turn.[16] Frederick West grew up in a tiny rural cottage in cramped conditions shared by parents and seven children. His first home as an adult was even smaller – a simple caravan in which he, his wife Rena, two teenage girls and two female children all slept; there were not even beds for all of them. When he moved to Midland Road with Rose, it was to a ground-floor one-bedroom flat which served to accommodate the two of them plus three female children. And at Cromwell Street in the early 1970s, there were parents, four children and four to six lodgers distributed among four bedrooms. Anne Marie occasionally shared with a lodger, and the other children were often in one bedroom. Individual privacy was never a factor in the West household. While it would be misleading to compare 25 Cromwell Street to the chronic conditions which exist in some Latin American slums, wherein incest is rife, the relative overcrowding that the Wests were used to did present classic circumstances in which the incest idea might take root.

The second staple of an incest narrative is usually the geographical or social isolation of the family.

114

Geographical isolation speaks for itself, in that a cohesive family group which is denied interaction with other groups and is rarely, if ever, exposed to strangers, is likely to turn in upon itself for sexual experimentation; such conditions apply to people who live in inaccessible mountain regions, or remote islands, or in areas which are periodically cut off from the rest of the world by hostile weather. Paradoxically, the taboo against incest is often strongest amongst such peoples (northern Canadian Indian communities, for example), precisely because its danger is recognized and its frequency acknowledged by the taboo. Rural Gloucestershire can hardly compare in isolation, yet it is common enough for tight little village communities to close ranks against the rest of the world and find solace amongst their own number, simply because they do not venture out but cling happily to an era before public transport when there was never anywhere to venture to. Incest in such rural communities does not seem so peculiar. (A more modern view holds that incest in higher-income families living in an urban environment is simply better concealed.[17])

I remember visiting the graveyard high on the cliff overlooking the fierce, perpetually inimical North Sea at Inverallochy when I was looking into the background of Dennis Nilsen, murderer of twelve young men in North London. Inverallochy is the small, grey, windswept village in Aberdeenshire where Nilsen's maternal ancestors lived for hundreds of years. It has a population of a few thousand, but the gravestones bear only five family names, repeated over and over again across the centuries. People in the community had continued to marry one another until they formed one homogenous unit, and I was told that incest was not especially frowned upon.

Even if the geographical isolation of a Gloucestershire village was stark, the city of Gloucester itself was large, fairly cosmopolitan, busy with people and activity, and it was here that Frederick West settled with his growing family. But even before he had moved into Cromwell Street the social isolation of the family, entirely self-willed, was already strong, and it grew worse with time. Despite the gregariousness of Fred and the constant supply of tenants at the house, and despite the Wests' reputation in the street as a fairly nice couple, they were curiously self-contained and mysterious. Rosemary's sister-in-law, Barbara Letts, was the only regular visitor; otherwise, the house was like a small fortress, packed with transients but psychologically impregnable. The children were seen going to and from school, but they always went together and returned together, with no friends in tow. Schoolmates were told not to call at the house, lest Rosemary bark at them, and the West children were never seen playing with others in the street. Rosemary sometimes went to pubs to pick up men, and Fred to tell tall stories or advertise his wife's services, but they did not go out together. It was as if a drawbridge had been raised and they were socially self-sufficient. In such an atmosphere incest breeds and is maintained.

Until comparatively recently, incest was not treated as a crime at all. Though it was always considered to be wrong, it was regarded as an offence against God (a sin rather than a crime, in other words), and was dealt with by ecclesiastical courts from the Middle Ages into modern times. Such courts also dealt with witchcraft, bestiality and adultery. At the end of the nineteenth century there was some pressure to make incest a criminal offence, but it met with strange resistance, successive Lord Chancellors advising against it on the grounds that it would draw attention to a subject better left alone, and might give people ideas. Eventually the Punishment of Incest Act came on to the Statute Book by Private Member's Bill late one Friday afternoon in 1908, when the House of Commons was almost empty. This remained the law until more up-to-date legislation was passed in 1956, under the Sexual Offences Act, which prescribed a maximum sentence of seven years' imprisonment for the offence, unless the girl be under the age of thirteen, when life imprisonment might be imposed. This remains the law today.

Not many cases come before the courts, however, because this is the most secret of crimes. Of all indictable sexual offences incest is the least reported, less even than buggery. It has been estimated that over 1,500 incestuous offences may be committed every year, but only 300 of these ever come to the attention of the police.[18] Even then, the case may be dropped due to the reluctance of the victim to see it through to conviction, as indeed happened with the West family in 1992. Such a massive amount of attention has been paid to child abuse in the last ten years that it has given rise to the suspicion that much of it arises from wilful exaggeration or a desire for vengeance on the part of children, who are suddenly aware of the great destructive power within their grasp merely as the result of a word. According to this perception, incest is still rare, but press obsession with it is rampant. Roland Summit is impatient with this view. 'An image persists of nubile adolescents playing dangerous games out of their burgeoning sexual fascination,' he writes. 'What everybody does not know, and would not want to know, is that the vast majority of investigated accusations prove valid and that most of the young people were less than eight years old at the time of initiation.'[19]

On the other hand, it must surely be true that, historically speaking, the opportunities for incestuous assault have diminished with the advent of compulsory education and the removal of daughters from the family home for several hours a day. As recently as the last century, when girls were kept at home and the father's authority over them was absolute, their vulnerability must have been far greater than it would now be, and with the collision of other circumstances mentioned earlier (overcrowding and social isolation), their sufferings were unlikely ever to be discovered. Nowadays, there is a much greater awareness of the dangers children face and a whole department of Social Services dedicated to their well-being.[20]

Nevertheless, the psychological pressures upon the incestuous victim are as powerful as ever, and the experience of the West family amply illustrates how they can prevent disclosure. In a normal family atmosphere the members are bound together by ties of love, affection, loyalty and trust, and each will flourish with the unspoken, tribal support of the rest. The incest family distorts this process by kidnapping those same values and wrenching all true meaning from them. The members will stick together out of loyalty, and to protect the only security and honour they know, but the loyalty they feel is born of fear, not affection, and the honour they protect is based upon a lie. What they have is an unnatural cohesion, a pathological cohesion which renders the family totally turned in upon itself and unable to form relationships of any sort beyond its tight frontiers. It becomes an 'incest family' with an 'incest secret which binds the members together in ties of dependency' in an atmosphere of stifling and noisome conformity.[21] One incestuous father has described the effect as 'really love in the inner circle'.[22]

Such a family is rigidly patriarchal, with the father ensuring his dominance by making repeated threats about the dangers of anyone outside knowing anything about them. This makes the abused daughter of such a family hopelessly dependent, for she must choose between her submission or collapse of the family structure. She is intensely vulnerable to coercion and intimidation, and easily persuaded that what is happening to her must be kept secret, because her father says it must, and it is from him and her (perhaps) complicitous and acquiescent mother that she learns moral boundaries. These are, a) it's for your own good, b) it's secret, c) don't tell, or we shall all suffer. She complies out of obedience and a natural wish to please, and the rest of the family echo the

118

subservience, subsuming it into their repertoire of ordinary conduct. Their greatest fear is desertion and the dissolution of the family unit.[23] They are terrified of being abandoned, and will keep quiet rather than risk it. It is significant how uncommonly quiet the West children always were, silently fusing together.

The daughter who is the object of abuse will have the greatest burden, extending beyond the endurance of the assaults themselves. There are two additional crosses she must bear. One is the corruption of her affectionate guile, for she will have learnt that sexually provocative conduct and sexual availability are her best means of obtaining the parental attention and love she needs. Secondly, it is on her that responsibility for the family's future, and the happiness of her siblings, depends. The police sometimes disastrously misunderstand this cohesion, attributing it solely to obstruction directed at them, and they unwittingly serve to reinforce it. 'Some of the police took the attitude that the whole family were scum,' says Stephen West.[24] They were not angels, and they had learnt by long example to regard policemen as enemies, but they needed very gentle treatment indeed if they were to be prised loose of the hell in which they lived. One policewoman in particular was aware of this and it would be to her gentle persistence that revelation finally came about.

Disclosure is usually made by the daughter, in a gradual sequence of events. She will first attempt to hint to her mother, who very often disbelieves her, tries to hush the matter up, or blames her. She will then try to tell outsiders, all the while feeling deeply disloyal and hoping that nothing will happen to break up the family. One girl described her dilemma in this way: 'You see, I had this kind of magical thing – if someone would say the word, I'd talk about it, but I couldn't bring the subject up . . . If I did and my dad went to jail, it would be my fault. But if someone else brought it up and I talked about it, it would be their fault!'[25]

Once disclosure has been made, the family is thrown into huge crisis the outcome of which threatens catastrophe. The father could lose his job, his wife, his daughter, his freedom. The wife could lose the breadwinner and the man in her house. The daughter could lose her parents and family home. All of them will become objects of prurient curiosity. Worst of all, the rest of the family could ostracize the daughter and make her feel she has ruined herself as well as them. Faced with all this, it is small wonder that the incest victim often retracts her accusations, and that the incest family coalesces once more around its poisoned nucleus.[26]

All of this was seen to operate when the Wests were arrested in 1992. The charges arose out of an event at Cromwell Street which, in Mae's vivid account, combined elements of the banal and the awful in a way which characterized life in that doomed, surrealistic house. In a highly significant aside, Mae reveals the detail that Rosemary had gone out of the house that afternoon, leaving Fred upstairs while five young children sat downstairs watching television.

Fred came down and asked one of the girls there to make him a cup of tea. At the same time he contrived an excuse to inveigle another one to follow him upstairs. Once she had entered the bar-room, he closed the door behind her and began his assault. The other children were aware that something was happening, and sought tentatively to intervene. One of them knocked on the door and said, 'Your tea's ready, Dad.' He was annoyed at the interruption and came storming downstairs. Mae says that the girl had been penetrated four times.

The girl was severely shaken. In a halting manner, she revealed to one of her schoolfriends the gist of what had occurred, and this friend went home and told her mother. The mother was sufficiently alarmed to inform the Social Services, who in turn passed their concern on to the police. The girl was gently interviewed, eventually making a statement which was harrowing and specific.

Hence it was that on 6 August 1992, police arrived at 25 Cromwell Street with a warrant to search the house for evidence of child abuse. They took away with them trunkloads of dildos, leather underwear, whips, straps, and ninety-nine pornographic videos, some of which Fred had required his daughter Mae to watch with him, to her disgust. The videos were both commercial and home-made. Fred was charged with three offences of rape and one of buggery. Charges against Rosemary came later – causing or encouraging the commission of unlawful sexual intercourse, and cruelty to a child – which were, on the face of it, difficult to comprehend in view of her supposed absence from the house at the time.

After that, the authorities moved swiftly and decisively, removing all five younger children from the custody of their parents once and for all, and precipitating the crisis which demonstrated all too clearly what can happen to an incest family threatened with fragmentation. It also demonstrated something the court in 1994 was never fully to examine, namely some unsuspected aspects of the personality of Rosemary West.

Police intrusion into their lives sent the older Wests scuttling like a myriad of ants in a disturbed ant-hill. Fred and Rosemary warned Stephen and Mae that questions would be asked and that they must stick together. Fred was then taken into custody, leaving Rosemary bereft in an empty house, contemplating the now useless décor of a family home which, in her own view, she had cherished, and the waste of motherhood, the only thing she thought she was good at. She was in turn belligerent and pathetic, the former in the presence of police whom she blamed, as usual, for the ruin of her life – she was in addition charged with obstruction when she lashed out and hit an officer in an obstreperous fit – and the latter when she frankly admitted to herself that she was lost without her brood. The author Howard Sounes relates how Rosemary's sister-in-law Barbara Letts went to No 25 to comfort her and help her pack some clothes to send to the children. 'As they sorted through the bedrooms, putting tops and trousers into a bag, Rose broke down and cried.'

She went further. One evening, after much smoking and drinking, she swallowed forty-eight Anadin tablets. Stephen found her collapsed on the floor and summoned an ambulance. At 1.50 a.m. on 13 August, only a week after the family break-up, Rosemary West's stomach was pumped clean at Gloucestershire Royal Hospital. The depression, however, did not lift.

Police watched in dismay as the family rallied round to diffuse the calamity which had befallen them. Reasoning that he could serve time more easily than his father, Stephen made a statement that it was he who had committed the offences (he was then nearly twenty years old). The girl who brought the charges in the first place began to backtrack, and Mae also announced that she would withdraw her statement supporting them. The police were witnessing the self-protective re-gathering of forces within an incest family to prevent that which they regard as worse than abuse – their own dissolution. The effect is best seen at work in Mae's own untutored words: 'She [the girl] said she didn't want Dad charged. She thought that she would be allowed to go back to her home if the whole thing went away. I was in a similar position so we agreed that, *to keep the family together*, I'd lie to the police. We thought that if the charges were dropped then all our younger brothers and sisters could come back to Cromwell Street and *we'd be a family again* . . . She didn't want to give evidence against Dad, and she wanted her life to *return to normal*. I couldn't say anything against him myself because I thought – well, he's our dad after all. I was also *scared of losing my mum*, who was sticking by Dad. It put us all in a very difficult position over loyalties and doing the right thing'[27] (all the italics have been added).

The two children who were to be witnesses in the trial were prepared for their evidence by staff at the home where they were staying, but on the day itself they declined to testify. The judge then had no alternative but to direct that the trial could not proceed. All charges were dropped and formal verdicts of not guilty were entered. The whole business had taken three minutes. Fred was elated, because he thought he had done nothing wrong in the first place and it served the police right to get their come-uppance. Rosemary was more subdued.

One of her first acts was to sign an authorization for the police to destroy the pornographic videos and sexual aids which they had seized. As Mae put it, 'She didn't want them in the house again because it had lost her her children.' From that moment there was a subtle estrangement between the pair. For the first time in her married life Rosemary had made an autonomous decision. She declared what was to happen and would no longer allow herself to be persuaded by glib tongue and winning manner. His pornography had, in effect, destroyed her home, so it would have to go. 'He was livid about losing all his stuff,' says Mae, noting, by striking omission, that he did not seem to care one way or the other about losing the children; rarely can the difference between these two people have been so marked. He also wanted Rosemary to resume prostitution, once more with a startling lack of recognition of what this might mean or imply about his priorities, or about his ability to understand the emotional content of anything at all. Mae: 'He wanted her to go back on the game, but Mum refused to have anything to do with it. She stopped everything completely and never gave into him again.'[28]

But it was too late. She was not to know that a sequence had been set in motion which would erupt, two years later, into something infinitely worse. The engineer of this sequence was a policewoman of remarkable tenacity, Hazel Savage, who had interviewed Anne Marie and heard the terrible story which she had kept to herself for so many years. Anne Marie, too, would retract at one stage, but Savage instinctively knew that the matter could not be laid to rest and that there was probably more to the West household than child abuse. In particular, she began to wonder what had happened to Heather West. She received little encouragement from her colleagues and superiors, who were professionally bound to tread cautiously before making unsubstantiated allegations. Yet she intuited the turmoil and degradation of spirit which must sweep in the wake of repetitive incest and had some understanding of how the 'incest secret' is buried. It was her patience with Anne Marie which enabled this secret, and others, eventually to be prised out of Cromwell Street.

Savage must have realized that the five children removed into care wanted to abscond and run home to 25 Cromwell Street (they occasionally succeeded), and may well have wondered what was the glue which could ensure such a degree of loyalty in such extraordinary circumstances. Once again, it was conversation with Anne Marie which offered the clues.

The exploited daughter in the incest relationship is initially confused by what has happened to her. 'Bed covers take on magical powers against monsters, but they are no match for human intruders.' As she grows older and more accustomed to it, this translates into anger because she has been made to feel that any complaint could lead to disintegration of the home, and loss of love and security are far more frightening than violence or sex. Her anger cannot be expressed, because it is accompanied by guilt. The girl loves her father as the main source of nurturing in the house and her principle moral example, and at the same time despises him for what she gradually perceives as his betrayal. The conflict is a terrible weight and wear, and she repeatedly surrenders to it. 'The child cannot safely conceptualize that a parent might be ruthless and self-serving,' writes Roland Summit; 'such a conclusion is tantamount to abandonment and annihilation. The only acceptable alternative for the child is to believe that she has provoked the painful encounters and to hope that by learning to be good she can earn love and acceptance.'[29]

We heard this voice in court. Anne Marie Davis told us that she remembered feeling she should not be so ungrateful, but at the same time wondering why the experience felt so like punishment. 'What had I done? I hadn't done anything wrong.' Her love for her father is painfully manifest even in retrospect. 'I would try so hard to please him and would be over the moon if I achieved the ultimate – his praise and attention,' she writes. 'I wanted Rose to love me because it would please my dad.' When the intercourse became regular, she said, 'I didn't object because it was the only way I knew of getting his affection.'[30] Mrs West said in court that Anne Marie 'thought the world of him'. The act itself was for her, at that age, devoid of sexual content – it was a way of receiving interest from a parent. And the guilt which she later felt derived from the disruption she had caused, not from the incest itself.

This guilt is worth examining in some detail, for it is multi-layered. In many respects, variations of it protected Frederick West from discovery and, by extension, frustrated the revelation of his murderous activities for so many years.

While it should feel good to earn one's father's attention and love, the pervasive secrecy which surrounds incestuous behaviour conditions the child to feel ashamed of having earned that love, without quite knowing why. Her moral understanding is turned upside-down. As Summit puts it, 'Maintaining a lie to keep the secret is the ultimate virtue, while telling the truth would be the greatest sin.'[31] She is perplexed and regards herself as irredeemably bad, because the right thing can only be the wrong thing, and she is 'likely to spend a lifetime in what comes to be a self-imposed exile from intimacy, trust and self-validation'.[32] It is impossible to exaggerate the ghastliness of this position or the dramatic, destructive measures to which the child must resort in order to deal with it. Typically, there are unnatural and unpredictable alterations of mood, and other indications of depression such as fatigue, loss of appetite, disturbance of sleep, inability to concentrate. There are often threats of or attempts at suicide, coupled with severe delinquency and trouble-making subconsciously designed to bring down punishment upon her. She will continue the complicity with her father by maintaining silence to shelter him, and at the same time seek chastisement for her other behaviour in lieu of the punishment she should receive for submitting to his love. Faced with insoluble conflicts, she will run away. It has been estimated that about half the females in juvenile detention for running away are incest victims.[33]

Almost all of this could be seen in the history and demeanour of Anne Marie West. She gave evidence as if trapped in a trance-like state, her voice the very definition of lassitude – flat, monotone and lifeless. She had ripped out emotion and taken refuge in blankness. Her behaviour at home became uncontrollable, and at school she was a disruptive bully. She embraced sexual promiscuity, seeking attention from a succession of anonymous suitors with the only asset she thought she had – her body. She was often brought to the attention of police. And she ran away from home four times. She tried to kill herself when charges were brought against her father, after his own suicide in prison, and mid-way through her evidence at her stepmother's trial.

Terrified of the risks involved in revelation, Anne Marie castigated herself for even *wanting* to reveal, treated herself like dirt because that's what she thought she was, and behaved in such a way as to attract the punishment she knew she deserved. Her only means of expression was self-criticism. All of this grew directly out of the incest to which she had been subjected and accounted for the fact that it went completely unnoticed. It also accounted for her subsequent retraction of statements, as the dangers she had always feared loomed like foul, uncharted terrors before her. 'Whatever a child says

about sexual abuse, she is likely to reverse it.' In exactly
the same way, it accounts for her sister's retraction
before the case against her parents could be brought
before a jury in 1992. Nor is the West family unusual in
this regard. 'Most ongoing sexual abuse is never disclosed, at least not outside the immediate family.
Treated, reported or investigated cases are the exception,
not the norm.' And, worst of all insults, when a child
does have the courage to report what has happened, her
adult hearers, more often than not, refuse to believe such
a wild, incredible tale, notice her shiftiness and guilt, and
side with the parents who have been so outrageously
defamed. 'The child of any age faces an unbelieving audience when she complains of ongoing sexual abuse. The
troubled, angry adolescent risks not only disbelief, but
scapegoating, humiliation and punishment as well.'[34] She
will end up an orphan, in mind if not in fact.

When Heather West told a schoolfriend that her
father was having sex with her, the friend immediately
responded by asking whether she had told her mother.
She said that Rosemary would not believe her.[35]

It is axiomatic that the offender is generally the father.
Cases of incest perpetrated by mothers are so rare as to
hardly figure in statistical analysis.[36] It is even (surprisingly) true that the mothers do not generally know the
incest has taken place. 'Contrary to popular myth,' writes
Summit, 'most mothers are not aware of ongoing sexual
abuse. Marriage demands considerable blind trust and
denial for survival. A woman does not commit her life and
security to a man she believes capable of molesting his
own children. The "obvious" clues to sexual abuse are
usually obvious only in retrospect. Our assumption that
the mother "must have known" merely parallels the
demand of the child that the mother must be in touch in-
tuitively with invisible and even deliberately concealed
family discomfort.'[37]

From what we already know of Rosemary West, it
may be pitching her standards too high to ally her with

the sort of woman who 'would not commit herself' to a man like Fred, were she aware of his incestuous assaults. Anne Marie's testimony, as we have seen, affirmed that she not only knew about the incest but encouraged it and took part in it on two specific occasions. Hers, however, is the only voice to allege Rosemary's active involvement (we do not know what allegations were made in advance of the 1992 case, as they have not been divulged, although it is clear there was much alarming medical evidence to support them). The other children said she turned a blind eye. Fred used to touch Heather and Mae on the chest or between the legs and tease them when they objected, and Stephen said he was embarrassed by his mother's non-intervention: 'She never told him to stop doing it.' Mae said, 'There was no point in appealing to Mum. She knew about it, but she ignored it. She'd just say that Dad was playing, she never really put it down to much. I think she thought that, as he wasn't really hurting us, there was nothing to worry about.'[38]

This passage makes it abundantly clear that Rosemary was aware of Fred's vulgarity, lewdness, overt sexual play with his own daughters, but not necessarily of his incestuous attacks. She thought he was a rogue obsessed with sexual matters, and that the girls would have to learn to put up with it as long as it caused them no real harm. It is, alas, also conceivable that she thought incest with a pre-pubescent child was harmless, and would examine a child after the event to make sure she was all right.

There are other authorities, however, who aver that mothers merely *pretend* not to know what is going on. According to these, the mother is usually a passive and dependent creature, whose excessive dependency has arisen from inadequate parenting in her own childhood, and who will put up with anything for the sake of her marriage. She may have been a victim of sexual abuse herself, and her apparent collusion in the incest which occurs within her own family may be an attempt to resolve her own experience by 'normalising' it.[39] There is some reason to suspect that Rosemary may have nursed bitterness against her own submissive mother for not having protected her against Bill Letts' attentions, and have worked this out in indifference to her own daughters' needs ('I put up with it, so you should'), or projected on to the daughters the 'bad' part of herself.[40]

Another reason for the mother's denial of incest may be her own promiscuity, that she is prepared to tolerate her husband's infidelity with their daughter in return for his indifference to her lovers. While Rosemary was promiscuous, the evidence is that she was so initially in obedience to Fred's requirements. That would not prevent her, of course, from feeling guilt about it, and resisting any interference with his incestuous activities as a result, but this is a very speculative view. Much more applicable is the observation that 'these mothers are often intimidated by their husbands and fear violent retaliation if they should try to intervene in the incestuous relationship'.[41]

What evidence is there that Rosemary might have been ignorant of incest under her own roof? Anne Marie stated both in court and in her published account that over the years during which she had sexual intercourse with her father in his van, in houses, in fields, he had always insisted she keep it from Rosemary at all costs. 'He would sometimes give me a few pounds not to tell,' she said.[42] Rosemary herself said that Anne Marie was too fond of her father ever to 'tell on' him. On the other hand, Anne Marie recounted a conversation from more than twenty years previously, when Rosemary had absolved Fred from any blame for what had happened. She quotes her as saying, 'I'm sorry. Everybody does it to every girl. It's a father's job. Don't worry, and don't say anything to anybody. It's something everybody does but nobody talks about.'[43] The sentences frankly sound too polished, too complete, too well edited to admit of genuine memory, and were perhaps the product of assistance from her journalist collaborator.

If so, it would be in keeping with a very common experience of incest sufferers, that of profound reluctance to blame the father – stretching so far as a need to exonerate him – with its concomitant requirement to heap much of the blame upon their mother, who should have known, who should have helped, who should have protected. 'Although these girls felt abandoned by both parents, they verbalised most of their hostility against the mother. They often idealised the father . . . and absolved him of guilt.'[44] It is no disrespect towards Anne Marie to suggest that her response now to her appalling ordeals of many years ago may be recognized within that summary. Her stepmother's counsel at the trial would put this to her in so many words. She denied it, and the jury believed her.

What she finds very difficult to acknowledge, and what is the crucial gradation leading from incest to murder in this case, is the essential violence of her father's attentions. It would be wrong to assume that all incestuous relationships are identical and easily understood. There are some psychiatrists who would even make a distinction between benign incestuousness and malign incestuousness, with the claim that the former is a 'normal, transitory stage of development',[45] though it is only to point out that this would be more akin to incestuous thought than any overt incestuous act. When the victim of actual incest is herself an adolescent with developing sexuality, then the damage done is less than it would be to an eight-year-old girl to whom excessive sexual stimulation is strange and frightening.

It is a disturbing statistical truth that most incestuous fathers initiate sexual contact with their daughters when they are between the ages of eight and twelve, that is, before they can have any real notion of what is going on. It is quite obvious why this should be so. The child cannot understand and therefore will not object. She can be controlled. The man's utter dominance will not be challenged. He is taking advantage of her infancy not to make love to her, but to exercise his needs for violence and supremacy upon her unresisting body. She has become for him almost a thing, like a doll he could buy in a sex-shop, a masturbatory aid. She is a sex toy, and unlike a woman who may object to being played with, she will keep quiet and submissive, and submission is what he wants above all else. In this regard at least, such a man resembles the paederast who is too scared to attempt contact with a grown person, except that the paederast is sometimes tender in his attentions. The incestuous act is therefore an act of extreme pathological violence, with marked sadistic undertones. It is ruthless, selfish and blind. There is nothing of love in it.

No wonder Anne Marie would not see her father in any of this. 'She thought the world of him.'

In a case which came before Liverpool Crown Court in 1988, June and Hilda Thompson, sisters in their thirties, revealed that they had each had full sexual relations with their father Tommy Thompson since their childhood. It had been a joyless, sordid routine, sandwiched between television programmes and signalled by a slight nod of their father's head to indicate to one of them that she should go upstairs, undress and prepare herself for him. Their mother had been pummelled into docility and was powerless to intervene. When Thompson was about to kick his wife in the shins or punch her in the face, June and Hilda would stand closely either side of her to prevent her falling. That the sexual assaults had more to do with sadism and control than with passion was demonstrated by Thompson's ordering of his daughters' daily lives. They had to place their cups five inches from the edge of the table, or they would be punished. They had to pull the curtains at 7.35 in the evening, not a second before or after, or they would be punished. They had to wash up without a single piece of cutlery or crockery touching any other piece, in complete silence, or they would be punished.

Tommy Thompson too was a hoarder, with cupboards full of meticulously labelled and positioned provisions. The cruelty of his conduct is evident, as is the sadistic impulse which informed it. Incest was merely one cold expression of it.

One day June and Hilda took a shotgun and executed their father. The jury inevitably found them guilty, but Mr Justice Boreham released them with a mild suspended sentence. He said, 'I accept that in many ways your life has been a form of torment, and in a sense you have taken your punishment before the event.'[46] Tommy Thompson's sadism was terminated. Frederick West's was not. When incest failed to satisfy it, he found other methods of forcing submission.

5
Control

While it is obvious that a father who forces sexual relations upon his own daughter is vicious, it is perhaps less acceptable to regard him also as pathetic. Yet the very fact that he has to rely upon enforcement, and must choose the one person in the world who is the least likely, because of fear, bewilderment and trust, to resist him, must indicate an extraordinary ineptitude.

Frederick West's sexual relations with women, from his adolescence on, had always been functional (empty of emotion) and violent (based upon attack), and he seems never to have experienced the mutuality of desire or the comfort of a loving embrace. The first assault upon a thirteen-year-old girl, when he was himself barely a man, set the pattern. In Rena he found a woman who was, initially at least, ready to accept his arid and quick love-making, possibly because her life as a prostitute had prepared her for it, and she was not necessarily shocked or let down. Anne McFall made the mistake of asking for love rather than sex, which Fred would find threatening because it undermined him and invited him to lose himself. It is highly significant that this man never 'lost' or surrendered himself in the act of love-making, but remained always the copulating animal, knowing what he was doing and doing it when and how he wanted to. (In police interviews he would make frequent reference to his murder victims having started the 'love stuff' which, however insultingly untrue, at least reveals his fear and incomprehension.)

Rosemary was the first girl he met who both put up with his rough approach and seemed to admire him the more as a consequence of it. She did not smother him with soppy love, but was content to be available for him when he needed to ejaculate. She later made it clear that sex with Fred had never been anything but perfunctory. Upon the mysterious glue of this relationship the prosecutors of Rosemary West would build many speculative assumptions to make a connecting thread between the nature of her marriage and the fate of her husband's victims. It is, I submit, much more fruitful to look upon the nature of Fred's sexual demands and to what extent they were satisfied, over a long period, by incest with Anne Marie on the one hand, and by the ritual subservience of his wife on the other.

The man who cannot relate to others in the biophilic way, that is through love or creative helpfulness, is left floundering without anchor unless he can find other ways of relating which accord with his quasi-autistic needs. It does not matter whether the people he is relating to appreciate this or not. They are simply there to have things done to them, to enable him to exist and be effective. Incest is one route by which effectiveness is guaranteed, for it requires no pretence of love from the victim, but rather looks for obedience and acquiescence as proof that the perpetrator can function. The daughter is his property, and he is exercising right of ownership by relating to her as her conqueror. This is no mere academic theorizing – Fred himself used words which support the proposition when voicing his rights over his daughters. Another method of relating is through sadistic force, wherein the pain and suffering of the victim offer proof of effectiveness; the victim may be indifferent to you, but your treatment of her will cancel that indifference and make her take notice and acknowledge your existence. A third is destructiveness, the need to force one's existence upon the world by annihilating it; this is the path of murder and necrophilic delight.

It should be manifest that all three – incest, sadism, murder – are essentially different expressions of narcissism, the abject inability to relate to any other person with mutuality. They are expressions of self, arid self-propulsion and self-protection. The victim's only purpose is to validate the selfness of the perpetrator. Anne Marie was pitifully deluded if she thought that she could earn her father's love and attention by submitting to his lusts – their only point was his own satisfaction, the triumph of his effectiveness. Erich Fromm has expressed this need with great clarity:

> The ways to achieve a sense of effecting are manifold: by eliciting a sense of satisfaction in the baby being nursed, a smile from the loved person, sexual response from the lover, interest from the partner in conversation; by work – material, intellectual, artistic. But the same need can also be satisfied by having power over others, by experiencing their fear, by the murderer's watching the anguish in the face of his victim, by conquering a country, by torturing people, by sheer destruction of what has been constructed. The need to 'effect' expresses itself in interpersonal relations as well as in the relationship to animals, to inanimate nature, and to ideas. In the relationship to others, the fundamental alternative is to feel either the potency to effect love or to effect fear and suffering.[1]

I think, further, that incest, sadism, murder and dismemberment are different stages in the development of this narcissistic absolutism, that one stage might herald another, and that in West's case there is a definite progression which begins with incest and ends with the hacking of bodies. The trigger which propelled him from one stage to the next was the constant need for fresh stimulation.

Once again, the need for stimuli is not in itself reprehensible or even unnatural. Any parent will confirm that the baby and growing infant thrive on different and constantly escalating stimuli being presented to them for exploration; it is their way of discovering the world, and if they are thwarted, they may well risk a dangerous degree of autism and withdrawal. (Apropos of which, it would be interesting to know if Fred West, as an infant, had been denied the stimuli which would have enabled him to become aware of the needs of others as well as of his own.) But when the hunger for stimuli extends into adulthood and is exacerbated by a rampant narcissism developing at the expense of every other growth, then its unrestrained character can wreak havoc.

We know that Frederick West displayed stimulation-need in his ordinary quotidian life. He was restless and nervy, unable to sit still for long. He was an impulsive thief, stealing whatever happened to be at hand whether he wanted it or not, simply for stimulus, for the excitement of the hunt. In other words, he was very easily bored. The person who is bored is implicitly making a complaint, namely that the world does not give him the stimuli he craves. He will deal with it by snatching at stimuli, by stealing them in fact, sucking the world's energy to feast himself.

In sexual matters, the need for ever-increasing stimuli makes it impossible for the narcissist to be pleased with the repetition of a pleasure – such is the province of the satisfied and the mature – but on the contrary condemns him, if you will, to seek heightened pleasures in a never-ending quest for novelty. Fred wanted his wife to have fresh lovers so that he could spy on them or listen to them. He then seduced his eldest daughter and continued with consequent assaults upon other daughters. Other young girls were enticed into his company, and upon them he developed his sadistic lusts. It is a sad and troublesome characteristic of the sadistic impulse that it is the most prone to this escalation of stimuli. The sadist must move forward with each experience, ever deeper into perversion.

The older West children would periodically notice an increase of tension in the house, as their father grew moody and quiet. This might last several weeks, until the tension suddenly lifted as if a cork had been released. They never understood why.

Studies by Mark Gresswell of the District Forensic Service in Lincoln suggest that there are close similarities between the pathologies of the addictive gambler and the repetitive murderer, in so far as both habitually seek to repeat a peak experience and, failing, are moved to increase the degree of stimulation they require in order to attain it or go beyond. The gambler wants a repetition of that special feeling which accompanied the first big win, the lust murderer a repetition of the 'high' which followed his first taking of life.[2] A sexual sadist has confessed that, after his first murder, 'I never thought it would be so easy to kill a person, or that I would enjoy it. But it was easy and I was enjoying the feeling of supremacy. A supremacy like I have never known before.'[3] And never would again, unless it could be improved. It is more instructive to term such people 'addictive' rather than 'serial' killers.

There are dozens of examples of sadistic murderers whose appetite for conventional sexual intercourse is, like West's, limited and who are driven by boredom into experimentation. The most obvious parallel in the public mind must be with Ian Brady and Myra Hindley, the so-called Moors Murderers who tortured and killed several children in 1963 and buried them on the bleak, windy moors of Lancashire. I hope to demonstrate that the points of comparison with the West case are indeed few, but as far as sexual boredom is concerned, Brady and Frederick West were soul-mates. Hindley indicated that Brady had not shown a great deal of interest in her sexually, preferring to be masturbated by her, and that in a desultory manner.[4] W. McCord thought that Brady and Hindley illustrated the psychopathic craving for excitement, that 'they explained their actions as simply ways to

137

attain new levels of excitement, a new "consciousness" and temporary escape from boredom.'[5]

As so often occurs, the pathological is no more than a deplorable exaggeration of the ordinary. Happily married couples also engage in experimentation, and for similar reasons – to save a tired marriage which is threatened by lack of novelty. They might buy sex aids from shops which do huge business with run-of-the-mill customers, or watch pornographic videos, or join a wife-swapping group, or find where they might attend an orgy, where several couples play with each other and change partners repeatedly. Curiously, the only certainty they demand is that no emotion should contaminate the proceedings, that they should merely 'have sex' with as many people as possible in a great variety of ways. This is precisely the frame of mind which I have identified as belonging to those, like Brady and West, who are incapable of true emotional feeling. It is as if normal couples wish to escape their maturity and responsible attitudes in order to let Dionysus rip from time to time. The difference is, of course, that they revert afterwards to responsibility and mutual caring, whereas the Bradys and Wests do not and cannot.

A study made at a boys' training school into the personalities of the internees and what behaviour had occasioned their being admitted showed an astonishing degree of destructiveness which appeared to result from *the boredom of being insensate*. One boy threw rocks on to his garage roof and let them roll down on to his head. He said it was the only way in which he could feel something. In the school he made several attempts at suicide, always cutting himself where it would hurt most. He explained that pain proved he could at least feel. Another boy used to walk the streets with a knife up his sleeve and lash out at passers-by, enjoying the look of terror on their faces. He also took dogs into an alley and killed them with his knife 'just for fun'. Note his remarkable choice of words in explanation: 'Now I think those dogs felt it when I stuck the knife into them.'⁶

It should be clear from the above that there is a direct link between emotional blankness and the various forms of substitute effectiveness which are employed to compensate it. Incest, sadistic torture, murder, are all ways of doing something *to* someone rather than *with* someone, and all validate the doer at the expense of the person to whom it is done. The incestuous father, the torturer and the murderer are enabled at last to imagine they can *feel*, too, as other people apparently do, and because they are afforded this benefit, they further imagine that the individuals whom they are raping, torturing or killing are likewise deriving pleasure from the experience. They have no other way of comprehending the event. Frederick West was one such man. Like Ian Brady, he needed victims to make himself *felt*, and his method was to exert absolute control over them.

Opinions still differ as to the motive force of sadism. Some, following Freud's initial insight, hold that the sadistic impulse is essentially a perversion of the sexual instinct and has its base, therefore, in the libido. In Freud's own words, 'Thus sadism would correspond to an aggressive component of the sexual instinct which has become independent and exaggerated and, by displacement, has usurped the leading position.'⁷ This is tantamount to saying that an obsession with one aspect of sexual behaviour can elevate that particular until it is the *only* aspect which can achieve arousal or provide satisfaction, and overwhelm all the others, 'And hence one master-passion in the breast, Like Aaron's serpent, swallows up the rest.'⁸ According to this reckoning, a little bit of sadism does nobody any harm provided it is part of the repertoire of shared love-making, but is highly dangerous when it is exaggerated for the single pleasure of one partner, 'when the libido becomes misdirected or perverted so that the act of inflicting pain becomes in itself an object of sexual gratification'.⁹ This also carries the implication that non-sexual manifestations of sadistic behaviour, such as humiliation in argument, merciless teasing and the denigration of subordinates, is still sexual in origin, although it is not always easy to see how.

The alternative view is that sadism has nothing whatever to do with sex, but arises from a desire to cause pain as an end in itself, without there being a necessary sexual component. At the beginning of the century the deviation was called 'algolagnia', from a combination of words meaning the lust for pain, a term coined by von Schrenck-Notzing. The use of this word is now rare, because it is both clumsy and inaccurate, making no distinction between the lust for pain caused (sadism) and the lust for pain suffered (masochism). The modern term is named after the Marquis de Sade (1740–1814), a writer, revolutionary and sometime judge, whose novels are not particularly good and would have long been forgotten but for their subject-matter – the degradation of young girls. These novels and others like them fuse the two sources of the sadistic impulse, for while it is obvious that Sade's cruelty to his victims is based upon sex, it also looks likely that the cruelty eventually overrides the sex and becomes the principle purpose. Hence we have come to see nowadays that the crucial element in sadistic behaviour is the secret exercise of power by a weak man, be it sexual or crudely psychological, and that the sadist is inevitably psychopathic. 'It is transformation of impotence into the experience of omnipotence; it is the religion of psychical cripples.'[10]

In examining this 'experience of omnipotence' it will be important to discern whatever echoes there may be of Frederick West's behaviour, as far as we are able from the little he has himself vouchsafed and from the forensic evidence discovered with human remains at 25 Cromwell Street. We must bear this in mind throughout, for upon the strength of it must rest any picture of what happened in that house.

On the face of it, there is a remarkable resemblance between the staple of sadistic literature and West's presumed predilections. The usual plot involves a great deal of bondage, of girls being chained, shackled or restrained in some way, and an aggressive male 'hero' who forces them to submit to his will. But it is the 'conversion' which is the leitmotif of these plots, that is to say the unwilling virgin, having been forced to submit and endure rape, comes to welcome such aggressive attentions and beg for more of the same. There could hardly be a more vivid example of male fantasy than this, involving as it does the recognition of the man's superlative power and ability to enchant the female with his sexual technique, to 'give her a good time' as nobody else can. It is also a perfect illustration of the way Fred saw himself. We know he imagined that virtually every woman he saw was 'begging for it', as he frequently told his children so. We also know that the truth was just the opposite. He was just the sort of man who needed fantasies to cancel this truth.

Let it be said now that there are very many people who indulge in sadistic acts for pleasure and who would regard the linking of their preferences with acts of cruelty and murder as offensive. The sadist and masochist consenting couple please one another mutually, and theirs is a living fantasy, a pretence of power and submission often at odds with their polite daily lives. When asked, many of them claim that sadistic acts are more natural to them than any other sexual connection, because they resurrect the earliest sexual thoughts that can be remembered, those of early childhood. It is also true that those of us who do not regard ourselves as sadists nevertheless can bite our lovers with sufficient force to cause pain and leave a bruise, and we should be less than honest if we did not admit that the sensation of pain heightens the mutual pleasure involved. Even in 1902 a writer was able to say, 'What is more common than to find playful pats and slaps, the mimicry of blows, given and received as privileged tokens of affection?' The same writer suggests that these ripples of sadism are left-overs from our prehistoric past, 'exaggerated revivals of ancestral tastes', though this is not a view to gain respect in an age which has forsaken the image of the cave-man dragging his mate by her hair.[11] The fact is, however, that the married couple who enjoy a touch of battle, and the sadomasochistic pair who elaborate it into a ritual, are far removed from the sexual sadist who acts alone, has no thought for the other person present, and does not desist when real pain is caused. On the contrary, this is his signal to begin.

The Marquis de Sade's dictum that 'cruelty is one of the most natural human feelings, one of the sweetest of man's inclinations, one of the most intense he has received from nature' is nicely paradoxical and worthy of debate, but is mortal in the mind of an emotionally vacant psychopath. Ian Brady was known to read de Sade, and to gain succour from his assertion that murder was also in the natural order of things, thereby confirming his already highly developed sadistic impulses. Frederick West was nearly illiterate, and would not waste time with books even if he were not, but the video films he watched were the equivalent of Sade's indoctrination. There on the screen he saw the representation of his imaginings. He had not the intellect to recognize that they were, and must remain, no more than fantasies. For secure people, cinematic or literary fantasy offers healthy enjoyment of a forbidden lust by proxy, and may well prevent overspill into reality. But not for Fred West.

Various attempts have been made to categorize the kind of man in whom a potential multiple murderer may be lurking, and all of them are helpful to some extent. The Federal Bureau of Investigation has a specialist unit devoted to the study of criminal minds, at Quantico, Virginia, called the Behavioural Science Unit. Its famous study of thirty-six killers identified common traits among them which are now assumed as a matter of course by police investigators who are trying to track down an habitual murderer. They include, for instance, a possible history of arson or at least minor fire-setting, a tendency to wet the bed even into adolescence, a long period as 'mother's boy' in the family, a preference for the solitary pursuits of a 'loner', and so on. The trouble with these lists is that they point to characteristics which might innocently apply to a significant proportion of the population, and that they signify very little unless and until the person so described commits a crime. In retrospect, however, such lists can be astonishingly accurate.

It was the FBI who came up with the term 'serial killer', to denote a man who murders several times over a period of years and to distinguish him from the mass murderer who kills a lot of people on just one occasion. Perhaps the best summary of the murderous character came in a paper published long before serial killers had been heard of, by Dr Robert Brittain in 1970. Brittain based his findings on twenty years' experience of dealing with offenders who killed for no apparent motive apart from enjoyment, and his conclusions are still useful to this day. It must be stated that nobody would expect to find *all* these characteristics repeated in *every* multiple murderer, amongst whom there is the same span of differences as one would find in the general population. On the other hand, an accumulation of several features in one person does give one pause.

Brittain's sadistic murderer was a withdrawn, antisocial man with no close friends, studious and pedantic, uncommunicative, meticulous in appearance, reticent and shy. On the face of it, none of this can possibly apply to the garrulous and vulgar Fred West, but there are other indications which suggest the murderous part of him was revealed in tangential ways which could not have seemed relevant at the time. Brittain describes his composite man as:

> [a] vain, narcissistic, egocentric individual who, through his vanity, may be convinced that he can commit murder and escape detection by

being more clever than the police. He would rather be notorious than ignored . . . there can be a peculiar arrogance about him . . . his fantasy life is in many ways more important to him than is his ordinary life, and in a sense more real, so diminishing the value he puts on external life and on other people. It is almost as if he were forced by practical realities to emerge unwillingly from fantasy at times, but returns to it as soon as he can.[12]

Fred is clearly recognizable in this, although it is only now that we can appreciate the significance of some of it. There was in addition a strange emotional frigidity in Brittain's man, which would be strong enough to be remarked upon by those close to him and would be unexpected, and also a tendency not to drink alcohol. This last observation is a curious and accurate one as far as West is concerned, for he hardly drank at all; his family always thought this was because he preferred to retain control of himself and his household.

That word *control* will occur again. It lies at the root of the sadistic disorder. 'For the sadistic character there is only one admirable quality, and that is power. [He] is afraid of everything that is not certain and predictable, that offers surprises which would force him to spontaneous and original reactions,'[13] writes Fromm. The sadist must transform living people into 'slaves' who will do his bidding, whether they want to or not and especially if they do not, as a means to assert his power. He objectifies the living, turns them into things which have no will or preference but will only respond in the way he dictates and decides, exactly when he dictates and decides. It is for this reason that he usually kills by strangulation, because this method will permit him to increase pressure or release it, giving back life when he feels like it, as a cat might play with a mouse. There is no better way to ensure control than this, and death comes as a disappointment, for it demonstrates that control has been lost. Dennis Nilsen and Jeffrey Dahmer both strangled their victims, for they were sexual sadists, whereas Peter Sutcliffe and Jack the Ripper each stabbed or beat their victims to death, for they were destroyers. For the destroyer, death is the point and purpose, whereas for the sadist, some tiny residue of life must remain in order for him to exercise his mastery over it. He is stimulated by helplessness, not by extinction.

Forensic science was unable to determine how the girls under 25 Cromwell Street met their deaths, but I think it is reasonable to conjecture that they were strangled. Fred admitted strangling the last victim, his daughter Heather, as well as several of the others whom he did not name, and his account accords well enough with the effects of asphyxia for it to be believed.

I have already suggested that West's tendency to hoard things, be they tools, videos, bicycle clips, vegetables, or even (though this cannot be certain) fingerbones and knee-caps, is a mark of the anal character which is closely allied to sadism. Some manifestations of anal character are risibly absent from Fred's repertoire, notably excessive tidiness and punctuality, yet he revealed something of it in other ways. He was, for instance, stubborn and intense, holding himself rigidly against the danger of letting anything of himself slip away to be stolen by others. Intimacy (as opposed to sexual congress) was a threat to him, which was why he was ever afraid of affectionate closeness. The line from anal to sadistic character is here clearly drawn, for both types must either be remote and safe from intrusion, or be in possession and control. Security eschews unpredictability.

It is not difficult to see how these attitudes might be a residue from infancy and denote a severely immature person. The child requires security before all else, and only gradually does it learn that the richness of relationship requires some diminution of that security in return for adventure and love. If the child never does so learn, and his affective development is thereby stunted, he will only be capable of relating to another person if he is in control of that person, just as he had been in control of his mother. 'Individuals who exhibit sadomasochistic attitudes, or who are preoccupied with sadomasochistic fantasies are, therefore, demonstrating the persistence of an immature picture of interpersonal relationships. Such individuals seem unable to conceive of mutually rewarding relationships on equal terms. In the eyes of the sadomasochist, one must necessarily give the orders, whilst the other submits. It is a child's-eye view of the world.'[14]

It is no surprise, then, that the sadist requires his victim to regress to the helplessness of a child, who will be instructed, given orders, made to obey, and punished when he, the instructor, decides. Such people might make good generals, industrialists and captains of sports teams, where their success conceals what would otherwise be seen as a defect of character. In domestic life, they can always terrorize a wife or be cruelly manipulative towards a dog. The latter will not suffice, however, for the sexual sadist, who needs more than obedience; he wants despair.

The desire of the sadist has rarely been so well expressed as in the words of José Marcelino, a brutal murderer arrested in 1973 in Veracruz, Mexico. 'It made me feel good to see the women suffer,' he said, 'and the fear and horror in their eyes fed something in me that was sometimes even more pleasurable than having sex with them.'[15] Frederick West was never so honest. Though he described to police in repellent (and sometimes fanciful) detail what happened to the girls who perished at his hands, he never admitted to sadistic pleasure, and went so far as to maintain that they had been enjoying themselves and died accidentally. The artefacts found with their remains speak clearly, however, and allow us to suppose that he would recognize himself in Marcelino's words had truthfulness been within his scope.

Freud held that the ego was the libido's original house, by which I think he meant that the sexual drive arose from the ego's need for projection and fulfilment, and that sex was essentially selfish. If that is true, then it is easy enough to see how the sexual function may evolve, in a deranged personality, into incest and sadism, both of which are perfect instances of blind selfishness. But if Freud was wrong, and the desire to inflict pain may be an end in itself without a sexual component – in effect a replacement for and improvement upon sex – then perhaps even stable and unselfish people may harbour the sadistic urge in a tight little corner of their souls, never to give it air. That this might well be the case was demonstrated by an experiment conducted by Stanley Milgram at Yale University in 1963. The results were first published in an obscure specialist journal, later in book form, and later still were spread across the world by journalism. They were intensely alarming.

Forty males from in and around New Haven were picked at random or volunteered to take part in the experiment. They were told that the purpose was to test the effect of punishment upon learning and memory. In front of them was a man strapped to a chair with an electrode attached to his wrist. He was given some words to learn by heart, and each time he made a mistake he would receive an electric shock, which increased in intensity with each repeated mistake. The administrators of these shocks were his forty 'teachers'. Each of their switches was labelled to indicate the level of electricity to be pumped into the man, so they all knew what they were doing. What they did not know was that there were no electric shocks at all and that all the men who occupied the chair in sequence were actors who could simulate pain and terror according to the level of his supposed ordeal, from grunting at 75 volts, to an agonized scream at 285 volts and imminent death at 450 volts. The undeclared purpose of the experiment was to discover how far the 'teachers' would go in causing visible pain to another human being in compliance with instructions. Would they become sadists if they had official sanction to smother their inhibitions?

Two-thirds of the teachers obeyed most of the instructions and many went to the final hurdle of shooting 450 volts into a man already in acute distress. One of the actors was told to reveal that he had a heart condition and was worried about the effects of the experiment. Having been reassured that, though the shocks would cause pain, they would do no lasting damage to his heart, he 'agreed' to continue. At 150 volts he begged to be set free, and complained about his heart as the voltage increased. In spite of this, twenty-six of the forty experimenters went so far as to administer the maximum voltage of 450, when it must surely have occurred to them that they were causing great suffering and might even cause death. They would not consider themselves murderers or sadists because they were acting under orders and had been told they were doing good; the point was, were they sadists and potential murderers in *secret*, whose deeply buried desire to punish had been released by the simple nod of authority?[16]

I mention the Milgram experiment not because there is any suggestion that Frederick West acted under orders, but to show that the capacity for sadistic behaviour is latent within many people who would never consider themselves to be cruel. Indeed, the cheering effect of the experiment was to demonstrate how strong were the consciences of all the teachers, both those who desisted despite orders to continue, and those who continued in great travail of heart and broke down with self-hatred afterwards. It seems that, when authority permits the impermissible, the sadist goats separated pretty quickly from the compassionate sheep.

It is also instructive to see how frequently in contact magazines used by recreational sadists to search for suitable partners, the terms 'master' and 'slave' occur as totemic words which have an erotic charge almost by themselves. They show how strong a part the giving of orders must play in the sadist's repertoire, and how the notion of sanction to do that which one's conscience would normally forbid is central to the sadistic creed. Myra Hindley saw Ian Brady as her master, whom she must serve whatever private misgivings she may have had – the function of the master/slave relationship being precisely to stifle them. That is its joy, its triumph and its erotic core, as if the conquering of conscience and inhibition were the most exciting, liberating experience in the world. The evidence in the West case, such as it is, points to Fred having sought to make Rosemary his obedient partner but, having been disappointed, dominated his daughters instead and eventually found slaves among strangers whom he could control for his private pleasure far more severely than he dared with Anne Marie.

True sadists, as opposed to recreational and fantasy-inspired sadists, are very rare. They are intensely private and cannot easily be spotted. Who would have thought that jolly Fred West, boasting about the number of illegitimate children he had sprinkled about the land, talking with ribald abandon, touching women's bottoms and legs with total ease, belonged amongst men described by Anthony Storr as 'those who cannot sustain relationships with women, feel rejected by them, and become suspicious, hypersensitive and resentful as a result. Such men revenge themselves for supposed rejection by inflicting pain and humiliation, and feel potent only when they have their victim entirely at their mercy.'[17] Only the manufactured, inauthentic danger of the master/slave relationship could enable Fred to perform well in his own eyes and imagine what was happening in the minds of his victims. It is interesting to note that, etymologically, the word 'danger' is derived from Latin *dominarium*, which means power over others.

To assist him in creating this imaginary inauthentic world of domination into which seven poor girls would stumble, West relied heavily upon pornography.

At the time of the 1992 arrests scores of magazines were seized, similar to those which Heather or Stephen (or both) had taken with them to school and been roundly punished by their mother in consequence. They depicted scenes of sexual congress in a variety of guises and with assorted objects. Some involved bestiality. In addition there were ninety-nine videos of an explicit nature, almost all commercially obtained but a few of which were home-made by Frederick West. A large proportion of them were sadomasochist in nature. It was this collection which Mrs West asked should be destroyed after the case against her and Fred collapsed.

Material of this kind is widely available in most advanced Western cities, and themes of dominance and submission are not at all unusual in the fantasies of so-called 'normal' men.[18] Nor are underground networks of men and women who meet for spanking and bondage sessions. The common image of bondage and domination pornography is of women bound with ropes, handcuffs, chains, shackles, and clothes which cannot be removed. Gags, taped mouths, blindfolds and hoods are to be found in almost all such videos and magazines. The torture does not vary much. It shows clamps or some constrictive object attached to the breasts or genitals, hot wax dripping onto the skin, and occasionally the picture of a woman or girl hanging from a beam by the wrists or ankles. (It would have been part of the prosecution case against Frederick West that the notches in beams of the cellar at 25 Cromwell Street were used to suspend living girls, and one of his confessions contains a grotesque and, one must hope, fantastical account of the death of one specific girl in circumstances closely resembling this type of video. It is worth pointing out, however, that the murder of the girl in question took place several years before the acquisition of the video and that Fred's distorted imagination was probably working in retrospect. It is to the Crown's credit that such evidence was not adduced against Rosemary West.)

In an extensive study of commercially available pornography published in 1982, Dietz and Evans concluded that 'the degree of violence depicted ranges from a stern glance to apparent murder. Some photographs are such that it would take little suspension of disbelief to imagine that the woman was dead.'[19] It is understood in crime prevention circles that some of these pictures do indeed show a murder being committed, and that the model hired for the purpose is killed in the process of photography or film-making. Such films are known as 'snuff movies'. It is significant that bondage films and magazines are the ones which, in a shop dedicated to the sale of all kinds of pornographic material, are most in demand from customers. When asked if there was anything with blood in it, a shop-owner declared, 'It sells out so fast we can't keep it in stock.'[20]

Such material is generally used to arouse a man who can achieve no semblance of potency without it. If this be insufficient, he may take recourse to brothels which specialize in bondage techniques and flagellation, wherein some women are prepared to have objects entered into them as well. For the true sexual sadist, this, too, will be inadequate to the purpose, since the element of force will be missing. A prostitute who feigns fear is no match for the frightened girl who shows it, and in her case the objects used upon her body are likely to be inserted with brutal determination, in mock substitution for the erection he finds it so difficult to muster. The sufferings of girls in such a situation must be beyond comprehension.

It is a fact that this degree of sadism is unheard of in so-called 'primitive' societies, and only occurs in sophisticated Western countries where sexuality is habitually the source of guilt and frustration, fostering negative attitudes towards the ability to attract and perform. Historically, too, it is a comparatively recent phenomenon, entirely missing in preliterate societies. That these fantasies of domination should be so widespread is in itself cause for true alarm, if one assumes, as I believe one must, that the progression of this disorder bodes ill for the future. But for the present, it remains the case that the man who acts out a bondage fantasy to the point of actual death is extremely rare. The few cases we have on record resemble one another to an astonishing degree. If we look at some of them, we shall recognize Frederick West in each.

Gary Heidnik was arrested at his apartment on North Marshall Street, Philadelphia, in 1987. He was then forty-three years old. His ambition was to capture ten women, make them all pregnant and keep them in the basement. He had so far collected five, who were subjected to a daily dose of beatings, rape and prison diet of oatmeal and bread. Two of them died, one from exhaustion after being suspended from the ceiling by her hands for a whole week as a punishment for trying to escape, the other from being held in a water-filled pit and tortured with shocks from a bare electric wire. The body of the first was then put through a meat grinder and cooked. Heidnik pushed a screwdriver into the ears of the remaining three in an attempt to damage the eardrum and prevent them hearing any rescue attempt. All of the unfortunate women were prostitutes, either in professional reality or in his mind – he had to feel that they were 'inferior' for him to be able to exercise power and control over them, and to achieve sexual arousal. He was convicted on eighteen counts, including two of first-degree murder, in July 1988, and sentenced to death.

Three years before, a thirty-four-year-old lorry-driver from Turin called Giancarlo Guidice had routinely abducted, tortured and murdered seven middle-aged prostitutes who had accepted lifts from him. Two of them were whipped to death as they hung by the wrists. Another two were eviscerated in the manner of Jack the Ripper. All had fingers and toes chopped off (as had the West victims) before their bodies were flung into ditches.

After his arrest, a search of his flat revealed a collection of handcuffs, shackles, knives and scissors. In this case, the psychiatrists who examined him determined that he was irrevocably mad, and he is now detained in an institution for criminal psychotics.

Colleen Stan, aged twenty, was abducted as she hitch-hiked from Oregon to California in 1977 by a man called Cameron Hooker, who was accompanied by his rather dim wife Janice. Once Hooker had got the girl in his apartment, he placed a purpose-built wooden box over her head, shutting her in complete darkness, and enclosed both her and the head-box in a larger wooden box which was to be her home. She was taken out of this only to be chained and hung from a beam, whipped into unconsciousness, held under water until she nearly drowned, photographed in agony and given electric shocks. She was told that she was a slave and that Hooker was the master, whose orders had to be obeyed at all times. These included the admonition not to wear underclothes and to keep her legs apart in his presence. (Several witnesses would testify that Rosemary West did not wear panties and often spread her legs apart, but she was not asked whether this peculiar conduct had been at the behest of her husband.) This treatment went on for an astonishing seven years, during which she was gradually allowed out of her box for an hour a day to help with house-work, and eventually permitted to leave the house and get a job. She made no attempt to escape, having by then accepted her lot as a sex-slave and submitted to regular sexual intercourse when she was tied down to the bed and gagged. Most amazing of all, after the first four years of her captivity Hooker drove her to her parents' house, introduced himself as her fiancé and let her stay overnight. Colleen then returned to her almost casual torment.

The ordeal came to an end when Colleen and Janice took up Bible reading and revealed all to their pastor. It was Janice who, having confessed to Colleen that there was no truth in the idea that she was an actual slave and that in effect her husband was a pervert, insisted on spilling the beans to the police so that the young woman could gain her physical and, in the longer term her moral, freedom. We shall look at the complicity of Cameron Hooker's wife in this long terror in a later chapter, when we have to examine the degree of involvement of Mrs West in Frederick West's depravities. Hooker was sentenced in 1985 to one hundred and four years' imprisonment.[21]

Lawrence Bittaker and Roy Norris abducted several young girls in southern California and subjected them to days of degradation before giving them release in death. The girls were either hitch-hiking or simply walking home. Bittaker and Norris had a van they called 'Murder Mac', which was fitted with a sliding side door to facilitate snatching victims off the street, and it was generally in this van, with the radio blaring, that they committed crimes remarkable for their brutality. All the girls were repeatedly raped by both men, demonstrating their obsession with dominance and submission (the sexual act being not an end in itself but a means to humiliate). One had her nipples ripped off, another was stabbed in the ear with an ice-pick then strangled with a coat-hanger. Some were not despatched in the van but taken to a mountain retreat and kept captive for days before being killed.[22] It has been suggested that Frederick West may on occasion have had a male accomplice, but for legal reasons this possibility has never been explored.

The elements of control, domination, self-aggrandizement and pitiless cruelty are evident in all these cases, to such an extent that they may be seen as the unifying thread which places such criminals side by side in the category of 'lust murderer'. The distorted ego rules triumphant, and the people who are used as dramatis personae in these sordid tales have to be dehumanized, completely stripped of any vestige of dignity in order to be treated as objects, dispensable things which can serve

154

a purpose and be discarded. Even Hooker, who held on to his 'property' for seven years and never did willingly discard her, obviously regarded Colleen as an object to be penetrated and tormented for his sole satisfaction. I know of no more chilling illustration of sadistic control than his sending her to her family after four years as his slave, knowing she would return in utter compliance. Her will had been surrendered, cancelled out by the force of his.

From the evidence found at Cromwell Street it is possible to deduce the kind of torment suffered by seven young women who also ended their lives as the play-things of a demented sadist. The remains of Lynda Gough, Carol Cooper, Lucy Partington, Thérèse Siegenthaler, Shirley Hubbard, Juanita Mott and Alison Chambers were all found without clothing. Since one would expect some traces of material to have survived interment, the only correct conclusion was that the girls were naked when their bodies were disposed of, and there-fore probably naked when they died. What happened to the clothing was never fully explained; it was part of the Crown's case against Mrs West that she 'must have' done the tidying up and cleared out anything which had belonged to the victims; Fred West, on the other hand, admitted several times during his confession that he put everything in dustbin bags and left it for the refuse collectors. (Stephen and Mae remember seeing extra dustbin bags left out a couple of days after Heather dis-appeared.)

With each set of remains were found artefacts point-ing to various kinds of restraint. Rope tied around the wrists or the body, sometimes under the crotch and around the legs, in one case so complex that the victim had evidently been trussed up. Each skull was found either under or on top of other bones, tipped into a hole like rubble from a wheelbarrow. The role of dismember-ment in these crimes will be looked at in due course, but for the moment it is the condition of the skulls which is most eloquent. Each was encompassed in brown sticky tape, of the kind used in parcelling, always across the eyes and mouth, sometimes under the chin and over the top of the head, often winding a dozen times from back to front. It cannot be that this tape was applied after death, for there would be no discoverable reason for such an act, so it was applied to living young women, and it can only have been for the purpose of terrorizing and immobilizing them. In one case the tape covered the whole skull, apart from a small opening at nostril-level, from which issued a hollow tube; that girl was kept breathing not for her sake but for the sake of the sadist who was abusing her body. Another girl may have endured abuse for a week; this is suggested by the lapse of seven days between her disappearance and the treatment of Fred West at hospital for lacerations to his hand, from which it is deduced that he may have been busy with dismemberment on that day. At any rate, there can be little doubt that these girls suffered appalling treatment.

Fred West told police that he had no intention of killing them, that the deaths were accidental. 'You see, you've even got the killing wrong,' he said. 'You're trying to make out that I just went out and blatantly killed somebody . . . nobody went through hell. Enjoyment turned to disaster.'[23] This says much about the thinking of a sexual sadist. 'Fred considered himself to be a perfectly normal, rather nice man.'[24] Death is not his purpose, for it puts an end to enjoyment. And so intense is the personal pleasure that he feels, so complete and engrossing and exclusive the satisfaction, that he is emotionally unable to comprehend an expression of fear as anything but complementary to that pleasure. It is divorced from the person who expresses it.

To make sure, then the person must be depersonalized, and one way of achieving this is to black out the windows of humanity – the eyes, mouth, face – which is the whole purpose of hoods and masks used by recreational sadists in their make-believe. The harmless sadist still wants to feel that his partner is so helpless as to be anonymous, that his or her identity does not matter and can easily be squashed out of existence, to be replaced by a pulsating thing which is his to command. The difference between this and the psychotic sadist is that the latter is not playing games.

Photography is another tool in the fantasy. To take a photograph of someone is in a way to freeze him, objectify him, render him unable to budge, turn him into the photographer's property. The subject of a photograph still has some autonomy, but the photograph itself is a means whereby it is stolen and appropriated by someone else. It is an expression of power, of purloining. Dahmer photographed every one of his victims, in poses which he could control. Nilsen's camera was his most prized possession. Ian Brady took photographs incessantly, his model often posed naked except for a dehumanizing hood, that symbol which turns a person into a sex aid. He and Hindley took pictures of little Lesley Ann Downey before killing her. Then they took pictures of one another standing on her grave on the moors.

Any pictures which Fred West may have taken of his victims disappeared with the débris after the 1992 clearout. We do know that there were some of his wife, intimate close-up vaginal shots which were intended to display her sexual function and erase her personality. Was she, too, in some measure a slave of this man?

A curious undated document offers a palpable clue. It is in Mrs West's handwriting and it says, 'I, Rose, will do exactly what I am told, when I am told, without questions, without losing my temper, for a period of three months from the end of my next period, as I think I owe this to Fred.' It is signed R. P. West, and beneath that is Fred's own signature, F. West. This is typical of the kind of contract which a sadist requires of his 'slave', to be found in most of those cases involving the subjugation of a spouse by a dominant male. It is further typical of the man to place his own signature on such a document to signify that not only is his woman obedient, but her obedience is published. He owns her. Her humiliation is acknowledged in writing. Another similar document cannot be quoted, due to the repugnance of its vocabulary; beginning 'I, Rosemary West, known as Fred's cow', it goes on to list all the bodily orifices which she is bound to make available to him to do with as he wishes when he wishes. On a certain level, it is childish. Yet case histories clearly demonstrate that those sadists who proceed to crime and murder often start by abasing their wife, mistress or girlfriend in this way.

Those same case histories also show that the 'slave' is forced to submit to sexual intercourse with other men at the behest of her husband, often with perfect strangers, and is expected afterwards to describe the encounter in lewd language.[25] The parallels with the West marriage are too obvious to ignore. Fred told the police that he demanded a wide and open vagina and guilelessly admitted, 'I met Rose at sixteen and trained her to what I wanted.'[26]

Anne McFall was killed because she resisted his control, she would not do as he said in everything and made herself a nuisance with her pregnancy and her talk of love. He had to keep her in line. Independence on her part would be a threat to his manhood. Moreover, he buried her in the field he had known since he was a boy, keeping her close by as if she still belonged to him and he still exercised control. She would lie where he dictated, and nowhere else. That, surely, is the point of placing the other girls beneath the house of which he was so proud.

Was Rosemary clever enough always to keep in line? Not according to Kathryn Halliday, the neighbour from No 11, who visited her every morning for months to chat about teenagers and knitting, and occasionally to have sexual contact while Fred was at work. She told the court that Rose placed a pillow over her head and whispered, 'What does it feel like not being able to see?'

'They played with me and the idea that I was frightened,' she said. 'They got their thing from seeing other people frightened.' Far from keeping in line, Rose was an active participant in the assault upon Mrs Halliday, she said.

Virtually everyone who has studied aberrant sexuality has been of the opinion that sadistic behaviour is the province of men and not of women. It is, after all, an exaggeration of the attacking gesture which is part of maleness. Moreover, women are not fetishists or fantasists, preferring reality to an imaginary construct. Consequently, all empirical research into the sadomasochistic subculture has tended to concentrate on men, in the belief that women only take part in the victim-role, either professionally as prostitutes, or through specialist contact magazines; the former would suffer for profit, the latter for amusement, but neither would be likely to *inflict* suffering. Those who admit to enjoying the masochistic role say they were introduced to it by men. Masochistic females tend to be bisexual. The only study to prove that 'nonprostitute females do participate in sadomasochistic sex' was unable to show that they took the sadistic role *against women*; they would do so when pressed into it by men who desired to be the victim, cowering beneath their whips.[27]

The most provocative and least palatable reflection upon all this is that people like Bittaker and Norris, like Heidnik and like Frederick West are demonstrating aspects of their *human* condition when they behave with such contemptible cruelty, for it is only human beings that are capable of it. Animals are innocent by comparison, and to say that West 'behaved like an animal' is the opposite of the truth. Whether we want to allow it or not, West behaved like a human. 'With the exception of certain rodents, no other vertebrate habitually destroys members of his own species,' writes Anthony Storr. 'No other animal takes positive pleasure in the exercise of cruelty upon another of his own kind. We generally describe the most repulsive examples of man's cruelty as brutal or bestial, implying by these adjectives that such behaviour is characteristic of less highly developed animals than ourselves. In truth, however, the extremes of "brutal" behaviour are confined to man; and there is no parallel in nature to our savage treatment of each other. The sombre fact is that we are the cruellest and most ruthless species that has ever walked the earth.'[28] Fromm agrees: 'What is unique in man is that he can be driven by impulses to kill and to torture, and that he feels lust in doing so; he is the only animal that can be a killer and destroyer of his own species without any rational gain, either biological or economic.'[29] The point here is not that West can be excused because his sadism is part of his (and our) inheritance, but that he has to be explained in the light of it, and not written out of the scene as some kind of monster. To give comfort is none of our purpose. Mercifully, the number of men who tap into that reserve of cruelty is exceedingly small, as we have said, but that they do so is in response to a human need which has been distorted by a peculiarity of their personality and circumstances to overwhelm the rest of their nature. That need is one for closeness and related-ness to others. Denied the option of ordinary mutuality of need and shared satisfactions by a malignant quirk of character, they find it instead in the intimacy of torture.

The relationship between torturer and victim is, says Michael Ignatieff, 'the most intimate of all relations between strangers; eye to eye, hand to hand, breath on breath, torturer and victim are as close as lovers'.[30] And that, in the poisoned mind of Fred West, is exactly what he and his captives were, which is why he can still express astonishment that others of us cannot see it. In torturing them, he is making them feel, and the surge of pleasurable power which such control bestows makes him feel at the same time.

The victims will play their part by reducing themselves to quivering, hapless, helpless proof of that power. The more they scream, the less human they appear and the more easy it is to punish them. The ultimate cruelty is to oblige them to assist in their own degradation. Their anguish 'serves to aid the one who inflicts that anguish', and the victim soon 'loses his human status as he wails in his utter nakedness'.[31] This is precisely what the professional torturer acting on behalf of the State must do if he is to convince himself that his victim is sub-human and therefore not worthy of compassion or even concern.

Josef Stalin is perhaps the most vivid example of the sadist in our time. Able to kill and to spare, to reward and condemn, to banish and embrace, sometimes all at once or within the same hour, his was the demonstration of control 'by whim and mood'. He never betrayed the slightest indication that he considered the millions who suffered by his decree anything but pawns in the game of personal satisfaction. I think we can be fairly certain that Frederick West was a smaller-scale sadist of the same kind, pitiless in his moment of power. The police apparently told his son that West had pulled out the nails and cut off the fingers of his victims while they were alive, as well as stubbing cigarettes on their flesh. There is no support for this theory in the confession, although it is difficult to distinguish fantasy from fact in his ramblings, and the police may have been led to interpret him by the advice of the criminologist they asked to assist them. I prefer to believe his fevered boastings augmented the actual truth, harsh as that was.

If West's captivity and torture of seven girls is indicative of cold control, his murder of his mistress Shirley Robinson and his daughter Heather were substantially different in nature. These two incidents resemble the deaths of his wife Rena, his mistress Anne McFall and his stepdaughter Charmaine in that they result less from Stalin-esque deliberateness than from a severe lack of impulse-inhibition. Countless repetitive murderers have said that they felt they were in the grip of something foreign, that 'something strange came over them' which

161

they could not resist at the time of the offences. In this they reflect the common experience of a sudden change of character, illustrated by an access of rage which afterwards seems inexplicable – 'I don't know what got into me'. Priests do know, of course, and they call it the Devil. It seems to be the very opposite of the sadistic control we have been talking about, but I think it is a different manifestation of the same urge to be right and to eliminate any danger of being thwarted by the will of others.

It is this need of Fred West to 'sort things out' that led to the unexpected deaths of Shirley and Heather.

6

Shirley and Heather

Shirley Robinson came from a broken home. Her father Roy was an RAF corporal living with her mother Christa in Lincolnshire, but within three years the marriage faltered and Christa left home, taking baby Shirley with her. When that arrangement too failed, the little girl went to live with her father in Wolverhampton. Lacking discipline and structure, Shirley fell into delinquent behaviour, was selling herself as a prostitute at the age of thirteen, and ended up living in children's homes. Her last one was situated in Gloucester.

In April 1977, when she was eighteen, Shirley Robinson became a lodger at 25 Cromwell Street. It is not known who introduced her there, but since the house was well known to drifters and unhappy youngsters, it was no surprise that this extremely withdrawn and damaged young woman should have found her way into a ménage which afforded her some attention. She had apparently already demonstrated some lesbian tendencies, a not unusual trait in a girl who has been used for sex and craves affection, and this may have made her attractive to Mrs West, at that time two months pregnant with Tara. As for Fred, he appreciated a complicated sexual cocktail better than anything.

Anne Marie was then thirteen with a maturing body. She had already been introduced to sex, which was likely to have been thought a natural development in that house. She had posed naked, in a rigid standing position, hands by her side, as if to measure her progress towards womanhood. Rose took the picture, and Fred probably showed it to his mates by way of advertisement.

Eighteen-year-old Shirley was a reassuring companion for Anne Marie at this moment in her life, who responded to her friendship. 'She was nice and took me ice-skating,' she said, 'so I remember her better than the others. Sometimes I would walk down to the unemployment office with her. She was a bubbly girl and I spent quite a lot of time talking to her. I would sit in her room and chat.'[1] No longer withdrawn, Shirley blossomed in the free atmosphere of this unconventional house.

By September she had conceived a child by Fred, when Rosemary was seven months advanced in her own pregnancy. There is some dispute as to whether Rosemary realized what was going on. Witnesses would testify that the relationship was open and that Fred introduced the two women as his 'wife' and his 'lover'. A neighbour, Mrs Greening, said that Rosemary had told her, without embarrassment, that her husband was the father of Shirley's child, and Anne Marie maintains that it was 'common knowledge' he was. Questioned about this in court, Rosemary would claim that 'Fred told me he was covering as the father of the baby to help Shirley out until she got on her feet. I believed it. I believed she was silly enough to get herself in a scrape like that. The real father was a businessman, and Fred was protecting her.'[2] Given that Shirley had a promiscuous history there was no immediate reason why Rosemary should doubt such a story, and she well knew how much Fred liked to boast about his magnetic influence upon women, and thought it would amuse him, in a harmless way, to use Shirley's pregnancy as proof.

Shortly after this period, Rosemary and Anne Marie had signed a 'Bull Artist's Certificate', bought commercially and filled in by them, which they presented to Fred. It said:

This testifies that the bearer, namely Frederick Walter Stephen West, is declared the world's greatest bull artist and is known to the fair sex

as 'God's gift to women'. He is hereby acknowledged to be fully qualified to lie, overstate,
understate, and generally dabble with the truth
on any subject referring to himself that he may
find necessary to win himself a sort.[3]

She knew the measure of her man, and it was entirely in
keeping with this that she should acquiesce in his
charade of paternity if it suited him. Besides which, in
the second week of his confession in February 1994,
when he had been given no opportunity to confer with
his wife and neither of them had had any reason to pre-
dict, at the time of his arrest, that the subject of Shirley
would come up (police were then only looking for
Heather and had never heard of Shirley Robinson), Fred
himself corroborated Rosemary's version. He stated that
he needed to conceal that he was the father of Shirley's
baby from Rosemary.[4]

This is important, as it was the Crown's case that Mrs
West knew it was no joke, and was intensely jealous. A
motive for murder was thus established. There was little
evidence for it (it appears that Shirley often called the
Wests 'Mum' and 'Dad').

Tension did arise, but largely because Fred did not
know how to deal with Shirley's growing attachment. She
'became too loving', he told police. She wrote to her
father, then living in Germany, with the news that she
had met a wonderful man whom she was going to marry,
and that she had never been happier in her life.[5] With the
letter she enclosed a smart photograph of herself and Fred
together, both properly dressed and looking proudly at
the camera. It might almost have been an official engage-
ment picture. Why Fred acceded to this pretence is a
mystery, unless it be that he was too dim to realize its
implications. As soon as he did realize, he panicked.

Shirley's closest friend in the house was Liz Brewer,
who had been living there before she moved in and
would continue as a lodger for four years. She recalled

that everything had been happy and carefree at first, but that the atmosphere deteriorated seriously in the spring of 1978, as Shirley's term approached. 'She became frightened of Mr West and wanted to keep away from him,' she told the court. Eventually, Shirley shared Liz's room for safety, her incipient happiness having now turned into a dangerous liability. Fred admitted to Jim Tyler (husband of Rosemary's sister Glenys), 'She wants to get between me and Rose. She wants Rosie out so she can take over and take her place. I'm not having that. She's got to fucking go.'[6]

On 9 May 1978, Shirley and Liz posed for a jolly snapshot in the photo-booth at Woolworth's in Gloucester, one grinning, the other poking out her tongue. One morning shortly afterwards, Liz left 25 Cromwell Street to go to her job as a lunch-time waitress. 'Shirley seemed depressed,' she said. 'I asked her to come along, to meet some friends, but she was too tired, she just wanted to go back to sleep. I said, see you later, and left. When I came back that afternoon, she'd gone. I thought that perhaps she was downstairs making it up with Mr and Mrs West. I did not want to go down and get drawn into one of their explicit conversations about sex. I was sure she would be there in the morning and would tell me how everything was normal and happy again with them.'[7]

Fred told the police that on that day he met Shirley at an allotment and then went with her first to Painswick Beacon and then back to Cromwell Street. A row had developed. According to Fred, Shirley had called Rosemary a bitch and a cow 'and I had warned her a lot of times about that'. When they got back to the house, Rosemary had taken the babies to the park (there were now four of them, ranging from Heather aged seven down to Tara aged six months), and only Anne Marie was at home. She was shut in her room, and being by this time deaf in one ear, she would not hear what was going on in the back room on the ground floor. The row continued.

Fred claimed that Shirley had threatened him with revelation. 'I'm going to tell Rose that this is yours,' she said. He was furious, because 'it was stated right from the word go that the baby that she was carrying was not to be mentioned to Rose and it was hers, nothing to do with me'. Suddenly, the secret was to be betrayed. 'It was going through me mind at the time,' he said, 'she's going to absolutely ruin my marriage.' His rage thrust aside every other consideration, including his wife's imminent return to the house. 'I wasn't that bothered whether they [she] were dead or alive, you know, I mean it was just to get rid of them [her].'[8]

'I hit her onto the floor and then I just strangled her,' Fred said. In a police interview on 28 February 1994, he gave a cold and detailed account of how he strangled, dismembered and disposed of Shirley Robinson in a style so detached and irreverent that Detective Hazel Savage admitted to being shocked. It would serve little purpose to repeat it here, save to illustrate the void which exists at the centre of a 'serial' killer, the separation from that relatedness which ties the rest of us together. He used a brown serrated bread knife to cut her up – 'that was how I found out that the bone would come out' – dug a hole outside the back door, put the body in first, then threw the head and legs on top. Forensic evidence revealed that these were the only remains to be found without any restraint materials such as gags, tapes or ligatures. But the dismemberment had been ferocious. The thigh bones had been chopped through with nine mighty strokes of a cleaver, as if the murderer were in a hurry or in a rage, and several bones, including kneecaps and finger-bones, had been removed. Further, Fred's child, the eight-month foetus which Shirley carried, had been removed from her body and interred with her. This, of course, is exactly what had happened eleven years earlier with Anne McFall and her baby, two years before Rosemary came upon the scene. The pattern repeated.

To the police, Fred prevaricated, suggesting the baby

might have fallen out. 'I never touched the baby at all.'[9] Yet he did let slip that it was a baby and not an embryo, which at least indicated that he had seen it.[10] Rosemary's reflection in court was that 'it would take a really sick mind to do something like that'.

Fred was bound to have been in a considerable mess by the time he had finished, and would have needed to clean himself thoroughly. It was the Crown's case that Mrs West, his accomplice, assisted him in this, but she maintained that she noticed nothing amiss. Nor did Anne Marie, who was in the house throughout this crime and its aftermath. Neither mother nor stepdaughter appear to have observed a fresh hole outside the back door, or if they did, they ascribed it to yet more of Fred's odd-jobbing. 'If Rose had come out at all I could have said make me a cup of tea and she'd have went straight back in and made it . . . she had no suspicion I was doing anything apart from building that washroom.' She had, of course, come home after the murder and before the interment, when Fred calmly had his tea and she proceeded to 'bathe the little ones and everything there, with Shirley just behind the wall, not even knowing.'[11] (This does rather stretch credulity.)

As for Shirley's vanishing, not one person appears to have thought it odd. 'I didn't really miss her when she disappeared,' said Anne Marie. 'She was just another transient member of the household.'[12] Mrs West said in evidence that 'it was an everyday occurrence for us, people came and went. She was only there on a temporary basis. She just wasn't around one day.'[13] Fred volunteered the information that Shirley had suddenly decided to go to Germany, which was perfectly possible in theory, since her father lived there. This is what he told Rosemary, who had 'no reason not to accept it', and what he told Liz Brewer, catching her in the hall at the foot of the stairs one day as she came down with her boyfriend. Rosemary, who had heard the explanation before, nodded. But Fred added a touch of his own fertile fancy to the story later on. Making a special visit to Liz's room to tell her privately, he said that Shirley had to go because she was getting too randy and was planning to rip Liz's knickers off her. 'He went on so much about her wanting to get my knickers off,' said Liz, 'after that, to be honest, I was quite glad she'd gone.'[14] As a result, there took place another shuffle of rooms at 25 Cromwell Street and Liz's boyfriend Peter was able to move in.

Another lodger was Clare Rigby, whose room was opposite Shirley's and who had been living there for about two months when Shirley vanished. One day a week or two later she noticed the door was open, and inside Mrs West was stuffing clothes into black bags. She presumed they must have been Shirley's, although she knew she did not have many belongings. Rose pushed the door to, and that was that. But she had not bothered to lock it from the inside, as one might have expected her to do if concealment had been necessary or desirable. In the witness-box, Rosemary said that lodgers would often abandon bits and pieces behind, and it was 'up to me to clean up the mess and prepare the room for the next person'.

This was a perfectly rational explanation. Packing clothes need not in itself be a suspicious undertaking. It was, however, very peculiar that when Mrs West was first questioned about Shirley Robinson she professed never to have heard of her, never to have met her, then gradually to remember her vaguely as somebody who visited from time to time but never lived at the house. While it would have been understandable for her to forget many of the lodgers who stayed for a week or two seventeen years before, and we already know that the police traced one hundred and fifty people who had lived there at one time or another, it was simply not credible that she should obliterate from her memory the girl who had lived in her house for over a year, who was heavily pregnant, whom her husband at least proclaimed he had impregnated, and with whom she may have had some

169

intimate connection herself. As Brian Leveson QC said in his opening statement at her trial, 'It is ludicrous for Mrs West to pretend that she does not remember such a dramatic and disturbing part of her life.'[15] To which one might add that it would still be strange even if she did not regard Shirley Robinson's tenancy as dramatic or disturbing. It was only as the trial approached that her recollection was repaired. Her daughter Mae has pointed out that 'Mum has a memory like a sieve', but its selectivity was to do her much harm and to raise many doubts as to her honesty.

There is something else, not evidential but suspect. Why was Mrs West never tempted to hang on to some of the clothes which these various lodgers left behind when they moved on? She cannot be blamed for not doing so, but it can be pointed out that such scrupulosity is unusual, to say the least. It is part of human curiosity to want to make use of something which has been abandoned, to turn it to advantage. Indeed, Mrs Gough claimed that she saw a woman she took to be Mrs West do precisely that, wear her daughter's slippers. Why should she throw out everything that had belonged to Shirley, and save not a scrap? It smacked of the abnormal or the guilty.

In the coming weeks Fred told Liz Brewer that Shirley had given birth in Germany to a lovely boy whom she had called Barry, and that Rosemary was going to look after the baby for a while to give her a break. This may have been a simple lie to deflect any anxious enquiry, but since there is no evidence that anyone wondered anything, I think it more likely to have been an instance of Fred's unbridled myth-making. He was just making up a story because it sounded like a good one.

Nine years later he would do precisely the same when his own daughter Heather disappeared. This time it eventually led to his undoing.

The little girl whom Rosemary told the court she loved

'very, very, very much' and whose beautiful eyes Fred said he most missed when he was in prison during the first months of 1971, grew into a sturdy and self-willed adolescent. She had to, in order to keep her father's attentions at bay and her mother's temper cool.

Heather was more resistant and argumentative than her half-sister Anne Marie had been. It is not known whether she was aware of Anne Marie's treatment at the hands of her father, but when Fred made casual remarks about it being 'your turn next', Heather froze. She shared a bedroom with Mae when they were both in their early teenage years, and the sisters protected one another against Fred's suggestions and innuendoes. He touched both of them indecently and repeated his adage that a father's rights included the taking of his daughters' virginity, whereupon Heather and Mae promised each other that they would leave home as soon as they reached the age of sixteen, and that meanwhile they would fight him off if he ever tried anything.[16]

Heather's ambitions were tellingly escapist. She wanted to live alone, preferably in the Forest of Dean, even as a hermit if possible. She loved the feeling of freedom and openness in wild nature, the sense that everything was ordered as it should be and worked according to healthy rules, the safety and sanctity of the forest, above all its privacy. There she could be left alone and undisturbed. She would rather be with animals than people anyway. Scarcely could one imagine a more robust message of claustrophobia than this. Heather felt stifled and trapped at 25 Cromwell Street, threatened by nameless terrors. She walked around the house barefoot, a symbol of her yearning to tread the sweet-smelling leaves of the forest.[17]

She became a resentful and solitary girl, smoking surreptitiously and responding sullenly to enquiries. She was once arrested for shoplifting. Rosemary told the police, 'She was a stubborn girl, you ask the rest of the family, I mean she didn't want to do her own washing, she didn't want to move up off the seat, she didn't want nothing, she was so negative.'[18] Mae said she used to bounce back and forth on a chair 'like a kid',[19] a type of compulsive repetitive pattern common in disturbed young people (and reminiscent of Rosemary's own behaviour as a little girl). She sat around the house doing nothing, deep in thought. Rosemary suspected that Heather had turned against her because she realized her mother was a prostitute. 'I believe she disliked me because I had these other men,' she said. Significantly, she never had a boyfriend of her own and declared that if any boy were to touch her she would put a brick over his head. It was hardly to be wondered at that she should eschew any idea of sexual encounter, but Fred put a typically blunt interpretation on it. He told Rosemary and anyone who would listen that Heather was a lesbian. He was not being mischievous; he genuinely believed that if his daughter resisted his advances then there must be something wrong with her. If it were true, one would expect Rosemary to sympathize, but she nursed a rather naïve and foolish notion that her own lesbian activities were irrelevant or different in some way. Besides, she could not have talked to Heather even if she had wanted to; Heather would not listen.

She was so good at classes that her friend Denise used to copy out her homework on the bus. She passed eight GCSE examinations at school in the summer of 1987 and immediately saw her chance to escape. She would get a job and leave as soon as possible. But first there was a shock awaiting her which plunged her further into despair. Denise found her crying on a wall and asked her what was the matter. Heather had just found out that the father of another schoolfriend was also the father of two of her sisters. She further revealed that Fred had been abusing her and that Rosemary had done nothing about it. The man concerned heard that Heather had been blabbing and went to Cromwell Street to remonstrate. As a result of this, Heather received a tremendous beating.

She told Denise that her father had beaten her, and Denise repeated this to her parents. They were old friends of the Wests and said it was impossible Fred would do such a thing.

On 17 June the whole family went to Anne Marie's home at 52 Sapperton Road for her daughter Michelle's third birthday party. Heather was in the group, but not of it. It was clear to everyone that she was miserable and morose, and the mothers of other children at the party complained of her swearing. This caused a rupture between Anne Marie and Heather which was to prove fateful, for shortly afterwards Heather told her half-sister she was desperate to get out of Cromwell Street and asked if she could stay with her. Anne Marie, with her own memories of Fred coming to fetch her every time she had run away from home, thought that the same would happen if she encouraged Heather. So she refused.

Matters were reaching a climax for this unhappy girl, when rescue came in the form of a job offer from Torquay. She was to be a cleaner of chalets at a holiday camp, and presumably would have her accommodation provided. Then one day, without warning or reason, the job offer was cancelled and Heather sank into hopeless despondency. 'To be honest I felt sorry for her', said Rosemary, 'because it was the first time she'd shown an interest in anything since she left school.'[20] All accounts, from each parent and from her brother and sister, agree that she spent that night in floods of tears. Mae was in the same bedroom. It was she who told her parents that Heather had not stopped crying all night long. 'Heather looked as though she had had a rough night,' said Fred, 'so Rose said let her go, she said I'll go and draw the money out and let her go.'[21] Rosemary concurs. She drew out £600 from her accumulated family allowance and gave it to Fred, who was to have one last talk with her to try and dissuade her from leaving so abruptly. He wanted to tell her that she was too young to go just like that, and to talk it over with her. Rosemary went shopping, having first extracted a promise from Fred that if he failed to stop Heather from leaving, he would at least delay her until she came back so that she could say goodbye. Her things were there in the hallway, ready.

Rosemary estimates she was out for two or three hours. Fred said, 'When Rose goes shopping you can guarantee three to four hours, I mean she looks around the shops.'[22] When she returned, Heather had left. Fred explained that a woman had come in a red Mini to fetch her, and that was that. Rosemary says she hit the roof, and it was during this part of her testimony, recounting the day of Heather's departure, that she was so racked with sobs as to be barely audible at times. 'Fred seemed rather ashamed of having let her go before I got back home,' she said. He then announced that he had made arrangements for Rosemary to spend the night with a regular man in Pembroke Street. 'I didn't want to leave the house, because I thought the kids would miss her,' she said, but she nevertheless followed instructions as usual and did not return to Cromwell Street until around seven the next morning, in time to see to the children's breakfast.

Fred told his son-in-law Christopher Davis (Anne Marie's husband) his version of Heather's disappearance, and added this postscript when questioned about it by the police, 'Well I told Rose the same story anyway.' He further professed to having found it difficult 'to have to lie to Rose and Mae and Stephen, especially Mae, even more so . . . I mean Rose believe anything I tell her anyway, always have done, I mean that, done ever since I can remember with Rose, so I mean but with Mae, I mean it was, Mae was always a bit special to me because of her being educated and she was going places.'[23]

'We were expecting to hear from her. Fred said she'd promised to keep in contact. I thought she's bound to get in contact at Christmas, she wouldn't let it pass without saying Happy Christmas to Mae and Stephen. But we heard nothing. I thought she'd turned her back on us. I didn't think I was that bad a mother. I was so upset about it I told my mother. She said these things happened in families.'[24] A letter from Mrs Letts to her daughter confirms they were in touch on the matter. 'Have you heard from Heather yet Rose? It's a worry when they go off. I would love to see her.'[25] When in his turn Stephen left home a couple of years later, Mrs Letts wrote, 'Isn't it funny Rose, you can give them everything but they would rather rough it.'

'Mum cried a lot when Heather left,' said Mae. 'We asked Dad why she was crying and he said it was because of Heather. It was an unusual sight to see, because she was usually quite hard.'[26] From that day, Rosemary never swiped the children in anger again. It was a tacit acknowledgement that she could lose them.

Meanwhile Fred had spent the £600 on a transit van, telling his wife that he was paying for it by weekly instalments.[27] 'So you nicked £500 from your wife,' exclaimed Detective Constable Savage.[28]

From time to time Fred would say he'd seen Heather in the street or spoken to her on the telephone. Some of his stories were so fanciful as to be ludicrous, but others were sufficiently ordinary to merit belief. On one occasion he handed Rosemary the telephone, and she heard a drunken voice against a background of other chatter and noise; she thought Heather must have been in a pub somewhere. Stephen was present at the time. He now assumes his father must have got somebody to pretend to be Heather, and that his mother was deceived. Even as late as 1992, when Fred was in a bail hostel in Birmingham after the younger children had been taken into care on the grounds of his abuse, he was saying that Heather had visited him and that she would be home within a week. Rosemary simply told him to shut up.

What really alarmed Detective Sergeant Terence Onions, who conducted the first interview with Mrs West, was not so much her readiness to accept these stories, but her apparent indifference to the fate of her first-born child. Time and again she was asked why on earth she had not reported Heather as missing, or had made no attempt to locate her, and policemen seemed unable to comprehend that anyone should not wish to involve them. Rosemary looked upon this in quite a different way. As I have said before, she was from a family that had always regarded the police with caution, had married into another such family, and had several times been on the wrong end of a police enquiry. For her the police spelt trouble, not help. So when asked why she didn't report the matter, she astonished officers with the reply, 'So I have to snitch on my own daughter now, do I?' Though she may lament Heather's turning against her, she would never have sided with a police force against her. In her view, it was Heather's business what she did with her life, not theirs.

This attitude is audible in the first interview, which took place in the first-floor front room at 25 Cromwell Street, the so-called 'bar' room with its Caribbean mural and louche ambience, on 24 February 1994. Rosemary West makes it quite clear she regarded Onions and his colleague, WPC Willetts, as unwelcome intruders bent on giving her 'hassle'. She is uncooperative and resentful, mumbling, muttering and swearing, apparently convinced that the police were making fools of themselves yet again and were tormenting her for no reason. In her heart she knew why her five youngest children had been removed from her and Fred eighteen months before, but on the surface she took pleasure in blaming the police and interfering busybodies for having stolen her family. Occasionally, she shouts her responses contemptuously. She is on her own ground, in her own home, and not beset by doubts.

DS Onions is perplexed by Rosemary's vagueness and obviously does not believe her. Where did she get the £600 she says she gave to Heather to help her on her way? 'I was upset at the time, I cannot fucking remember,' she replies. 'It's a bloody long time ago.' When pressed further, she erupts, 'What do you think I am, after all that's happened? What do you think I am, a bloody computer?' DS Onions insists that all he is trying to do is gather information which will help locate Heather and confirm that she is alive. 'If you had any brains at all you could find her,' says Rosemary, 'it can't be that bloody difficult.' She reminds him that the police have resources at their disposal which she could not possibly match, so if anyone is to find Heather it should be them rather than her. When DS Onions warns her that 'the whole patio will be dug up, and the garden will be dug up and, you know, everything', she retorts, 'There's nothing you'll stop at, is there, hey?' These are the responses of a woman at once angry and astonished.

The officer points out that there have been rumours within the family for a long time that Heather was buried beneath the patio. The rumour first came to light as the result of a chance remark of no especial weight made by one of the children during the 1992 investigation. It was something of a family 'joke' that if they did not behave they would end up like Heather under the patio. Apparently none of them took it seriously, but police officers were curious and tried to trace whence such a peculiar joke could have come. They thought they had worked out the original source as being Anne Marie and her boyfriend Phil, and when DS Onions put this to Mrs West, he elicited a reply which bore all the marks of long antipathy between the two women. 'This is a girl who goes round stabbing other people', she said, 'and breaking up families and all the rest, and I'm going to take any flipping notice of it? Am I hell!' In point of fact, of course, the original source of the story can only have been Frederick West himself, the one person who knew where Heather was because he had put her there. Whether he said it in a confidential manner, as a real threat, or in a moment of absent-mindedness one can only surmise, but say it, at some point, he did.

It is not conceivable that Rosemary had not also heard this family 'joke', but there is no evidence that she took it any more seriously than the others. The police officer probed whether or not she had more specific knowledge. 'If you knew, let's talk hypothetically,' he said; 'if you knew, hypothetically, where she was, now, would you tell us?' The reply this time was still distrustful, but canny as well: 'Don't know that, I'm not in that situation.' Onions presses further: 'I've got a very strong feeling that she's been dead a long long time, a long long time, and whether she's under the patio or not is neither here nor there, but she's somewhere dust and bones, isn't she?' To this Rosemary's reply is packed with contempt: 'Oh you're lovely, aren't you?' Her voice is still sure, though tired and oppressed.

On the following day, 25 February, Rosemary West was placed under arrest and her interrogation continued at Cheltenham police station (Frederick West was simultaneously being questioned at Gloucester police station). The same ground is covered, with the same incredulous scepticism expressed by Mr Onions, who has a daughter of his own and cannot imagine not moving heaven and earth to find her if she left home. Mrs West is more subdued, but retains her firmness of mind in the face of what she considers to be harassment. Then comes the moment which electrified Winchester Crown Court when the tape of this interview was played, and which had caused me grave misgivings when I had first heard it at the committal proceedings eight months previously. DS Onions announces that there has been a 'major development' in their enquiry. 'Fred', he says, 'has confessed to murdering Heather.'

At this, Rosemary West shrieks, '*What?*' in a tone of unmistakable anguish, not pronouncing the final consonant and not pausing to reflect on how she should react. It is instantaneous and from the stomach. There follows a gabble of voices as question and answer interweave, DS Onions perceptibly embarrassed by the effect of his revelation. The transcript unravels the interchange in this way:

Mrs West:	So you know where she is?
DS Onions:	He's told us where she is.
Mrs West:	So she's dead? Is that right?

The police officer appears momentarily confounded by this candour, realizing he has just announced to a mother, one with terrible defects but a mother none the less, that her daughter has been killed by her husband. What if she really did not know? The whole exchange takes only a few seconds, but it radically alters the enquiry as far as Rosemary West is concerned. She is sobbing by the end of it, and is offered a break. Thereafter for the remaining tapes she is a chastened woman, speaking softly and deferentially, with no trace of the former defiance, until after four interviews she withdraws altogether into silence.

Immediately following the revelation, however, DS Onions has told her that Fred's confession 'automatically implicates' her, and her quick retort, through her tears, shows the steely logic with which they would have to deal. 'Why', she asks, 'does it automatically implicate me?'[29]

Here is an edited version of what Frederick West told the police: 'She's standing there against the drier with her hands on her hips . . . she had a sort of smirk on her face like you try me and I'll do the business. I lunged at her like that and grabbed her round the throat like that and I held her for a minute, how long I held her for I don't know I can't remember because for that few minutes I can't even remember what happened to that extent, I just, I can just remember lunging for her throat and the next minute she's gone blue. I looked at her and I mean I was shaking from head to foot, I mean what the heck had gone wrong? I put her on the floor, blowed air into her mouth and that, and pumped on her chest and she just kept going bluer, so

I mean at this I didn't know what to do. I mean Rose was due back, I mean I didn't know when Rose was due to walk in or when anybody else was due to walk in . . . and I've got her on the floor there and I mean I tried everything to try and get her to breathe again, but she just couldn't breathe. So anyway I tried to put her in a dustbin to cover, to get her out of the way . . . till I could get to do something about it . . . she started to go cold by then and she already wet the floor . . . I mean I never intended to hurt her I mean I just went to grab her and shake her . . . so anyway I tried to get her into the dustbin, I couldn't get her in there, so at that time we used to have one of those big ice saws for cutting big blocks of ice, so I cut her legs off with that . . . and then I cut her head off and then I put her in the bin and put the lid on and rolled it down the bottom of the garden behind the Wendy house and covered it up and left it there.'

Rosemary confirmed that there used to be in the house a knife designed for cutting large pieces of frozen food.

Fred went on to describe how he dismembered his daughter in the ground-floor bathroom, which formed part of the extension at the back, getting some blood on his hands only, then dug a hole in the garden (this was before the patio was extended to cover the whole garden). The digging, he said, happened at night, after he had sent Rose away. Between her returning from shopping and leaving for Pembroke Street, Heather's body had lain in the bin. 'I dug this hole and buried her down behind the fence, then . . . we had some of that blue membrane polythene you know they use on the floors that blue stuff think blue plastic . . . I put it on the top to cover up, to show there hadn't been any digging done there, to cover up the digging.' A police team had started excavations under the patio and had to be redirected by Fred, who told them they were at the wrong spot. They asked him what sort of grave they should be looking for. He said just a hole in the ground.

Savage:	And what's going to be in this hole in the ground?
West:	Heather.
Savage:	In how many pieces?
West:	Three.
Savage:	What?
West:	Two legs and a head and a body . . . I think the main bulk of her body is in the middle and legs are on the side, the head's on the front.[30]

He described how he ran a knife round his daughter's neck and then twisted the head round until it made a breaking noise, having first closed her eyes because 'I just couldn't look at her face and do it to her, you know what I mean?' He continued, 'I put the children to bed, locked the back door, went down behind the fence with a torch and dug the hole.' It took him 'two and a half hours perhaps.'[31] He chucked out her clothing and books for collection in St Michael's Square, behind the house. It was already packed in the hallway, ready for her departure to Devon.

Readers may be surprised that such an account should be so bereft of feeling, as were those present in the courtroom when the tape was played. A brief snivel as he mentioned decapitation passed unnoticed, the rest delivered in a flat monotone. In another interview, he said, 'She fell back on to the drier and then slid forward, she was making funny noises from her throat or chest for a little while.' Yet another remark which the jury did not hear established Frederick West's emotional blankness more vividly than ever. 'It is surprising', he said, 'how long you can hold someone round the neck before you know.' In another interview he said, 'I had one heck of a job to pick her up.'[32] For sheer effrontery of detachment and clinical insolence the remarks are breathtaking. They reminded me of an almost identical reflection made by Dennis Nilsen in conversation with me in 1983, all unaware of how shocking it was. 'It is surprising', he said, 'how much a head weighs when you pick it up by the hair.' These are the voices of derangement.

West appeared to be without remorse of any kind. Though he said it had been difficult to live with the knowledge that he had murdered Heather, it was clear that what he was most afraid of was losing his wife's support. 'I was thinking, God if Rose walks in, that's it, I'm had.' He admitted that he had constantly to deflect curiosity about Heather. 'I used to make excuses up and then of course when it came up over the trial, you know the other trial [in 1992], like then I had to cover it again then by meeting her in Birmingham.' Now that the actual fact of Heather's death was out, Fred knew perfectly well that Rose would hate him, and he pitied himself for it. 'Once Rose finds out about this then I'm finished . . . at least I had her behind me before with the other case, somebody, but now I mean my daughter and son and wife I mean they made it quite clear last night.' What they had made clear was that he was henceforth on his own.

He told police that he regarded Heather's death as an accident, and that he used ever afterwards to sit at night on the patio contemplating her. He would 'stand and say prayers by her' and 'tell her to rise and come up, you know'.[33] He had indulged in similar gazing before burying, but after dismembering her, an image which prompted a shocked DC Savage to observe that he 'stood there looking at her in pieces in a bin'.[34]

Asked rather crudely what she was feeling when she had just heard that her husband had confessed to murder, Rosemary confirmed his fears. 'Put it this way,' she said, 'he's a dead man if I ever get my hands on him.' After the 1992 case she was determined never to follow his instructions again and she put a decisive end to the informal prostitution which he had imposed upon her. She had planned to leave him then, but Mae had dissuaded her from that course. This time, she would have nothing more to do with him. When they appeared periodically in the dock together at the magistrates' court, as police continued to gather evidence, she would not even look at him.

The police were anxious to tie Mrs West's knowledge of the patio to the date of her daughter's disappearance. If she were to confirm the date it would show that it had been a matter of some importance, or if she were to prevaricate and give a false date, that too would indicate some knowledge that she needed to conceal. But she had not noticed. Despite persistent questioning, she simply could not recall when the patio had been extended, because Fred was always doing something out there. 'He only had to say to me, oh I've laid a new path or I've took some stones up because they were unlevel or whatever, and that would have been good enough for me.' We now know that the patio was extended in order to cover Heather's body. Had Mrs West known that, she would have had some more positive response, however evasively phrased, to the question put to her.

'Do you feel that perhaps you've been a bit naïve over this eight-year period?' asked DS Onions. 'Looks like it, don't it?' she said. Pursuing, the detective told her, 'You are the wife of the person who's confessed to killing her. You live in the house on whose land the body is allegedly lying at this very moment . . . Fred has described to us the steps taken and what's happened to Heather, and that it didn't take minutes, it took somewhat longer, and you'd have been in that house in between time, or at the time things were happening, and either you're blind, extremely naïve, or totally trusting of your husband – or you're a liar.'[35]

This, succinctly put, was one of the main planks of the prosecution case against Mrs West and has been throughout the principal public perception of her involvement. Detective Onions may well have believed that she was a liar. The public shared that belief and the jury acted upon it.

Mae and Stephen were fifteen and fourteen at the time of Heather's disappearance. They were not told they were naïve or blind or liars. Stephen may even have innocently helped dig the hole that his sister's remains would later fill (he recalls helping his father on such a task, but there were many like it).

Rosemary West sank into a lethargic condition as the interviews progressed. For very good reasons her young family had been kept away from her for nearly two years. She had lost much of her point for living, but was cheered by the support of her older family, particularly Mae. Now it was confirmed that Fred had murdered her first child. She told the police where to find pictures of Heather upstairs in the house, some of which dated from not long before she was last seen. For three consecutive days of interrogation, she refused all food offered her. During the fourth interview she was told, for the first time, that preliminary indications suggested there may be more than one body in the garden, to which her response was, 'Oh this is getting all too much.'

By the close of the fourth interview the detective was faltering. It had begun to occur to him that the person before him was quite possibly not involved in murder. 'Obviously this is a very traumatic experience for you,' said DS Onions, 'and I can only apologize if you, as you say, have no knowledge of this, it must be tragic to hear about your daughter.' He went on to ask her 'to look at our view on things', which amounted to the conviction that 'she must have known', particularly since her husband was by now hinting at the possibility that Heather's body remained for some days in the house before interment, a matter of a few feet away from where Stephen and Mae slept. This would indeed make it that much harder for Rosemary or her children to claim total ignorance, but the evidence was thin, depending upon what Fred was saying on whichever day, and he remained the only possible source of information. The likelihood that he disposed of the body the same night, when his wife was packed off to Pembroke Street, must remain the stronger. Onions clearly thought they were about equally balanced at this stage. 'Obviously if you're as naïve as you possibly might be, gullible, I can only apologize for the trauma that you've suffered over the past couple of days,' he repeated. In all subsequent interviews Rosemary West said nothing, save 'I'm innocent' to each of the charges as they mounted against her day after day, and once, 'I'm innocent, by the way.'

If the police view of her involvement hardened, it was not because of any new evidence. On the contrary, their secret monitoring of her every conversation over a two-month period merely underlined her declared lack of knowledge. It was firstly because the more they uncovered about child abuse from the 1992 case and the renewed statements of Anne Marie, the more they disliked her and thought her capable of complicity; and secondly because investigators intensified their belief that 'she must have known' with a misplaced certainty that 'she must have seen' a change in her husband's demeanour. 'You must have noticed a personality change, I would have thought,' Mr Onions told her, 'and that's the way most of us think, so therefore that's the reason you're here.' The day before, there had been this exchange:

Onions: Seems like you've been, and I don't mean as any insult whatsoever . . . a bit of a mug, doesn't it, if we're to believe what you're saying? I would have thought that you'd have seen something, something that would have aroused your suspicions, heard something, saw some behavioural change if we're to believe what you're saying. For Fred slaughtered his daughter, didn't he? He'd have changed in

	some way, wouldn't he? Unless he's a man without a personality, without feelings, without remorse, without anything, wouldn't he?
Mrs West:	I don't know that. I don't know how they work or not.
Onions:	Or perhaps you're not perceptive, are you? Can you tell his changed moods, his depressions, his anxieties? Or is he like a lump of stone and . . . never changes whatever's happening to him?

One may sympathize with the frustration in the detective's voice, and one must also remember that in this early part of the enquiry the police were not yet aware with what manner of man they were dealing in Fred West. Had this been a domestic murder of the kind most policemen are used to dealing with, and West an ordinary man who had lost his temper in a blazing row, then yes, there would have been a discernible alteration of personality, a descent into torpor or post-traumatic paralysis. But there were already signs that another body lay beneath that patio, and there would soon be more of the same; police knew fairly quickly that they were not faced with a domestic crisis gone wrong. The fact is, so-called 'serial' killers do not betray changes in emotion after the crime, because they feel no emotional response to it. Being indifferent to the meaning and content of what they have done, the disposal of remains is simply a task to be performed before resuming normal routine. In Dennis Nilsen's ugly phrase it is 'the dirty platter after the feast'. One of the principal reasons serial killers are so adept at avoiding detection is precisely because their behaviour does not alter; there is nothing about them to attract attention or cause disquiet. They slip back into the flow of things without qualm, because they do not feel repulsion for what they have done and therefore cannot show it. This is true of Nilsen, who resumed life at the office and walked his dog while heads were simmering on the stove; of Bundy, who charmed some girls the day after he slaughtered others; of Christie, who brewed his tea and papered his walls all unperturbed by the fact bodies were immured within them; of Sutcliffe, who drove his lorry before and was sweet to his wife after an attack of manic ferocity. There is no reason to think West was any different from these men, and it is therefore entirely believable that wife, children, lodgers and workmates would notice nothing odd about him. He was back at work the following day, 'bullshitting' as usual.

The only time serial killers do experience a change of personality is *when they are committing the crime*, at which point there is a surge of emotional strength which quite overwhelms the event and the participants in it. If he is acting alone, then only his victim will see it. Rosemary West's guileless reply above, 'I don't know that, I don't know how they work', rings true. She is not an educated woman, and could not have said this as an evasion. She is right. Only professionals in criminal psychology 'know how they work'. Even without her husband's confession, this remark would testify to her absence from the scene of the crime.

It was not suggested that Heather had been subjected to torture, although two pieces of cord found with her remains gave rise to the possibility that her father may have tried to rape her and it was her resistance which led to her death, a view held by her sister Mae. The absence of clothing in the hole lends support to this. The cords, 15 and 22 inches long, had trapped within them some carpet fibres, which pointed to Heather having been lying on the floor when they were applied. Twenty-two of her finger- and toe-bones were missing (out of a total of seventy-six), as was one kneecap. The head had been severed with a sharp, fine-edged knife, the thighs had been chopped more crudely. Legs were found on top, covering chest, vertebrae, arms, and skull at the bottom, with lots of hair and some loose finger- or toe-nails. (The possibility that nails had been pulled out before death is not sustainable from the evidence, though it cannot be ruled out.)

I have described Heather's remains with a purpose. If the description makes you shudder, it is because of all the indignities inflicted upon the people who died nothing is worse, perhaps, than the manner of their interment, because though we respond to cruelty and torture with fear, we react to this dreadful disposal of bits and pieces with pity. A. N. Wilson, who attended the trial, wrote that our need to reverence the dead was a profound one. It is also true that somebody who does not, or cannot, reverence the dead displays in that, more than in any other way, his divorce from humankind. I recall Dennis Nilsen's terrible reply when I told him how his treatment of corpses made me wince with horror. 'There's something wrong with your morals', he said, 'if you are more alarmed by what I did to a corpse, which cannot be hurt, than what I did to living men, which is unforgivable.' The logic is seductive. But human beings are more than creatures of logic, and though it may be absurd to weep over a pile of bones, it is deeply human, and Nilsen was wrong to mock the moral inversion.

Something else he said to me is also relevant here. I had wanted to protect the families of his victims by giving them numbers rather than names, so that the precise nature of their suffering should not be revealed. He told me that I would be treating them in exactly the way he had, reducing them to abstractions, and that I should not compound the offence by robbing them of their humanity. This time he was right. I do not want the Cromwell Street girls to be left as the pile of bones which they became when Frederick West had finished with them. They are more than just victims of murder. They must be allowed to come up for air. John Kilbride, the twelve-year-old bespectacled little boy who fell into the

188

clutches of Ian Brady, was found on Saddleworth Moor with his head down a hole and his feet near the top. Yet more than thirty years later he is not the anonymous victim of the Moors Murderers. He is John Kilbride.

Carol Ann Cooper was from a broken home. She was only three years old when her parents separated, and her mother died when she was nine. Thereupon she went to live with her father, but his remarriage set up frictions with which he could not cope. When Carol became rebellious, she was placed in a children's home in Worcester, where she was famous for her sparkle and good humour. She liked to be called 'Caz' and had this nickname tattooed on her arm. On 10 November 1973 she went with her boyfriend Andrew and some other youngsters to the Odeon cinema in Worcester and then on to a fish and chip shop. They finished the evening in a pub and left Caz at the bus-stop. She was due to catch the No 15 to go and stay with her grandmother, who worshipped her. Her friends waved goodbye and never saw her again. For days afterwards Caz's grandmother questioned neighbours in the street whether anyone had spotted her, and an appeal was put out on local television. Whenever her name was mentioned, her grandmother would burst into tears. Caz was fifteen years old.

Thérèse Siegenthaler was brought up in Switzerland with her parents, brother and sister. It was a happy, harmonious life, and Thérèse was a fine student, intelligent and curious, her head always in a book. She came to London to study sociology at Woolwich College, and to perfect her English, which she soon spoke fluently, though with a heavy accent. She shared a flat in Lewisham with another Swiss girl, and helped her finances with a weekend job at Bally shoe shop in the Swiss Centre on Leicester Square, in the heart of London's West End. In April 1974 she went to a party in Deptford, where she told friends she planned to hitchhike to Holyhead and catch the ferry over to Ireland to meet up with a priest with whom she shared an interest in South Africa. It was to be a brief holiday, for she had bought tickets for a West End theatre on a dáte after her expected return, and also an airline ticket to Zurich to see her family. One of the friends warned her about the perils of hitch-hiking. She assured her that she could look after herself because she was a judo expert. On 15 April she set off, but never got as far as Ireland. Though Gloucester is not on the route to Holyhead, she found her way into Frederick West's van somehow. Her disappearance was reported to Scotland Yard and her brother came over to England to retrace her steps. Thérèse Siegenthaler was twenty-one years old. West constructed a fake chimney-piece above her grave, and his younger children later slept close to it. Her parents never recovered from the shock of their grief, and died without knowing for sure what they came to suspect, that their daughter lay dead and unmourned in a foreign land.

Shirley Lloyd's parents separated when she was only two and she was placed in care. Fortunately, however, she was later fostered by council worker Jim Hubbard and his wife in Droitwich, and was so contented with them that she announced her intention of changing her name to Hubbard; she never did, but in deference both to her and to her new family, it is as Shirley Hubbard that she is known on the files. She went to Droitwich High School and went for work-experience to the make-up counter at Debenham's in Worcester. She seemed to be one of the lucky ones, to have emerged from a broken home and settled into a secure one. With her broad smile and green eyes, she was something of a flirt, and was once discovered camping in a field with a soldier. Before long she had found a regular boyfriend called Daniel, aged eighteen. On 14 November 1974, Shirley and Daniel sat eating chips by the River Severn in Worcester, cuddling and planning future meetings. After seeing her on to the bus to Droitwich, Daniel arranged to meet her again the following day. In the morning, he waited forlornly at the bus-stop for every arrival from Droitwich, but Shirley never appeared and he never saw her again. Why she ever got off the bus to fall into the clutches of Fred West is a complete and utter mystery. It can only be that he was hovering where she alighted, and coaxed her into conversation. She was fifteen years old.

Juanita Mott was the daughter of a local girl from Newent, just outside Gloucester, and an American serviceman. She had two sisters. Her parents separated when she was little and the girls grew up with their mother. Juanita left home at fifteen and took a bedsitting room in Stroud Road, Gloucester, while she found work in a nearby bottling factory. It was there that she met Jasper Davis, whose own lodgings were at 25 Cromwell Street. She used to visit him there and it is possible that she moved in for a period, but there is no documentary evidence of this. By 1975 she was living with Jenny Baldwin in Newent, and on 11 April that year she left Jenny's house to hitch-hike into Gloucester. She was due back that night for a very particular reason – Jenny was getting married on 12 April, and Juanita had promised to look after her children while the wedding took place. She never returned, and was not reported missing. If she had been, perhaps investigation would have led to Cromwell Street. She was said to be a lovable rascal, mischievous and jokey. Presumably Fred recognized her when he saw her standing by the road. When Rosemary was shown a picture of her at the trial, she said she had never seen her before. Juanita was eighteen years old.

Her sister Belinda was a visitor to 25 Cromwell Street four years later. She now realizes that Juanita was lying beneath the cellar of the house in which she sat giggling. Her parents have reconciled, mother spending some of her time nursing the ailing Mr Mott in Texas.

Lucy Partington was a clever girl, intellectual, artistic and sensitive. She played the violin and wrote poetry. In 1973 she was in her final year at Exeter University studying medieval English and was expected to get a degree with First Class Honours. Her father was an industrial chemist, her mother an architect, and though they had separated, Lucy got on well with both of them. Sir Kingsley Amis was her uncle. Lucy spent Christmas with her mother in the Cotswold village of Gretton, near Cheltenham, reading *Wuthering Heights* and drinking the odd half of Guinness – her only extravagance. Lucy had converted to Roman Catholicism and was a very pious young lady, serious and reflective despite her light-hearted nickname Luce the Moose. On 27 December she spent the evening with an old friend in Cheltenham, Helen Render, who was confined to a wheelchair. The two girls discussed their future and composed a letter of application for Lucy to attend an MA course in Medieval Art at the Courtauld Institute in London. She left Helen's house at 10.15 p.m. to catch the bus to Gretton. It was a simple journey; the bus-stop was only three minutes away, and if perchance she missed the last one, she could easily come back and ask Mr Render to give her a lift. She was never seen again. As Mr Leveson was to say, with stark, sad emphasis, 'There was no trace of her. She had no future.'

Because Lucy Partington was not a runaway or de-linquent like many of the other girls, the discovery of her remains at Cromwell Street implicated Rosemary West by sheer power of suggestion. She was not the sort of girl to get into a car with a strange man, it was said, ergo Mrs West must have been in the car when she was abducted. However comforting the thought may be to her grieving family, this must remain mere speculation. (On the one occasion when we *know* she was in the car as an abduction took place, that of Caroline Owens, the young woman lived.) So, too, is the tentative conclusion that she died a week after her disappearance, supported by the hospital record of Frederick West's admission to the casualty department of Gloucestershire Royal Hospital shortly after midnight on 3 January with a deep laceration to the hand. It is possible that his wound occurred as a result of dismemberment of a corpse, but it is just as possible that it did not, which is the inference I should prefer her family to make. All that we do know is that she went to Cromwell Street, and that Fred drove her there. It is reasonably safe to assume she was dismembered on the premises rather than elsewhere, as a knife was found with her jumbled remains. She was reported missing and extensive searches were made. She was twenty-one years old. Her cousin Martin Amis dedicated his novel *The Information* to her in 1995.

Alison Chambers was forever running away in search of adventure and the good life, like a bird breaking free of its cage. She had been born in Germany, where her father was a sergeant in the Royal Army Ordnance Corps and her mother a WRAC private. There were two sisters. When her parents divorced, Alison eventually went to live with her mother in Swansea, but she ran away from home so frequently that her mother despaired of her, and her stepfather would sometimes be out late at night looking for her. Once she managed to get as far as Paddington Station in London. Her mother decided that she would have to be placed in care, as she was too untameable for her to look after; she would be safer there, she thought. When she was sixteen she transferred to Jordan's Brook House in Gloucester, a home for delinquent teenage girls. Frederick West's Ford transit van was sometimes seen parked outside or cruising by.

The girls at Jordan's Brook remembered Alison as a fantasist, full of stories and hopes and plans. She would spend hours meticulously drawing sketches, presumably imagining the kind of life she wanted for herself. In nine months she absconded eight times. According to her friend Sharon Compton, on some of these occasions she went to 25 Cromwell Street where she became familiar with both Fred and Rosemary, who showed her an estate agent's picture of a farm, which entirely captivated her. There was a girl they knew at the house, who may have been Anne Marie. (The Crown had intended to call

Sharon as a witness, but decided not to.) Alison had a part-time job as a lawyer's clerk, but she failed to turn up for work on 5 August 1979. She was reported missing. Then her mother received a letter in Swansea, telling her that Alison was with a nice couple and family, and would be working as their nanny, so enquiries about her were pursued no further. The letter had been posted in Northampton.

These girls, and Lynda Gough before them, died as the result of sadistic assault, their bodies used as objects for depraved enjoyment and their faces bound to blank out all reminder of their human status. Interviewed by the police, Frederick West variously stated that they were all 'girlfriends' with whom he had been having affairs and who threatened to tell his wife, or that they were too much in love with him. He even claimed that the affair with Lucy Partington had been going on for three months and that she wanted him to meet her parents, a risible and insulting invention easily refuted by the facts of Lucy's known movements. Heather and Shirley Robinson were clearly different; they were problems which had to be solved, like Anne McFall, Rena and Charmaine. There was one other victim, with whose murder Fred was not charged through lack of evidence and his resolute denial, though Gloucester police are reasonably sure that he is her killer. Her name was Mary Bastholme.

She was born on 14 March 1952 in Gloucester, the youngest of three children. In 1967, when she was fifteen, Mary was seen in the company of teenagers who frequented a café in Southgate Street called the 'Pop-in', and during the course of that year she took a job as waitress there. Frederick West was a regular visitor to that café. It is no wild conjecture, therefore, to suggest that Mary served him tea on a number of occasions. In addition, Fred did some building work behind the café, and Mary was seen in the company of a young woman who resembled Anne McFall. There was a witness who claimed to have seen Mary in Fred's car more than once. And although Fred denied any involvement, he appears to have told his son Stephen that he would reveal all when he was good and ready.[36] Mary disappeared on the evening of Saturday, 6 January 1968. She had been waiting at a bus-stop in Bristol Road on her way to visit her boyfriend. Some of the monopoly set she was carrying was found scattered by the kerb. Her body was never found. Frederick West described the weather as snowing on the night that Lucy Partington disappeared. It wasn't. But it was snowing when Mary Bastholme disappeared from the bus-stop.[37]

Rosemary Letts was a little over fourteen years old when Mary Bastholme disappeared, and she had not yet come into contact with Frederick West, facts which did not deter this deplorable man from telling his confidante Janet Leach in prison that it was Rosemary who had killed Mary, not he.

7

Destruction

On 25 February 1994, Frederick West told his questioners at Gloucester police station, 'I've never harmed anyone in my life.'

What did he mean? He was engaged upon a lengthy explanation of the strangulation and disposal of a number of young women, and yet his moral compass appeared to be so warped that he could not reach into the iniquity of what he had done. They were mistakes, or 'enjoyment turned to disaster', bloody nuisances, problems to be sorted out. All this he related in a voice bereft of colour or intonation, with an apparent detachment which chilled the blood. Could it be possible that this man did not *know* he had done wrong?

Not quite. He was able to recognize that killing people and cutting up their bodies was socially and legally unacceptable, which is one of the reasons why he was secretive about it and was at pains to point out that his wife had had nothing to do with it. But he did not really think that it mattered all that much. A man in the grip of an aberrant sexual mania is not likely to agree that his mania is qualitatively different from anyone else's. He might know that the general opinion would be against him, but he cannot see why it should be so.

There are all manner of peculiarities in sexual arousal which are to the majority of mankind appalling. They are known as paraphilias, an uncommon word until it was adopted by the American Diagnostic and Statistical Manual after lying in desuetude for most of the century. The layman would refer to them as sexual perversions. They include zoophilia – a preference for sexual relations with animals – commonly known as bestiality, which researchers believe is more common amongst people who work on farms. Paedophilia is a sexual attraction to children, gerontophilia a preference for elderly sexual partners, coprophilia involves sexual arousal by faeces, urophilia by urine, and klismaphilia by the use of enemas. A fetishist replaces an object for the person desired, such as a shoe or a handbag or even a drawing-pin, while the partialist desires only a bit of the person – the ear, the toe, and in extreme cases (Jeffrey Dahmer) the intestine. There are frotteurs, who are more excited by rubbing against strangers in a public place than they are by ordinary sexual encounter; voyeurs who like to watch; some who can only be excited by making obscene telephone calls and others by strangling themselves until they pass out.

Three observations may be made of the above brief summary. First, there is a great deal of guilt and secrecy underlying all of them, indicating that they are substitutes for real sexual attraction, the development towards which has been arrested by some circumstance or particular event in childhood or at puberty. All the paraphilias are representative of some kind of immaturity. Second, though most people would profess to be disgusted by them, the amount of commercial exploitation of paraphilias shows that they are quietly indulged by legions of men (women are hardly ever afflicted by them).

The third observation is that Frederick West indulged in some of these himself. He told his son that he had sexual relations with animals on the farm where he grew up, and instructed him on how to go about it. His voyeurism is beyond dispute, the spyhole in Rose's 'special' room permitting him to watch and his elaborate wiring to loudspeakers permitting him to hear. His frotteurism is indicated by his compulsive touching of every woman who came near him, and his continuous scatalogical talk is a variant on the telephone mania which inflicts sexual innuendo upon those who do not want to hear it. All these manifestations of paraphilic disorder contain elements of sadism within them, albeit mild and disguised, for they all involve forcing attention upon unwilling partners. They are all intrusive and selfish. West's further interest in urine is demonstrated by the videos he made of his wife displaying her genitals and urinating, which his son knew about and which the police had as exhibits not produced in evidence.

His most significant disturbance from the point of view of this case was his necrophilia. The word is often understood in too narrow a sense. From Greek *nekros* (corpse) and *philia* (love, liking, friendship), it is handily translated as 'love of the dead', but it can take various forms and is not restricted to sexual congress with a corpse. 'Necrophagy' is the ingesting of dead human flesh, a kind of cannibalism which offends the most tenacious of taboos. There are men who like to be in the presence of death, and try to spend the night in cemeteries if they can manage it (a policeman told me he would frequently have to move people on when he found them hovering near a tombstone). Others get jobs as morgue attendants or embalmers. Some feel a need to dig up corpses. Sergeant Bertrand, a twenty-seven-year-old soldier in the 74th Regiment in Paris (1848), was so in thrall to his obsession that he would swim across an icy river in order to reach a graveyard.

The most innocent form of necrophilia is a refusal to accept the death of a loved one, demonstrated by Romeo when he hurled himself into Juliet's tomb and held her to his breast. In such an instance, it is a desperate extension of mourning, and has been held in high regard by many civilizations. Herodotus tells us that Periander continued to have intercourse with his wife after her death, and in some parts of Europe until the seventeenth century it was considered proper for a man to consummate his marriage even if the bride had died before the wedding day.

More subversive is the necrophile who prefers to

perform the sexual act when the partner is so passive as to feign death. Apparently some happily married women are prepared to do this occasionally if the husband is in such a mood, and there are plenty of brothels which will cater for men who can only get an erection if the whore is in a black shroud and lying in a box. In the most extreme case, a mild and apparently gentle man like John Halliday Christie will kill the woman he wishes to have intercourse with in order to be able to function. Christie indulged his necrophilia six times before he was caught, tried and hanged in 1953.

There is a kind of necrophilia which is more intense than all the others, and which is virtually always an extension of lust murder. This is the disorder which revels in destruction for its own sake, being a continuation of the murder after the killing itself is done, as the lust seeks additional expression. The American author M. Hirschfeld described it as 'a frenzied intensification of the aggressive and destructive impulse. The murderer is not satisfied by merely killing his victim; he also wants to possess her and destroy her beyond death.'[1] This is what von Hentig called *lebendige Zusammenhänge* ('the tearing apart of living structures').[2] It far exceeds the practical need to dispose of a corpse, and even murderers who confess to killing are reluctant to allow any inference of necrophilic passion afterwards. This is not because they are ashamed of it, but because it remains the one relationship with the body which is still private, theirs and theirs alone; no amount of interrogation can prise open this secret, and in such a way the connectedness to the dead body is inviolate, its possession by the murderer irreversible and undilutable.

Frederick West was one such individual. He mutilated and dismembered his 'girls' as an act of self-regard, to assert ownership of his possessions. They were like the victims of one of Dr de River's studies, 'a playful, sadistic dissectionist, the objects of the caprices of a butcher'.[3] For Fred, the moment of dismemberment was the triumph of his power, and it is likely that he would savour it in solitude, enjoying the ultimate degree of control which it afforded him. Nobody could deny that he was the master then, nor that his girls were finally robbed of all resistance. Howard Sounes wrote, 'It was like performing an operation',[4] which perfectly conveys the intensity, the solitariness, and the cold, quasi-professional monstrosity of it, all typical of the destructive necrophile. Sounes even suggests that Shirley Robinson may have been scalped, because no hair was found with her remains.[5] The fact that the body of Lynda Gough was *unnecessarily* dismembered when the grave into which it was put would have easily taken a whole corpse allows the very firm inference that West cut it up because he enjoyed doing so. Moreover, the catalogue of missing bones to which we have referred several times in the course of this account can only point to the painstaking performance of a dissectionist. Kneecaps, finger-bones, toe-bones, ribs, vertebrae, their absence implies dozens of individual acts of dismemberment. In one case, a whole shoulder-blade had been removed and taken away, which the pathologist at the subsequent trial assured the jury would take a very long time and considerable patience. The removal of a foetus is a vivid expression of contempt for life itself.

Decapitation is a sure and symbolic way of dehumanizing human remains, for it removes the identity and, with it, the soul (at least in the necrophilic scheme of things). Every one of West's victims had been decapitated, from Anne McFall in 1967 to Heather West in 1987, and it is worth noticing that this, too, was not strictly necessary for the purposes of interment, even in a vertical hole; it was an expression of will. It is here that one may discern the difference between the sadist and the necrophile. Sadism and necrophilia are both malignant expressions of the desire to control, but whereas the sadist requires his victim to remain alive in order that her pain may be visible and stimulate his flagging libido, the necrophile exerts final control by chopping up a corpse; he wants to destroy utterly; his enemy is the impertinence of life. Given the importance of escalating stimulus and addiction mentioned in an earlier chapter, it is almost certain that this kind of necrophilia develops from sadism. They are different stages of the same descent into madness, and the lust murderer who is not yet necrophilic will soon become so.

The various paraphilias mentioned above are frequently interrelated. Jeffrey Dahmer's necrophilia emerged from a previous stage of partialism, in which his fascination was restricted to the internal organs of a sexual partner – the heart, which he would hear thumping with his ear against a man's chest, and the intestines, which he liked to hear churning and gurgling within. It was the machine that he was listening to, not the person who inhabited it. In adulthood, when this partialism erupted into full-blown necrophilia, it was the intestines that he wished to see and the heart he wished to possess. Paul de River cites the example of a man who fell upon the body of a dead girl because he wanted to have her bladder, which is an extreme example of urophilia leading to necrophilia. The cannibalistic impulse, if unchecked, can lead to such awfulness as exemplified by the Düsseldorf sadist Peter Kürten, who could rip off a swan's neck in order to drink its blood, and the Sacramento madman Richard Chase, who mixed internal organs in a blender.

Since Frederick West committed suicide in prison before a proper psychiatric and historical study could be made of him (although one would have been prepared had he lived to stand trial), it is difficult to be precise about which of his abundant paraphilic disorders could have led to the necrophilia which consumed him in the end. A voyeuristic tendency is unlikely to become so malignant owing to its essentially passive nature, nor is an interest in copulating with sheep. Obviously sadistic torture is very close to the destructive urge, but that must come much later in a series of developments. If we wish to find the first step, we have to look earlier, and there is little to help us, apart from his mother's fixation with him, which might induce an inability to relate to other females who saw him as less heroic than she had done, and which might then poison him against all females, reducing them to objects of his pleasure. Yet this is not sufficiently specific and could well alarm many a doting mother. It is more likely to have been some fetish of Fred's which grew diseased and vicious.

There is one tiny clue. When he was living in Scotland with his first wife Rena and being consistently unfaithful, West had an affair with a young girl who had been injured in a factory accident. As a result of this, she had lost all of her fingers and both thumbs on each hand in a guillotine. After her liaison with West, she married and had four sons, but is now dead. No useful purpose would be served by giving her name, as her mother is still alive.

The fetish for amputees is not unknown to psychiatry or, for that matter, to a certain public. There have been private exhibitions in New York of the use of a man's leg, amputated below the knee, as the penetrator in sexual intercourse; such spectacles do not want for interest on the part of the audience. If Fred had a fetish about amputation, and its earliest expression had emerged in puberty, so linking the act of masturbation with the pleasure in seeing an amputated limb, this would go a long way towards explaining the florid necrophilia which he displayed later. In the absence of fact and professional assessment, this can only be speculative, but I do not think West's attachment to a fingerless girl in his youth, and his removal of fingers and other bones from the women he killed in his maturity, can be entirely coincidental.

Such a theory makes sense when considered in tandem with what is already known of West's distorted relationship with women, borne out of his mother's disproportionate admiration for him. He was never able to feel that effortless superiority with a female which his mother's love had unwittingly led him to expect, and so he always felt gauche and inadequate. Many people have been struck by the ferocious touchiness he displayed when talking about women. It was as if he was always spoiling for a fight, and had constantly to defend himself against them. Fighting a woman did not appear as abnormal or reprehensible to him as it would to most men. On the contrary, it was to be expected, they had to be taught a thing or two, kept in their place. Women were seen by Frederick West as some kind of threat, and the only way he could deal with it was to subdue them. His beatings of both wives – Rosemary as well as Rena – is well attested.

It would be much easier for him to feel superior to a woman who was somehow 'incomplete' by virtue of her lacking fingers. The attraction of the amputee lies in the comfort she can offer to a hesitant ego. She is not so fierce or frightening if she is not whole. He would then hold and protect such a fetish both to enhance his self-image and to improve his performance. In normal intercourse West ejaculated so quickly in order to establish and 'prove' his ability before the woman discovered how poor he really was. With an amputee he would not suffer that inbuilt disadvantage. (A 1992 Birmingham psychologist's report that he could no longer get an erection was mistaken – West answered multiple-choice questions which he could not read.)

Another indication of West's preference for 'incomplete' females is afforded by his experience working as on odd-job man at Stroud Court in Gloucester, a home for autistic young women. They were impoverished, unthreatening, subdued and docile, with scarcely any will of their own at all, and to Fred they were exciting. He fantasized about having sex with them, as he did also about nuns, because their very lack of strength made him feel masculine.

Some experts on fetishism have suggested that damage

to the temporal lobe can cause a dysfunction which gives rise to the sudden nurturing of a fetishistic fixation. In 1960, A. W. Epstein wrote in the *Journal of Nervous and Mental Disease* that a factor in fetishism may be 'a primary state of increased organismic excitability . . . the product of cerebral pathophysiology'.[6] This is another way of saying that brain damage can influence sexual appetite. Frederick West's motorcycle accident at the age of eighteen *might* have caused damage to the temporal lobe which *could* have contributed to the development of a fetish. In the absence of diagnostic records we can say no more than that. But there is no dispute whatever that West's obsession with sex was uninterrupted and far above the average. It included other minor fetishes so bizarre and repellent that they have not been publicly disclosed.

While admitting (gradually) to murder, Frederick West was quite unable to allow that he had ever raped anyone. Apparently, however, he told his son Stephen that he had sex with the girls only *after* having killed them,[7] which would point to necrophilic behaviour of the second order as well as destructive necrophilic dismemberment. But there is no corroboration for this and no way of testing the reliability of the information.

What evidence there remains is anecdotal and forensic. Mae and Stephen have each given full authentic accounts of their father's love for gadgets and machines, the complex wiring of the house to enable him to eavesdrop on his wife's sexual activities, his casual treatment of his wife's vagina as an object to be touched at will, the all-pervading wish to witness by stealth rather than participate, to steal rather than share, to intrude rather than be invited. All these are possible necrophilic traits, although it might be argued they are nebulous and inconclusive by themselves. The forensic evidence of human remains, on the other hand, speaks very plainly.

At this point we shall jump ahead to one of the expert witnesses at the trial, Bernard Knight, CBE, consultant pathologist to the Home Office for thirty years and Professor of Forensic Pathology at the University of Wales College of Medicine in Cardiff for twenty-five years. With a clutter of letters after his name, it would be difficult to find anyone more experienced or distinguished in his field. He has lectured in London, Newcastle, Hong Kong, Kuwait and China, was President of the British Association of Forensic Medicine, belongs to corresponding associations in Finland, Germany and Hungary, and has written widely on the subject (as well as publishing detective novels in both English and Welsh). It was important for both prosecution and defence that the matter of the missing bones be properly addressed, and everyone was prepared to concur that Professor Knight's opinion would be the most reliable in this respect.

Knight first explained the difficulty of excavation at Cromwell Street, due to the fact that the water table was often higher than the floor of the cellar, which obliged the diggers to work in waterlogged soil. No sooner was a cavity emptied than it filled with water again. This suggested that it was possible for bones buried there to have moved around in a semi-liquid medium and changed position relative to one another. He then told how everything was carefully removed and examined by him and all remains precisely counted. That was why he was able to tell, in the case of Heather (the first to be excavated), that twenty-two finger- and toe-bones were missing out of a total of seventy-six, and that one kneecap was missing. Describing the chop-marks made on thigh bones, he held a femur aloft in court by way of demonstration. It was a macabre moment, and I was not the only one in court to wonder whether Mrs West assumed it was actually Heather's bone that the professor was waving around; she spent most of this part of his testimony quietly weeping, as she did whenever Heather was mentioned, and resolutely looked at the floor of the dock. Generally, she watched witnesses, but this time she averted her gaze and bowed her head low.

Passing through the sequence of remains as they were excavated, with five skeletons uncovered in nine and a half hours, Professor Knight gave details on each (sixty-three finger- and toe-bones missing, both kneecaps, forty-two finger- and toe-bones, both kneecaps, twenty-four finger- and toe-bones, left collar-bone missing, shoulder-blade missing, left kneecap, fifty-two finger- and toe-bones, fifty-eight finger- and toe-bones, thirty-five, forty-seven, and so on), and also detailed what he did find. This included description of the tape wrapped around skulls, a knotted cloth, lots of hair, some hair trapped in the knot, some degenerate brain tissue, a black-handled knife, a plastic rope similar to a clothes line, and much else. When he came to the baby that Shirley Robinson was expecting, most of whose bones were matchstick size and very brittle, the jury were visibly shaken. One man looked disgusted, and the woman on the front bench who had spent the whole trial leaning forward in concentration, suddenly sat back as if to place distance between herself and the evidence.

Professor Knight said that dead bodies would begin to smell after about a week, and Chief Superintendent Bennett later confirmed that all the remains, save for those of Lynda Gough, still gave off an odour so many years later; it was a smell he recognized, as he had once been a diver and had, coincidentally, dived in the un-successful search for Lucy Partington in 1973. This was potentially important information, in the light of the prosecution's case that Mrs West 'must have known', because presumably she must also have smelt something. Yet the same inference could be drawn in respect of all the other people living at the house. They smelt nothing, because all the bodies had been pushed down to a depth of six feet and then covered over with concrete (in the cellar) or slabs (in the garden). Knight gave details of the exhumation of Charmaine as well, confirming that both her kneecaps and forty-seven bones were missing, and at the request of the defence he further reminded us that the remains of Rena West and Anne McFall had been found in a similar condition: Anne's legs had been disarticulated at the hip, thirty-six of her bones were missing, the foetus she had been carrying had been removed, and, most significantly, cord had been tied around her wrists.

As if in recognition of what everyone in court was trying not to think about, the professor declared that it was impossible to say whether any of the dismemberments had taken place before or after death. When pressed to clarify, there took place the following exchange:

Leveson:	Could that knife have been responsible for the cut marks you saw?
Knight:	Possibly some, but not all. Not for removing the thighs.
Leveson:	How difficult is it to disarticulate legs and remove a head? How long would it take?
Knight:	A good many minutes if you're not used to it.
Leveson:	While the victim is still alive?
Knight:	There would be massive arterial blood loss.
Leveson:	And if she was dead?
Knight:	The blood would be oozing, but not that much.
Leveson:	Is it easier after death, or before?
Knight:	After.
Leveson:	Easier two or three days after, or immediately after?
Knight:	It would not make much difference, except for rigor mortis.

Questioning then moved to the central issue of the bones which were not there. Knight said that this was not the first time he had found skeletons with some bones missing, and, invited to explain what could account for this, he said there were four possibilities. The first of these was degeneration. 'Eventually', he said, 'most skeletons will disappear as the bones disintegrate over time, and usually the smallest and most fragile bones will disappear first. That was not the case here, however.' The bones which had survived, especially those under the cellar, were in very good condition, and some of the smaller bones, like those of the foetus, which one would have expected to disappear, had not done so. 'If those which remained were in very good condition, there was no reason why others should have disintegrated. It was just not possible.' This theory was therefore discounted.

The second possibility was that a failure to excavate properly had missed some bones, which were still lying where they had been interred. This was also quickly discounted by Professor Knight, who had been present at Cromwell Street and had seen for himself that the police search was thorough to a fault, recovering even some loose fingernails. Every centimetre of ground was carefully sifted until there could linger no doubt at all that nothing of interest remained.

The third possibility was that the bodies had been removed from one burial site to another and that some of the bones had fallen off in the process. This, too, was discounted. Professor Knight pointed out that bones are held together by strong ligaments and tendons, over which there are muscles, fat and finally skin. The ligaments are much more resistant than soft tissues (muscles, fat and skin) and will survive much longer. If the bodies had been buried elsewhere and then moved to Cromwell Street, there would have been the possibility of animal predation. Knight looked specifically for evidence of animal interference (tooth marks) and found none. He said that it would take a couple of years for a skeleton to reach the stage of consisting only of dry bones, besides which the black soil which surrounded the remains proved that there had been a substantial quantity of soft tissue present, which meant that the limbs must have been whole when buried, that is to say with flesh and gristle intact.

Asked how strongly a patella (kneecap) was attached to the leg, Professor Knight replied that it was very strongly indeed. 'It cannot become detachable until the thigh muscles and shin muscles have rotted away. Most of this would have had to go before the kneecap could fall off.'

There remained only one other possibility to account for the missing bones. They had been removed as the result of deliberate mutilation. This would have been possible. 'Fingers and toes are very easy to remove,' said Knight, 'and a kneecap is quite possible to remove with a sharp knife.' The shoulder-blade, on the other hand, would have been very hard, and the professor found it difficult to explain why such a huge bone should be missing, attached as it was by lots of tendons to shoulder-joints and the end of the collar-bone. 'Is it possible to cut out a shoulder-blade?' Mr Leveson candidly asked. 'I could do it,' replied the professor, with the implicit understanding that a non-professional could not. And yet the shoulder-blade was not present, and it could not have fallen off until after years of decomposition. Therefore, had it become detached after those years, it would still be in the ground with the rest of the young woman's remains. The fact that it was not could only mean that the murderer, with great effort, had dislodged the bone and taken it away.

Frederick West told police that one of his dismemberments had taken him one and a half hours. And he had once worked at a slaughterhouse where he could have learned some of the techniques required. He was asked how he could cope with such a task. 'There are no words to describe it actually,' he replied. 'You actually feel terrible. I mean there is just no words to explain what you go through, I mean there is so much pain in it, it's unreal. Both mentally and physically like, you are absolutely shattered.'[8] He further informed the police that he would lay a body on the ground with its head over the prepared hole before decapitation, to enable the blood to flow straight out and minimize the risk of staining himself or his clothing.[9]

When he said that he had nothing to do with missing bones, however, it is possible to detect awkwardness and deviousness in his words. For instance, he denied amputation even before he was asked about it. The exchange went like this:

West: Cause I mean I never, I never cut no toes and fingers off.

Savage: Did I suggest you had?

West: Well, I mean you said they're missing, so —

Savage: Yeah?

West: Well I mean you —

Savage: They might be in another place?

West: No, no no no.

Savage: That's what I'm asking you.

West: No no, every, everything is in one place, there ain't no, there wasn't, all, all if they were cut up it was just their head and arms, and legs, nothing else took off.

Savage: You're sure about that?

West: Yeah . . . when you push them down with a spade I mean it's quite possible for something like that to happen.[10]

There is a variant on the third theory which DC Savage touched upon here. It made little difference to the evidence which the court had to consider, but the vehemence of West's denials give it weight. While the missing bones could not have become accidentally detached during transit from one location to another, they might still have been removed at another location and left there, while the body parts which were brought to Cromwell Street for interment were actually those found at the house up to twenty-two years later. The reason that many of the bones were missing was because they had never been there in the first place, mutilation having taken place elsewhere. The same would have been true of Charmaine's skeleton at Midland Road, and Rena's and Anne's in the fields by Much Marcle. According to this theory, the murderer would have enjoyed his grim and solitary task of dismemberment quietly, at leisure, in some remote spot known only to him. There was some talk from Stephen West that his father had told him he brought the bodies back home for burial, and that the crimes had been committed in a derelict farmhouse. One newspaper printed a photograph of a farmhouse which might have been the one intended, but no police enquiry has followed. It could easily be a red herring, another instance of West's myth-making.

On the other hand, it could explain why the debris of mutilation has never been recovered. It is not conceivable that so many bones should simply disappear without human agency. When one accepts that they were deliberately removed, one must also accept that they were deliberately sequestered somewhere by the mutilator. The very fact that they are *not* to be found at Cromwell Street strongly suggests that they are still to be found somewhere else. That is a secret which Frederick West took with him to his grave.

It would be typical of the necrophile to take 'souvenirs' in the form of body parts to keep for private delectation in some secret place. Ed Gein in Wisconsin had used human skin to make lampshades and human nipples to decorate a belt. Jeffrey Dahmer had a collection of eleven skulls and heads, one of which was in his refrigerator, human genitals in a bottle of formaldehyde and two complete skeletons which he had 'defleshed' (his word) and reassembled. The difference is that Frederick West's grotesque collection was not discovered.

The return of body parts to Cromwell Street must also appear reckless and bizarre, and for this reason police officers were reluctant to credit it. And yet that would be typical behaviour of the destructive and possessive necrophile who needed to demonstrate, if only to himself, that he was in complete charge and that these body parts were possessions to be kept near him.

Certain it is that when police took their warrant to 25 Cromwell Street on 24 February 1994, suspicious about the disappearance of Heather West and the recurrence of a family 'joke' that she was under the patio, they had no idea of the manner of man they would be dealing with.

8

Arrest

The seed for the investigation which peeled unsuspected layers of concealment from the West household in 1994 was sown nearly two years earlier in the summer of 1992, and even that was very nearly blown away by circumstance. A police constable on the beat in Cromwell Street was approached by the mother of a little girl who had told her an alarming tale of what went on at number 25. She had been repeating what she had heard from one of the children in the house, but was uncertain about the surname. It was Chest or Guest or something. Had the Social Services not made a thorough search of the electoral roll, or had they been swamped by other work that day, they may not have discovered that the name they were after was West.

They made the effort because the complaint was not routine or trivial. If the little girl was telling the truth, then they might be dealing with a very severe case of sexual abuse. Social Services informed the police, and together they acted swiftly. The very next day, 4 August 1992, they applied for a warrant to gain entry to 25 Cromwell Street and remove the children for interview. The warrant having been granted, police went to the house at nine o'clock in the morning on 6 August and took the children away. They were questioned that day and the following day, and as a result of what they said, an Emergency Protection Order was issued, followed by a Full Care Order. The children never spent another night in the house.

For their sake, it is not possible to detail their allegations. Nor is it desirable. We know that medical examination of the children yielded disturbing signs of intrusive adult behaviour, and the Bridge Report published by the Gloucestershire Area Child Protection Committee after the 1995 trial twice abandoned its normally bland and formal style to record its anguish. 'The detailed descriptions given by some of the children about their lives to date', says paragraph 69, 'makes painful reading and, in fact, is quite appalling.' Paragraph 122 concludes that 'the surviving children have had the most dreadful experiences, of a kind which it is quite beyond the comprehension of professionals and general public alike.'

They were also worried about the children's mental health in view of what they had been through, and it was this consideration which initially caused social workers to pay little heed to their offhand remarks about Heather being 'under the patio'. Gradually, however, as the story was repeated and enlarged, it seemed likely that the patio had been laid at about the same time as their elder sister had reportedly left home. Consequently, social workers informed the police of what they had been hearing. Detective Constable Hazel Savage was appointed in August to investigate Heather's whereabouts. It was, at that stage, just one small enquiry among dozens which were under way, and its relative importance was not high.

DC Savage was unable to find any record of Heather West since her disappearance in 1987. She was not resident anywhere, had paid no taxes to any authority, had claimed no benefit or signed on with any unemployment office. She was on no doctor's list and had visited no hospital. She had apparently vanished without trace. Hazel Savage then became suspicious and suggested to her superiors that application be made for a warrant to dig up the patio at 25 Cromwell Street. This they were reluctant to do, for a variety of reasons. First, no complaint had been made, and the Wests were very quick to allege harassment; it would be a considerable risk to offer them ammunition for further allegations against the police if in fact the contents of the garden were perfectly innocent. Besides, the cost of excavation would not be slight, and it would be difficult to justify such an expense on the hunch of one constable and the unguarded tattle of children. So no action was taken.

Hazel Savage would not let the matter drop. Her interference elicited interestingly contrasted responses from Mr and Mrs West, Fred choosing to dismiss her as of no importance and even attempting to flirt with her, Rosemary turning her foul-mouthed wrath upon the woman who, in her view, should be made to leave them alone. She was heard to call the policewoman a 'bitch'. These were earthy, emotional reactions of a woman who knew she had done wrong and was resentful of the punishment inflicted upon her – being separated from her family; Frederick West's airy and cheerful indifference to the policewoman's persistence showed what a fragile hold he had upon reality.

During the months from August 1993 until February 1994 the Wests were together more than they had been in all their married life. As we have seen, Mrs West refused any longer to go out and sleep with other men at her husband's command or whim, and her own 'special room' was not used. He started to discourage her friends from calling. Her sister-in-law, Barbara Letts, had been supportive, but Fred was now anxious that his control was slipping and he sought to maintain it by isolating his wife from everyone else. She had, for instance, formed some reliance upon the solicitor who represented her during the abuse case, Leo Goatley, and Fred did all he could to prise her away, speaking ill of Goatley and undermining her confidence. The point was that her solicitor was one of the few connections in her life made without her husband's direction; he signified a degree of autonomy on his wife's part which West fought hard to forbid.

According to Howard Sounes, they tried to start a new family. Rosemary had been sterilized after the birth of a daughter in 1983. She now attended Gloucestershire Royal

Hospital for an operation to reverse the sterilization, and did succeed in becoming pregnant late in 1993. But she miscarried, and told her doctor she was depressed.[1]

In the early days of 1994, Hazel Savage again asked to see senior officers and made her case for application to search the West house. She was supported this time by indications from the children that they were frightened to speak about what had been going on at home, and by written statements from social workers. Gloucester magistrates were therefore asked to grant a warrant under Section 8 of the Police and Criminal Evidence Act 1984 to look for evidence relating to the disappearance of Heather West. Application was granted on 23 February, and the search would be made the following day.

On Thursday 24 February Hazel Savage called on Anne Marie Davis at home as she was getting her children ready for school. She told her that police would be digging up the patio at her father's house later that day, and they would be looking for Heather's body. Anne Marie says she was not able to absorb this shattering information, and assumed only that they would be searching the house for clues. At 1.25 p.m. five plain-clothes police officers turned up at 25 Cromwell Street to serve the warrant. Mae had returned from her work at an insurance office to watch *Neighbours* with her mother and have some lunch. It was she who opened the door. Detective Chief Inspector Terry Moore, Detective Inspector Tony James and Police Sergeant Tony Jay pushed straight past her and went to the living-room to find Mrs West. The two collies, Benji and Oscar (acquired only since the removal of all the children in 1992), were barking furiously.

Handed the warrant, she read it, handed it back, and muttered, 'This is stupid,' whereupon DCI Moore placed it on the table in front of her. At that point she became hysterical, hurling foul abuse at the policemen who, she said, were invading her home. 'I thought the police were being bloody-minded, going too far,' she would tell the court. 'It seemed so silly at the time.' Mae was told she could not go back to work, but would have to go to the station and make a statement. Then Stephen turned up, and he, too, began shouting at the officers and demanding that they should wait until his father arrived. They told him they were going to dig up the patio whether his father was there or not.

Stephen told Mae to refuse to go with them, while he tried to reach his father on a mobile telephone. His mother was by now in a state of shock, staring at the floor. Stephen said he had only seen her look like that once before, at the time of the 1992 arrest. She seemed transfixed. Then she telephoned Fred's boss and, sobbing, said, 'I don't care where he is. I want him home now.' Fred was finally located at 1.50 p.m., twenty-five minutes after the police had arrived. He said he would leave the job he was doing and come straight home. They expected him within twenty minutes.

But he did not come straight home. The weather was foul, rain pouring down from a gloomy sky, and the atmosphere inside 25 Cromwell Street seemed to match it. Police were taking pictures of the back yard and preparing to excavate, though they could see that large slabs would have first to be removed, and that since night would fall soon after 4 p.m., there was little chance of making progress that afternoon. Inside, Hazel Savage told Mae quite frankly that they were looking for her sister's body and were quite sure they would find it. When Mae asked if that meant Heather was dead, DC Savage replied, 'I think you know what I'm on about.'

Everyone was wondering where Fred was. Hours passed and still he did not appear. Mrs West had sunk into a kind of paralysis. 'Mum remained sitting down and wouldn't look outside,' recalled Stephen. 'She never once peered outside from the moment they started.' The team assigned to the garden eventually departed at 5.30 p.m., with one officer left on the spot to stand guard all night. West's boss reported that he had left the site where he was working about an hour after he had been told to rush home, and it was about three hours after that when he did turn up. It has never been established what he was doing all this time, nor where he went. DCS John Bennett gave the opinion that this was 'thinking time' for him. The other possibility, unfortunately only speculative, is that he used the time to dispose of bones that he may have hoarded elsewhere. His own ludicrous explanation may be discounted. Having left the lids off some paint pots, he said, the fumes affected him, he pulled into a layby and passed out.

Frederick West arrived at 5.40 p.m. 'He didn't whistle or call out as he usually did,' says Stephen. 'He just strolled in.' Having been told by Stephen what had been going on, he appeared to be more worried about the electricity meter than anything else. For years he had been interfering with the electricity supply, routing it directly from source in such a way that it did not show on the meter, then routing it back through the meter a couple of weeks before it was due to be read. As the policeman lingered at the bottom of a garden which would be destroyed on the morrow in a search for the remains of his daughter, Frederick West was frantic lest he should walk in and discover him fiddling with the meter.

At 7.40 p.m., West made his own way to the police station and was interviewed on a voluntary basis by Hazel Savage. This is when he said he had seen Heather in Birmingham. Rosemary West refused to go to the station, so she was interviewed at home, between 7.55 p.m. and 8.20 p.m., by Detective Sergeant Terence Onions and WPC Willetts. West went back home at 9.30 p.m. and took the dogs for a walk in the park, possibly accompanied by his wife. Then he took a shower and watched the television news. Stephen and Mae said their parents had some desultory conversations in whispers. What they may have said to each other was the subject of intense enquiry the following day. 'What sort of discussion went on when you were all back together last night about Heather?' Onions asked Mrs West.

'That she must be around somewhere,' she replied. 'We were getting some idea that there was going to be some publicity of what was happening in our back garden, and the next thing we heard it was going to come out on the news. I thought she might contact somebody if it's been in the papers or on the TV.'

'You thought she must be around somewhere?' said DS Onions. 'Not around the house somewhere?'

'No, outside. Out in the big bad world.'

'That's what you're hoping for, is it?'

'Well of course I am.'

Onions went on to ask about the patio. 'Was the patio mentioned last night?' he said. 'About what might be in the patio? Did Fred talk about the patio or anything like that last night?'

'We was just waiting for them to do the job and go away again . . . we hoped they'd put it back the way they found it. That it was going to rain today, and general things.'

Frederick West's version as to what was said on the evening of 24 February is a little more specific. He said he was most worried about his standing within the family if the investigation were to uncover the truth. 'Once Rose finds out about this, then I'm finished,' he said. 'At least I had her behind me before with the other case, somebody, but now I mean my daughter and son and wife, I mean they made it quite clear last night.' What, exactly, they made clear he did not vouchsafe. It is implicit that they, and especially (one may surmise) his wife, told him that this time he was on his own, and that if he was hiding anything he could no longer look to her for loyalty. Once more revealing his tenuous grip on reality, he consoled himself with the thought that the house itself would survive: 'Me marriage has gone, me home's gone, but at least me home's done up that they've got something to sell or keep.'

At 11.15 on the morning of Friday 25 February, DC Savage and DC Law went to 25 Cromwell Street and spoke to Mr West at the front door. He invited them in. They said they were going to question other members of the family, including Rosemary's mother Mrs Letts, whereupon Rosemary exploded in anger. 'I don't want them to speak to Nan,' she said. 'I'll kill that bitch Hazel Savage if she ever speaks to my mum. Nan is ill and I don't want her to be involved.' The police account of this meeting states that 'Mrs West was unco-operative when asked for her mother's details'. Fred then took his wife aside and went with her into the hallway, closing the door behind him. 'The police were in the living-room,' she said. 'Fred came into the hall and told me to go upstairs. So I did, and I waited. Nothing happened.'

Stephen says he caught his father staring out of the bathroom window at the garden and the digging which had resumed. He turned round and gave his son a look 'that sent a shiver down my spine. His eyes bore straight through me. It definitely wasn't normal.' One writer says his face was 'contorted with malevolence'. According to this account, when West restored his composure he told his son, 'I shall be going away for a while. Look after Mum and sell the house. I've done something really bad. I want you to go to the papers and make as much money as you can and start a new life.' Stephen's own recollection is that he said, 'Look, son, look after your mum and Mae, I'm going away for a bit.'

Frederick West then presented himself to officers with the words, 'Can we go to the police station?' Once in the squad car, he admitted for the first time that his daughter was buried in the garden, but said the police were digging in the wrong spot. It was then that he was arrested for the murder of Heather West.

Rosemary West, at the house, was sobbing heavily. 'I don't know what's going on, I don't know what's happening,' she wailed. She had been told by Fred to keep out of the way, and now he had left without explanation. 'He told me to go upstairs and keep out of the way,' she said to DS Onions, 'that he'd sort something out.' In court much later, she said, in a little-noticed aside during her evidence, 'Fred didn't tell me he was going to the police.' Recalling the events of that morning, she stated that 'Steve came in [to the room] shouting, where's Dad? I said he was here a minute ago. His girlfriend [Andrea] said she'd just seen Fred leave with police in a car. I didn't know what was going on.'

One hour later, Rosemary West was herself arrested on suspicion of Heather's murder and taken to Cheltenham police station. Now only Mae and Stephen remained at the house, all unaware of what their father had confessed in the police car and what was about to unfold before them. They watched from a window as the digging continued, eating crisps and drinking tea, and when a chicken bone was held aloft, they giggled and made derisory clucking noises. In the early evening their father was brought back to the house and taken into the garden. He pointed out where they should be digging. If they did not know before, Mae and Stephen certainly realized at that point that something serious was afoot. Subdued, they went to the police station where their father's solicitor, Howard Ogden, said, 'I'm sorry to tell you this, but your dad has admitted to the killing of Heather.' They spent that night alone in the house, sleeping fitfully in the same room. We have already heard how Mrs West was informed of her husband's confession and of her reaction to it.

Heather's pitiful remains were unearthed on Saturday, 26 February. Stephen and Mae asked if she was whole, and an officer replied, 'You wouldn't have wanted to see her.' A woman police officer telephoned Anne Marie Davis that afternoon, in the midst of a birthday party for her little daughter, to inform her that her half-sister's body had been dug up. Meanwhile, Fred had retracted his confession, only to retract the retraction three hours later. The most significant event of the day was, however, the discovery by accident of another human femur in the back garden of 25 Cromwell Street. Both femurs for Heather were accounted for. It was at this moment that the possible scale of the enquiry dawned upon startled police officers.[2]

It was determined that a man of quiet but solid experience was needed to take charge of what was certain to be a long, difficult investigation. Detective Superintendent John Bennett, aged forty-nine and a policeman since the day he left grammar school, was duly appointed. He was the one person to co-ordinate the various strands of the enquiry and to make all pertinent decisions as to the direction it should take. It was a huge responsibility, which he bore with calmness and a certain frigid dignity necessary to maintain the straight course of logic and analysis. One way or another, the entire force of Gloucestershire Constabulary was to become involved in an investigation unprecedented in its scope in the county. Eighty-four officers were directly engaged upon it, and they were supported by clerical, analytical, forensic and computer staff who generated enough documentation to fill a lorry. There were, for example, over 1,200 statements taken and over 2,000 reports made. The entire contents of 25 Cromwell Street – 130 items of the domestic debris of family life – were removed, tabulated, analysed (and mostly destroyed in the end to avoid the attentions of freaks, newspaper editors and souvenir hunters). The Incident Room devoted to this one investigation was manned by two detective inspectors, two police sergeants, two detective sergeants, twelve police constables, twenty-three detective constables and five civilians.

The logistics of the excavation team working in the garden and eventually beneath the house for weeks on end escaped the notice of the public. Under the direction of Sergeant Peter Maunder, the Police Search Advisor, the team worked in difficult conditions every daylight hour, and they had to be fed two meals a day by a specially organized catering corps working on the spot in co-operation with Asda supermarket. The entire premises were excavated to a depth of seven or eight feet below ground level, to the hard Severn clay beneath, a task which had to be undertaken with great care lest the house collapse upon them. As each area was dug out and its contents sifted, taken away and examined by the pathologist, so ready-mixed concrete was poured down a chute from the street outside, the hole filled and allowed to set before the adjacent area was dug. Ground-penetrating radar was employed to detect the likely location of human remains, which required another specialist team. Exhausting hours (8.00 a.m. to 10.30 p.m.), combined with the uniquely distressing results of the dig, made it essential that individuals be given a day off at intervals, but there was never a day when work was not continuing at Cromwell Street. Out of respect for the Seventh Day Adventist Church next door, an attempt was made to minimize the disruptive nature of the work on Saturdays.

Then there was the intense difficulty involved in the identification of victims. Only the identities of Heather West and Shirley Robinson were immediately obvious. For the others, although the murderer was able to indicate where officers should dig to find them, he could put names to none of them. One, for example, he knew as 'the Dutch girl'. Accordingly, extensive enquiries were made in Holland to no purpose. Interpol and continental police forces were called in to help with missing foreign nationals, and, correlating the age of the girl at her death with lists of foreign girls living in England and missing at the relevant time, a total of over 130 possible identifications came up. These were gradually eliminated by other explanations until only one name remained – Thérèse Siegenthaler. The process had been laborious and meticulous. Not many murder enquiries need to stretch both ability and endurance so far.

The final cost to the police force was nearly £2 million. In return, there was acute satisfaction at having identified all the victims, for which John Bennett and his colleagues deserved the most unalloyed praise, together with a tangential delight – the fact that enquiries into missing girls succeeded in tracing 110 of them and placing them once more in touch with their families.

Meanwhile, after nearly three days of questioning Mrs West had been released on police bail on the evening of February 27 1994, under Section 47 (3) of the Police and Criminal Evidence Act 1984, to report back on 25 April. They had no cause to hold her any longer, which implicitly meant that the 'suspicion' that she had murdered her daughter could not at that time be sustained. She, Mae, Stephen and his girlfriend Andrea spent one last night together at 25 Cromwell Street, because she said she did not want to be alone. They all slept in one room, Stephen and Andrea in the double-bed, Rosemary and Mae on a mattress on the floor. The cat and two dogs were also there with them. They could hear the sound of digging outside, but could see nothing, as the windows had been covered with black plastic.[3] On February 28 they moved to a police 'safe-house' and never saw Cromwell Street again.

Mrs West and her daughter did their best to make the rather spartan house seem cosy, and Stephen put up some curtains. But his volatility of character and lack of judgement very quickly disturbed the peace, and there were squabbles, rising to physical fights, with his sister and girlfriend. Mrs West went so far as to call the police to say she would rather be behind bars if her son was going to act like his father, and to his face she said, 'You're as nuts as he is.' What annoyed her most was that Stephen had already made an arrangement with the *News of the World* and seemed interested only in his own gain. He said that he wanted to visit his father in prison, and she thought that his motive was not filial but commercial – his newspaper owners wanted him to report back to them after the visit. The media corruption of this sensitive case had already begun.

The *Daily Star* for its part was in touch with Anne Marie, against all legal rules governing interference with potential witnesses, and some newspapers had placed anonymous advertisements in the local press asking for anyone who knew the Wests and 'could help with their enquiries' to call a certain number. The use of police jargon was deliberately deceptive, and DCS Bennett was understandably furious as well as frustrated that a serious investigation should be thwarted and trivialized by this kind of wanton intrusion. As he and everyone else was soon to realize, the lower end of the British press regards both the law and justice with lofty scorn and will not hesitate to undermine the judicial process for its own ends.

As a direct consequence of Stephen's betrayal to the *News of the World*, Mrs West and Mae were moved to another house in Dursley and Stephen was banished. He sent flowers to his mother through the police in an attempt to ingratiate himself, but she would not have him back. The journalists were not pleased, as Stephen without his mother was a less valuable commodity. It did not work. Thereafter Rosemary West and her daughter lived alone together, not daring to go out for fear of being recognized (Mae could venture forth much more easily than her mother), playing Scrabble, watching television, cooking, and telephoning all and sundry. They did not know that every one of their conversations, with each other and on the telephone, was recorded. Mae has written that 'at night Mum would sleep with me, and sometimes in the night I would wake up and hear her crying. Then she used to sort of rock herself to sleep again, like she did with us when we were babies.'⁴

Frederick West was meanwhile feeling isolated in prison. He chatted to guards and to his special visitor Janet Leach – the 'appropriate adult' provided at police request by Social Services – with his usual tales of invention, fancy and obfuscation, but he knew that he had lost control of events, and therefore of the family he owned. 'I can now think of what Rose is feeling,' he said in his confused grammatical staccato, 'now I've got that out of my mind, and Stephen and Mae, what everyone is feeling at this moment in time. You know, as before I couldn't think of what they felt, I was making sure they didn't know.'[5]

Rosemary West was taken back into custody on 20 April 1994, and arrested on two charges of rape against the same victim, in company with two separate men. As these charges were later dropped by the Crown Prosecution Service, it is neither possible nor proper to name the men in question.

From that date for a period of six weeks until 2 June, she was interviewed fifty-nine times. At each interview she remained silent, save to declare her innocence of charges as they were brought against her. The first charge, on 23 April, was for the murder of Lynda Gough. This was fully seven weeks after Frederick West's verbal and written confession (in his own hand), and six weeks since he had been remanded in custody on eight separate counts of murder. Mrs West was charged on 26 April with the murder of Carol Cooper, on 28 April with the murder of Lucy Partington, on 30 April with the murder of Thérèse Siegenthaler, on 4 May with the murder of Shirley Hubbard, on 6 May with the murder of Juanita Mott, on 18 May with the murder of Shirley Robinson, on 23 May with the murder of Alison Chambers, and on 26 May with the murder of her daughter Heather, whose remains had been the first to be disinterred in February.

It is instructive for an understanding of Frederick West to trace how his mood altered through the relentless hours of interrogation almost daily over many weeks. At first he was cocky and confident, telling DC Savage that her suspicions over Heather were groundless. 'I think we better pack it up, Hazel,' he said, 'we're talking rubbish, aren't we?'[6] Even after Heather's remains were found, he was seen to hide a smirk with his hand, as if holding on to something or playing games with his interrogators. Some of the time he did not understand a difficult question, and the meaning of specific words escaped him ('Fascist', 'witches' coven' and 'impotence' are three examples). He volunteered much useless information, but tended to react to police discoveries rather than help in advance (apart, that is, from indicating where they should dig). As Hazel Savage put it, 'You tell us nothing at all until we plug you. It's like pulling teeth.'[7]

As soon as police came to him with a new line of questioning, West responded with a new kind of answer. Officers grew increasingly wary of his inventiveness. 'You've got that silly look on your face again,' said DC Savage after eighty-five interviews, 'that sort of gawky look that always brings, I'm just about to shoot off on another story now. I've got to recognize it over these weeks.'[8] DC Morgan likewise grew frustrated with the prisoner's myth-making. 'I don't want you making up a story to keep me happy,' he said, 'because that wouldn't keep me happy at all.'[9] In an attempt to force honesty out of shiftiness, Morgan told him, 'Can you look at me, Fred, when you're working this out. I prefer to sort of have eye contact with people when I'm talking to them and then we can assess things, can't we?'[10] The detective was understandably reluctant to credit many of the things he was hearing, especially when West insisted that he dug a hole and interred a corpse when the house was full of people and he could hear footsteps on the stairs above him; the soil was clay and ash, he said, and shovelling it did not create much noise. Or when he brought a dead body back to the house while his wife slept upstairs. But they were all compelled to believe when he gave a classic description of lust murder, committed during the act of sexual intercourse, when Fred West the storyteller obviously gave way to a genuine memory.

As the weeks went by and oceans of information came

pouring into the incident room, West lost his cheerfulness and began to sink. He became less co-operative, more sullen, more recalcitrant. When he was told that his mother Daisy West, normally a resilient woman, had broken down with sobbing in 1967 because she knew that her eldest son had murdered a girl and buried her in a field (Anne McFall), he was becoming a broken man.

It was shortly after that, on 27 April, that West was told for the first time that his wife Rosemary was facing two charges of murder (in respect of Lynda Gough and Carol Cooper), and that he had a meeting on 28 April with his then solicitor Howard Ogden and counsel, in consequence of which on the following day he handed a note to police officers which stated, 'I have not and still cannot tell you the whole truth . . . From the very first day of this enquiry my main concern has been to protect another person or persons.' The language was obviously not his, but seemed as though it had been dictated for him by somebody else. Nor was it apparent who were the person or persons to whom the note alluded. It may well have been other males, some of whom had been charged with other offences. But the prosecution held on to the idea that the note was intended to implicate Rosemary West, and that her husband had been protecting her. Nobody sought to explain how the plural 'or persons' could be construed as pointing solely to her.

The remains of Charmaine West were recovered from 25 Midland Road on 4 May. Frederick West was charged with her murder a week later, on 11 May. No charge was brought against Rosemary West in respect of Charmaine. This can only be because the police were satisfied that she had nothing to do with the slaughter of Charmaine. They knew, then, that Fred West was at liberty when Charmaine disappeared, and they had already charged him with the murder of her mother.

Thereafter West denied everything and would simply say 'no comment on that' when directly challenged with evidence of murder. The police turned fiercely upon him.

DC Savage taunted him by withholding what evidence there was against Rosemary, hoping to make him wonder and worry. Relentlessly she described the condition of Charmaine's skeleton in order to shake him, referring to 'this little kiddie whom you loved', and asking, 'What happened to her clothes when this poor little mite went down there? Where are they? Who undressed her? And why was she undressed?' The interview became harrowing, quite rightly so if police officers were to uncover the truth, but so harsh that West was unable to listen. 'This is horrible, isn't it? This is a child. You told us that other people wanted your body, wanted sex, fell in love with you, threatened to tell Rose that they were pregnant by you. Charmaine doesn't seem to fit into that story to me. Does she to you? What went on there that night? Where did you undress her, this little girl, your daughter? You didn't cover her up and anything in that hole, you stuffed her in there. She's not wrapped, she's not clothed, and she's not in one piece.'

For the first time, West was reduced to tears, mumbling about 'Charmaine my child . . . I just got that fear that you're gonna take Charmaine away', and giving way to what the police officer referred to as 'this terrible internal grief'.[11] Why was it? Why was he suddenly so upset about a stepdaughter whom he said he treated as his own but whom others claimed he neglected in favour of Anne Marie? Was this self-pity in disguise? Or could it have been a chink of humanity pushing through the armour of madness, a tiny recognition of stifled emotional truth leading to a real remorse?

A week later he had retreated into adamant denial. 'I had nothing to do with these girls' deaths at all,' he said. 'I have lied through the statements and at this moment I am not prepared to change that . . . you do know a vast amount of the truth. And what I'm saying is, for God's sake put it together . . . My life means nothing to you, but it means a lot to me . . . and if the police sorts it out then I haven't said anything, it's as simple as that.' He appeared to be frightened, but of whom or of what he would not say. 'No, I can't do it, sir, there's no no no no way I can do it.' By this time the officer (Detective Inspector James) is calling him 'Mr West' and there is a sense of anxious urgency in the room. DI James asks what is on West's mind, is he still thinking what to do about it? 'Yeah, yeah, got to do summat,' says the prisoner. Then, 'No I can't do anything at the moment, it's too dangerous to try, too dangerous.'[12] Is this fantasy, fear or insanity? Begging for the interview to be terminated (and it was), West muttered, 'Nobody spares a thought for what I've lost in this. I've lost more than anybody else . . . my ex-wife, my daughter, my daughter, two unborn children, how much more do I need to go?'[13] And that, I think, is both self-pity and exhaustion.

Police officers were exhausted, too, but at the end of the day they were convinced that West's earlier confessions represented the truth. It was he who had told them there would be coal found with Charmaine's body, that there would be a knife found buried with Lucy Partington, and he who left the identical 'signature' on every set of remains they found. DC Harris said, 'I think our investigation to date has tended to confirm what you originally said to the police.'[14]

It was on 30 June that the Wests appeared together at Gloucester Magistrates' Court and that Rosemary refused to speak to or look at her husband. She asked that a police officer be placed between them, and this was repeated on all subsequent occasions when they appeared together and were remanded. 'I saw him as not the same man I had known all those years,' she said. 'He just seemed to grin, like it was a joke or something.'[15]

Frederick West was found hanged in his cell at 12.55 p.m. on New Year's Day, 1995. He had not been thought a suicide risk, because his relentlessly cheerful manner seemed to indicate that he was far removed from a realistic assessment of his position. At times he was unconcerned, at others he saw himself as a man to be pitied for having lost two daughters and a wife. Nevertheless he was accompanied by two guards virtually all the time. It was rare that he was alone for very long. One of those occasions was the lunch-hour, when prison staff were changing shifts and taking their own breaks. West was locked into his cell at 12 noon with his food, and would be seen again to deliver his crockery and cutlery at 1.00 p.m. During that hour, he stripped his bedsheets to make two ligatures and looped them around a small air-vent above his door. From this he hanged himself, his body preventing the door from being opened rapidly. It was estimated that he would have died within five or six minutes, and after frantic efforts to revive him, the doctor declared him dead at 1.22 p.m.

Mrs West's solicitor, Leo Goatley, was immediately telephoned and asked to inform his client. As it happened, January 1st was the wedding anniversary of Mr and Mrs Goatley, but any intention to celebrate had to be dropped immediately. Through her daughter Mae, Mrs West later sent a bouquet of flowers to Mrs Goatley by way of apology for the fact that her day had been spoilt by Leo's summons to Pucklechurch Prison on her account. That aspect of Rosemary West which delighted in large families, and which would befuddle the public perception of her when she came to trial, was most evident in her dealings with her solicitor, to whom her first greeting was invariably, 'How's Cath? How are the children?' The Goatleys also had eight children.

The suicide of Frederick West remains mysterious. As his wife's counsel Richard Ferguson would later say, when it was suggested that he had killed himself to save his wife from prosecution, 'He was not the stuff of which martyrs are made.' Every ounce of effort he had ever expended had been for selfish ends, to such an extent that he was not aware that selflessness was possible in the human breast. No such conception was possible to him. The looking-outwardness of self-sacrifice was a notion that a man like this could not have comprehended, still less formulated as an intention. Nor did he have conscience. There was no indication he felt guilt for what he had done, which would have been a clue to the presence of conscience and responsibility in his make-up, and such an emotionally flat man would not know remorse. Yet these are among the common motives for suicide, which has led many people to wonder whether perhaps West had a conscience after all.

There are other possibilities, all frankly conjectural. One of them is cowardice in the face of what lay in store for him, though I suspect this, too, accords more with a comfortable notion of what we think a man ought to feel than with what we observe that he does feel. There is no more evidence for cowardice than there is for guilt and remorse. West had been playing pool the morning of his death and showed no especial signs of fear and foreboding. Self-pity is another motive which does not survive scrutiny. The self-pitier wants above all to live and experience the pity from others which he feels he deserves. He will attempt to earn pity, but not to remove the pleasure of it by being dead. Only the most profound order of self-hatred, that which besets people who believe themselves to be worthless, a burden to all, a blight on the universe, occasionally leads to suicide, and West was in no measure a man who despised himself. He lacked the smallest degree of introspection, without which self-hatred is implausible. One must, after all, know oneself before one can hate oneself.

Or he may have been driven to despair by Rosemary's rejection of him. He is known to have been astonished that she refused even to acknowledge him.

Perhaps Frederick West's distortion of soul was so remote and private that it is beyond both our and his comprehension. The disorder of the lust murderer and the necrophilic destroyer does not answer to intellect, logic or reason; it is compulsive, secret, bizarre and ungraspable. Its power need not be understood to be felt. The Düsseldorf sadist Peter Kürten in the 1930s murdered anyone to hand when his compulsion took hold. His victims included men, women and children, and his behaviour involved sadism, dismemberment, even necrophagy (cannibalism). He derived gratification from strangulation, whether or not his victim passed out, from stabbing sheep as he sodomized them, or from being near to a road accident, when he would ejaculate involuntarily. After his trial and condemnation to death, he said he anticipated the final act with extraordinary pleasure, for he looked forward to being able to hear the sound of his own blood spurting from his body.[16]

Is it possible that the ultimate aim of the necrophilic character is to experience his own destruction? The true springs of such a character are undeniably mysterious and little understood. Dennis Nilsen made himself up to look like a corpse long before he killed anyone, as if he had been dreaming of such an end all his life and the murder of others was a repeatable rehearsal for the real thing. By this reading, Frederick West, illiterate and backward though he was, could have held his final secret from everyone. He could have killed himself because he enjoyed it. We shall never know.

West's death threw the judicial process into consternation. Quite apart from the negligent security arrangements which allowed such an event to occur, and the fury of the police officers whose laborious work in bringing this man to justice suddenly came to naught, there was the very tricky matter of deciding how to proceed against Rosemary West. On seven counts which she faced there was virtually no evidence against her, and it had been intended that she would face them jointly with her husband and be contaminated by the evidence against him. On another two charges there was precious little to implicate her save motive and opportunity. Much had been discovered during the course of the year about her enjoyment of recreational sadism, and some witnesses had been assembled to suggest, according to the Similar Fact rule examined in Chapter Two, that her behaviour could go beyond the recreational and become distinctly dangerous. In the absence of her husband as co-defendant, however, there was nothing to point to murder, and it might very well have been necessary, in strict legal terms, to drop charges. The Crown Prosecution Service was naturally reluctant to do this, both because public anger needed to be assuaged, as it most certainly had not been by a suicide; and because there was the very definite feeling that Rosemary West had much else to answer for anyway, and should be made to answer for it somehow.

It was then that the decision was taken, eight months after the last count of murder had been lodged against her, to charge Mrs West additionally with the murder of Charmaine. This was formally done on 13 January 1995. If it could be shown that she was solely responsible for this death, and a jury could be so convinced, then the imputation that she was involved in the other murders would be more difficult to resist with or without evidence. Mrs Giles would have to be interviewed again, and her memory of what occurred in 1971 re-examined.

The police showed no overt embarrassment at the implications of this manoeuvre. For it meant that, if they were to carry the case against Mrs West in respect of Charmaine's death almost entirely on the grounds that Fred West could not have killed her because he was in prison at the time, they ought to face up to a very awkward question. Why, for the past eight months, had they been prepared to see Frederick West go to trial for a murder which, by their own assertion, he could not have committed?

In the meantime, press intrusion into the case had broken all bounds of decorum. So desperate were newspaper editors to have gruesome details to store up for the circulation battle which would inevitably follow a guilty verdict, that they broke their own rules of conduct, bribed witnesses with large sums of money, kidnapped the corpse of Frederick West, and treated the judicial process with bold contempt. Their unspoken purpose was subtly to establish Mrs West in the public mind as the new object of general detestation. Such figures are symbolic in the public consciousness and vastly useful for the sale of sensationalist newspapers. Whether she was a murderer was entirely beside the point as far as the generation of sales was concerned. It was sufficient that she be despicable. The tabloid press must do their best to ensure that she was denied a fair trial, even though they dared not publicly bruit this intention.

There were no witnesses to murder, but several witnesses to character upon whom the Crown would largely depend. Every one of these was bought by newspapers.

Anne Marie Davis was clearly going to give crucial testimony as to her stepmother's acquiescence in her father's incest with her. She had given statements to the police two years earlier in respect of this incest, then withdrawn them. It was obvious that her tortured relationship with her father had left terrible scars upon her personality and undermined her capacity for stable relationships with anyone. Added to which, she was devoted to her father and had always been somewhat in awe of him, a circumstance which rendered her attitude towards him cruelly ambivalent. With his arrest in February 1994 she found herself racked by conflicting emotions and was, not surprisingly, in a very confused state. The *Daily Star* managed to track her down within forty-eight hours of the arrest and sent a journalist, Virginia Hill, to interview her. There emerged from this encounter a long and loyal friendship which I should not wish to subvert. Miss Hill is a sympathetic and helpful listener, and Mrs Davis was much assisted in her hour of need by the patient companionship of a decent-minded stranger.

On the other hand, the *Daily Star* was not interested in her welfare, only in her cash value. They offered her money for exclusive use of her 'story', no matter how relevant it might be to the fate of a citizen about to stand trial. Virginia Hill instead entered upon a close relationship with the witness which endured throughout the months preceding the trial and beyond it, and resulted in a book written by Miss Hill and based on confidential conversations with Mrs Davis. Mrs Davis was said to be expecting £60,000 as a result of this contract.

Anne Marie had always detested her stepmother. Her earliest memory had been of Rosemary's intrusion into the family, coming between her and her beloved father, and her earliest endeavours had been to steal precious time alone with her father. As a child she had been jealous of Rosemary, who was only ten years her senior, and in adolescence she became unmanageable, promiscuous, rebellious and troublesome. This was hardly surprising in view of the lengthy sexual relationship she had had with her father, but because she loved him, it was against her stepmother that she had vented her anger and hurt. Now, in warm and relaxing conversations with Miss Hill – contrasting so vividly with the harsh factual rigidity of a statement made to police – she might have felt free to visit that wrath once more upon her stepmother.

Virginia Hill regarded herself as a humble foot-soldier doing her job. In fact, she was much more, as she must have realized. She was an unofficial therapist, without whose support Anne Marie might have found it much more difficult to give her appalling evidence in open court. What she had to say was dreadful to hear, but irrelevant to the charge of murder. If Mrs West had done to her what she alleged (and no corroboration was ever offered), then she was indeed a wicked woman. At the very least, the parading of this wickedness before the jury helped establish prejudice against the defendant, a prejudice encouraged by the wilful participation of a newspaper which needed a good story. Thus a private vendetta, however justified it may have been, was used to improve the attractions of an 'exclusive'.

Anne Marie Davis was closer to Miss Hill and to anonymous toughs provided by the *Daily Star* than she was to the police who were conducting the enquiry. When she came to give evidence, it would stretch over three days, during which time she would be entitled to police protection. She would decline it. She had better friends. And they might be able to help remind her what to say if some anecdote about her stepmother's wickedness slipped her memory.

Mrs Agius had been a neighbour of the Wests when they had lived at 25 Midland Road in 1970. The police had not interviewed her when, reading of Frederick West's arrest, she telephoned the *Sun* newspaper because, she said, she could not get through to the police. They were always engaged, so she thought the *Sun* might help her do her duty and contact a police station to give her information where it was most needed. The *Sun*, of course, did nothing of the sort (nor could anyone reasonably imagine that Mrs Agius expected it to); it sent round a reporter, who was the first to hear, several months before the jury, Mrs Agius' allegation that she was privy to a conversation with Mr and Mrs West in which they revealed they liked to motor round in the evening picking up girls, the younger and more lonely the better, to recruit into prostitution. It was always easier to do this, they said, when they were together, as a girl was more likely to jump into a car when a woman was present. This conversation was unique. Nobody else, in the twenty-four years that had elapsed since it took place, had anything remotely similar to report. The extremely damaging allegation stood alone. But it was the kind of allegation which newspapers loved to print.

Mrs Agius denied she had received any money from the *Sun*, but acknowledged that after an interview with a television company she had found £750 left on her mantelpiece. Later, she did the proper thing and gave a statement to the police. In court she would be exposed as a liar, for she had resolutely maintained that she had never been in bed with Mr and Mrs West together, whereas she had admitted as much to a police officer but warned him that she was prepared to deny it on oath for fear of her husband's reaction.

We have already had cause to look at the evidence of Caroline Owens in the chapter on Similar Fact. Her first statement to the police is dated 26 February, two days after the arrest of Frederick West and before any bodies had been found. This must remove any suspicion that she tailored her testimony to make it match the allegations of torture which would emerge later. Her evidence related to one incident of sexual assault in 1972 which had been dealt with by the courts and which did not involve torture or rape. Her statement of 1972 had disappeared. There survived, by sheer chance, the notebook of Police Constable Price who had taken that statement at the time, in which no reference was made to torture or rape. The new allegations, now restored to her memory, were much more serious, and she wrote them out in manuscript form and offered it to the *Sun*. Cannily, however, she kept back one page of the manuscript as a teaser. After an initial offer of £500, she revealed that there was much more to say of a sensational nature which would interest them. The price rose to £15,000 upon which she produced the additional page. On this basis alone, her evidence should have been suspect. There would be no doubt that an incident had occurred in 1972, but its florid nature had been, perhaps, improved by the lure of newspaper money. On the other hand, there was no significant dispute between her official statement and the newspaper story. Even if her evidence were to be allowed against all legal precedent, as mentioned in Chapter Two, then there might still be cause to disbar it on the grounds of its possible influence by the press.

Having posed for pictures, Mrs Owens' story was spread all over the *Sun* on 2 January 1995, the day following West's death, under the title I WAS FRED WEST'S

SEX SLAVE. The mention of the woman with him at the time he assaulted her was clearly Mrs West, though she was not named. It had not yet been announced whether Mrs West would face trial alone.

The witness known simply as Miss A was to offer a graphic account of sexual degradation at the hands of the Wests some twenty years before. No matter that she had never mentioned the attack to anyone during those twenty years, despite having been in psychiatric care and in a position to reveal an event of major emotional and psychic importance to her. No matter that she had been infatuated with Mrs West's brother and invented a story of being with child by him. No matter that she had hallucinations and an imagination of pathological proportions. What mattered was that she had a revolting story to tell and, true or false, it was perfect stuff for squalid papers. She persuaded a friend to telephone the newspapers 'out of curiosity', she said, despite the fact that she already had contact with a police officer engaged on the West case, and one might have thought he would be better placed to satisfy any curiosity she might feel. She contacted Caroline Owens to find out how much she had been able to get, which was at least more honest. Then she said she had asked to see a journalist because she was worried about her kids, which was less so. Miss A was paid £30,000 by Express Newspapers to dredge her memory exclusively for them.

Kathryn Halliday's story of being another sex slave to West appeared in the *Daily Mirror* on 3 January, together with a specially posed photograph. No mention was made of Mrs West. However, when the time came for her to make a formal statement she would transpose everything she had said to the newspaper on to the surviving defendant. She was a neighbour and friend of Rosemary West. She lived at number 11 Cromwell Street and for a period of many months used to visit Mrs West in the morning, after the children had been taken to school, for gossip and tea. Sometimes they would engage in lesbian activity, to their mutual pleasure, and very occasionally Mr West would be present also. Her evidence would be that the sexual encounters with Mrs West became too frightening and painful for her taste, notwithstanding that she always went back for more and her visits were voluntary. Still, stories of dangerous sex are far more interesting to *Mirror* editors than stories of chat about knitting and children, as she well knew. She contacted the press, with a local reporter acting as her agent to bump up the price, before she contacted the police. The best offer she could get was £8,000 from the Mirror Group. When she came to give evidence, it consisted entirely in impugning the moral nature of the defendant coincidentally to the satisfaction of newspaper requirements. It was also manifestly rehearsed, with journalists' clichés tumbling from her mouth. Richard Ferguson, Mrs West's counsel, would suggest that the prosecution found this nasty witness 'embarrassing', and when he came to give his final address to the jury, he disdained even to mention her name.

In a case brought before them in 1991, the Court of Appeal condemned the interviewing of prosecution witnesses before the trial took place. Three witnesses had given interviews to a television company. The court said this amounted to a dress rehearsal, and the prosecution ought to have forbidden any co-operation with the makers of the film.[17]

The most shocking of all was a woman who never expected to be called as a witness. This was the 'appropriate adult' who had sat in on eighty of Frederick West's police interviews for nearly three months and had private conversations with him in his cell both before and after. We shall see later how she came to be called, but for the moment it is enough to note her duplicity. Janet Leach never told the police what West had revealed to her in private conversation, because she said it was her duty to respect the confidentiality of those conversations. Hence the police did not know that West had claimed to be lying to them all the time in order to cover for his wife.

However strong Mrs Leach's loyalty to West when it came to giving information to the police, this same loyalty was somewhat weaker where newspapers were involved. Shortly after her period as 'appropriate adult' had ceased, she contacted the Mirror Group and offered to sell them exclusive rights to her highly privileged story for a series of escalating sums which finally mounted to a dizzy £100,000. The monies would be concealed by being paid not to her, but to her lover, who did not bear the name Leach. As it was suggested to her by the defence counsel, in return, she had to maintain the exclusivity by revealing nothing to the police, who were the ones who *should* know what she had to say, thereby clearly subverting the course of justice. It was important to keep the relationship with West going, even though its official nature had ended, in order to get more out of him. So she continued to visit him and to receive letters, as well as having regular telephone conversations with him. West had no idea his new friend's loyalty had found its price, but he was perfectly happy to string her along with as many stories as she was prepared to listen to. The Mirror Group did not mind who said what, as long as it was said only to them.

Perhaps the most questionable instance of press ethics occurred when the funeral of Frederick West was due to take place. This, at least, could not affect the course of impending proceedings against Rosemary West, as the purchase of witnesses listed above most certainly had done, but it revealed at what level tabloid newspapers pitch their moral peak. The *News of the World* had bought Stephen West, and by now Mae had been sucked into the vortex of corruption with him (which, incidentally, removed the possibility of her appearing for the defence as she had wanted, and might itself have subtly influenced the course of the trial). Anne Marie, on the other hand, had formally identified her father's body and taken charge of arrangements. This was not sufficient for the *News of the World*, which insisted on having paid for exclusive coverage of the funeral. Stephen West was prevailed upon to remove the body from Birmingham Morgue clandestinely, on 28 March 1995, in order to keep Anne Marie Davis and the *Daily Star* away from what promised to be an opportunity for more dramatic pictures. There was nothing illegal in this manoeuvre, but its taste is questionable.

As it happened, the *Sun* got wind of the funeral due to take place the following day, so the *News of the World* tried to have it postponed. To their chagrin, this could not be done. When the *Sun* photographer snapped away at the hearse, his rivals grappled with him to tear the camera from his hands, and there was a general free-for-all which brought credit upon nobody. In like manner a few months later, reporters would hand eggs to school-children to hurl at the van conveying the defendant Mrs West, as yet unconvicted, away from Dursley Magistrates' Court.

It was against such an atmosphere of journalistic behaviour that the committal proceedings against Rosemary Pauline West took place in the quiet village of Dursley. They would last over a week, because the defendant had elected for an 'old-style' committal, which meant that the Crown would need to present its evidence to the magistrate before he could decide whether it warranted sending her for trial. (A 'paper' committal is a mere formality, without evidence, conducted in a matter of minutes.) It was Mrs West's contention that she did not have a valid case to answer, and her counsel prepared to argue vigorously to this end.

9

Committal

The committal proceedings at Dursley were bound to be complicated, due to both the legal points which needed to be resolved and to attendant public clamour. The two were manifestly in conflict, and somebody would have to decide which was the more important – the rule of law or the satisfaction of what is loosely known as 'public opinion'. Hence the choice fell upon the most senior Metropolitan Stipendiary Magistrate in the land, Mr Peter Badge.

Proceedings opened on 6 February 1995, almost exactly a year after Frederick West had first been arrested for the crimes at issue. Sasha Wass, appearing for the defendant Rosemary West, immediately proposed that the magistrate should stop matters going any further, on the grounds that the cardinal principle of fairness which underpins the criminal justice system had already been compromised, by: the amount of time that had passed since the alleged offences were committed, the absence of certainty with regard to evidence, the absence of documentation to support it, and the adverse publicity the case had already received. She said that all this amounted to an 'abuse of process', which it was in Mr Badge's power to correct by discharging the prisoner without hearing the prosecution evidence. 'If there cannot be a fair trial in Mrs West's case', she said, 'then there should not be a trial at all.'

Abuse of process is a serious matter and not just (as the public was bound to imagine) a legal technicality designed to get somebody off the hook. If there has been delay in bringing a prosecution, of such magnitude that a proper defence cannot be conducted because witnesses cannot be expected to recall relevant events and the accused cannot possibly know whether he or she had an alibi at the time, then the magistrate may halt the proceedings forthwith, whether or not the delay has been the prosecution's fault. It is sufficient that he be convinced that the mere fact of the delay is productive of unfairness. A case in point was the proposed prosecution of police officers involved in demonstrations outside newspaper printing works at Wapping in January 1987. Officers were not served notice that they would be charged until eleven months later, and the committal proceedings were delayed until May 1989, over two years after the alleged offence which had itself occurred in a few seconds. The magistrate duly decided that it would be an abuse of process to hear the charges. 'It was perfectly proper, in the circumstances, to infer prejudice from the mere passage of time.'[1]

In the case of Mrs West, it was not two years that had elapsed, but twenty-four years in respect of the first charge, and eight years in respect of the last.

This is not to say that undue delay in bringing charges must *always* constitute an abuse of process. When two defendants were accused in 1990 of having sprung the spy George Blake from gaol in 1967, they applied for proceedings to be stayed on grounds of the unreasonable delay of twenty-three years. In the meantime, however, they had published a book (in 1989) setting out in great detail how they had accomplished the feat, so that a plea of failing memory could hardly be advanced without a smile. The application was not granted, and the trial went ahead, though the jury eventually acquitted the two men.

In that case, the book they had published offered a great deal of documentation. In the case of Mrs West, there was no documentation to assist the forgetful at all.

Sasha Wass was blunt in her submissions. She called the case 'stale' and made the highly valid point that the

244

delay resulted from the concealment of the crimes. If one were to accede to the Crown's suggestion that Mrs West was herself the cause of the delay, it would be to argue in a circle, for 'Mrs West is responsible for the delay only if she is held to be responsible for the crimes themselves'. But that had yet to be shown. An innocent woman would not have known that anything *had* been delayed. 'This case', she said, 'turns almost exclusively on remarks or observations, trivial at the time, which Mrs West cannot be expected to remember twenty years later . . . It is too much to expect anyone to remember what slippers she was wearing when she answered the front door twenty-one years ago.' Moreover, the time lapse not only hampered the defendant's memory, but also 'deprives her of the opportunity of seeking alibi witnesses who might have been with her at the material time'.

The Crown suggested that Mrs West was never apart from her husband, and that in particular she was house-bound throughout the relevant period when eight murders took place between 1973 and 1979. 'In my sub-mission to you, that is ludicrous,' said Miss Wass. The defendant had constantly to leave the house, for the purposes of taking her children to school and to the doctor's, for shopping, for recreation. She was con-stantly seen in local pubs without her husband and had friends with whom she went dancing. All these were commonplace events, but they were 'impossible to recall in sufficient detail after so long in order to give an alibi', and there was 'no way of demonstrating that she was not there when Frederick West was killing'. (Miss Wass found the opportunity later to point out that Mrs West was excluded from the house on diverse occasions to sleep elsewhere with her husband's friends.)

So much for delay. As to lack of documentation, counsel listed the loss of Caroline Owens' 1972 state-ment and the absence of medical records to support her version of events. The only document was a note made by PC Price in 1972 which made no mention of the vivid ordeal Mrs Owens now alleges took place, including having her genitals whipped with the buckle end of a two-inch-wide brown leather belt. It was odd that she did not remember this in 1972, but did in 1994. 'She has elaborated and sensationalized, but she will simply deny that she has, and her denial cannot be challenged.' As for the evidence relating to the death of Charmaine West, it was 'in a state of disarray'. There was no document to demonstrate when she disappeared, and reliance upon eye-witness accounts after so long would be intrinsically unfair. One witness claimed that Charmaine was living in Cromwell Street in 1973. 'That, by any account, cannot be right, but it highlights the danger of relying upon eye-witness statements which are so old.' In other words, if that witness can be wrong, so might Mrs Giles be.

As Judge Stephen Tumim wrote, in another context, 'Our legal system is based upon the curious notion that people can remember whole sentences for a remarkably long time'.[2]

Sasha Wass slipped in one of the most crucially significant points of the whole case almost as an aside (probably because it did not go to abuse of process so much as to abuse by police). I mentioned it towards the end of the last chapter. Frederick West had been charged with the murder of Charmaine. The case now brought against Rosemary West relied upon Mr West being *incapable* of having killed Charmaine by reason of his having been held in custody at the relevant moment. Why, then, had he been charged with a crime he could not, according to the Crown, have committed? The point passed unnoticed and was not reported in the press. It implied that the charge against Mrs West in respect of Charmaine had been concocted.[3]

Counsel then went on to consider the 'unremitting, sensational, inaccurate and misleading' publicity the case had received. The due administration of justice, she said, must rely upon freedom from bias. Yet the press had

246

been so excited by this case that they had let in through the back door evidence which would not normally be admissible. 'The press has prejudged the evidence of Caroline Owens', by which she meant that the press had already decided that Mrs Owens' testimony was truthful in every regard. By writing so much about Frederick West, his 'sex slaves' and his sadism, the idea that Mrs West 'must be' involved had already implanted itself in the public mind. 'If the prejudice is national and continuous,' said Miss Wass, 'the defendant has literally nowhere to go' (to receive a fair trial).

If at the end of the day a defendant could not receive a fair trial because the publicity had made him or her so notorious that nobody could approach the case with an open mind, then this was an abuse of process. 'I want to make it clear', she continued, 'there was never any suggestion that Mr West implicated his wife.' (This was months before we were to learn of the tales he had been telling Janet Leach.)

Mr Badge interrupted to point out that there was no precedent for a magistrate stopping a trial on the grounds of prejudicial publicity, and that such a ruling could only come from the trial judge, to which Miss Wass retorted that it was high time the principle was extended.

She also listed four instances of real prejudice in the newspapers, rather than mere extensive coverage:

1. The description of Caroline Owens as the girl who got away was based upon a conclusion which it was proper only for a jury to make.

2. The magistrate who fined Mr and Mrs West for the assault against Caroline Owens in 1972 had said publicly that he made a mistake in being so lenient and regretted it. This prejudged acceptance of her newer version of what happened.

3. Articles in the *News of the World* which purported to carry confessions by Frederick West to his son that he had carried out illegal abortions at 25 Cromwell Street

247

and that 'two or three' victims were buried with a foetus by their side gave rise to the assumption that Mrs West 'must have known' what was going on in her own home. I would add that this assumption spread like a fast-moving fog from the North Sea until it engulfed the land and could not be dissipated. It was also inaccurate, there being only one foetus at Cromwell Street, and one other in a field, relating to a crime with which Mrs West was *not* charged. Accuracy, however, seemed to be of relatively little concern to the *News of the World*. The same paper printed Stephen West's assertion that his sister had been strangled in the hall and dismembered on the spot, again implying that Mrs West would know what happened, whereas the defence would be that dismemberment could have occurred not at Cromwell Street, but somewhere else.

4. The suggestion in the *Daily Mirror* that Mrs West was due to make a fortune of £10 million by selling her story, placed next to another which stated that the mother of Alison Chambers could not afford a decent burial for her daughter, was designed solely to make the defendant detestable in the public mind.

All the above newspaper reports had been referred to the Attorney General, who had declined to act upon them. Sasha Wass would not say so, but there were many present who could not resist the reflection that the Attorney General was a politician, and politicians like to keep newspaper editors happy lest they forget their traditional role at election time. 'It is in the public interest that such charges as these should be tried,' she agreed, but the evidence being wholly circumstantial, the absence of prejudice would be crucial to a fair trial. 'The interests of the defendant must be maintained.'

In the afternoon, Neil Butterfield QC rose to answer Miss Wass's submissions. On the matter of the very long delay between the date when crimes were committed and that when charges were brought, he had three different remarks to make. First, the delay had not been the fault of the prosecution. Second, it operated to the advantage of the defendant anyway, and to the disadvantage of the Crown. Third, the defendant had contributed to that delay by her own conduct. On the matter of publicity, he had two responses: that it was not prejudicial, and that it was not for this court to decide upon.

Turning to the matter of alibis, Mr Butterfield had a telling point to make, which effectively demolished the significance of Sasha Wass's claim that Mrs West could not account for her whereabouts after so long a period of time. Only the killer or killers, he said, would know the day and time that these deaths occurred. Even after only three months it would not have been possible for Mrs West to conceive an alibi as to where she was, because the prosecution were unable to specify a date and an hour to which any such alibi would apply. So, she would never be able to have one, however long the delay.

He agreed that the disappearance of Caroline Owens' 1972 statement was disadvantageous to the defence, and said that doubtless the trial judge would take this into account, but of itself it was not sufficient to justify a stay of proceedings. As for Charmaine, much depended upon the date of Mrs Giles' visit and whether or not Frederick West was in prison at the time, and though her recollection was not altogether reliable so long after the event, it would still need to be examined, and the jury would be reminded of the difficulties inherent in such evidence.

Mr Butterfield then returned to the problem of delay with some fairly contentious assertions. It would be entirely wrong, he said, to suggest that a murderer who managed to conceal the body of his victim for twenty years could not be charged with or tried for that murder. From this general principle he jumped to a particular conclusion. 'The delay has been caused by the defendant herself,' he said. 'It is her fault that the bodies were not discovered for twenty or twenty-two years. "I say I am not guilty", she says, "therefore you cannot try me." In 1992, two years before Heather's remains were found, she lied, informing the police that her daughter was alive and well and that she had spoken to her on the telephone. Thus, on the single occasion when Rosemary West had the opportunity to speak the truth about the bodies concealed on her property her reaction was to conceal the truth. By her own conduct she contributed to the delay in bringing charges. There is plain evidence of active concealment.'

Many questions were hereby begged. What Mr Butterfield had to say would be true only if Mrs West were guilty as charged, and that was for a jury to decide. Assuming that she was innocent, then she could not be accused of concealing the existence of bodies on her property if she did not know they were there. Assuming she believed her husband's explanation for Heather's leaving home, then she could not be blamed for preventing discovery of her remains when she did not realize Heather was dead. She could be accused of lying, but not of lying as to the death of her daughter if she thought she was alive. One cannot conceal the truth unless one knows what the truth is. Besides, it should be remembered (as Miss Wass later reminded the magistrate) that questions about Heather were put to her mother during the course of an enquiry into child abuse; there was then no question of murder, so Mrs West's answers could not be construed as evasive of the issue as to murder, which did not come up. Both interviewer and interviewee assumed Heather was alive, but neither knew where she was.

Rosemary West's defence, concluded Butterfield, boiled down to three words – 'I know nothing.' This was a fair summary of her position, and it was not satisfactory or conducive to enlightenment on these very serious charges. The publicity, said Mr Butterfield, had given widespread attention to Frederick West's confession and affirmation that his wife had nothing to do with the murders. This was prejudicial to the prosecution, not to the defence, a point which he undermined slightly by an impromptu aside to the effect that nobody believed what the *News of the World* printed anyway.

It had taken a whole day for these arguments to be heard and elaborated. When the court rose a little before 4.00 p.m., Mr Badge said he would reflect upon what had been put to him and would deliver his decision the following morning. There was not a single one among the journalists present from various parts of the world who imagined that he would stop the case going to trial. The cruel deaths of those girls and young women demanded that some explanation, at least, be offered in a public theatre.

On 7 February, Peter Badge gave his ruling in the following words: 'I am satisfied that firstly I have the power to stay proceedings on the grounds that their continuance would be an abuse of court process; secondly that it is a power to be exercised very sparingly and only in exceptional cases; thirdly, even more rarely should the power be exercised in the absence of fault on the part of the prosecution; fourthly, each case must be decided on its own facts; and fifthly, where the defence has caused or contributed to the delay, a stay of proceedings for delay would not be justified. Applying these principles to the facts of this case, I prefer the arguments of the prosecution to those of the defence where they conflict. I find that the delay in this case is not the fault of the prosecution; that there is evidence that it was at least contributed to by the defendant. I also find having regard to the nature of the case and the likely defence that the absence of documentation does not mean that the defence would suffer serious prejudice to the extent that a fair trial could not be held, and such prejudice that there might be could be dealt with adequately by the trial process. Finally I am persuaded that the press cuttings I was given did not provide evidence of prejudice, actual or potential, against the defendant, and in any event the time to consider such a risk is at the commencement of the trial, if there is a trial after committal proceedings.

Accordingly, I decline to declare a stay on these proceedings.'

An impartial observer would be bound to agree that Mr Badge was right to conclude that the extraordinary lapse in time between the commission of crime and arrest of the accused was in no way attributable to fault in the prosecution. On every other point, however, such an observer might wonder what chance an innocent person might have when the dice were so heavily loaded against him. It seemed that the fact that sensationalist newspapers, in which Britain was unnecessarily rich, had published Rosemary West's name and face across the land together with the name and face of an alleged victim, did her no harm whatever. That would certainly be true if she were guilty as charged.

It seemed that Rosemary West's assertion that she knew nothing of her husband's murderous activities, her declaration of innocence, in fact, was to be held against her as having delayed the bringing of this case to trial. That would certainly be true if she were guilty as charged.

It seemed also that the absence of any evidence against her (apart from circumstantial and conjectural) was no more than a nuisance and could not be regarded as unfair. That would certainly be true if she were guilty as charged.

The assumption of Rosemary West's guilt preceded her trial. It would prove an insurmountable obstacle for her and her counsel to overcome. The offences were so horrible, and the defendant's character so suspect, that the hallowed principle of innocence before the law would need, for once, to suffer some dilution.

Neil Butterfield began his narrative of events leading up to the arrests for the first time that day. Those of us who attended both the committal and the trial would hear this narrative, subject to different emphases and interpretations, a total of seven times, and the public would become familiar with its salient points through newspaper reports once the trial was under way. They heard and read nothing, of course, at this stage, for evidence placed before the magistrate is there merely to help him reach a decision whether or not to send the defendant for trial, and it cannot be reported. The central rule (subject to certain modifications) is that newspapers shall report that which a jury has heard, but not that which has not been sent to a jury for their consideration. So none of the evidence presented in these preliminary hearings over the following six days could be repeated in public print or on the airwaves. (There would be not a little fuss in the course of the hearings when foreign newspapers and television channels, not beholden to English law and custom, felt free to report what they wanted.) Though the police team knew what was to come, and there had been rumours from journalists who had been engaged on their own parallel investigations in past months, most people in Dursley Magistrates' Court were quite unaware of what Mr Butterfield would say, and their shock was palpable.

He was right to use colourful language in order to sear into our minds exactly what the case was about. He spoke of 25 Cromwell Street as being a 'charnel-house, a graveyard, where over a period of something like fourteen years young girls were sexually abused in depraved and appalling circumstances.' They had spent their last moments of life as 'the sexual playthings of this defendant and her husband.' He was right also to bring vivid phrases to bear when describing the alleged indifference of the defendant to death in the midst of family life. Charmaine was 'dead, buried outside the kitchen window'. Sexual torture had taken place in the cellar 'without the knowledge of the children and lodgers in the house'. When Carol Cooper was interred, 'her head was thrown in first'. Another victim was 'a prisoner in the cellar, horrible to contemplate, kept alive for whatever hideous purpose for some days before finally meeting her end.' The remains of the girl found with a breathing tube in her nostril told 'the most powerful and chilling story of all. She was kept living but restrained so that her body could be used at will. How long she survived, how her body was abused, how exactly she died, the prosecution cannot say.' By 1975 or 1976 the cellar was full up with bodies – five of them – 'so the floor was concreted over and the area used as bedroom accommodation for the children.'

All this was unpalatable enough, infecting the imagination with a remorselessness which we were powerless to resist. No mechanism exists in sane persons to exclude information they do not wish to hear, or discard it once it has been heard. And we were there, in any case, precisely because we felt it was our duty to be informed. But when it came to the precise allegations made by Miss A, Caroline Owens and Anne Marie Davis (née West), we were as though skewered to the wall by unwelcome knowledge. A few of us were in the courtroom itself, where we sat paralysed by disgust and pity, and often stared at the defendant in disbelief (she, meanwhile, was without expression, except when Heather was mentioned, at which point she turned her head away and appeared to weep). The majority were in an adjacent room, into which the proceedings were relayed by loudspeakers. There we were in one another's company, out of the sight of the magistrate, police officers and court officials. Yet I have never known journalists to be so subdued.

We grabbed our brief coffee-breaks and one-hour lunch recess as though they were gifts from beneficent providence, and though for most of the time it was pouring with rain, we all went outside for a cigarette and trooped down to the pub for jolliness and relief. Nobody talked about the evidence in detail. It was as though to repeat it would be to contaminate the soul, but I recall hearing one reporter say that 'if any of this is heard in open court, then she's had it', a remark which turned out to be prescient.

I remember also the one moment of mirth in court, embraced by us all as a reminder of ordinary human weaknesses. The court was hearing the tape-recordings of Mrs West's interviews with DS Onions when at one point he said that it was 'an occupational hazard in our job that people tend to lie to us.' In the annexe we all roared with laughter. I imagine those in court were controlled.

To this day, I do not believe that the precise evidence of Anne Marie and Miss A has been disseminated to any degree. The BBC's correspondent Joshua Rozenberg addressed a meeting of the Corporation's senior staff months later to give them a comparison between one item of evidence as it was heard and as it had been reported, in an exercise designed to show them why it was necessary to hold back. A written account of his speech has been published in the *British Medical Journal* but not, to my knowledge, anywhere else.

Other slivers of important evidence were detectable in the statement made by Anne Marie Davis on 7 August 1992, when the enquiry into child abuse was under way, which were not sensational and of no interest to the press. She said that her half-sister Heather had left home at sixteen and would now be about twenty-two years old, thus indicating that there was no real suspicion within the family that she might not be alive. Mrs Davis said she had been trying to locate her ever since. She also said that her father did not want her stepmother to know about her incestuous relationship with him, that he did not go to pubs but was at work seven days a week, and that Rosemary sometimes did go out at night and not return until the following morning. There was the tiny domestic detail that the garden at 25 Cromwell Street had contained three apple trees and a pear tree.

When he came to deal with Heather West, Mr Butterfield was spared the need to sniff deeper. It was her disappearance and her mother's acceptance of it which earned his eloquence. 'None of her possessions has been recovered,' he said, 'not a single one. None of her belongings, none of the impedimenta of adolescence of a sixteen-year-old. No trace. Nothing. It has all been disposed of, cleaned out.' On the other counts, he boldly invited inferences which were strictly beyond the strength of the evidence to support, but he made the distinction between allegation and conclusion, the one for himself, the other for a jury. 'If the Crown is right that these inferences *may* be drawn, properly and reasonably,' he said, 'then only a jury will decide if they *should* be drawn.'

He summarized what he would expect the jury to do in two sentences. One, they would have to make a leap from the evidence as it was to the evidence as they imagined it could be. 'If a jury is satisfied that Rosemary West was party to such [sexual] abuse, it is but a small step to infer she was also party to the acts, whatever they were, which led to the deaths in each case.' But since we did not know what these acts were, it was impossible to say whether or not they were similar to any other acts. It was established, he said, 'that one of the acts which both Frederick West and Rosemary West found particularly exciting was the involvement of Rosemary West in violent lesbian acts with helpless victims.' It wasn't. It was merely alleged.

Second, Mr Butterfield would expect a jury to realize that Mrs West, living at 25 Cromwell Street and collecting rent from lodgers, 'could not have remained ignorant' of what was happening. This was the 'argument from residence', the simple but eventually damning assumption that 'she must have known'.

Sasha Wass dealt with these assumptions and inferences head-on when she resumed her argument to Peter Badge on Monday, 13 February. She spoke with a new passion, an ardent but disciplined anger, as if provoked by the emptiness of the Crown's case and their cheek in trying to fill it with guesswork. 'There is', she stated flatly, 'no evidence that Mrs West had any sexual relations with any of the murder victims in this case. There is no evidence at all that Carol Cooper, Lucy Partington, Thérèse Siegenthaler and Shirley Hubbard had visited Cromwell Street or ever met Mrs West at any stage. There is just inference upon inference, but these are not inferences based on factual evidence. An inference of participation in murder is one thing, but what I suggest the Crown is doing is inviting the court to consider a theory as to what might have happened, because the truth may never come to light.'

For the first time, we were made aware that we had been listening to a string of possibilities, untested by fact and unsupported by logic.

To bolster this theory, the prosecution had to introduce evidence from so-called 'surviving witnesses' which had nothing to do with murder. 'It is lurid, sensational and of a highly emotive character,' she said, 'calculated to lower Mrs West in the eyes of a right-thinking person. An application will be made to exclude it.' It would be ridiculous to invite a jury to make inferences from something which was not relevant or probative. 'There is no direct evidence of any knowledge by her of the killings, or any involvement in the burials. Very little is known of how and where the victims died. Yet the Crown relies on the suggestion that all the victims met their deaths at Cromwell Street, particularly as Mrs West was resident there. It is far from certain that they did. The missing bones may indicate that they died elsewhere, but the Crown does not consider this.'

There were only three victims, Charmaine West, Shirley Robinson and Heather West, with whom the defendant had any connection. Because there was no evidence as to motive with any of them, the Crown would suggest a variety of motives. Shirley was killed because Mrs West was jealous; Charmaine because she didn't like her; Heather because of lots of possibilities, among them adolescent arguments. As for the other seven cases, a motive can only be guessed at. 'What the

Crown has done is to make guesses, then elevate these guesses into the category of evidence before you.'

'What in fact do we know?' asked Miss Wass. That all the victims were dismembered. That they were buried at either Cromwell Street or Midland Road. And that Frederick West pointed out where they were buried. There was no doubt that Frederick West was the killer. The point at issue was, was Mrs West his accomplice? 'The Crown relies on the fact that as she was married to the man who committed the murders she must have participated in them.' The evidence, such as it was, did not point that way. There were four strands to the case against Rosemary West:

1. That she had a bad character and propensity to commit murder. This would only work if the court were to accept the Similar Fact evidence of other unrelated offences. It was, said Miss Wass 'an impossible leap'.

2. That she lived at the house.

3. That she was married to the murderer.

4. That she was the mother of one victim and the surrogate mother of another, making her knowledge and participation inevitable.

I shall pass over the rules regarding admissibility of similar facts, which counsel summarized, as they have been dealt with in Chapter Two. Miss Wass said that the prosecution wanted us to concentrate on this evidence, from four witnesses – Caroline Owens, Miss A, Anne Marie Davis and Kathryn Halliday – and 'seek out similarities'. By all means let us do this, she said, but we must look at them in rather closer detail than the Crown would like.

In the first place, they say that a striking feature is the recurrence of hitch-hiking. This applies only to Caroline Owens, not to the other three. The inference was that victims were picked up as hitch-hikers 'just like Caroline Owens'. In fact, only one of them do we positively know was hitch-hiking, and that was Thérèse Siegenthaler. Lynda Gough was not hitch-hiking, nor were Carol

Cooper, Shirley Robinson or Alison Chambers. Shirley Hubbard was put on a bus by her boyfriend, not left to hitch-hike her way home. Juanita Mott sometimes hitch-hiked, but was not necessarily doing so the night she disappeared. As for Lucy Partington, it was supposed she must have resorted to hitch-hiking when she missed the last bus, but we do not know. 'It is mysterious how she came into Frederick West's hands, but the Crown must not be allowed to indulge in detective work unsupported by evidence.' So, of the ten victims in this case, one was certainly hitch-hiking, two might have been, five were not, and in respect of the last two – Heather and Charmaine – the theory did not apply.

The second similarity the Crown pointed to was that the victims were all connected to 25 Cromwell Street. In fact, two were resident there, two were visitors, five had no known connection, and with one (Charmaine) the theory did not apply.

Third, three of the 'surviving victims' complained of lesbian assaults by Mrs West. Yet there was no evidence of any sexual connection between the murder victims and the defendant, save the merest suggestion of a possible *ménage à trois* with Shirley Robinson. It was said that Mrs West used penetrative instruments, yet there was no evidence that any such implements were used on the murder victims.

Fourth, seven of the victims appeared to be gagged at the time of death. The prosecution agreed that Frederick West was instrumental in the killings, and that it was his habit to wrap tape around the heads of his victims. It was highly significant that Caroline Owens' tape was *removed* by Mrs West, who wanted to kiss her. Therefore the tapes found with skulls did not point towards the defendant, but away from her.

Fifth, Mr and Mrs West were always together, the Crown had claimed. Yet the evidence of Anne Marie, who had intercourse with her father on countless occasions, pointed in the opposite direction. He instructed her not to tell Rosemary. If the Crown put her forward as a witness of truth, why was she not put forward as a template? It was obvious that Frederick West kept secrets from his wife. Anne Marie also confirmed that he kept the binding tape in his van. In short, if the Crown wished to show evidence of similar fact which went well beyond propensity, as they would have to, then they had already fallen far short of their goal. 'The connection between sexual proclivity and murder is not sustainable,' said Miss Wass. 'Even if it were, it would point to Frederick West, not to his wife. The Crown has not even made out a case for similarity. Mrs West's sexual activity and the ways in which the victims died were not similar at all.' She continued, 'Rosemary West is a peculiar woman, but the Crown can do no more than raise suspicion against her. In point of fact, in all cases where she participated, the victims survived.' Furthermore, there was plenty of evidence that Mr West picked up young women alone. In conclusion to this section of her argument, Miss Wass spoke with solemnity and respect as she said, 'We do not doubt their ends were gruesome. We have not come to argue that.'

She went on to examine the second strand of the Crown's case against Mrs West, namely that she was resident at the house. Nine sets of remains were found there. It was inconceivable, said the Crown, that she did not know her husband was burying people. Miss Wass asked us to remember that there were tenants at the material time and that their suspicions were never aroused. Frederick West dug Shirley Robinson's grave in the garden, yet not one of them noticed. They even helped him with his building work. There were various children living in the house at the time, and Mrs West was often away whole nights. The Crown proposed that one victim was kept alive and captive for a whole week, yet this was highly unlikely in a house full of lodgers. It was just as likely, perhaps more so, that she was killed elsewhere. The remains of this young woman had a shoulder-blade missing. 'It was not a small bone,' she said. 'It had certainly troubled the pathologist. I suggest it is something that should trouble this court.' In other words, such a difficult piece of surgery could not have taken place in a house packed with people. The argument from residence was insufficient and erroneous, and there was 'no evidence that the murders were committed at 25 Cromwell Street.'

The third strand of the Crown's case was the argument from conjugation, which amounted to little more than implicating Rosemary West because she would have known her husband extremely well. It was put plainly into words by DS Onions, who spluttered with disbelief at Mrs West's insistence on ignorance. Sasha Wass dismissed it out of hand as contradictory on grounds of common sense alone. The dismemberment of Shirley Robinson was a hard physical task. Fred was used to it. He had done it before he met Rose. She was seen clearing out Shirley's room a week after her disappearance, with the door open, which would suggest she thought she had left, as her husband had told her. The Crown, said Miss Wass, inferred too much and wrongly.

The last strand was the argument from motherhood. Frederick West's explanations for the departure of Charmaine were in keeping with what had long been expected, and Rosemary, at just over seventeen, would not question what she was told. The evidence on this count was in such confusion that a committal for trial would be unsafe. Besides, the Crown accept that Frederick West murdered Rena West without assistance from Rosemary. (Privately, some police officers are unwilling to accept this, and think Rosemary had a hand in that as well.) As for Heather, the only evidence was a failure to show concern at her departure. On this count, there was simply no case to answer at all.

Sasha Wass was not quite finished. Mindful perhaps of the strong prejudice abroad, both inside the court and out, which wanted the defendant to be tried and found guilty, and aware that her advocacy had fallen upon some ears already closed to its import, she sought to remind the court not of the law, but of the meaning of words within the law. '*An inference is a conclusion to which one is driven by facts of which one is sure,*' she said (author's italics). There were no such facts, of which one could be sure, in this case. None concerning the circumstances of death and none to suggest that more than one person was involved. With such a scarcity of evidence, only speculation remained.

The committal hearing, like a dress rehearsal for the real thing, was drawing to a close. Neil Butterfield allowed the possibility that Rosemary West would not be sent for trial for murder when he asked the magistrate to consider committing her for trial instead on the lesser charges of indecent assault and rape. At that moment there seemed a very real chance that Sasha Wass might have persuaded Mr Badge that he could not, in justice, allow the West case to go any further. But the Crown had one more throw to make. The similar fact evidence, said Mr Butterfield, would not be introduced merely to establish identity, but to show that the killings were the result of joint venture. 'We do not put before you the proposition that Rosemary West was an accomplice,' he said, 'but that they were in it together.' There were only three possibilities: that Frederick West acted alone; that Rosemary West acted alone; that both Wests acted together. If the evidence pointed only to the first option, then you could not commit Mrs West for trial. But you could and should do so if the evidence pointed to either of the other two options. Even if she was involved in sexual abuse of the victims, and had let her husband finish them off, that would still be sufficient to commit her. As for the evidence of Caroline Owens, Mr Butterfield reminded the magistrate of the specific threat made by Mr West, in Mrs West's presence, to falsely imprison her and to bury her underground, anticipating events which would happen a few months later.

'At the end of the day', rejoined Miss Wass, 'nothing physical happened to her that was life-threatening. Her life was not endangered. That's the point.' She added that it did not follow from the fact that a woman was lesbian that she must be having lesbian affairs with all and sundry 'any more than two heterosexuals who met would necessarily embark upon an affair *because* they had met.'

Peter Badge reserved his decision until the following day. On 14 February 1995, Rosemary Pauline West was committed for trial on ten charges of murder. Mr Butterfield then announced that charges of rape which she had faced with two men, who were brought into the dock, would be dropped forthwith, and the men left as free citizens. (These charges were added to the indictment against Mrs West alone.) That was to be Neil Butterfield's last connection with the case, for he was shortly thereafter raised to the Bench to become Mr Justice Butterfield. His place as chief counsel for the prosecution was taken by Brian Leveson QC. Sasha Wass would see her commitment through to the trial and beyond and would be led by Richard Ferguson QC.

The defendant appeared for the first time at Winchester Crown Court on 12 May 1995, for the formal arraignment, at which she pleaded Not Guilty to each charge.

On 7 July, Mr Ferguson appeared before Mr Justice Mantell with an application that the four additional charges of rape and indecent assault be 'severed' from the main indictment of ten murders, as being too complex for the jury to consider. To this request the judge assented immediately, presumably because he realized that accusations of rape against the defendant would weigh heavily with any jury struggling to maintain an impartial view with regard to evidence of murder.[4] In the event, this would serve but cosmetic purpose if allegations of rape were allowed in anyway under the 'similar fact' rule. Thus Mr Ferguson came to grips with the application for inadmissibility of evidence, which Miss Wass had unsuccessfully attempted before the magistrate. He made exactly the same points, with some added touches of his own. There was no precedent, he said, for a delay of twenty-four years between crime and indictment except in cases of war crimes. The judge interjected. The same argument could have been put forward had Frederick West been alive, he pointed out, and was standing here in court. All of us felt very keenly, at that moment, that no such application would have been granted.

As an example of the impossibility of an honest witness recollecting events of long ago, Mr Ferguson indicated that witness Mrs Gough had misplaced the disappearance of her daughter Lynda by a whole year, and that she had seen a woman at the door of a house in Cromwell Street who was older than her daughter Lynda, whereas Mrs West, whom the Crown alleged was this woman, was in fact six months younger than Lynda. (He might also have mentioned that Mrs Gough had told a policeman of her acquaintance that Lynda had disappeared, but had made no mention of visiting a house in Cromwell Street.) The judge declared his reluctance to stop the case; it was very rare, he said, for a court to intervene when there was no fault in the prosecution. Again, he made a simple point which had awful resonance in the midst of legal reasoning, and showed that his pulse pumped in tune with the public's. 'These ten girls did not die natural deaths,' he said, 'they were murdered.' It was, in other words, unthinkable that no-one should stand trial.

Turning to the attendant publicity, Mr Ferguson drew the judge's attention to a recent copy of the *Sunday Mirror* comparing the present defendant with Myra Hindley and inventing a yarn that they had become close friends in Durham Prison where they were both incarcerated (they had not). No clue could be better placed to indicate what some newspapers intended to do with

Rosemary West, whatever the verdict. 'It appalls me,' said Mr Justice Mantell, but he would not allow his distaste for such things to rule his head.

Giving his ruling, Mantell said, 'I am content to adopt the approach of Mr Justice Garland in the Birmingham Six trial, who faced a similar application and refused. I bear in mind the power of the judge to regulate the admissibility of evidence during the course of the trial and to direct the jury accordingly. I have come to the conclusion that a fair trial may still take place, but that the clearest possible direction to the jury will be necessary.'

And so the problem was again shelved. It remained to be seen whether Mr Justice Mantell would remember his pledge to give 'the clearest possible direction to the jury' with regard to the defence's misgivings about irrelevant and prejudicial evidence being admitted. The date for the trial was set for 3 October.

10

Trial

One of the principles of English justice which earns most respect is the calm expedition of jury selection. It is held as axiomatic that a citizen must account for his actions not to his accuser, nor even to a judge, but to twelve other citizens chosen at random, whose opinion, having heard the facts and been guided as to how the law deals with those facts, will decide his fate. It is therefore crucial that these twelve people should be independent of any bias, influence, personal knowledge or animus. It is not important that they be blank, stupid or incapable of thought.

In the United States, the courts have become so cautious of admitting any juror who may have an opinion of any sort that they will allow weeks, even months, to be spent on cross-examining prospective jurors with a view to weeding out those who think. This calamitous system has evolved through the bullying of over-scrupulous lawyers who misunderstand the point of a jury and imagine their job is to ensure that their client be tried by an approved committee instead. I mention this because some American journalists present at Winchester were astonished that the jury in the West trial were chosen and empanelled in just over four minutes.

What the Americans did not recognize was that it was essential we know nothing about these twelve people. We must not care what opinions they may have, or where and whether they were educated, or what they do in their spare time. They must be anonymous, the better to reach an impartial and incontestable verdict born of their secret deliberations. The defendant can only be promised justice if there is no connection between him and the twelve people he faces, by which I mean not only that there is no historical or familial connection, but that no superficial connection be temporarily established in court by virtue of any knowledge of what kind of people they are.

A panel of potential jurors is chosen by taking their names and addresses from the electoral register entirely by chance, almost with a pin. These are then summoned to attend court. The summoning officer has no idea whether any of them might fall within a disqualified category (convicts, clergymen, lunatics, judges), and must therefore rely upon their honesty in revealing the fact if it applies. Should a potential juror fail to reveal grounds for his disqualification, then we should have one liar on the jury, which, out of twelve, may well help to represent a cross-section of the community as a whole. In addition, a potential juror may be excused for service on request if he has good cause. The clerk of the court shuffles the cards on which names and addresses are written, and calls out the first twelve who turn up. If he runs out of potential jurors for one reason or another, the court may send the clerk out to pick up anyone from the street to serve, though this rarely occurs. Eight men and four women were called to try Rosemary Pauline West. None of them asked to be excused, and Mr Justice Mantell, presiding, warned them that if they did so ask, he might well not grant the request anyway. He then told them that they had a heavy responsibility ahead of them and that they must bear it alone, for they could discuss the case with no-one. 'The chief danger lies when you go home,' he said. 'Don't allow members of your family to offer their views to you. You may discuss the case as the trial proceeds, but only if all of you are present and can each hear what is being said.'

It was possible only to guess who they were (although we had all heard their names). One woman appeared pro-fessional and middle-aged, smart, attentive, with an extensive wardrobe and discreet jewellery. Another was probably a housewife in her thirties, worn with care but cheerful, most likely a 'good sort'. Two of the men were stout, white-haired, probably getting on for seventy, and another two were barely twenty years old, one wearing an ear-ring, the other always in open-necked shirts. But, coming together in these unnatural circumstances, they were immediately ennobled by the trust that was being placed upon them and, as the weeks passed, they would congeal into a unit. Mr Justice Mantell was clearly aware of this strange but essential process whereby ordinary people don a cloak of power and responsibility such as is given to no other in the land, not excluding cabinet ministers. He demonstrated by his avuncular and confiding manner that he trusted them and that he would help them as best he could through the ordeal ahead. He gave the impression that he and they would suffer it together.

However, they could not start straight away. Legal arguments would have to be heard in their absence before evidence could begin, and no sooner had they taken their places on the jury bench than they were told to go home and await further instructions.

The first ruling the judge made might have been thought redundant. At the request of Richard Ferguson, QC for the defence, he said, 'I prohibit the interviewing of witnesses about their evidence until the trial is over.' In view of the fact that most of them had already spilled their beans to various journalists, the prohibition could have applied to the proverbial bolted horse. The judge also reminded the court of another prohibition that was not generally appreciated, namely that counsel were not permitted to express an opinion in any circumstances. We knew that they could not (again, unlike in the United States) give press conferences or chat to journalists during the course of the trial on the merits of the evidence, but Mr Justice Mantell reminded us that they could have no opinion even within the trial context, in court.

Mr Ferguson then made application to exclude the

'similar fact' evidence which the Crown wished to introduce. 'I call it disputed evidence rather than similar fact,' he said, 'it is prejudicial in the extreme. It cannot be admissible if its only purpose is to prove propensity.' You could not, he said, weigh disputed evidence from living witnesses against inferred evidence from human remains, which was 'much more difficult to evaluate because it is silent'. These were not 'facts' that were 'similar'. 'We're not comparing like with like, but two kinds of evidence which are not comparable.'

Mr Justice Mantell intervened to tell the story of Bluebeard, who murdered his wives. If one of them had escaped, he said, he would have regarded her evidence as relevant. Mr Ferguson quarrelled with this, on the grounds that there was no evidence of any attempt to kill the living witnesses, so they could not be said to have escaped death in the way Bluebeard's imaginary fortunate wife might have. The judge resisted him still. There was only a limited number of purposes for tying up a young girl and stripping her naked, he said, implying that the experience of living witnesses could have been a prelude to death and that they did, arguably, escape. Ferguson replied that the bodies of the dead girls may have been stripped not for sex but for dismemberment, which again would make the fact of their remains not 'similar' in any real way to the ordeals of the living witnesses, and on three counts, not remotely 'similar' at all. Perhaps, he suggested, these three counts should be tried separately from the other seven.

Mr Ferguson moved on to make another point. There were two murders in which the Crown did not suggest that Rosemary West was involved (at which point the row of three police officers shook their heads defiantly) and of the total of twelve sets of remains, five of them bore none of the striking similarity which the Crown suggested should allow in similar fact evidence. 'These five counts present grave problems for the Crown,' he said. 'They cannot pick and choose. They cannot say that of the twelve instances they will pick seven and draw inferences from their common features, then blithely ignore the other five where they cannot.' On the matter of Mrs West's sexual assault against Caroline Owens in 1972, Mr Ferguson said that evidence from other witnesses *would* be admissible if the defendant was being tried for sexual assault. But she was not. 'Evidence of sexual abuse is *not* probative of any allegation of murder.'

Ferguson went on to challenge the prosecution's string of speculations. They wanted us to think that the victims 'found their way to Cromwell Street', yet there was no evidence they ever did. They may have been taken there after death and dismemberment. This speculation was 'plucked out of the air'. Further, they each suffered sexual abuse at Cromwell Street? Not so. This is imagined merely because the remains were found without clothing. In conclusion, Richard Ferguson asked the judge to exclude five Crown witnesses (the only five who were important to their case, as it happened), on the grounds that their 'similar fact' evidence went only to previous bad conduct and character of the defendant, and only then in respect of five counts of murder. 'If you do allow these five to testify, my lord, then they will talk about sexual abuse and in so doing will raise the question of a fair trial in respect of the other seven counts. It is very problematic.'

In reply for the Crown, Brian Leveson QC made the astonishing remark that, with regard to the murder of Rena, 'I do not concede that Mrs West was not involved.' And with regard to the murders of Heather, Charmaine and Shirley Robinson, 'We admit that motive distinguishes these three from the other seven.' He then responded to Ferguson's objections. 'The fact that the victims are dead and the witnesses as to similar fact are alive is neither here nor there,' he said. 'Similar facts in a murder case are likely to be from live witnesses.' And the fact that they went to Cromwell Street was 'abundantly clear, because that's where they were found'. There was no reason why clothing should be removed just for dismemberment, therefore the deaths must have occurred at Cromwell Street. This was a rather shaky series of *non sequiturs*, which evaded rather than addressed Ferguson's points, and made one wonder whether the unthinkable was still possible – that this evidence would be excluded by the judge.

We had to wait forty-eight hours to find out, for the court rose at that point and it had already been announced that it could not sit on 4 October. It was on the morning of Thursday, 5 October that we assembled to hear Mr Justice Mantell's ruling. It went squarely in favour of the Crown. The evidence of the five witnesses illuminated both the purpose for which the victims were brought to the house and the complicity of the defendant in that purpose, and was 'of such probative value that fairness does justify its admission'.

Mr Ferguson then returned to his other application, that three counts of murder be 'severed' (i.e., tried separately from) the other seven. 'The jury cannot reach an unbiased view on these three counts if they have heard similar fact evidence on the other seven. You would be asking them to perform a series of mental gymnastics. They will be influenced by the evidence on seven counts which is prejudicial when they are deliberating on the other three counts where such evidence is irrelevant.' In other words, if they are persuaded by similar facts that the defendant had something to do with the deaths of seven strangers, they will have this thought in their heads when they come to consider the deaths of Charmaine, Shirley Robinson and Heather, wherein none of these similar facts relating to sexual abuse would be remotely pertinent.

The judge refused this, also. Provided always that clear direction was given (by himself), there need not be the prejudice which Mr Ferguson anticipated. It would be several weeks before we were able to determine whether this clear direction was given by Mr Justice Mantell, and whether it was clear enough.

Thereupon, after the announcement that forty-six witnesses were due to appear, the jury was brought in and the stage was set for the case proper to begin.

Two distinct and contradictory images of Rosemary West were already looming in the public imagination by the time she came to stand trial, and neither was matched by the enigmatic woman who sat in the dock. One, nurtured by the popular press, was of a satanic, Borgia-like creature gloating with voracious sexual appetite, keen of eye and terrible of aspect. The other, perceived by those few who were already familiar with the evidence, was of a pretty but rather dim young girl aged between seventeen and twenty-five (the age of the defendant at the time all but one of the crimes alleged against her were committed), a Lolita-type nymphette, sexually aware and suggestible. The accused was not a fusion of these two, but a third, unimaginable version, a dull, unexciting, uninteresting, matronly woman clad in boring black.

She marched in with firm stride and purposeful gait, nodded a perfunctory bow to the judge, and sat flanked by two policewomen. She never spoke to either of them. Her hair was thick, shiny and black, cut sensibly short, and she wore heavy round spectacles. Simple ear-rings dangled, and a simple chain hung from her neck. She was dumpy, almost fat, and severe. Every day for seven weeks she would wear the same black jacket beneath which was just visible a white blouse. She looked more like a schoolmistress or a supermarket manager than the embodiment of evil. A psychiatric assessment of Mrs West dated 13 June 1995, found her 'pleasant, open and friendly, with a quietly spoken voice, readily forming rapport'. She manifested 'no sustained abnormality of mood, thought or perception' and 'no evidence of mental disorder'. She was, however, visibly upset when reference was made to her husband's abuse of children, to Charmaine, or to Heather, whose departure had 'shattered' her. When she reiterated that Fred's strict instructions could never be disobeyed, she added that he sometimes turned the children against her, in order to make her feel different and ostracized and stupid, so that she would obey him to make him desist. She said that he treated her 'like shit'.[1]

The imagination was quickly shattered by the cruel reality of Mr Leveson's two-day peroration. Assuring the jury that they should not trouble themselves to remember all the names, as they would hear them often enough in the days to come, he took them through a narrative of the defendant's life and crimes, in the Crown's version, which he warned would contain evidence 'more terrible than words can express'. 'The picture I shall describe is in places horrific and harrowing,' he said. 'I do not do this to shock or provoke sympathy. Emotion has no part in this case or in this court whatever. It is the one faculty which has nothing to do with analysis.' Nevertheless, Mr Leveson's two key assumptions, which he introduced now and would repeat as leitmotifs in the coming days, had little to do with analysis and were much influenced by unspoken emotion. They became the 'sound-bites' of the prosecution's case – 'they were in it together', or at least 'she must have known'.

The jury were handed a bundle of exhibits, photographs, plans of the house and maps, to consult when following Mr Leveson's address, which he began with the birth of the defendant on 29 November 1953 and traced through various stages to her arrest.

Mr Leveson's purpose was to paint an outline for the jury, the details of which would be filled in by witnesses to be called. He therefore dealt with the counts chronologically rather than in the order they appeared on the indictment, the better to establish sequence and flow. His task, after all, was to tell a story, and to tell it in such a way as to make a cumulative point. It would require considerable skill to navigate the shoals of this unpleasant voyage without acknowledging they were there.

Charmaine came first, including her brief and tragic life, her disappearance, Mrs West's delight in seeing the back of her, Mr West's prison term at the material time. The defendant 'blanked out any questions about what had happened to Charmaine. It was as though she never existed.' Mr Leveson conceded that it was not known how, when or why she died, and that it was impossible even to date when she vanished. One might think, then, there was little or nothing on which to bring a charge, but counsel was adamant that 'you can be sure that she was involved in Charmaine's death and that her lies were to protect herself, not just him. Her wish to be rid of Charmaine had been granted.' Thereafter, the Wests were bound by a terrible shared secret and they became as one – a morbid sex-obsessed duet. 'At the core of this case', said Mr Leveson, 'is the relationship between Frederick and Rosemary West: what they knew about each other, what they did together, what they did to others and how far each was prepared to go.'

Counsel went on to give a detailed description of the original house at 25 Cromwell Street, and in a completely unexpected move, produced plans drawn to precise scale which he then superimposed upon the plan of the courtroom in which we were sitting. 'From front to back, the house is only as long as this court is wide,' he said. 'Its maximum width is from the front of the clerk's desk to the back wall of the court behind my lord. The sitting-room is the size of the two rows of the jury box squared. The scullery and the kitchen together are only the size of the court clerk's desk.' This extremely adroit scheme had the effect of impressing upon the jury how small the house was, and consequently suggesting to them in a subliminal manner that the accused could not have been unaware of what was going on in so confined an abode. It was to be hoped that they would not also wonder how the lodgers could remain in ignorance of murders being committed a few feet away.

Mr Leveson summarized the evidence the jury would hear from Caroline Owens, which was 'highly relevant, that's why I'm telling you, although Rosemary West is not charged with any offence against Caroline Owens in this court.' He said that when Caroline was hitch-hiking home from Tewkesbury it was 'perhaps by coincidence but perhaps not' that Mr and Mrs West drove up and offered her a lift. The ordeal which followed illustrated how the couple could alternate between cruelty and kindness, offering cups of tea one moment and sexual indignities the next, and, more importantly, pointed to features which the members of the jury would be invited to conclude were replicated in subsequent murders. These were:

1. The age and sex of the victim. Caroline was seventeen. All subsequent victims were girls between fifteen and twenty-two years old.
2. The way in which victim was obtained, hitch-hiking, offering job as child-minder.
3. The place to which victim was taken, 25 Cromwell Street.
4. The manner by which victim was bound, with adhesive tape around the face to form a mask.
5. The joint sexual behaviour towards victim of Mr and Mrs West.
6. Mrs West's interest in girls 'together with the pleasure and gratification she obtained from sexually assaulting a restrained and immobile girl with the pain, humiliation and indignity which that involves.'

Caroline was permitted to go home, said Mr Leveson, 'but the Wests would not be so trusting again.' A few weeks later Lynda Gough would find herself in the same situation, he said, but this time she did not survive. Whether or not Lynda Gough did suffer the same treatment as was meted out to Caroline Owens, and whether or not Mrs West was present when she did, was of course guesswork, but the evidence of the girl's remains were potent enough to fill in some of one's gap in knowledge. 'Think for a moment about the absence of clothes and the presence of tape with hair still on it after twenty years', said Mr Leveson, 'and the picture becomes clear.'

He continued with a graphic account of the next five victims, buried clockwise in a circle under the cellar over a period of seventeen months from November 1973 to April 1975, when the 'pattern' was repeated with 'a vengeance'. At every opportunity counsel alerted the jury to the 'striking similarity' between the forensic evidence found with the girls' remains and the painful experience of Caroline Owens, clearly in preparation for the time, should it occur, when appeal might be made against the decision to include these 'similar facts'. Readers will recall that they are admissible only in rare instances, and only if the similarity is 'striking'.

'Picture, if you will, the constant excavations to bury another victim,' said Mr Leveson. First, Carol Cooper. 'We do not know how Carol came to get off the bus without returning to her grandmother. What we do know is that she ended up in Cromwell Street.' Strictly speaking, as he well knew, Mr Leveson should have said that we knew her dismembered body ended up in Cromwell Street and no more. The materials of restraint found with her indicated that she had been bound and gagged somewhere by someone, so counsel's duty was again to remind the jury that her fate appeared to repeat that of Lynda Gough and (nearly) Caroline Owens. 'The more it happens,' he said, 'the more and more crystal clear and obvious the conclusions which can be drawn.' Furthermore, 'Rosemary West could not have remained ignorant. She was party to her imprisonment and subsequent death.'

With Lucy Partington's remains was found a knife. That, pointed out Mr Leveson, strongly suggested that the dismemberment had taken place at Cromwell Street and not somewhere else. 'Why bury it with the body if it had not been?' It would indeed be very difficult to posit an alternative explanation, and for the first time the almost inconceivable scenario, that killing and dismemberment could take place in a small house stacked with people, was built on more than earnest conjecture. But Leveson went further. He put forward the proposition that Miss Partington had been held captive for a week in the same place, for which there was no evidence at all. 'Both must have been involved in that,' he said, for it would certainly have been too much to credit that Mrs West could have been unaware of what was going on for seven whole days. But he did not consider (nor was he required to consider) the possibility that she had been held elsewhere and her dead body brought to Cromwell Street shortly before it was dismembered. It was essential for the Crown to keep Mrs West in the front of the frame at all times. 'If Lucy was picked up from a bus-stop, Rosemary West must have been involved; she would have provided both reassurance and, if necessary, assistance when it became necessary to subdue an unwilling victim.' That was the baldest conjecture. Never mind. It was again 'striking' that the pattern should repeat itself, and while we pondered this we were given pause to reflect that no pattern had been established with anything approaching certainty.

On Thérèse Siegenthaler, counsel said, 'Here, then, was the naked, dismembered body of a hitch-hiker, with the now familiar accompaniment of some form of gag. The only reason to abduct her must have been so that she might be abused either sexually or physically or both. Having regard to all the circumstances, this can only have gone on in Cromwell Street. If that is so, the Crown contend that it is unthinkable that Rosemary West would not have known of it and been involved in it.' The same paucity of knowledge required the same creative thought to replace the 'unthinkable' with regard to Shirley Hubbard. 'Where she went and what she did we simply do not know,' said Mr Leveson, 'but we do know that she fell into the hands of those at 25 Cromwell

Street . . . she was picked up from the streets in some way, just like Caroline Owens, Lucy Partington and others. Once picked up, she was then taken to Cromwell Street, perhaps willingly, where she was kept in secret, murdered and buried in secret. Precisely when we cannot say; she may have been on the run for some time.' None of this would be supported by any evidence at all. What, however, was forensically decipherable was that this fifteen-year-old girl had been subjected to a frightful ordeal somewhere, at the hands of someone. Mr Leveson spared no feelings in describing it, and for the first time demanded that the jury look at a photograph of human remains. He concluded, 'How long it was before the blessing of death came to her, we cannot say.'

Juanita Mott, said counsel, 'died while she was being degraded'. When at Cromwell Street, she was bound and gagged. 'No other explanation possibly fits. The cellar is now full up. The floor was concreted over.'

To account for the fact that there appeared to be no more victims for a period of two years following this frenzy, Mr Leveson indulged in a different sort of guess-work. 'Perhaps when the cellar became full', he said, 'the Wests felt, at least for a while, that enough was enough.' This is highly implausible. The kind of compulsive, repetitive, ritualistic murderer who had been responsible for six deaths in two years would not be capable of logical reasoning and rational decision. He would not, could not, say to himself, well, I think I'd better stop doing this now; it doesn't seem such a good idea when there's nowhere to put the bodies. He may hope that his activities will be curtailed or possibly even permanently halted by changed circumstances. When Dennis Nilsen moved from a ground-floor flat, where he had been able to place bodies beneath the floorboards and eventually burn them in the back garden, to an attic where no such practical advantages obtained, he felt certain that his murderous impulses would be contained. They were not, and three more young men died in the attic before he was caught, their bodies sliced into pieces and flushed down the lavatory. When Jeffrey Dahmer was caught, his apartment was littered with bodies, three of them murdered within the last four weeks; this was despite the fact that he had lost his job, had no money left, and would be required to move out within days. Logical thought would have stopped him weeks before, but his compulsion was heedless of reason.

Similarly, it is not possible to imagine a conversation between Frederick and Rosemary West in which one tells the other that the cellar is full so they had better not kill anyone for a few years until they can think how to dispose of remains. I do not think such a conversation could take place, or, if it did, that it could be acted upon. Either the murderer did not interrupt his activities, and the bodies of his unknown victims are buried elsewhere, or the murderous impulses subsided for reasons unaccountable, to surge forth again much later. As the first possibility is utter conjecture, I prefer the second. It at least accords with what forensic evidence we have.

Other activity was taking place during that two-year period, said Mr Leveson, which was both sexual and cruel. He referred to the evidence which would be heard from Miss A, and told the jury that it was included because it fitted with all the requirements of 'striking similarity' that he had mentioned earlier. Miss A was of the right age, was assaulted at 25 Cromwell Street, was assaulted by both Mr and Mrs West, was bound and taped, and was humiliated by Mrs West who derived pleasure from dominion over a helpless female. Why was she not killed? Because the Wests did not feel threatened by her, said Mr Leveson. 'They obviously made an assessment that this girl would not go to the police. They were right.' The same mistake in crediting serial killers with logic applies here. They do not make 'assessments'. They act in the grip of magic. While they can plan the abduction and captivity meticulously, with that part of the brain which decides how to cash a cheque and how to catch a bus, the moment of murder is not so much the result of a plan as of a psychic explosion. It cannot be resisted by discussion as to likely outcomes.

Something of the kind happened the day Shirley Robinson died. The way Frederick West described the murder in his interviews supports the notion of a sudden access of rage, ungovernable by reasoned deliberation and not subject to strategy. Her entreaties and pleas for affection became too much for him. But because her death did not fit the template 'just like Caroline Owens', Mr Leveson had perforce to paint a different picture of her place at 25 Cromwell Street, one supported by plenty of anecdotal evidence from lodgers and neighbours. It was common knowledge, he said, that Shirley was carrying Mr West's child. She was so much a part of the family that she signed a card of congratulation to Mrs West, along with Stephen and Mae, on the birth of her daughter Tara. Mrs West had been perfectly able to tolerate this seemingly intolerable situation, he said, because she had been attracted to Shirley herself. There may well have been a tripartite relationship involved. But it grew too intense, and jealousy erupted into flaming arguments. Shirley took refuge in the room of another lodger, Elizabeth Brewer. 'It can only be that Shirley was seeking sanctuary from jealousy and friction,' said Mr Leveson.

It was impossible to be precise about the date of Shirley's death. On 9 May 1978 she was photographed in a Woolworth's booth with Miss Brewer. On 12 May she withdrew her claim for benefit because she was moving to Scotland. Yet a claim for unemployment benefit was made on 26 May. 'I say immediately that I cannot say Rosemary West was involved in any of this for there is no source of information at all,' said Mr Leveson. The Department of Health and Social Security sent her a letter dated 14 June asking her to call. There was no response. On 4 August Mr Gregson from the Department called at 25 Cromwell Street to enquire after her and was informed that Shirley had gone to Germany. 'The lady to whom he spoke was almost inevitably Rosemary West. What she said to him was a lie. Shirley Robinson had been murdered.'

Why did she die? 'The Crown does not have to prove motive,' said Mr Leveson, 'but it was probably to remove the threat to the stability of the relationship between Rosemary and Frederick West. On any showing Rosemary West had a much stronger motive for ending the life of Shirley Robinson than did her husband.' This was debatable, and the opposite view would be put by Mr Ferguson a few weeks later. When Mrs West was questioned about Shirley, shortly before her body was found, she denied ever having known such a girl. 'Even when prompted that the police were talking of the girl whom Frederick West had made pregnant, that rang no bells. We submit that it is ludicrous for Mrs West to pretend that she did not remember such a dramatic and disturbing part of her life.' Indeed it was, and the accused had unquestionably been lying when she said so. Why she should lie at that moment, and what conclusions could or should be drawn from it, would also wait until the defence case opened much later.

Counsel for the prosecution made another telling point when he came to the death of Alison Chambers in 1979. Again, forensic evidence indicated restraint, with a belt 'clamping closed her jaw, to stop her screaming, to keep her silent', dismemberment, missing bones. But it was the implication of domestic aftermath which clearly made the jury think. 'What happened to her possessions?' he asked. 'Who cleared them away?'

An entirely different implication, one that Mr Leveson probably did not intend, was carried in his reminder to the jury of the ages of various family members at the time. Heather was just nine years old when Alison Chambers died, he said. Eight years were to pass before she joined all the other skeletons. This would mean that the other children, Stephen and Mae, were seven and eight, and Tara was still a baby. When the other girls died, Stephen and Mae had been babies themselves, then infants. The only one of the family to be of discerning age when Shirley Robinson and Alison Chambers disappeared was Anne Marie, a sturdy if difficult teenager. And she had for a long time endured an intimate sexual relationship with her father. What, if anything, she may have known about what was going on in the house in which she lived was never explored.

And what of Heather? Did she know anything? 'There is no direct evidence that she knew what had been going on or what an examination of the cellar or the garden would reveal,' admitted Mr Leveson. But there had been growing friction between the Wests and their eldest daughter, possibly the result of normal problems of adolescence, possibly of something more serious. It was perhaps significant that she had never had a boyfriend. Counsel rehearsed in some detail the various conflicting accounts that Rosemary West had given of the day Heather disappeared and of the argument which had preceded her departure, accounts with which the reader is already familiar. They were, he said, 'all lies'. The truth was simple and brutal. 'The fact is that some four months short of her seventeenth birthday she was murdered, chopped up and dumped in the back garden of 25 Cromwell Street. She had been living at home. All her possessions must have been left in the house. All suggestions of contact by telephone from Rosemary West are lies. There was no contact by Rosemary West with any authority to enquire after this missing child who makes no attempt to call home. The precise motive for the death of Heather West is to a degree speculative. It could be because she knew too much about what had gone on and could not be allowed to leave home. It could be because there was a blazing row as Rosemary West said and that Rosemary West did give her a hiding and rather more than a hiding. It could be that Heather was resisting attempts to involve her sexually in the household.

She participated in the killing of her own daughter. Why else the lies?'

Mr Leveson had warned that he was going to be speculative 'to a degree'. In fact, this mounting indictment with regard to Heather was wholly conjectural. Although he had mentioned that ropes had been found with her remains, sufficient to bind hands and legs (but no gag), and that there had been the by now usual dismemberment and removal of bones, he did not point out that these were the signature of Frederick West, identifiably ascending to a time before he had met his future wife. Nor, of course, was he obliged to do so. Anticipating the objections that might be raised by the defence, he allowed that 'what she did with her husband and what she did with others who consented, is, of course, entirely up to her and does not *of itself* mean that she was involved in sexually abusing anyone, either to the point of death or otherwise.'

What it did mean, however, was that her relationship with Frederick West was of such closeness that 'she must have known about those who were brought to Cromwell Street and buried there.' That, succinctly put, was the burden of the Crown's case. She had become a 'perfect companion' to him.

After a weekend break, Mr Leveson continued his opening address to the jury on the morning of Monday, 9 October, with a description of the difficult task of investigation into the Cromwell Street murders. After the skeleton of Heather West was unearthed on 26 February 1994, he said, eight other sets of remains were discovered in less than two weeks. There followed the enormous problem of identification and, in tandem, the mystery of the missing bones. Here he summarized the opinions of Professor Knight, the pathologist, with regard to the various explanations which could account for the bones, and was particularly concerned to discard the possibility that the victims had been murdered in another place. Such a possibility would, of course, have considerably diminished an already thin circumstantial case against the defendant. 'What on earth would be the purpose of moving a body from a site at which it has not been discovered for months or years presumably away from Cromwell Street into Cromwell Street where it could inevitably be linked to the West family?' asked Mr Leveson. 'Why is each carefully placed in its own individual hole in the ground? It is absurd, isn't it, to visualize nine removals, each one months or years after the killing and each one carrying its own risk of discovery, for no additional purpose.'

Here one might interject two remarks. First, while it might appear surrealistic to disinter and rebury nine bodies many months after death, it would not be nearly so absurd to commit murder and dissection somewhere else and to bury the remains at Cromwell Street within a day or two, at dead of night. Besides which, we know that the limbs were whole when they were placed in the ground, for the discoloration of the earth around the bones indicates the presence of decomposed flesh, which would have been much less evident if the bodies had already partially or fully decomposed before re-burial. Mr Leveson's purpose in introducing this problem was to dismiss the possibility that some bones went missing in transit. That, eventually, was accepted by both sides, and agreement would be reached that only mutilation could account for the disappearance of kneecaps, vertebrae and finger-bones. But he was understandably reluctant to envisage the other possibility – of more or less immediate translation from place of death to place of burial.

The second observation one might make is that astonishment at the apparent nonsense of moving bodies from one place to another is only tenable if one expects a compulsive serial killer to behave logically. As I have suggested earlier, he does not so behave, or rather he is beholden to a private internal logic which defies the common sense of the sane person. What on earth would

284

be the purpose? To keep that which belongs to him close by, with him for ever on his property, in order that he might gloat with secret knowledge and power. It is crazy, but it fits with what we know of such people. In this case, it can only be a plausible idea. There is no proof, and Frederick West was silent on the matter.

None of the above can apply in the case of Heather. Mr Leveson was right to point out that 'she was last seen by her mother at Cromwell Street and she was found at Cromwell Street, and she also is missing bones from her hands and feet as well as her right kneecap or patella. She was not moved to some other place and left to rot until she could be brought home, was she?' This was true. So far as I know, Frederick West's account that he killed his daughter in the house has not been contested. All that is contested is his wife's complicity in the murder, not where it took place. From this particular counsel expanded to envelop all the counts. None of the victims was found in any sort of bag, he said, 'because each was buried where she died.'

In which case, the murderer must have been in a terrible mess. 'What was Frederick West wearing as he carried out this task? However he did the task, Mrs West could not, we submit, have remained in ignorance.' At the very least, she must have helped him clean up.

Finally, Mr Leveson came to the indictment itself. The Crown had to show, on each of the ten counts, *either* that Rosemary West was one of the girls' attackers *or* that she was part of a joint enterprise with Frederick West, the ultimate result of which was to be the girls' murder. Therefore, even if she did not partake of the murder, but did partake in activities which led to murder, she would be guilty as charged. 'They were in it together,' he said. He reminded the jury that it was she who touched Caroline Owens, she who collected Lynda Gough. 'It must have been' Mrs West who enticed the victims to Cromwell Street. It was she who was interested in sexual abuse and violence. 'Consider how much time it must have taken after death to deal with the remains, dismember the bodies, dig the hole, fill in over the remains, dispose of excess soil, clothing and belongings, tidy up and clear up the mess . . . even assuming Rosemary West did not, in fact, participate in the disposal and hiding of the bodies, she must have known it was going on.'

From a charge that Rosemary West was ten times a murderer, the accusation had imperceptibly weakened to the point where she might have been ten times an accessory before or after the fact. In other words, that 'she must have known'.

In 1916 Judge Avory made a classic ruling on the conduct of prosecuting counsel, which has found its way into all the legal textbooks and is invisibly engraved above the door to each set of chambers in the Temple. 'Prosecuting counsel', he said, 'ought not to struggle for the verdict against the prisoner, but they ought to bear themselves rather in the character of ministers of justice assisting in the administration of justice.'[2] It is because this decorum and discipline is so deeply entrenched in the behaviour of barristers that the criminal justice system, on the whole, earns such respect. It is also why the same system is regarded with scornful derision by colleagues at the American Bar, where if a lawyer does not 'struggle' to win the case at all costs he is deemed unfit for his job. There, the adversarial habit has grown into a monster of battle and strife, in which lawyers will apparently stop at nothing to win a case, not excluding hurling abuse at their opponents and attempting to seduce a jury with falsehood and histrionic fervour. In England it is more important that justice should be done and fairness observed than that a particular barrister should be given a stage on which to show off.

This may sound pious, but it is relevant. The Rosemary West case was already a difficult one to try by reason of the sordidness of the allegations and the fragility of the evidence available to support them. It would have been far worse had barristers on opposing sides made a point of detesting one another and rubbishing their arguments. To foreign observers the proceedings at Winchester appeared quaint. They were astonished that all four barristers (Ferguson, Wass, Chubb, Leveson) sat together on the same bench, and chatted amicably to each other before and after each session of the court. They were disappointed that more shouting and arm-waving did not take place. They were frankly impatient with the coded language of the courtroom – the judge asking counsel what help they could offer when he meant that they had said something unintelligible and counsel being most grateful to his lordship when they meant that they wished his lordship would interfere somewhat less. But this studied politeness is essential to the administration of justice, in which personal animosity plays no part and disgust at the evidence wields no influence. When Mr Ferguson and Mr Leveson referred to one another as 'my learned friend' they meant what they said.

Only three times in seven weeks did Ferguson object to a line of questioning which Leveson had initiated (in the United States it is customarily once every ten seconds). He knew, without having to be told, that Leveson was in no way motivated by malice towards the defendant or ambition for himself.

I say this because Brian Leveson conducted the prosecution case with exemplary patience and tact. His difficulty did not reside in overcoming sympathy for the defendant, for there was none, but in grappling with evidence which he knew to be insubstantial. A lesser barrister would have used the animus against Rosemary West to cement together the rather loose bricks of his structure and deflect attention away from the legal vacuum on the edge of which he was constantly poised. He resisted this easy route. Twice only, as I shall indicate, did his personal abhorrence reveal itself, to be swiftly checked. He mapped out the course of his narrative and kept firmly in view that he had to present the case for the Crown with clarity, however wobbly it might be in legal terms. It must be said that he was much aided in this task by Mr Justice Mantell.

Charles Mantell, a man of great girth and avuncular manner, quickly established a rapport with the jury for which they were visibly grateful. He was considerate towards them, always explaining what was going on, what was meant by the term 'admissions' (matters of fact which were not in dispute but admitted by both sides, as, for example, the accused's date of birth), gently apologizing to them when they had to be sent out for him to hear legal argument. It would be no idle cliché to suggest that he had a twinkle in his eye, for he did smile at the jury whenever he had something to say to them, and raised the right corner of his mouth to emphasize a point. One had the impression that he was looking after them, that he would make sure their requirements were met and their comfort assured. Of all those involved in the legal process, they were the most important. Not once did Mr Justice Mantell allow this cardinal precept to be forgotten. He went further. It seemed that, very subtly, he was able to make them feel that he and they were saddled with this burden together and that they would all suffer emotionally as a result of it. Thus, when weeks later he came to give them advice on how to interpret the evidence, they were ready to heed it. They had forged a bond.

Very early in the proceedings, for example, a spokesman for the jury complained that they were constantly distracted from listening to witnesses by the habit of pressmen of getting up and leaving whenever they felt like it. The judge ruled that it was more important that the jury should concentrate than that members of the press should telephone their editors, so he forbade any departure from the court during testimony. Even before that, however, when Mr Leveson had finished his opening address, Richard Ferguson rose to inform the judge that two newspaper editors had been summonsed to appear, in order to reveal what information they had elicited from witnesses, but had not had the grace to reply. The judge did not appear much concerned by this. Throughout, his attitude towards press involvement in the proceedings over which he presided vacillated from irritation to indifference.

The first witness to be called was a frail white-haired old lady, Daisy Gwendolyn Letts, mother of the defendant. Rosemary was the fifth of her seven children. Mrs Letts told the court that she had only met Frederick West once and did not take to him. He had boasted of owning a string of hotels, which she knew could not be true, and she didn't trust him. Her husband had placed Rosemary in care when she was fifteen precisely in order to keep her away from West, but she had run to his caravan as soon as she was legally free to do so. She was not told when her daughter became pregnant, nor when she gave birth, nor when she married. She had not known of Heather's existence until Rosemary brought her home one day, aged about four months. She had had an argument with Fred and walked out. Mrs Letts remembered one part of her conversation with her daughter that day. Rosemary had said, 'You don't know him, Mum. There's nothing he wouldn't do.' She wasn't sure, but she thought her daughter had said Fred was capable of murder, or something like that. He turned up in the afternoon to take her back, and she went very meekly.

The rest of her evidence was devoted to establishing that she had had very little contact with her daughter over the years. She had been to Midland Road three times, and to Cromwell Road probably about seven times. They had not met for the past seven years.

Cross-examining, Mr Ferguson encouraged the witness to recollect Mrs West's childhood and her affection for children. She had gone to live with Fred because of it. 'I thought it was the children who attracted her,' she said. 'She adored small children. She never actually said she loved him.' There was also this brief but telling exchange:

Ferguson:	Was she frightened of him?
Letts:	Oh yes.
Ferguson:	But she went back to him?
Letts:	Yes.

The witness confirmed that Frederick West was especially close to his daughter Anne Marie, and that Rosemary was still a child herself, 'so babyish in her ways'. Nevertheless, she said, the little girls were in a much better state than they had been when she first took them in; she 'kept their hair looking nice'.

Mrs Letts stood down after less than half an hour. She had not once glanced to her left to look at her daughter. Rosemary West, on the other hand, stared at her mother throughout. No mention was made by either Mr Leveson or Mr Ferguson of the letters they had exchanged over the years and the little gifts of money and flowers which Rosemary had been wont to send her mother.

The second witness was the defendant's sister Glenys Tyler, who told the court she had run a small café in Southgate Street at one time, and Fred was a frequent visitor. He had told her that Shirley Robinson was pregnant with his child, a piece of news which appalled her, she said. As Rosemary was not there at the time, and Glenys did not recall her sister ever having visited the café, this was redundant information, for it did not go to whether or not the accused knew that her husband was the father of Shirley's baby. In cross-examination Mr Ferguson again got the witness to confirm that Rosemary had been childish for her age and 'absolutely devoted' to her two younger brothers. As to Heather's disappearance, Mrs Tyler said, 'Heather told my daughter that as soon as she was sixteen she would leave home.' 'So it came as no surprise to you when she did,' said Ferguson.

'Absolutely not.'

The third witness was the most crucial, not as to character but as to opportunity. This was Shirley Ann Giles, on whose recollection of precise dates twenty-four years earlier would depend nothing less than the jury's perception of the defendant either as a young girl who was living with a murderer or as one who had independently become a murderer herself.

But first there was the story of the wooden spoon. Mrs Giles lived above Frederick West and his unorthodox household at 25 Midland Road. Her daughter Tracey was the same age as his step-daughter Charmaine, and they were 'first best friends'. One day before breakfast Mrs Giles sent Tracey downstairs to ask Rosemary if she could borrow some milk. The little girl came upon a scene which troubled her. Charmaine was standing on a chair with her hands tied behind her back and Rosemary held aloft a wooden spoon, as if about to strike her with it. When Tracey went back up to her mother she was in 'a very distressed state', whereupon Mrs Giles remonstrated with Rosemary, who told her that Charmaine had been naughty and had to be taught a lesson.

The story was not inherently improbable. It accorded with Rosemary's plea in a letter to Fred that she did not see why she should have to be the one to handle Charmaine 'rough', with the implication that she was not used to it and did not like it. The question was not so much whether this event occurred, but when.

The Giles family moved away from Gloucester in the course of 1971. There was a tearful parting between the two girls, Charmaine and Tracey, assuaged only by Mrs Giles' promise that she would bring her daughter back to Midland Road for a visit. It was known that Charmaine was due to leave the family for good, since her real mother was coming to fetch her as she had always wanted. Shirley would make sure the two friends could see one another once more to say goodbye properly.

When they turned up, however, Charmaine had already left and Tracey burst into floods of tears. She was comforted by Anne Marie. Rosemary did not offer them a cup of tea. In fact, they proceeded no further than the hallway, but Mrs Giles noticed, on the left, a wooden caravan which Fred had made in prison and which Rosemary had collected on a visit. Mrs Giles much admired it, and wrote to Fred asking if he would make one for her. According to this sequence, then, Charmaine's disappearance had pre-dated the release of Frederick West from prison.

Richard Ferguson, cross-examining, immediately questioned the reliability of this sequence. 'There is no reference to Charmaine in this very friendly letter you wrote to Mr West [quoted in Chapter One],' he said, 'no expression of regret, no question as to where she is, no request for an address where she could be written to. Why is that?'

'I didn't think of it,' the witness replied.

Mr Ferguson allowed a silence to fall before continuing. It was indeed a weak response to a very telling point. If the whole purpose of the visit to Midland Road had been to see Charmaine, and her departure had caused such acute disappointment to Tracey, then it was simply not credible that the letter she wrote immediately afterwards should contain no mention of Charmaine at all. On the other hand, if Charmaine had been present at the time of the visit, there would have been no especial need to mention her. Mr Ferguson allowed the jury to work this out for themselves.

'You have changed your evidence about the date of this visit,' he said, with a gentleness and respect far more provocative than a bark would have been. 'Why is that?'

'Because I wasn't sure.'

'I'm trying to test how accurate your memory is, Mrs Giles. Once Rosemary accidentally got the kitchen on fire and came upstairs to you for help. Do you recall when that was?'

'I can't remember dates, no, it's too long ago.'

'The police sought a second statement from you to change the dates on the first. They told you you got your dates muddled. Confusion arose. You discussed it with your daughter, and your recollection changed as a result of what your daughter said.'

The witness agreed that the police had called on her to change her statement. Mr Ferguson pressed on. 'Charmaine was still alive in June 1971, but you were told she had gone in March. You were getting muddled again. Could your visit have taken place in September?'

'No.'

'Rosemary lent you Heather's baby clothes for the baby you were then expecting, Claire, and asked you to return them when she was expecting Mae. Right?'

'I don't remember.'

'It was after the birth of Claire that you visited Midland Road.'

'I don't think so.'

Ferguson did not need to continue. The witness had prevaricated sufficiently for it to be questionable whether reliance upon her memory on such an important issue would be safe. She had also agreed that she had not seen the wooden spoon incident herself, and told Mr Leveson that she had never seen Rosemary hit the children.

There was no need to repeat the evidence as to the same events given by Tracey herself, now Mrs Hammond, looking so frightened that she asked to be allowed to sit. On the wooden spoon incident she told Mr Leveson, 'I still find it quite disturbing,' and she remembered Rosemary's reply when, on the return visit, she asked what had happened to Charmaine – 'Gone to her mother and bloody good riddance.' Mr Ferguson established two points in cross-examination: first, that by the time Tracey Hammond made her statement to the police on 1 July 1994 she already knew that Charmaine's remains had been found (and her recollection was not, therefore, as free from emotional influence as it would have been had she not known she was dead); and second, that there was a baby in a pram on the visit to Midland Road, which would place it after Claire was born in August.

The day closed with further argument about newspaper interference, in the absence of the jury. Both the *Sun* and the *Mirror* had questioned witnesses before the trial, and Mr Ferguson wanted the judge to order both editors to surrender to the court documents relating to what these witnesses had said. A young lawyer representing the *Sun* stutteringly denied that he knew of any documents. It was probable neither newspaper intended to comply with a court order. It might be less embarrassing, therefore, not to make one, but nobody dared say as much.

Proceedings on Tuesday, 10 October, opened with a reading to the court of three letters between Fred and Rosemary during his 1971 custodial sentence served at Leyhill Open Prison, and followed with the establishment of the dates of that custody, given by prison officer David Whitcomb. The index card of Frederick West 401317 confirmed that he had arrived on 21 January 1971, and been discharged on 24 June of the same year. That was his earliest possible release date, which would have been delayed had there been cause for any disciplinary action. There was no evidence of absconding, though Mr Whitcomb agreed that it was not difficult to abscond. Richard Ferguson wanted him to go further and admit that absconding was a frequent occurrence. Prisoners were at liberty within the open prison between 5.00 p.m. and 9.00 p.m., and there was nothing to stop people leaving, he said. 'Prisoners sometimes went out all night leaving their clothes under the bedsheets?' Mr Whitcomb admitted that 'it has been known'.

It was perhaps a mistake in strategy for the defence to pursue the possibility of West's having walked out of the prison on an unspecified date before his official release, for there was no actual evidence that he had, and the proposition implied an acceptance of the prosecution's case that Charmaine had died before 24 June. Since the burden of the defence case on this count was that she had died after 24 June, this new line of questioning seemed to let in unnecessary doubt on the matter; if the defence was sure, it would have ignored Whitcomb's evidence and asked no questions of him.

It was the next witness who was to provide the first of many dramatic moments in this unsettling trial. Mrs Elizabeth Agius had lived in Midland Road in 1971. She was now coming from her home abroad to testify in court as to what she knew of her neighbours then. She had clearly been crying before she entered the witness-box, was extremely nervous and agitated, breathing heavily, sighing, sniffing, as if every eye upon her was a shaft of accusation and every word addressed to her a body-blow. Wearing a brown, gypsy-like shawl and large dangling ear-rings, her mass of curly brown hair, long sharp nose and thin lips gave her the air of the archetypal fortune-teller.

Answering Brian Leveson, Mrs Agius recalled how she had met Frederick West one day when he offered to help her as she struggled up the steps with her pram. He introduced himself as the man who lived next door. Her husband was abroad at the time. She accepted an invitation to go to West's flat for a cup of tea. There she met Rosemary, who she thought at first was his daughter because she looked about fourteen years old. They got to know one another very well, and Mrs Agius used to go into their flat about twice a week. Twice she baby-sat for them when they were out in the evening. But it was a particular and very curious conversation she had with them which brought her to give evidence today.

'Fred said they had been riding around looking for young girls,' she told Mr Leveson. 'He said having a woman in the car made it easier to pick up a girl, and he preferred young runaways because they had nowhere to go. Rose was in the room. I couldn't believe it. He sometimes went as far as London, but said the best place for pick-ups was Bristol way . . . Fred brought up the subject of sex when Rose was not there, but later she admitted that he wanted to have sexual intercourse with me. It's the truth, she said. She would have liked me to go to bed with him. They wanted three in a bed as well . . . he told me Rose was a prostitute and that he liked to watch or listen to everything she did. If he wasn't there, she would tell him exactly what had happened . . . he said if he got me into bed he would tie me up and I could do the same to him, but nothing happened. It was all just talk.'

In 1972, said Mrs Agius, she had visited the Wests at Cromwell Street, and been shown a trap-door leading to a cellar which Fred said he wanted to turn into a playroom for the kids or make his torture chamber. She told him he was dreaming, she said. Finally, in a perfect echo of the Crown's 'in it together' theme, she said this: 'They were such a close couple, really close. They were the type of people who didn't hide anything from one another.'

Even before Richard Ferguson stood up to challenge Mrs Agius, she was fierce, cornered. Her limbs stiffened and her first reply was shouted in defiance. With his destabilizing tranquil tone, Ferguson pointed out that the trap-door she claimed to have seen at Cromwell Street was not there until 1975. 'It *was*. That's the *truth*,' she said. He implied she had made it up. Why? Because she had been to the press before going to the police. 'I tried to phone the police,' she protested. 'My mum said phone the *Sun*.' She said she had tried the police three times, but they were always engaged. (This is not entirely implausible, as the Gloucestershire constabulary were much frustrated in their efforts by ceaseless telephone calls from the world's press.) The *Sun* then sent a man to visit her. By this time, she had seen about the West enquiry in the newspapers. Mr Ferguson put it to her that she had tailored her memory and testimony according to the allegations she had read, but she said she hadn't paid attention to what was in the newspapers.

'You weren't curious?' he asked, incredulously. 'You wouldn't have believed it,' she responded, 'they were such a nice couple.'

This was not quite the impression which her direct evidence to Mr Leveson had produced, so Mr Ferguson brought her back to the compromising conversation about picking up girls, which she had not, until now, repeated to anyone. Why? 'I was shocked,' she said. 'Did you continue to be friendly with the Wests even after this "shocking" conversation? Did it not affect your friendship?'

'No, because I didn't believe it.'

'You thought it was a joke?'

'Yes.'

'Was it said in a joking fashion?'

'In a certain way, yes. I didn't take it seriously. They did no harm to me. They were such a nice couple.'

'And you were friends with them right up to the very end.'

Counsel went on to undermine the witness's credibility with a surprise question. 'Did you ever have sex with Fred?' he asked.

'I don't know.'

'What do you mean?'

'No, never.'

'You're not telling the truth.'

'I've never done *anything* what you're suggesting,' Mrs Agius shouted.

Ferguson reminded her that she had told a police officer, in what she took to be a confidential conversation not to be alluded to in court, that she had been three in a bed with both the Wests. This drew from the witness an explosion of fury. 'I have never *ever* been three in a bed with the Wests,' she screamed, emphasizing her denials with a shrillness of voice and telling counsel rather more than she had been asked, as if scared and tapping into a rehearsed script for self-protection. Ferguson was persistent and calm, telling her that he knew she had promised she would deny having sex with Frederick West if challenged in court. 'You're frightened that if you admit to having had sex with Fred it will destroy your marriage. I suggest to you that you did have intercourse with Frederick West at a time when Rosemary West was expecting her daughter Mae, who was born in hospital when you were at Midland Road.' The witness first avoided the question, put as a statement, by offering irrelevant information designed to enable her to wriggle free, then finally admitted that she remembered Rose had had a baby. Counsel reminded her that Rose had hammered on her bedroom door when she came out of hospital to find the two of them inside. The witness was reduced to snivelling.

Mrs Agius left the witness-box a shattered and trembling woman, yet it was difficult to feel sorry for her. Ferguson had succeeded in establishing that she could lie on oath to serve her own purposes. That she had also confirmed Frederick West's reputation as a storyteller whom nobody took seriously was a bonus. 'He was always laughing about everything, whatever he was talking about.'

Defence wanted to call the policeman to whom Mrs Agius had declared her intention to perjure herself. The prosecution was not keen. 'The Crown put forward this witness as worthy of belief,' intoned Mr Justice Mantell. 'If they now wish to suggest she was telling lies, because another Crown witness conflicts, it's up to them to resolve it.'

While the ordeal of giving evidence is palpably a misery for anyone, it was the next witness who earned the court's sympathy much more than Elizabeth Agius and who was much more difficult for the defence to dislodge. That witness was Caroline Owens.

She walked in like a timid but beautiful bird which had just adjusted its plumage. Her dark hair was swept back and secured with a bow behind the nape of her neck, leaving just enough to fall as a tentative fragile fringe across her forehead. She wore a dark suit with spotless white blouse beneath, gold bangs on her ears, and comported herself with an air of efficient resignation. In answering to her name she spoke clearly, with an impressive unfaltering voice, and her face broke into a dazzling smile; it was not a smile of cocky self-assurance, but one which promised that she would do her best. That smile happened only once.

Born in 1955, Mrs Owens was now forty and formidably attractive. The reader is already familiar with the details of her story, to which reference has been made several times, so that full repetition here would be wearisome. It was the details of her vivid recollection which swept aside the intervening years. When she recalled how Mrs West had admired her hair ('you've got lovely hair'), she ran her own fingers through it in the witness-box, enabling us to see a gesture of the accused snatched from the distant past. The words Frederick West had used when she was being abducted in the van – 'What's her tits like?' – were so precisely in character that their veracity could admit no doubt. On that journey towards Cromwell Street she remembered she could just make out, from her recumbent position, the passing yellow street lamps.

It took nearly an hour for Mrs Owens, gently prompted by counsel for the prosecution, to fill a chastened court with the narrative of the events of that night in 1972. We felt like intruders on her intimacy, just as her assailants had been. One sentence stood out amidst the list of indignities: 'I was scared they might operate or something,' she said. The vision of a gynaecological examination, the Wests nattering to one another as they performed it, was repellent to the imagination.

By contrast, she pointed out that Fred used to 'pick on Rose a bit. I tried to stick up for her. He told me to mind my own business.' The incongruity was striking.

Before leaving his witness to the deceptively generous Mr Ferguson, Mr Leveson made her admit dealings with the press. She had telephoned the police immediately news broke of the arrest on 24 February 1994, and her first statement was dated 26 February. A further two statements were given on 22 April and 1 July, but in advance of these, ten days after the first interview, she began her negotiations with newspapers, using a local reporter to pose as a friend in order to advise her on how to obtain the best price. She was due to receive £20,000. This confession was no doubt strategic, in view of what was to come, but it somewhat diluted Mrs Owens' value as a victim.

Ferguson ignored this for the time being. Going straight to the 1972 assault itself, he wondered why she had sustained no injuries. Within an hour of her escape from 25 Cromwell Street she was with her friend Doreen Bradley, when her injuries would be 'at their most visible', yet there was nothing to show. No obvious black eye, no bruises. Part of her evidence told how Frederick West had whipped her genitals with the buckle end of a two-inch-wide leather belt. How many times had he hit her, asked Mr Ferguson. About six. 'On your exposed body, in an overhand manner, coming down with strength?' he continued, lifting his arm above his head and bringing it down with a whoosh.

'Did it draw blood?'

'No.'

'Six blows delivered, and no blood?'

'Just bruises.'

'Bringing it down from behind his back, and no blood?'

'There were weals.'

'Did you show them to Doreen?'

'No.'

'To the doctors who examined you?'

'Yes, they would have seen it.'

'And did they make any comment?'

'No.'

'Was the area raw?'

'It hurt.'

'Not bleeding?'

'No.'

'Not at all?'

Counsel employed the same line of questioning about the punch which the witness alleged West had given her in the van, knocking her out. 'Was it with a clenched fist? Did it leave any marks? A cut on your face? Why doesn't it show on the photographs? Is there any mark that you can show us? Any bruises? Any way you can help us? Were there injuries to your mouth?' In the wake of negative replies to all this, he said, 'Is that because there was nothing to be seen?'

This relentless questioning quickly established a disquieting gap between the viciousness of the assault as described by Mrs Owens and the lack of any apparent physical effect as a result of it. She had been prescribed no medication of any sort, not even an aspirin; there had been no stitches required, no pads and no bandages. Exaggeration was clearly implied. So, too, was complicity. Mr Ferguson planted the suggestion that the witness had not been the innocent, inexperienced young girl she portrayed, and invited us, by implication, to imagine that she may have been a willing party to sexual adventure about which she subsequently complained. He did this with sardonic precision. When she was forced into the house, bound and gagged, the lodgers Alan and Ben were there.

'Prior to this you had had sex with both of them?' he asked.

'Yes.'

'Were they friends of yours?'

'Not close.'

'Close enough for you to have sex with them.'

'That was a mistake.'

'*Two* mistakes, Mrs Owens.'

Ferguson also established that she had had sex with another boyfriend when she had been living at 25

301

Cromwell Street, who had stayed overnight, and that on the day following her ordeal she had made no complaint to Ben Stanniland, who had found her using a vacuum cleaner with apparent nonchalance. 'Were you able to use the Hoover despite the physical trauma inflicted upon you?' he asked. 'In pain, but able to manage?' He also got the witness to admit that Mrs West had made no attempt to restrain her when she did eventually leave the house later that day.

He then turned to Caroline Owens' dealings with the *Sun*, which she might have hoped he had forgotten, and in particular with her sly withholding of one page of detail as a bargaining counter. The judge intervened rather harshly. 'Does this have relevance, Mr Ferguson?' he said. 'If it doesn't, I shall stop it.' Counsel replied that it showed how the witness had exaggerated for commercial gain. 'Your attack upon the character and use of this material will not be justified unless there is a gap between the witness's account and your account of what occurred,' said Mantell, who repeatedly during the trial gave the impression that evidence of press involvement was beside the point as far as he was concerned. Ferguson persisted, despite discouragement, in regarding it as central to the way the case had been brought. He told the witness in blunt terms that, though it was accepted that sexual advances were made, she had added details to make her story more dramatic and more commercial. 'You were not beaten, you were not knocked out.'

When he had finished, the judge leant forward again. 'I did not hear you challenge the evidence that she was taped, Mr Ferguson.'

Defence counsel had one more point to put to this witness. Quoting from her own diary, he was able to show that she had accepted lifts from strangers no less than eight times in the weeks and months following the ordeal which was alleged to have scarred her; one entry, in March 1973, proved she had got into a car in which there were 'two fellows'.

Mr Leveson was permitted by rules of evidence to resume questioning his own witness. He took the opportunity to lay emphasis on the fact that it was Mrs West who had been the first to lay hands upon her and that she had done so without coercion from her husband. Caroline Owens concurred. 'She seemed evil to me,' she said. Counsel also made it clear that when the witness had made her first statement to the police, no bodies had been found and she was therefore in no position to realize that her story would have any commercial value. He invited Mr Ferguson to admit that there was no discrepancy between her statement to the police and her account sold to the *Sun*. This he willingly did, which finally laid to rest any chance that the editor of the *Sun* would be hauled into court, at least in regard to tampering with this particular witness. 'The discrepancy', said Mr Ferguson, 'is between her 1972 account and both her 1994 accounts.'

Finally, Mr Leveson asked a question which unexpectedly brought a note of intensity and utter sadness into the court. If you did not come here for commercial advantage, he asked Mrs Owens, why did you come to court? Immediately her lower lip trembled, she fought stoically for a second or two to resist it, then an avalanche of sorrow erupted from deep inside her to capsize her features and shatter the self-control she had held on to for so long. Stammering through tears and mucus and impotent pity she cried, 'I want to get justice for those girls who didn't make it, because I feel it was my fault.' She was led from the court, her shoulders shaking with sobs, and at that moment those of us who had doubted her felt ashamed. We caught a tiny glimpse of what private thoughts she had had to endure, to what unendurable reflections she had been condemned.

The remaining witnesses of that week were heard out of order, probably for reasons of availability. Mrs Gough, the mother of Lynda Gough, appeared while the memory of Caroline Owens' breakdown a few moments before was still fresh. She was warm and decent, with straight silver hair and dressed in a smart olive-green suit. She declined the offer to sit, and spoke with open honesty and charm about the daughter she had lost. Again, the reader is familiar with the events surrounding Lynda's disappearance, which it would be oppressive to repeat. 'The last day I saw her was 19 April 1973,' said Mrs Gough. 'It is not a date I am ever likely to forget.' Rosemary West stared at her intently throughout her testimony, paying careful attention to everything she said, but giving nothing away. She talked about the visit to Cromwell Street and the lady who was wearing Lynda's slippers. She talked about Lynda's washing on the line. She said that she and her husband had gone to Weston-super-Mare in search of her but were told by the unemployment office there that information was confidential and even if Lynda had registered they would not say so.

Police officers were evidently worried that Richard Ferguson would question Mrs Gough closely upon the style, colour, quality and value of the slippers to which so much importance had been given by events, as well as on the clothes-line in the garden, which could not be seen from the front door. But he didn't. Perhaps he felt it would have been too cruel and that these points could be made later without having to force this plain, good woman to doubt herself. He put only one question to her, whether she had ever returned to 25 Cromwell Street since that day. 'I went past the house five years later and saw the cellar doors had been bricked up,' she said. 'I shuddered. I don't know why, but I shuddered. I never went past that house again.'

We already knew that there had never been cellar doors visible at the front of the house, and that nothing there had been bricked up.

On Thursday, 12 October, Ben Stanniland, now forty-one and grizzled but discernibly a good-looking spiv in the past, gave evidence in a deep, croaky voice. He had been a lodger of the Wests for nearly fourteen months, throughout their first year in residence and covering the period of Caroline Owens. He moved out in March 1973, just before the disappearance of Lynda, whom he had also known. In fact, it was due to him that Lynda first went to the house, for she was then his girlfriend, though she later became 'friendly' with others who lived there. Mr Stanniland told how on the first night that he and Alan Davis moved in to occupy a room on the top floor, Mrs West came upstairs and got into bed with both of them. They were 'dubious' about going down to face Mr West in the morning, but he made it quite clear he wasn't bothered. What they did not know was that he had put her up to it in the first place and would not have accepted a refusal. He confirmed that he and other lodgers regularly brought girls back to the house, and that Mr West was constantly engaged in building work of one kind or another. Most pertinently, he remembered Caroline being there with the Hoover, and meeting her at the launderette later the same day, when he neither noticed anything odd about her appearance nor heard her allude to anything unpleasant that had occurred.

Much the same kind of picture was painted by David Evans, a lodger in the top front room, now forty-five but looking much older, with a beard, jeans and grey hair. He had been arrested seven or eight times down the years for possession of cannabis. All the men living there had had sex with Lynda Gough and with the landlady 'because she liked it'. Mr Evans gave two conflicting accounts as to why Lynda ceased to visit. One was that she had had a row with Alan Davis, the other that Mrs West had told her not to come back. For the rest, his evidence was a repeat of Ben Stanniland's, which prompted the judge to suggest it might be curtailed. Leaning across to his right in cosy, confiding manner he said, 'There's no point, members of the jury, in witnesses saying the same thing over and over again if they're not challenged.'

Another lodger, Charles Jones, aged forty and looking sixty, confirmed that up to six or eight young men could be living at No 25 at once, each of them bringing girls to visit, and Terence Davis, blond, rugged, in a blue suit and with an insecurely knotted tie, told the court how much he had liked Frederick West and how he spent half a day helping him clear out the damp and muddy cellar. This witness was cross-examined, because he had seen a girl coming to the house late one night and spotted her again the following morning in the doorway of the land-lord's bedroom. This was, he said, 'nothing unusual', and the girl might have been Caroline Owens. She was not bound or gagged.

Later that week, Mr Justice Mantell was twice required to intervene at the request of counsel and in the absence of the jury. Mr Ferguson objected to evidence which the Crown intended to introduce to show that Lucy Partington had been received into the Roman Catholic Church, on the grounds that it was irrelevant. The judge agreed that being religiously inclined did not preclude the possibility of accepting a lift from a stranger, which was the point the prosecution wished to make, but said she was nevertheless abducted by some-one, so it was slightly relevant. 'I'm satisfied', he said, 'that it involves no prejudice to the defendant.' Then Mr Leveson drew his attention to the fact that a motorbike, presumably belonging to the press, had followed the police van taking witnesses away from the court, which he considered to be 'very serious indeed', for it 'amounted to harassment'. Once more, the judge was surprisingly unconcerned. 'I make no comment, Mr Leveson,' he said.

The next important witness was Elizabeth Brewer, a 'survivor' who not only lived at 25 Cromwell Street for four years without incident, but looked back upon the period as among the happiest of her life. She had taken a room in April 1977, by which time there were already six girls buried beneath the property. There were three other female lodgers at the time – Shirley Robinson, Gloria and Clare – and four children aged between four and fourteen, all sleeping in the cellar. They were moved upstairs during Mrs Brewer's tenancy, when the ground-floor extension had been completed. Liz described the Wests as 'friendly and generous', although their constant theme of sex as a subject of conversation embarrassed her. She remembered two specific remarks. Mrs West had told her that 'when she retired she would spend her whole time having sex', and on another occasion she said that 'no matter what Fred did she would never leave him'.

The remainder of her evidence-in-chief concerned the disappearance of Shirley Robinson and has been dealt with in Chapter Six. She concluded with the admission that she was due to receive £10,000 from a newspaper.

In cross-examination Mr Ferguson concentrated on domestic matters, eliciting the information that Rosemary West was always sympathetic towards her, despite the fact that she was either carrying a baby or having a baby more or less without interruption. There was an additional piece of evidence relating to Anne Marie which received little attention from the press. Mrs Brewer recalled that the teenager was frequently with boyfriends considerably older than herself, who came and went. Two of them, she said, more or less lived with her. They created problems and Fred had to throw them out. This information was not, of course, relevant to the matter on trial, but it did serve to confirm the steaming nature of this unorthodox household.

Further, Liz Brewer was experiencing a difficult time with her husband Peter, who was violent towards her yet whom she continued to love. Again irrelevant, but introduced by counsel for the defence by way of comparison. It was easier for Mrs Brewer to understand why Rosemary West should declare that she would never leave Fred, despite his treatment of her, because she, Liz, had been through the same emotions. This helped to contradict the prosecution's case that the bond between the Wests was solid and of equal weight on both sides, which they needed to establish to support the 'joint enterprise' theory.

A sequence of very rapid witnesses terminated the second week of the trial with varying degrees of clarity. The sister of a former lodger recalled the weird comment that Frederick West had made when introducing Rosemary and Shirley to her. 'This is my wife and this is my lover,' he had said. In normal banter it would have passed unnoticed, but the comment assumed its 'weirdness' in the light of a trial for murder. Mr Ferguson did not bother to cross-examine. Another lodger, Gillian Britt, pointed out how easy it was to become a resident at No 25. She was friendly with a girl who lived there. 'If anything comes up, give me a shout,' she had said. Something did come up, and she moved in in one day. There was no fuss about furniture. She remembered 'Rose's Room' on the ground floor and told the court that she saw men going in to that room, sometimes two or three at a time, after midnight. This time Mr Ferguson did object. 'Enough of this,' he said. 'It is accepted that Mrs West slept with other men, but it is highly irrelevant and panders to the worst possible element of salaciousness.' The judge did not agree, so Mr Leveson continued. He asked the witness what she thought about it all.

'I thought it was amusing to hear shrieks coming from this room,' she said. 'But sometimes it got beyond a joke and I had to turn up the radio to drown them out. The noises didn't seem to me to indicate any kind of pleasure.'

'Thank you,' said Mr Leveson, and sat down.

'You treated the noises as a joke?' asked Mr Ferguson.

'Yes, but I thought, I don't like living with this.'

'You did continue to live with it nevertheless.'

The court then rose for the weekend.

11

Trial (cont.)

Monday, 16 October introduced the most distressing
week of the trial. It began with the witness known only
as Miss A, and ended in the midst of evidence from
Frederick West's daughter Anne Marie. During this week
I saw lady journalists in tears, male reporters terrified of
turning a page lest it make a noise, jury members hiding
their eyes to blot out images created for them by the
words they heard, and Joshua Rozenberg, the BBC's
experienced legal correspondent, explaining to colleagues
and viewers why it was impossible to report the testimony accurately. A. N. Wilson wrote in the *Evening
Standard* that he wished he had not heard this evidence,
for it was not given to any of us to un-hear it afterwards.
There was contagion in the air.

Miss A wore a black-and-white-striped dress which
accentuated the pallor of her face, framed by short black
hair. She was extremely nervous, biting her lip and
swallowing hard throughout. Sometimes her answers
were reduced to a barely audible mumble, and what she
had to relate was of such ineradicable sadness that one
wished she could have been spared this ordeal of revelation and abasement.

She told how she had been placed in care at the age of
thirteen and ended up a resident at Jordan's Brook home
for girls in Gloucester. She hated being in an institution,
for it made her feel unwanted and embarrassed. Shortly
after her fourteenth birthday she was introduced to 25
Cromwell Street, where she met Rosemary West. 'She
was like a big sister-cum-young mum,' she said. 'She told
me I could go there any time, there would always be a
shoulder to cry on. I felt that there was somebody who

really cared at last.' She went to the house about nine times, usually on Friday on her way to spend the weekend with her mother. Oddly, she said she was never introduced to the children, which was surprising; on a Friday evening they would have been present. Several times she absconded from Jordan's Brook and lived on the streets. On one of these occasions she and another girl called Yvonne went to Cromwell Street and asked if they could stay the night. They were made very welcome, given hot drinks, and slept on the sofa. Nothing untoward happened.

It was on a subsequent visit that there occurred the terrible experience that we have had cause to refer to in previous chapters. It began with fondling by Mrs West and developed into an agony of intimacy. She was taken, she said, into a room where there were already three other people. One was Mr West. The others were two adolescent and unidentified girls. 'Rose started undressing me. I didn't know what to do. Everything seemed it was supposed to be normal, like we were all girls together. She was caressing this girl on her forehead and down over her body.' The witness's quiet, timid, frightened voice trailed away, yet contrived to fill every corner of the court. She cleared her throat frequently, and was close to tears as she resurrected harsh memories. Mrs West produced some packing tape, she said, which Mr West applied to one of the girls, wrapping it around her wrists 'as though bandaged'. There then took place some group sexual activity. 'The other girl didn't resist,' said Miss A. 'It was as though this was all normal to her.' Unhappily, it probably was.

Of the defendant, she said that she was one minute aggressive, and another all motherly again. She made encouraging remarks to her husband, such as, 'Is it turning you on, Fred? Are you enjoying it?' After this, said the witness, it was her turn, and she described to the court in graphic detail a series of acts performed upon her body. Several times she broke down in the telling of it. What was her attitude towards the defendant following this incident? 'I had felt that she really cared. I trusted someone and she used me.' Did she tell her mother or anyone else about it? No, 'because I felt so ashamed.' Besides which, she presumed she would be called a liar. 'Because you were in care you were regarded as bad.' She had not much left. She didn't want to see everything else taken from her. About six weeks later, she said, she went back to Cromwell Street with petrol and matches, intending to set the house on fire. And did she? Her voice strangled with regret, Miss A said, 'No, I didn't. I wanted to do it so much.' We were left with a feeling of overwhelming pathos, that this very lonely and vulnerable girl should fall into the clutches of predatory monsters.

The first person to whom Miss A told of her experience was Detective Constable Williams on 28 July 1994, five months after the arrest of Frederick West. The police had approached her, not she the police. At the committal in February 1995, her identity was inadvertently revealed by counsel in the course of a remark to the magistrate and immediately retracted. But it was too late. A newspaper contacted her and she had a friend negotiate on her behalf. She entered into a contract in March. She was due to receive £30,000.

'£30,000, Miss A?' asked Richard Ferguson as soon as he stood up. Showing none of the discretion which had kept Mrs Gough safe from scrutiny, counsel for the defence proceeded to demolish this damaging witness with a heavy heart. He clearly felt sorry for her, but her story, entirely uncorroborated, could not be allowed to stand as it was. Some of the sympathy she had aroused needed to be dispelled if it was grounded in falsity.

Having first exposed her deceit in giving spurious reasons for wishing to make deals with the press, Ferguson turned to her mendacity and her confusion. In her first statement to the police she said that she had never visited Cromwell Street. Now she says she had, up to nine times, but she could not describe anything in the house. There was worse.

'I apologize,' said Mr Ferguson, 'but I must ask some things. Were you abused as a child by your father?'

'Yes, not long before I went to Cromwell Street.'

'Your father had sex with you?'

'Yes.'

'And your brother?'

'Not full intercourse, no.'

'You've had a very unhappy medical background?'

'In what sense?'

'I'll try to help as best I can.'

The witness had been sobbing throughout this painful interrogation, and when Ferguson revealed that she had attended a clinic to be treated for gonorrhoea at the age of fourteen, and was about to launch upon her psychiatric history, Mr Justice Mantell intervened to put a stop to the ordeal. What was the relevance, he asked, and how far do you intend to go?

'It is relevant to her knowledge and ability to fantasize, my lord,' replied Mr Ferguson. 'She has had the experience, unfortunately, on which to draw for this account.' He intended to go as far as was necessary to show that she invented stories, mixing up personal history with imagination, and even that she was motivated by understandable rancour and malice. He was given leave to continue.

Counsel passed immediately on to the love affair between Miss A, aged fourteen, and Graham Letts, brother of Rosemary West. 'You were infatuated with him, weren't you?' he asked.

'Yes, I had a crush on him.'

'And you ran away with him.'

'Yes, I did.'

'You stayed with him in a flat above a tea-shop in Cheltenham, and you were having sex with him regularly.'

'Only a couple of times.'

Mr Ferguson then gave the witness her statement of 13 March in which she agreed she had been sleeping with Mr Letts on a regular basis. The statement included the lines, 'There are events from my life which I find difficult to talk about . . . why I distrusted adults when I was a child . . . I thought that no-one would believe me no matter what I said or what happened to me.' It went on to mention another man called Tom, aged about fifty, also living above the tea-shop in Cheltenham, who 'sort of looked after us both. I let him have sex with me three or four times. He threatened to call the police and tell them I was under age if I didn't.' As counsel read this out, our pity for the witness was in no way diminished by the gradual realization that she was not entirely reliable, especially when she said she had told Mrs West about her love affair with Graham, but Mrs West had not revealed to her that she was his sister.

Relentlessly, Mr Ferguson built up the portrait of a forlorn, abject, misused and manipulative young girl. She made up stories about boyfriends. She had several phantom pregnancies, three within one year. She attended maternity hospital continually for a period of four years with imaginary gynaecological complaints. She sent a photograph of a baby to Graham Letts falsely claiming it was his. Throughout the time she said she regarded Frederick and Rosemary West as friends, she was writing angry letters to Graham chastizing him for going with somebody else. At the age of sixteen she entered into a horrifyingly violent marriage which ended with her spending some time in a home for battered wives after her husband had tried to smother her with a pillow. She had tried to commit suicide and had sought psychiatric help, spending time in the psychiatric wing of a hospital. Without spelling it out, Mr Ferguson was able to suggest, to some of us at least, that Miss A was one of those severely damaged people who had been so deprived of love that they would do anything for some attention, however bizarre and however harmful that attention might be. Violence was better than indifference, jealousy preferable to emptiness, the pretended love of a doctor or a nurse infinitely more comforting than the featureless hostility of strangers. She was condemned to make herself lovable with lies.

Most alarming of all were the records of her history and background as revealed to the psychiatrist whose care she most desperately needed. She told him of the sexual abuse she had suffered at the hands of her father and brother, of her loneliness and despair, her disastrous affair with Graham Letts and her promiscuity, and of her violent marriage. But she had not once mentioned the ghastly ordeal which she now claimed she had endured at the Wests' home. Why? Because 'I didn't know how to talk about it,' she said. According to Richard Ferguson, it was because it had never happened. 'I suggest that when you were told what had been found at 25 Cromwell Street you fantasized that you were yourself involved . . . it was a complete figment of your imagination . . . you made up the story of masking tape after reading about it.' In other words, her invented testimony was yet another bid for charity.

Counsel finished with the damning revelation that Miss A had suffered from hallucinations. She imagined seeing people with other people's heads on their shoulders, and was haunted in particular by a man in black who followed her around. He did not exist. He was the construction of a fevered mind, the imagined tormentor who blessed her with his undeflected attention. She had undergone six sessions of electroconvulsive therapy. On occasions she walked out of her home and was found wandering in a state of blankness somewhere distant; only a year ago she had idly caught the first train from Basingstoke, which happened to go to Southampton, and been assaulted there at two in the morning.

Ferguson's final remark was addressed directly to the judge, thus subtly implying that this witness ought not to have been called. 'Mrs West has no recollection of ever

314

having met this woman,' he said. 'She never went to Cromwell Street at all, ever.'

Mr Leveson rose to point out that the witness did not discover that Graham Letts was related to Mrs West until after she had made her statement to the police, and also to elicit from her that the man in black she imagined was following her bore the face of Frederick West.

The final word belonged to this tortured woman herself, and it reverberated with emphatic defiance. 'I know what happened,' she said, without raising her voice. 'It wasn't a fantasy, and they know it wasn't.' Her accumulated tension burst out in tears. She had been in the witness-box the whole day.

An unusual witness opened proceedings on Tuesday, 17 October. Mrs Ruth Owen appeared in court at the request of the defence, with the result that although the Crown was still presenting its case, Mr Leveson had no questions to put to her. As the judge helpfully explained to the jury, she was 'a witness tendered for purposes of cross-examination'. It soon became apparent why. Mrs Owen had attended the same grammar school as Lucy Partington between 1967 and 1970 and had been friendly with her. It was her habit to walk with Lucy to the bus-stop on Evesham Road in Cheltenham, because she lived just round the corner from it. She told Mr Ferguson that she vividly recalled an odd incident one evening as she was walking between her home and the bus-stop. A car pulled up by her and the driver offered her a lift. She declined the offer because she was almost home anyway, but his manner was very friendly and persuasive and she felt she was being put under pressure to get into the car. She was anxious to move on and the possibility that the man might not take no for an answer frightened her. Eventually he gave up and drove away up the hill. She told her parents what had happened and never forgot the fear of that night. She said the driver was about ten or fifteen years older than she, with white skin and thick, dark hair, and though the evidence she put before the court could not be conclusive, it seemed very likely that she had been on the point of being abducted by somebody who could well have been Frederick West. Most pointedly, he was alone in the car.

Jane Hamer, who had been a lodger at 25 Cromwell Street in 1976 and early 1977, was called to give evidence on one point. She remembered that on two occasions she had heard a female child screaming in the cellar and specifically using the words, 'Stop it, Daddy.' It could have been Heather or Mae, she didn't know, but she told Mr Leveson that she found it 'unusual'. She also said that Mrs West hardly ever left the house, and seemed to be the dominant member of the family. Mr Ferguson ignored this last point when he rose to cross-examine, and asked one simple question of the witness: 'Did you report the screaming which you heard to anyone?' 'No,' she replied. Counsel stood at his place in silence for a full six seconds after this, as if pondering whether to continue, but in fact enabling the court to ponder the impact of the answer. Then, abruptly, he sat down without a word, leaving Mr Leveson to thank the bewildered witness and dismiss her. It was a clever device to belittle.

Erwin Marshall gave similar evidence, but was handled differently. He had been a boyfriend of Anne Marie's and had stayed one night in the house with her in 1980. (In his summing-up, the judge would refer to him as her 'lover', then apologize to the jury for using such an old-fashioned word.) Anne Marie was no longer living with her parents by this time, so it is not clear why they should have spent the night at Cromwell Street. Mr Marshall, too, heard a scream. At first, he said, 'I couldn't make out what it was', but it went on for ten or twenty minutes, interrupted by the words, 'no, no, please.' Mrs West later told him that it was Heather he had heard, and she was having a nightmare. (She was then ten years old.) Many years later Mr Marshall worked as a window-cleaner and his job took him one

316

day to the house next door to No 25. He struck up a conversation with Mrs West, during which she told him that Heather had run away from home and that there was not much she could do about it. Cleaning windows at the back, he glanced down and saw Frederick West laying the foundations for the patio.

Counsel for the defence concentrated on the scream. Reminding the witness that in his statement he had said it had lasted five to ten minutes, and that now it had expanded to between ten and twenty minutes, he asked, 'Are you just guessing, Mr Marshall?' The witness prevaricated. 'You didn't time it, did you?' persisted Mr Ferguson. 'You are guessing, aren't you?' The witness finally agreed that he was, and it was left to Mr Leveson to re-assert his value to the Crown. The point, he said, was that the total amount of time that elapsed was up to twenty minutes, during which time two separate screams had been heard.

Ronald Harrison, a life-long friend of Frederick West's and with a daughter the same age as Heather, was called next. He said that West had told him that Heather had run away after Rose had given her a good hiding, but kept in touch by telephone. West had also made the curious remark that Heather had 'put scratches on the faces' of the younger children. As before whenever Heather's name was mentioned, the defendant looked particularly unhappy at this testimony, kept her head bowed and sipped from a glass of water. Mr Ferguson strove to make two points, and succeeded with one of them. In the twenty-five years that the witness had known Frederick West, he agreed that he had had nothing to do with Mrs West, and had rarely even spoken to her. On the other hand, he had had countless conversations with Mr West over the years, and a vivid gesture of the hand to indicate that West was boringly loquacious brought a smile to many faces in court. Ferguson wanted the witness to agree that, from so many conversations, it was not possible for him to be sure that Mrs West was

317

present when one in particular took place, but Mr Harrison was adamant that she had been.

There followed a number of neighbours and acquaintances in quick succession throughout the day. Mrs Dix, who lived across the road at No 29 Cromwell Street, used to walk her grandchildren to school with Rosemary West, who took her daughter Heather. 'Fred thought the world of Rose, I know that,' she said with a distinctive Welsh lilt to her voice, 'I think she felt the same.' She was 'quite surprised' that Rose took Heather's departure so lightly. 'If it had been one of mine I'd have been worried sick.' She also told counsel how helpful both the Wests had been when she found her husband dead on the bathroom floor. Linda Tonks recalled that Mrs West 'always had the little ones with her when she went shopping', and got upset if Stephen West came in with muddy shoes. Mr West told her that his daughter Anne Marie had left home; when he found her she was working as a prostitute, so he put her over his shoulder and brought her back in the van, she said. A friend of Mae's and Stephen's said that Heather was often spoken about in the house after her departure, and that her brother and sister were keen on trying to find out where she was. This same witness saw Mrs West after a beating from her husband. Her spectacles had been broken and she had a black eye. 'All the things I've done for that man and he treats me like this,' she had said.

Then a thin, grey man, grey suit, grey skin, reading-glasses perched on his nose, gave evidence of meeting a woman called Mandy through a contact magazine. His name was Arthur John Dobbs and Mandy turned out to be Rosemary West, with whom he conducted an unromantic affair for eighteen months. Mr Dobbs went to the West household for sex three or four times a week, the first time with Mr West in the room. When Mrs West let slip that her husband had sex with children, he contacted the Social Services because he 'thought there was something funny going on'.

318

When Kathryn Halliday strode into the witness-box a certain *frisson* shivered through the court, for she looked hostile and seemed certain to be provocative. A tight little down-turned mouth with no lips, harsh face, hooded eyes and cropped hair added to the impression of purposeful antipathy which she brought with her into court, an impression in no way diminished by her addressing counsel as 'sir' with every one of her answers. Mrs Halliday had left her husband and was sharing a room at 11 Cromwell Street with a woman. When a leak appeared in her ceiling, she was advised to get Fred West down the road to have a look. He repaired it immediately. There was no secret about her sexuality, she said, and West said she should 'see my missus – she'll sort you out.' Thus began the lesbian affair with Rosemary West to which we have referred earlier. It started within minutes of her first visit to No 25. 'I'm not naïve,' she told the court, 'but I've never in my entire life been in a situation where it all happened so quickly.' The burden of her evidence consisted in a description of sexual activity which grew gradually more sadistic in nature, Mrs West cajoling with 'soft words' until she had one in her power. 'She wanted to make you vulnerable,' said Mrs Halliday, who broke down several times during her evidence and paused to sip from a glass of water. 'I'm sorry, I find this very difficult,' she said. Without being asked, she introduced the information that she found it shocking the Wests should allow their children to sleep in the basement above several dead bodies, and Mr Leveson had to bring her back to the subject in hand. Asked why she kept going back if she found the sex so offensive, she said it was like a moth to a flame; 'you get burnt, but still you go back.' It seemed obvious to all that the image and the words were not her own. Her contract with the *Sunday Mirror* was for £8,000.

Kathryn Halliday's description of the contents of a suitcase kept upstairs was the one piece of her evidence which was highly pertinent to the case. She was shown a collection of black clothing, including rubber suits and masks with slits for the nose and mouth, of the kind featured in pornographic magazines which cater to sadistic tastes and a predilection for anonymous partners. She was invited to wear them, but refused. She said that both Mr and Mrs West were present when she was shown these objects and some whips, and that she was only shown them once.

Mr Ferguson began his cross-examination by telling the witness that she had negotiated with newspapers and refined her story for them before she made her first statement to the police, and that she managed to extract another £1,000 out of them after the suicide of Frederick West. Why had she done this? 'Because I wanted the world to know I'm a survivor,' she said. And did she realize that there would be no publication unless the trial resulted in a conviction? Yes, she did. Ferguson turned on the witness with open contempt. 'You have cashed in on sexual activity which you enjoyed,' he said, 'then exaggerated that activity and tried to present yourself as a victim. The truth is that between October 1988 and June 1989 you kept going back to 25 Cromwell Street for more sex.'

Defence then argued in the absence of the jury that repetition of this kind of evidence was salacious and added nothing to the case. He further objected to the Crown's intention to introduce Frederick West's advice that the holes in the cellar beams were meant to suspend living bodies. A distinction must be made between inference and speculation, he said. The judge ruled in his favour. Three more witnesses, one of them in the form of a statement read out by junior counsel, were heard the following day, while discussion in the corridor outside focused on when and whether Anne Marie would be called. Since the committal in Dursley it was known that her evidence, if allowed, would be likely to prove catastrophic to the defence, even despite its total lack of information pertaining to the charges which her stepmother faced. Since Mr Justice Mantell had already ruled that it was admissible, the only question remaining was whether she would be able to stand the strain.

Anne Marie Davis entered the witness-box after the lunch break on Wednesday, 18 October. Her effect upon the courtroom was immediate. By her composed and rather shy demeanour she excited sympathy before she even opened her mouth. With her close-cropped tidy hair, full mouth, and the wounded eyes of an animal accustomed to fruitless punishment, she was unmistakably the daughter of Frederick West – dark and nomadic. She looked as if she had never smiled in her life and would not dare to for fear of the consequences. Largeboned and square-shouldered, there was none the less an air of appealing delicacy and fragility about her which called for protection, especially now that she was exposed, alone with every face turned towards her, about to be dissected and examined in public. She was simply dressed, with a white, fluffy, short-sleeved jumper and skirt, and a soft voice to match. Withal, Mrs Davis was polite and sweet, grateful for every consideration and correct in her behaviour. When asked if she would like to sit, she said 'May I?' She spoke barely above a whisper.

Brian Leveson displayed his skill with this witness as with no other, for he knew that he would be required to guide her through the most awful testimony, shirking no specifics, and was determined to do so in a strictly orderly, unemotional manner. He was patient and gentle with her, and I feel sure that, despite his wig and the unnerving formality of his office, he helped dispel her isolation. She might not have been able to testify with a less sympathetic counsel.

We drew breath as quietly as possible while Anne Marie gave evidence, and had we been able to regulate the pumping of our blood we should have done so. The danger was that we might be so stifled by awe as to let anomalies and contradictions pass unnoticed. At the very beginning, for example, she said that she vaguely remembered her mother Rena, whereas before her father's arrest she had no recollection of her at all and did not know her name. One may wonder what reason she could have for resurrecting a memory which had apparently been lost. Mr Leveson took her through early childhood, the love for her father, the recalcitrance of her sister Charmaine and Rosemary's often physical scolding of her. When she told how Rosemary had hit her over the head and drawn blood, because she had been angry with Char, she looked to her left at her stepmother in the dock, and held her eyes upon her. Mrs West looked down to her knees, but Anne Marie gazed in her direction for a few seconds before restoring her glance to Mr Leveson.

This happened half a dozen times. It made a powerful impression, as if the two women were conducting a private, silent colloquy from which the rest of us were excluded. For moments at a time, it was as though we were not there, the room dominated by Rosemary and Anne Marie embracing in the dark. For these long looks were not suffused only with hostility. They were difficult to interpret, but they seemed to be tinged with regret and sorrow, to contain an element of yearning, of endearment, even of frustrated affection. Each time Anne Marie referred to some painful memory involving intimate connection with her stepmother, often of a quite revolting nature, she appeared almost to apologize with her eyes. That, at least, was what this author thought he saw as this thirty-one-year-old woman, twice a mother herself, related the details of an experiment conducted upon her when she was eight years old and the admonition she was given that she should be grateful to have such loving parents.

Nine of the jurors had hands over their mouths. A male juror in the front row looked at the defendant incredulously and a female juror was close to tears. I felt we should not have been there, and should certainly not have been scribbling it all down for public consumption. In the corridor outside during the first break, Gordon Burn, who is writing a book on the case, said to me, 'We are none of us untainted.'

The witness told how she had regular sexual intercourse with her father, and that he gave her a few pounds not to tell Rosemary. Except once. Rosemary took her out for the evening when she was thirteen, helped dress her nicely and put make-up on. 'She was very nice to me, a different person. I felt happy. I drank barley wine and ate crisps, and by closing time I was a bit tipsy.' Then her father raped her in the back of his van, with Rosemary making sarcastic remarks. 'I kept thinking, what have I done? I haven't done anything wrong.' And here's another quiet but devastating sentence: 'When I was eleven or twelve I was introduced to coloured gentlemen.' She had finished her evidence-in-chief, but not been submitted to cross-examination, when the court rose.

At the end of the day, Nikki Gerrard of the *Observer*, who had visibly winced with pain in court, said outside, 'She was tremendous. Like cool, clear water.'

The following day, Thursday 18 October, the court moved to Gloucester for a view of the house, in response to a request from the jury to which the judge acceded with reluctance. After oaths were taken by two court ushers, that they would not suffer anyone to approach jury members, we set off from Winchester in three parts: the judge and his clerk left in a limousine; the jury were in a bus with curtains drawn at the windows and motorcycle police escort before and behind; and twelve people from the media followed in another bus, also with police escort but without the secrecy of curtains. We were selected by ballot, and I drew the straw to represent the authors – Gordon Burn, Geoffrey Wansell and myself. The jury bus disappeared beneath a canopy behind 25 Cromwell Street before jurors alighted, so that they were seen by nobody. Various helicopters hired by newspapers hovered pointlessly overhead. Once the jury had left, we followed exactly the same route through the house as they had, in single file, silently, prohibited from asking questions or making remarks, each with a note-book in hand.

We started on what remained of the patio, bare now apart from three chalked circles to mark where the remains of Heather West, Shirley Robinson and Alison Chambers had been found. Marching down the side of the house, we entered by the front door, walked in and out of the two lower rooms and up the pale-green stair-case to the bar-room and the former lodgers' rooms above. The squeak of the landing's floorboards made one wonder how much could be heard in that house. We finished with a grim view of the dark and dusty cellar and its dual purpose: the five chalk circles to mark the site of the graves; and the colourful scribblings on the wall to recall that this had once been a bedroom for children.

When we resumed at Winchester on Friday morning, it was announced that Anne Marie was unable to con-tinue with her testimony because she was 'indisposed'. In fact she had taken an overdose and was recovering in hospital. As she had declined to be looked after by the police while she was appearing as a witness, it was not clear who she had been with or how she had been ad-mitted into hospital. In the meantime, we heard evidence from her estranged husband, Christopher Davis, who recalled the birthday party in 1987 to which the entire West family came and at which Heather seemed more and more 'into herself', withdrawn and morose. It was the last time he saw her. Mr Davis also confirmed the existence of a suitcase in the bar-room containing sex videos and snapshots of Rosemary West naked. He was not cross-examined.

There followed legal arguments concerning the ad-missibility of these videos, not that they should be seen, but that they should be described to the jury. Mr

Ferguson objected on two grounds. The home-made videos which depicted the defendant were 'of an extremely personal nature, very private, and not relevant to issues in this case. They did not include bondage.' This was perfectly true. As for the commercial video which Mr Leveson wished to introduce because it depicted a woman tied to beams in a cellar, Mr Ferguson pointed out that this dated from 1992, whereas the events the jury were considering occurred twenty years before; there was therefore no probative connection. Mr Justice Mantell ruled that he would not allow description of a video showing suspension from beams, because no witness had ever mentioned suspension, hence there was no basis for it. (The only reference was by Frederick West himself during police interviews, about which the jury as yet knew nothing.) Others, however, he would allow. Mr Ferguson's reflection on this was that 'I accept there were home-made videos, but dispute they were ever shown to anyone. Also, one may find videos of many things in many homes, but it does not follow that people who have them behave in the same way.'

We were then told that Anne Marie was on her way to court by car, direct from the hospital. She had been photographed coming out of hospital. The judge was irritated that his order not to harass witnesses had been ignored, and made a new order prohibiting the use of the photograph or any news item identifying where the witness had spent the night. How it happened that any photographer or reporter should be in a position to know where she was, in the middle of her testimony, was not explored.

Anne Marie was back in the witness-box to face Richard Ferguson at 12.20 p.m. on Friday, 20 October. He, too, was gentle with her, but precise. 'I have a few questions to ask about your relationship with your father,' he said. 'I'm sorry, but it has to be done.' It was then that we heard for the first time just how extensively she had been her father's lover over a period of years, and that she had been made pregnant by him when she was fifteen. At that point, he said, 'No more details, Mrs Davis. Don't worry.' He passed on to her promiscuity, very briefly, and to her contract with the *Daily Star*, more exhaustively, then told her that she had put her stepmother into the story because she found it difficult to face the fact of her father's abuse. This elicited from her the final remark, 'I do know right from wrong.'

Brian Leveson was then afforded the opportunity to re-examine, and he discovered that the witness had more information to offer than he was prepared for. She told how sex with her father had been in the 'straight missionary position', with nothing unusual or unorthodox demanded of her (which, in the knowledge of Frederick West's bizarre tastes, was surprising). She said that her stepmother beat her for no reason, with whatever happened to be at hand, and that on one occasion Rosemary had asked her to stay home from school to keep her company when Fred came home. 'I wanted to be with her because she had been good to me,' said Anne Marie. 'I stood between her and Dad when he came home, trying to protect her. But she hit me, and said that'll teach you to be so cocky. I was trying to be good to her, I thought.' As Mr Leveson was bound by the rules not to have seen the witness since she was last in court, the question might have arisen how she had been reminded of these matters which she had neglected to mention during examination-in-chief, and whether anybody else had jogged her memory. The rules did not permit any further questioning by counsel for the defence. Mrs Davis left the court and was next seen with minders provided by the *Daily Star*.

The following week began with tapes of Mrs West's interviews being played, various admissions of fact, dates and documentation, and the door of 'Rose's Room', complete with peep-hole, being brought into court for all to see. Professor Knight gave evidence of human remains, specifying the missing bones in each case, and considered the possible explanations to account for these, which we looked at in Chapter Seven. He was followed by Dr Whittaker, with whose demonstration of the skull of Charmaine West superimposed over the photograph of the living girl this book began. The Crown rested its case against Rosemary Pauline West at 3.30 p.m. on Wednesday, 25 October 1995. Mr Ferguson asked that he and Miss Wass be given time to prepare the defence, and the judge rose until the following Monday. It was then that we heard for the first time that permission would be sought by the defence to introduce four of the taped interviews with Frederick West, a most unusual proceeding which, if allowed, would create a legal precedent. In the normal course the evidence of a dead man could not be heard, as the Crown would ipso facto be denied the opportunity to cross-examine. Mr Leveson warned that, to respond to four tapes he would need to play another thirty-one.

Over the weekend, one of the two young men on the jury was arrested on a minor charge and released on bail. Mr Justice Mantell asked him to stand and told him that he had automatically disqualified himself from service (without revealing the fact of his arrest to other jurors) and was forthwith discharged. He left the court without further ado, and Mrs West was thenceforth tried by eleven persons instead of twelve.

On Monday, 30 October, Richard Ferguson QC opened the case for the defence by reminding the jury that they had heard only half the evidence so far and they must suspend their judgement until they had heard it all. Turning to his left and speaking directly to them for the first time, he said, 'Some of what you have heard is shocking and some of it irrelevant to the issue which you have to decide . . . I want to tell you as loudly and as clearly as I can that Rosemary West is not guilty. She neither knew of nor participated in any of the murders, nor did anything to hide or conceal those murders. We are here because we believe in a system which holds you are innocent until proven guilty. The Crown must prove guilt beyond all reasonable doubt. I do not wish to be presumptuous, but all they have are allegations, accusations, and a superficially attractive theory. You do not have to accept it, and we place our trust in your integrity and independence. You will be fair and impartial.'

Mr Ferguson proceeded to set out some facts and some justifiable conclusions to draw from those facts, paramount among which was the indisputable knowledge that Frederick West was a murderer. He had told everyone he was, and had pointed out where to look for the remains of his victims. Two of these died before he met the defendant, and Mary Bastholme could well have been a third. 'If you think it is a fair assumption that Frederick West murdered even before he met Rosemary West, then the consequences are, 1) that he was capable of murder without her assistance, 2) that he was capable of dismemberment and disposal of bodies without her knowledge, help or assistance. You have heard evidence of sexual bondage, ropes and gags and so on. The same sort of articles were found with the remains of Anne McFall. What does that say? The Crown has built a careful but speculative case. The stack of cards on which it rests is that all the victims were sexually abused and that Rosemary West was a necessary ingredient in that mix. She must have enticed a number of victims to 25 Cromwell Street, lured them into a car. Who lured Anne McFall? . . . Even if you accept that Rosemary West was perverted, that is proof of that, and of nothing more . . . Because there can be no evidence as to how these girls met their deaths, the Crown have filled that void with prejudice and speculation . . . The defendant fell under the spell of Frederick West at the age of fifteen. He abused her as he abused everyone else during his evil life. It is because of her marriage to him that she is before this court now.'

Counsel then picked apart the elements of the prosecution case with precision, and with some Ciceronian relish. 'Mrs West may have been a lesbian, but that does not make her a murderer. She may have had sex with her lodgers, but that does not make her a murderer. She may have been forced into prostitution, but that does not make her a murderer. She may have had sex aids in the house, but that does not make her a murderer. What is the relevance of all this, except to excite prejudice against this defendant, and incidentally to provide interest to those whose appetites are so satisfied by it? These matters may offend your moral sensibilities, but they are not crimes. They may satisfy the media, but they do not add to the evidence with which you have to grapple.'

The Crown's second point was that the defendant was bound to know what her husband was doing in the home which they shared. 'This is an argument of doubtful validity in many marriages,' said Mr Ferguson, 'but in this house and in that marriage it is utterly without any substance whatever.' The jury must not be tempted to compare Cromwell Street to their own domestic situation. 'The absence of a familiar face would gain your attention. Not so at No 25, a refuge for the flotsam and jetsam of modern life. The sounds of digging, demolition and excavation would be a matter for comment in your homes. Not so at No 25.'

He conceded that the Crown was on firmer ground with the evidence of four witnesses – Caroline Owens, Miss A, Kathryn Halliday and Anne Marie Davis. They each made an impact upon the jury. 'Let us look dispassionately at what they had to say. One thing they have in common is involvement with the media. I'm not unduly cynical, but you may think perhaps they are not as unworldly as they would have you believe. There may have been an element of amateur dramatics in the way some of them gave evidence. One cannot blame these young women for selling what they have to sell, but it has this effect: you may think that, consciously or unconsciously, they are aware that the more sensational their evidence, the more the media will pay for their stories. No newspaper is going to pay out large sums if Rosemary West is acquitted . . . I accept the maxim that justice must be seen to be done and that there is legitimate public interest in this case. Lurid headlines do not serve that public interest, however. These proceedings alone will serve it.'

Taking the four witnesses in turn, Mr Ferguson identified what was lacking in each. All we have for certain about Caroline Owens is the fact that Mr and Mrs West were fined £50 each for what they had done, and that at a magistrates' court. She underwent no medical treatment whatever as a result. Miss A made no complaint for over twenty years, and then could remember nothing that would substantiate her account of having been in that house. She had been infatuated by the defendant's brother, had run away with him, had pretended to be pregnant by him. 'Pause before you accept the evidence of this witness,' he warned. Kathryn Halliday kept going back for more. Anne Marie was a tragic figure by any account and on any showing, irrespective of what the defendant did or did not do. She had always been resentful of Rosemary West coming into her family. 'Mrs West denies emphatically that she was ever party to the sexual exploitation of that sad woman.'

'You have heard her on tape,' he concluded. 'You have heard her shocked response on being told that her husband had confessed to murdering her daughter Heather. "So she's dead, is that right?" she said.' Mr Ferguson then sprung upon the jury a surprise, for which even the press benches had been prepared for only a matter of hours. 'You are now going to hear from her in person,' he said. '*She* will tell you, not me. For the first time in public she will say what actually did take place during her years at 25 Cromwell Street. This will be a considerable ordeal for her. This was *her* family, *her* home. I call Rosemary Pauline West.'

The rumour was that she herself had insisted upon her

right to speak in her own defence. She was thereby taking a measurable risk, for nothing could prevent her having to face the skilful and sardonic mockery of Brian Leveson. She made the brief walk from the prisoner's dock to the witness-box at twelve noon precisely.

She was surprisingly firm of voice. After all that we had heard about her, we expected, I suppose, a woman chastened by relentless exposure, beaten and subdued. She was certainly nervous, but sustained by a feeling of confidence in her ability to stand up for herself. This was to prove her undoing, for the swings between deference and defiance were to mirror, in the jury's mind, the switches they had already heard concerning her moods and behaviours. It was clear that meekness did not come naturally to her, and belligerence kept bursting through. When she addressed counsel as 'sir', it did not come across as a word she had used very often.

Responding to calm questioning from her own counsel, Mrs West told of her childhood, her younger brothers, her first job in a bakery, the two rapes she suffered before she was fifteen, and her meeting with Frederick West, all of which has already found its way into this book. She employed an unconvincing cliché to describe her reaction when West first invited her out ('shock, horror'), and a suspiciously prepared account of her succumbing to his seduction ('He promised to love me and care for me, and I fell for it. I was nursing old wounds. I just wanted someone to love me'). She was weeping at this point, and it was perfectly easy to imagine an affectionate teenage girl desperate to be useful, but this conflicted with the other image we carried of a sexually wise youngster eager for experience. Perhaps they were both true. Human character is, after all, more complex than is convenient for a court of law.

She cried again when she told how Fred's wife Rena came to collect Charmaine, and apologized for holding things up with her tears. Her voice trembled violently when recalling that Fred had made it clear to her he wanted her to sleep with other men as her contribution towards making their relationship work ('He said I had to play my part'). Her description of the state of the cellar at Cromwell Street when they first moved in struck an authentic domestic note which only a housewife would have noticed. 'Whatever you put down there would get soaking wet,' she said. That was a genuine memory. Her son Stephen was born in August 1973 ('our first boy . . . I spoilt him very much'), after which she was so exhausted she slept during the day and Fred thought she must be anaemic. She consulted the doctor about this. Some of us in court were tempted to reflect upon the parallel narrative of murder; Lynda Gough disappeared in April of that year, when Mrs West was therefore five months pregnant with Stephen. It was after his birth that she entertained thoughts of sexual contact with other women, she said. 'They were special to me, entirely different. Warmer, closer, more fun.' On the subject of her half-caste children, she said, 'It was Fred's idea. He called them our love children. I didn't want the fathers to know. I wanted them to be part of my family. But Fred told them anyway.' She added spontaneously, unprompted by any question, 'I certainly don't regret having them.'

After the incident involving Caroline Owens, which the witness unconvincingly insisted she could not remember properly, she revealed that she had tried to leave her husband. 'I knew in some way I had done wrong. I wanted it all to go away, and was terrified I would lose my family because we were in trouble. I wanted out of the marriage, to take my children away. I had them in the pram and was ready to walk out of the door. Then I thought, where am I going to go? Who would help me? Where would the money come from? I just felt so alone. Anne Marie loved her dad very much. If I took her away she would never forgive me.' In the end, her husband promised her he would never put her in that kind of situation again. 'I did not see that side of him', she said, 'before or since.'

The first indication that the accused's aggressive self-protection was to work against her came when she was asked about Lynda Gough. Answering more than the question demanded, she quarrelled with the girl's memory and her size in slippers, as well as with her mother's having visited the wrong house. These were points for a lawyer to make, not for the defendant to volunteer, but her counsel Richard Ferguson was unable to stop her.

Mrs West's solicitor Leo Goatley said that his client became progressively more tired as the afternoon wore on, and that accounted for her aggrieved stance. But she was at it again the following morning, 31 October, when questioned about Miss A. There was no truth in her story whatsoever, she said. It didn't happen. Then, inconsequentially and unnecessarily, 'Why didn't she tell someone if it was so terrible?'

I think it is not fanciful to have detected the first real sympathy for the defendant in court when questioning turned to the disappearance of her daughter Heather. For whatever reason, and her guilt or innocence must have a bearing on that reason, whenever Heather was mentioned she was visibly distraught. Now, as soon as Mr Ferguson introduced the subject, she could be seen to struggle for a moment, and then burst into tears without repair. 'I'm sorry, Mrs West,' said counsel, 'these questions have to be asked.' 'Yes, I know,' she replied. She proceeded to give her version of what happened, and when she came to her return to the house from shopping to find Fred had let Heather leave home without saying goodbye, she was shaking with sobs. There was no mistaking their genuineness.

The same could not be said, however, for her depiction of her marriage as a loose alliance between two people who led separate lives. It may have been true to some extent, as the facts themselves demonstrated (he always working, she sometimes sent out for the night, no-one ever spotting them out together for a social evening), but the insistence that she had always to report where she was and when she would be home, whereas his movements were a mystery to all, smacked of exaggerated contrivance to counter the 'in it together' theory of the prosecution. If one thought about it, however, the picture she drew would have been typical of the obedient checking-in and checking-out which sadistic controlling men demand. It merely did not sound convincing.

One felt that chess pieces were being moved about an invisible board. The defendant sobbed heavily again when she averred that she did not know her husband was a murderer. 'He fooled everybody,' she said. 'I don't know how he managed it.' Had she finished her evidence-in-chief on that note, she might have carried the day. But she added something entirely to the wrong purpose.

'I could not have lived with a murderer,' she said. 'I would not have known when it was going to be my turn.' A more proper response might have been that she could not have lived with a murderer because the very idea of murder was detestable. Fred's own reflection on this point was that, had she known what he had been up to, she would have reported him for the safety of her own children.'

Mr Ferguson sat down. Brian Leveson rose quietly to begin what everyone knew would be a merciless onslaught, based on the common-sense assertion that 'she must have known'. He began, 'Mrs West, between 1971 and 1994 you never saw anything which alerted you to the horror of what had been happening in your home? You never saw a body? You never saw human remains? Blood-stains on your husband? On his hands? On his clothes? In the bathroom after he left? Never heard any screams?' To each of these the defendant replied simply, 'No, sir', but the accumulation of implausibilities was overwhelmingly effective. Even before she had married Frederick West, said counsel, she had told her mother that he was capable of murder, hadn't she? 'Will you let me explain?' said the defendant. Leveson graciously allowed her room to damage herself. She said that she and Fred had argued over his insistence that she sleep with other men, which she had refused to do; he had grabbed her by the throat, and when she realized he was not going to let go, she had taken her words back, then fled to her mother with the children. That was why she had said, 'Mum, you don't know what he's like.' This in itself was also perfectly plausible, but her eagerness to get it in suggested preparation, and the extraordinary selectiveness of her memory, which was bright over this twenty-five-year-old conversation and inexpressibly dim on other matters, did not inspire trust.

After lunch, Mr Leveson turned to the alleged collaboration between husband and wife in every regard. 'You remained in love with him, utterly and completely devoted, at least until the moment of your arrest. You presented to the world at large as a perfect couple.' 'I don't know how I presented,' Mrs West replied. 'I wanted a home, and Fred to provide.' Leveson referred to an entry in her diary for 1977 on which was written, 'Go home to Fred, loved him very much'. When he was not making observations couched in language so direct as to suggest they were incontrovertible, he would use the device of a redundant interrogative at the end designed to show that the question really did not need to be asked. 'The evidence that you led separate lives is not true, is it?' 'Sexually you would do anything with any-one, wouldn't you?' 'You weren't going to have her [Charmaine] in your family, were you?' 'It's all piffle, isn't it?' This was sarcasm of a high order, meant to weaken the witness through derision. 'We can dance around this all afternoon,' he said, implying that nothing she said was worthy of serious consideration. And it worked, for he provoked her into another one of her damaging *non sequiturs* when, having three times denied that she killed Charmaine, beneath a barrage of accusations, she blurted out, 'Where would I hide a little girl's body at Midland Road?' Thus was she pushed into being indignant over the wrong thing, not at the fact of murder, but at the question of strategy.

Leveson saw the advantage he had, and determined to rile the defendant as often as possible when she began her third day in the witness-box on Wednesday, 1 November. He would be deliberately cruel, taunting, sardonic, and hope thereby to make her lose her temper. He launched into the (still irrelevant) allegations about her treatment of Anne Marie. 'You were concerned to improve her sex life, weren't you?'

'No, sir. It was me that took her to the doctor's when she was ill.'

'You shoved a vibrator up a little girl aged eight.'

'No, sir, that's not right.'

'You certainly did assist in the examination of the genitals of Caroline Owens, didn't you?'

'I don't know.'

'Are you saying it didn't happen, you can't remember, or what?'

'I can't say either way.'

'Because of what you claim are the limitations of your memory.'

'Are we talking about Caroline Owens?'

'We most certainly are.'

Again, Mrs West volunteered to say something without waiting for a question. 'Please carry on,' said Mr Leveson, with a mocking wave of the hand. She then launched into a legal argument about the seriousness of the charges in 1972, which was better left to her lawyer. Mr Leveson was content to let her get on with it, for she thereby increased the damaging impression of stridency which was already held against her.

As the day wore on, Mr Leveson's combination of withering contempt ('that was an immediate, spontaneous lie') and undermining ridicule ('I am not suggesting Lynda Gough was murdered for her slippers') gave way to questions loaded with catapults. Having established that lots of young girls came in to the house for a chat, then that the defendant could have no idea what Miss A looked like fifteen years ago, he said, 'Then how do you know she wasn't one of the girls who came in for a cup of tea?' (The point, that Miss A claimed to have done rather more than drink a cup of tea, was lost in the business of confusing a witness and tripping her into a denial of the obvious.) A similar catapult was hidden in the question, 'If they don't resist, then they are consenting, is that your view?'

On one point only did the defendant manage to make the court understand that she was, just possibly, being unfairly treated. Mr Leveson thought it absurd that she should pretend not to remember Shirley Robinson, as indeed it was, but she reminded him that she was questioned about Shirley immediately after having been told that Heather was dead, and that she was 'in a real mess'. If she was entirely innocent and ignorant of her daughter's death, then the point was a valid one.

Rosemary West was released from the witness-box at lunch-time. She had not been a convincing witness in her own defence. She had claimed a faulty memory at one moment, a clear one the next; she had been caught telling lies; she had been obstreperous (its derivative 'stroppy' conveys her attitude more vividly); and above all, she had denied any imputation of child abuse. Had she been able to admit this, and thereby establish some degree of honesty on a disquieting accusation which was only tangential to the ones she was being tried for, she might have been heard with more sympathy. But if she could not be believed on this, then it was easier to disbelieve her on the rest.

It was a measure of how far the assumption of the defendant's guilt had penetrated public consciousness that when she appeared in the dock on Friday 3 November wearing a Remembrance Day poppy pinned to her jacket, there were many who found the gesture offensive. The last word had been heard from Mrs West, but there was still one more surprise to spring upon the jury, and even that would have an unexpected coda.

The day before, 2 November, had seen a string of witnesses who testified to having been approached by or assaulted by Frederick West acting alone and trying to abduct women in his car. One of these was so dismayed by the memory that her brief evidence was one long howl of distress, and her screams could be heard in the corridor outside. What they did all achieve, however, was a clear indication that Rosemary West had nothing to do with the attacks upon them.

Then, extraordinary permission was given for four taped interviews of Frederick West, selected from a total of 145, to be played in court. In effect, the voice of the dead man would come to give evidence in defence of his living wife, and because he was treated as a witness, the jury were not allowed to keep transcripts of the tapes, as they would have been were they to be treated as exhibits. Defence counsel selected four of the few interviews which were useful, albeit unpleasant; the rest were tendentious at best, and at worst full of nonsense and gibberish.

The first to be played was interview No 3, dated 25 February 1994, in which the murderer gave his notoriously featureless description of the murder of Heather, complete with her loss of bladder control and his hacking off her head. Mrs West sat bowed throughout this, looking at the ground at her feet. Two jurors glanced across at her. The first and second row of journalists, who did not have a good view of her face, kept bobbing up and down, in the public interest, to catch sight of her weeping. There followed the interviews in which he claimed to have been having affairs with all the girls who died, in which he described the ambushing of Rena West and killing of Charmaine as an afterthought, in which he claimed Lucy Partington had first wanted him to meet

338

her parents, then demanded £1,000 to abort his child that she was carrying, and in which he described how girls would start messing about undoing his fly-buttons and threatening to tell Rose. The defendant in the dock sipped water and kept her face from view.

There were moments when he was clearly lying, others when he was lost in fantasy. The interview that assumed most importance took place on 29 April, when he proclaimed, following a meeting with solicitor and counsel the night before, that he was protecting other 'person or persons'. It was this contention that was to let in a surprise witness the following week.

Mr Ferguson completed on Friday afternoon, but did not formally rest his case until 10.30 a.m. on Tuesday, 7 November (the court did not sit on Monday in order to permit a juror to see a spouse in hospital). Immediately, Mr Leveson made six applications to call evidence in rebuttal of the assertions made by Frederick West. These were:

1. To hear the probation officer George Guest, who made a social enquiry report at the time of the Caroline Owens incident, lost it, but recalled some of the details. Mr Ferguson objected due to lapse of time since the event, but the judge allowed it in anyway. It is not reported here, there being no documentary evidence that Mr Guest had anything to do with the case.

2. To read the whole statement of Lucy Partington's mother, showing in detail all her daughter's movements throughout 1973, when it was literally impossible for her to have been having an affair with anyone. There was no objection.

3. To hear the evidence of Detective Constable Harris, to whom Frederick West on tape No 132 (page 5710 in the transcript) said he had nothing to do with any of the twelve deaths and asked him 'for God's sake to put it all together' as he would not tell whom he was protecting. There was no objection.

4. To hear the evidence of Dr James MacMaster, who

interviewed Frederick West at Winson Green Prison in Birmingham in August 1994, when West had become fearful after a disagreement with his then solicitor Howard Ogden regarding book and film rights to his story and claimed Ogden had manipulated him into saying things to the police which he ought not to have said. There was no objection, but Mr Ferguson reserved the right to cross-examine. MacMaster said that West told him his wife Rose had been running a brothel and tried to murder him, that Heather had helped dig her own grave, that Rose had been burying people without his knowledge and preparing his daughters for prostitution. Under cross-examination MacMaster agreed that he saw West two or three times a week between August and December 1994 and had determined that he presented no danger to himself. He killed himself on 1 January 1995.

Before the sixth and last application was made, exhibits 64 and 65 were admitted without dispute. They were letters written by Frederick West and taken from his cell after the removal of his body. 'Well, Rose, it's your birthday and you will be 41,' he wrote. 'The most wonderful thing in my life was when I met you. Keep your promises to me. You know what they are. You will always be Mrs West all over the world. I have no present. All I have is my life. I give it to you. Come to me, I'll be waiting.'

The sixth application, which was granted without argument, was that the 'appropriate adult' who had sat in on eighty of the interviews police officers conducted with Frederick West, and had formed a friendship with him outside of these interviews, be called in rebuttal of his own tapes. Thus it happened that the trial was rounded off with the appearance of Janet Leach in the middle of that morning.

Mrs Leach had been registered with a young homeless project in Cheltenham and her name placed on the rota of those likely to be summoned to act as an independent non-participatory witness at police interviews to ensure that no duress is applied during interrogation. When she drew the straw for Frederick West she had never heard of him, although it later became clear that she had known his brother John. There were, it is true, many witnesses at the trial of Rosemary West who appeared fearful, but none more so than Janet Leach. Aged thirty-nine with five children, long fluffy black hair, and a nervous disposition so intense that anxiety emanated from her pores and spread around the court, she sighed, breathed heavily, appeared about to be struck dumb, and would rather have been anywhere else in the world than Winchester Crown Court.

Here, in edited form, is what she told Brian Leveson: 'It was important to Fred that Rose be released from custody because they had made a pact that he would take the blame for everything. He told me that on 27 February 1994 and did not change it over several months. Other things he did change his mind about, but not the pact. Rose would never say anything, he said. Before the interviews he told me he was going to say a lot of nonsense, and went through it with me before he saw the police. I did not divulge all this to the police because it was not my place. I was told it in confidence. When Rose was released, he said the pact was working, and when she was re-arrested, he said the police were getting too close to her being involved. He told me he waited for the police to come up with something, and then would weave a story to fit round it. He was always at work when Rose killed, though he sometimes helped to dispose of the bodies afterwards. The deaths were all sexual, mistakes, they weren't meant to happen. The fingers were chopped off during dismemberment to prevent identification. He didn't say what he did with the bones. I kept in touch with him after my official involvement came to an end because I couldn't just leave it like that. The last time I saw him was on 16 December 1994, and I spoke to him by telephone on 23 December to cancel a visit due to bad weather. I was very angry that he killed himself and left me with all that knowledge, because he had promised me he would tell the truth.'

Mrs Leach frequently sniffled, blew her nose or broke into sobs during her testimony, especially when referring to the enormity of the responsibility placed upon her by confidentiality. She revealed that West often contradicted himself, first saying he murdered Heather, then that Rosemary had killed her by accident, or claiming to have been in prison when Charmaine died, then confessing to having killed her when he came out. It began to look as if he altered his accounts to her in exactly the same way as he said he altered them to the police – as a result of ideas suggested to him during interrogation. On the events of 24 February 1994, when the warrant to search 25 Cromwell Street was served, he told Mrs Leach that he was five hours late getting home because the van had broken down, and that Rosemary had told him that evening where the bodies were buried.

'He kept asking if he was shocking me,' she said. 'I was actually devastated, but I didn't want him to know how upset I was, because I was just doing a job to the best of my ability.' It does not seem to have occurred to her that he *wanted* to shock her, or to wonder what that said about his character and the content of his talk. She would not have known that the desire to shock, like exhibitionism, is a form of sadism and a route to non-consenting intimacy; that he was charming her; and that she was an unsuspecting victim of that charm. 'I told him he would have to cope by himself if he thought there was anything between us,' she blurted out. 'I was not prepared to put up with that.' But it was too late. She had been ensnared. (During the second week of interviews, on 4 March 1994, concern was expressed for the welfare of Mrs Leach in the light of what she had been listening to, and she had said that she wanted to carry on in order to give 'support' to Mr West, who had asked her to continue.[2])

In cross-examination Richard Ferguson reminded Mrs

Leach of other things she had forgotten to mention, as for instance that West had told her it was Anne Marie who brought young girls to Cromwell Street for him and knew what was going on, that he liked to break them in, and that many other people besides Rosemary West had been involved in the murders, including his brother, her father and several coloured men. 'Did you not think he was having you on?' he asked. 'He didn't come across that way,' she replied. She agreed that she had taken no notes of conversations which took place when she and Fred West were alone. Mr Ferguson looked worried, perplexed. He asked, 'In the police interviews, did you never interrupt?'

'No.'

'You sat there listening to hours and hours of lies and never told the police they were at variance with what he told you?'

'Yes.'

'You told the police you were concerned about his solicitor not being good enough for him, but you were not concerned about his lies to them?'

'It wasn't my place.'

'Was he using you?'

'I suppose he was, but I didn't think so at the time.'

When the court rose for lunch, Mrs Leach collapsed from the strain of her exposure and was rushed to hospital in an ambulance. It appeared she had suffered a stroke some months before, and was exhibiting signs of a recurrence. She had lost the power to speak or move her lips, and was completely immobile. We discovered all this when court resumed in the afternoon, and it was decided that, obviously, the witness could not continue with her evidence. Equally obviously, however, she would have to. Mr Ferguson was not prepared to leave matters where they were. He told the judge he still had more questions to put to Mrs Leach, and since the jury had heard her testimony thus far, and since it was potentially extremely damaging to the defendant, it was essential she be fully cross-examined. 'It is impossible to over-estimate the impact of her evidence', he said, 'which was a severe blow to the credibility of the defence.' Moreover, she had been presented to the jury as the first utterly honest and trustworthy witness who had refused to have any dealings whatever with the press, whereas the defence intended to show that she was already under contract to a newspaper.

The court would wait until she recovered. Nobody quite put it into words, but they would question Mrs Leach on a stretcher if they had to.

They waited six days. On Monday, 13 November, Mrs Leach was brought into the witness-box in a wheelchair, with a doctor sitting behind her lest she should suddenly collapse. Her expanse of fluffy hair was disciplined into a plait tied at the back, and her complexion was as white as flour. She both looked terrified and terrified those who were watching her. Mr Ferguson established immediately that the meetings which took place between the witness and Frederick West were unsupervised, and accused her of complicity with him. He rehearsed the various matters West had revealed to her, and which she had kept to herself, including a confession to the murder of Mary Bastholme who he said was buried in a field. He had also implicated other people with the allegation that girls were murdered outside the house and brought there for burial, and said one person in particular (not the defendant) had helped him murder Heather. 'I didn't ask things,' said Mrs Leach. 'He just talked all the time. By talking to me he was getting things straight in his mind.' Ferguson asked why she continued to maintain contact with West after she had been released from duty and after the police had objected to her interventions and expressions of disapproval about the advice West was receiving from his solicitor. 'I just wanted the other girls' bodies to be found,' she said. 'No,' said Mr Ferguson, 'you wanted to get more information out of him.'

Ignoring Mrs Leach's tears, Ferguson announced that a woman had telephoned the *Daily Mirror* to ask how a friend of hers, another woman, should go about getting a book about Frederick West's revelations published. A reporter arranged to meet this mysterious woman for discussions. 'You were that woman, Mrs Leach,' he said, 'you were the woman who planned to write a book.' She was barely able to reply, so he went on, quoting from the letter of 2 August 1994 which the *Mirror* wrote in reply to her proposal to pen an account of her dealings with West and offering £7,500 for the exclusive first option. He further revealed that payments were clandestinely made in August, October and December to a man called Brian Jones so that they could not be traced to her. 'Brian Jones is your boyfriend,' he said. 'It was his idea' that she could deny receiving any money, whispered Mrs Leach, but counsel had not finished. He told the court that she and Jones and three children had been provided with a chalet by the newspaper, that further payments had been made in the interim, and that in the course of a meeting with three men she had verbally agreed to accept £100,000 from them to tell all. Weakly, she replied that she had signed no contract.

Janet Leach looked as if she was ready to pass out. She swayed slightly, inhaled as if every breath was an effort and every drop of blood had been drained from her veins. The judge intervened to enquire how much longer Mr Ferguson thought he needed, and he said about an hour. He told the witness she had been lying, and her reply was so faint that neither the microphone nor the court typist picked it up, and I only heard it because I was sitting close and watched her lips. 'Sorry about that,' she muttered plaintively. He then attacked her so-called loyalty to the confidentiality of her role.

'You continued to see Frederick West even after entering into this agreement with the press.'

'Because he asked me to.'

'Because you needed to continue the relationship for

profit. You were unhappy when his solicitor advised him to make no comment, because you needed him to talk. You made conditions before giving a statement to the police to avoid being identified in the media as someone who had made a statement, as that would breach your agreement with the newspaper. You were prepared to assist the police to ensure a conviction against Mrs West. Did you help Frederick West make up his account? Did you assist in developing that account? Did you want to make it as vivid and lurid as possible to make a more valuable commodity to sell?'

Mr Ferguson terminated with an excruciating exposure of Janet Leach's friendship for Frederick West. 'Did you work your way into his confidence?' he asked. She had visited him privately once every week and he had telephoned her three times a week. In letters to her he had said, 'Keep it up, kid', 'you looked great', 'lovely to see you on Friday', 'let the world say what they will, think of me as you found me, I'll be looking out for you in court'. Mr Ferguson asked, 'Was Frederick West emotionally attached to you? Was he trying to impress you by playing down what he'd done? Were you romantically involved?' Janet Leach could not reply. She did not need to. Rarely could any witness have been so ruthlessly demolished in such dramatic circumstances.

'Last lap, Mrs Leach,' said Brian Leveson, who had one more question to ask before she was released back into the obscurity which she craved. In reply, she said that West had told her the bodies of another twenty girls remained to be discovered in fields. This was the one comment that the tabloid press thought worthy of their headlines the following morning.

Mr Leveson began his closing speech on Tuesday, 14 November. Part of his task was to remind the jury of the Crown's case, and there is no need to repeat it here. New points he made which were not available to him before evidence was heard included a clever attack upon

Rosemary West as witness. She was 'tough and resource-ful, not without intelligence, had clearly mastered the papers in this case and was keen to argue, she was able to make her points when it suited her. Where is the evidence that Fred forced her into prostitution? Why, only out of her mouth.' She was, he said, the strategist in this partnership, even at the age of fifteen. And she was still being strategic when, informed of Heather's death, she did not ask why, when, where, but how does that implicate *me*. She was full of 'complete humbug'.

As for the words from the grave, the 'high drama' of Frederick West's own evidence, its value was 'absolutely nil' and served only 'to create smoke'. He listed five of West's abundant lies by way of example.

The evidence of Anne Marie was 'overwhelmingly convincing', he said, and insisted on its relevance in this way: 'If you're sure what she says is true, that *alone* proves violence in the mind and behaviour of this woman.'

Mr Leveson was mocking in his treatment of the defendant's excuses with regard to Shirley Robinson. 'Is it really credible that Rosemary West never got around to asking Shirley who was the father of her child?' he said. 'Why did Frederick West tell everyone in sight that it was him?' The defendant claimed that was a joke, but 'not one witness testified that it was a joke. Anne Marie said her father and Shirley made no secret of their relationship, and the photograph of them together, all dressed up, looks like a wedding picture. Shirley walked around the house in bra and pants, for all the world as if she owned it. Liz Brewer says she saw her at 11.00 a.m. one day. When she returned four hours later Shirley had vanished.' Fred couldn't have done it alone in so short a time, he said. At the very least, Rosemary West was a party to this murder.

Mr Leveson invited the jury to entertain the same reflection when considering the murder of Heather West. 'He must have had a very busy three or four hours that

Friday afternoon. It was a truly impossible feat, unless they did it together. All those children were due home from school. The room had to be spotless, Fred had to be spotless.' As for motive, Heather died because 'she had become a liability'.

'The evidence that Rosemary West knew nothing is wholly unworthy of belief,' he concluded. 'She says she saw nothing, she heard nothing, she smelt nothing. Well, she certainly said nothing.'

It was fitting that Brian Leveson should finish on a note of indignant sarcasm, for that had been his major weapon in his attack upon the defendant's credibility. It had been very effective, to some degree because he was assisted by her own deviousness and want of honesty, but even his eloquence strove hard to conceal that the Crown's case still rested on the absolute, invariable but unverifiable certainty that 'she must have known'. There was much muttering in the corridor outside that Mrs West might 'walk', an American vulgarism to indicate the unfortunate acquittal of a guilty party, as some there suggested might have happened in the recently terminated case of the sportsman O.J. Simpson in Los Angeles. Nobody wanted to see Rosemary West acquitted; the issue of her guilt or innocence of the charges had receded into a semantic limbo, untouched by the heady and full-blooded partiality of 'gut reaction'. To this extent Brian Leveson had succeeded triumphantly; the defendant's fate rested on the perception of her character alone.

It was Richard Ferguson's task to try and shift the emphasis back to ascertainable fact.

'Rosemary West is not accused of cruelty to children, or of being a party to rape,' he said, 'but of the crime of murder . . . There are siren voices urging you to convict, but you have your conscience and your oath, for which you will need a clear head and cool judgement . . . it is very easy to feel morally superior to her. Her conduct as a woman and a mother falls far below the standard you would expect. One fact remains stark and clear – at the end of it all, when it comes to proof, they have not got the evidence. You cannot convict without proof. You cannot allow your feelings of shock, disgust, revulsion to affect your verdict. You are not being asked by me to acquit in the teeth of the evidence but because there *is* no evidence . . . And do not think that, by acquitting Rosemary West, you will leave a series of unpunished and unsolved crimes. Frederick West provided his own solution. His death lifted the burden from your shoulders. It is unfortunate the Crown did not see fit to let the matter rest there.'

Counsel then brought the jury's attention to the character of Frederick West, the man who should (he implied) be in the dock now. He was 'an evil, corrupt sex maniac, devoid of compassion, consumed with sexual lust, a sadistic killer who had opted out of the human race. He was not the stuff of which martyrs are made. To ask you to think that such a man should give up his life for another is an insult to your intelligence. And if there was a pact, why on earth betray it by telling Janet Leach?' Mr Ferguson pointed out that West only changed his tune and started to blame everyone else after his meeting with lawyers on 28 April 1994, and that the only witness to support his new version of events was Janet Leach. She was, he said 'an unmitigated disaster for the Crown . . . And what were the police doing in allowing this killer to be closeted alone with a woman?' They said that his earlier confessions, between 24 February and 28 April, in which he exonerated his wife, were unreliable in the light of his later retraction. But 'if Frederick West were alive and on trial, do you think the Crown would be telling you these confessions are unreliable? Because he is dead, it is no longer suitable for the Crown to rely on his confession. But if he *might* be telling the truth, then Rosemary West is entitled to be acquitted.'

Similarly, he asked the jury to think of the women whom they had heard testify they were attacked by

Frederick West alone. 'If they had died, would you now be asked to convict his wife of their murder?' (The strong and worrying implication was that yes, they would, and there would be just as much circumstantial evidence then as there was now.) 'Once you accept that Frederick West *could* have done these murders on his own, then that is fatal to the Crown's construction. Think long and hard about the death of Anne McFall.' There, at least, there was no doubt that he had acted alone, and that destroyed the Crown's case. Mr Ferguson paused. 'If there is a flaw in my logic', he said disarmingly, 'then one or other of you will point it out to the rest in the jury room.'

The police benches, exactly opposite the jury and in full view of them, at this point became agitated, for they saw the logic all too well and were not happy with it. Their furious fidgeting, scribbling and head-shaking was a fairly blatant device to distract the jury. No-one will know if it had any effect.

Mr Ferguson went on to face the lies that the defendant had told, and ruminated upon the possible reasons for this. One might lie because one is ashamed. Mrs West might feel ashamed that she did not make more effort to get in touch with her daughter Heather after she left home, and told lies to cover that shame. 'But that does not make her a murderer. It makes her a liar.' Or one might lie out of fear. 'The temptation to tell a lie when you are being questioned by the police about a crime must be enormous. I know I would be tempted. To distance yourself from trouble. You may be terrified that if you admit to anything you will be sucked in further.'

He referred also to the phrase which Mrs West was alleged to have used about Charmaine's departure – 'bloody good riddance' – and pointed out that we have all made such remarks and regretted them later when they came back to haunt us. Lawyers analyse such phrases in the light of knowledge which has come to them since, but they have little significance at the time.

Anne Marie was the most dramatic witness, he said. 'Imagine Mrs West standing trial on one charge of sexual abuse on Anne Marie, and that the only witness against her was Anne Marie herself. And then you hear about her father's relationship with her and about her contract with a newspaper. In those circumstances, would you ever convict on the strength of that evidence? Also, Anne Marie says she did not know her father was a killer. She was very close to him, closer in some ways than his wife. You believe her. Why, then, should you not also believe Rosemary West? And why is Rosemary West singled out for criticism for believing what Fred told her had happened to Heather? He told the same story to everyone else, and they all believed him.'

Ferguson did not refer to the evidence proffered by Kathryn Halliday. 'I shall not give her the honour of dealing with her,' he said. She had been an 'embarrassment' for the prosecution.

He said that Mr Leveson could not take the jury on a straight path which led from fact to conclusion. He had come upon a crevasse which separated the two, and had invited them to make the leap across from one to the other. 'Ladies and gentlemen of the jury,' he said, 'don't jump. Don't make that leap. If he cannot lead you along a straight path, then you must acquit this defendant. I understand the magnitude of the demands I am making of you. You will have to explain it to your friends. But you must do it fearlessly, without regard to the consequences.'

Mr Justice Mantell announced that he would begin his summing-up on Thursday 16 November.

12

Verdict

The judge's summing-up in a case as difficult and unpleasant as this is of paramount importance. Having heard conflicting interpretations of the narrative from counsel, the jury turn to the judge with some relief, hoping that he will clarify what it is they have to do and how they should find their way towards the truth. Secretly, they hope he will do even more than this, that he will tell them what to think. This can only be done very subtly. On matters of law, it is the judge's task to explain and the jury's duty to accept the explanation. On matters of fact, the jury alone can decide, and the judge may only offer advice, which they are free to reject.

The jury in the West case were confronted by a terrible dilemma. One suspects they were torn between what they felt was their duty to acquit (as there was not evidence to send the defendant to prison for life), and their desire to convict (on the grounds that she should still be punished for being who she was). Therefore, they looked to the judge to get them out of this quandary.

It is a mistake to believe that the judge must in no circumstances allow it to be known what he thinks of the merits of the evidence. Some judges are blatant in making certain that their opinion is known, although they must not bully the jury into accepting it. Others are so circumspect that the jury may have no idea what they privately think even after several days of summing-up. Most juries naturally prefer the first kind, and so do many other judges. In 1973 the much revered Mr Justice Lawton said this: 'In our experience a jury is not helped by a colourless reading out of the evidence as recorded by the judge in his notebook. The judge is more than a referee who takes no part in the trial save to intervene when a rule of procedure or evidence is broken. He and the jury try the case together and it is his duty to give them the benefit of his knowledge of the law and to advise them in the light of his experience as to the significance of the evidence.'[1]

Whether judges restrict themselves to analysing the issues and marshalling the facts, or make their own views on those facts known, they are equally required to put the defence case with clarity and impartiality. Lord Chief Justice Lane put it this way in 1989: 'However distasteful the offence, however repulsive the defendant, however laughable his defence, he is entitled to have his case fairly presented to the jury by judge and counsel . . . where the cards seem to be stacked most heavily against him the judge should be most scrupulous to ensure that nothing untoward took place which might exacerbate the defendant's difficulties.'[2] In other words, he cannot tell the jury what decision they should reach with regard to the facts of the case. It is a narrow path to tread.

Mr Justice Mantell dealt with the problem in his own manner. 'What I think about the evidence just doesn't matter,' he said. 'If I leave something out, you must bring it in. Do not be influenced by me or by my emphasis, for heaven's sake.' Then he told them how he would seek to disguise his personal opinion, and how they would recognize it. When he introduced a reflection with the phrase 'you may think that', he said, that meant he was about to tell them what his private view was. 'Watch out for it,' he said. 'What I think is of no consequence at all. I cannot stress that too strongly.' Nevertheless, he spent the next two days using that phrase with increasing frequency. Usually he would pause both before and after it, using it as punctuation to make sure the jury understood his intention and paid particular heed to an opinion he was about to express. Sometimes he went further and drew their attention with a mockingly self-deprecating interjection such as 'There I am doing it, members of the jury, did you notice?', so that they were left in no doubt. The avuncular alliance he had built up with them from the beginning now paid off, to the benefit of both judge and jury and, I think, to the detriment of the defendant. For he left no room for ambiguity. On one occasion, not certain his point had come across, he paused and said, 'All right, members of the jury?'

It does sometimes happen that a jury will resist this kind of seduction. In the case of Clive Ponting, the civil servant accused in 1985 of revealing state secrets which the Government had sought to suppress, the jury was more or less instructed to return a guilty verdict, but they decided that parliament should have been informed of these important matters and that the defendant had protected the interests of the state, though not of the Government, in revealing them. To great consternation, they acquitted.

Rosemary West, of course, did not have a jury prepared to exonerate her, nor could she expect one. Against her were her reputation, her character, her mendacity and the suspicions cast upon her by the evidence. But she could have expected a jury ready to set aside their dislike of her to determine whether there was evidence of her having murdered anyone. The judge saw the possibility of this.

He began by reminding them of the most basic principles of justice. 'The defendant never has to prove his innocence,' he said. The burden was upon the prosecution to prove the defendant's guilt, and this was only attained 'if the prosecution is able to make you sure of it.' These were fundamental precepts which would have carried even more weight had they been advanced at the end of his two-and-a-half-day speech and remained fresh in the memory. He also made clear from the outset that the fact that Mrs West had remained silent during most of her interrogation by the police 'could not be held against her. It was her right [as the law then stood], and you must draw no inference adverse to her from it.'

Having defined murder, and having pointed out that in a joint venture, Mrs West would be equally guilty even if she had only enticed girls to the house and Mr West had struck the blow which killed them, the judge clarified the facts of which the jury must be satisfied. They were, 1) that Mrs West either alone or jointly participated in the killing of those named in the charge, 2) that what she did either alone or jointly was both deliberate and unlawful, and 3) that she intended the people named in the charge should either be killed or suffer serious bodily harm. Because there was no evidence as to how any of the girls met their deaths, the prosecution were inviting the jury to infer what might have happened. 'You must draw obvious and irresistible inference,' he said, 'otherwise the prosecution have not proven their case.' Some of us were reminded of Sasha Wass's precise definition that 'an inference is a conclusion to which you are driven by facts of which you are sure.'

Mr Justice Mantell congratulated counsel on the total absence of rancour and ill-temper, 'which would have distracted us', and characterized Brian Leveson's closing speech as 'analytical' and Richard Ferguson's as 'using a broader brush'. This was the first clue we had to the judge's own preference. He compared Leveson to Canaletto and Ferguson to Van Gogh, and hinted, with the subtlest lift of the eyebrow, that precision was preferable to impression.

He warned them that there were many unanswered questions and that they must not speculate on what evidence there might have been, although, in truth, it was virtually all they could do. He then began his summary of the facts, starting with the meeting of Frederick and Rosemary West, pausing to reflect upon the murders of Anne McFall and Mary Bastholme, attributable to Frederick, and marching through the ten counts against Rosemary West to pick out the most telling circumstances in each. Regarding Charmaine, the judge reminded the jury that for two of the three crucial months following the taking of her photograph on 29 April, Frederick West was in prison, but did not also remind them that during those first two months she was still alive. He quoted the testimony of the odontologist that she died within 'two to three months', but failed to point out that, in the light of other facts, this must mean in the third month. He allowed that the evidence of Mrs Giles was confused, not only as to the month of her visit to Midland Road, but even as to the year, but sought to elucidate it with a fact which had not been emphasized during evidence. The letter that Mrs Giles wrote to Frederick West in prison bore a drawing of herself at the bottom of the page showing she was pregnant. Her baby Claire was born on 7 August 1971. Frederick West's due date of release was 24 June 1971. Therefore she wrote the letter before 7 August, even before 24 June. He did not, however, point out that there was no mention of Charmaine in this letter, and consequently no reason to assume that she had already vanished from the scene (in truth, that the letter was not evidence at all, but a red herring!). He did say that Charmaine had been due to be taken to visit her stepfather in prison on 15 June, but said the record was silent as to whether the visit took place. He made reference to the defence's contention that Mrs Giles' visit to Midland Road when Charmaine had disappeared almost certainly took place in September, as she was pushing a pram at the time, and her baby had been born in August. Mrs West fixed the date by the lending of baby clothes.

On the other hand, he said, Anne Marie had corroborated that Charmaine had disappeared while her father was in prison, and moreover, that her evidence on this issue was not challenged by the defence. This was a telling point, and one wondered why, indeed, Mr Ferguson had not challenged it. It was, after all, eminently challengeable, both because Anne Marie was a little girl of eight at the time and it would have been miraculous had she been able to recall dates and circumstances from that age; secondly, because she initially had no memory of the events at all and seemed only to rediscover them under interrogation by the police and in other conversations.

Then there was this contentious reflection: 'At what point did Mrs West remember or decide that it was after Frederick West came out of prison that little Charmaine was taken away?' The suggestion that she had altered chronology was the reverse of the truth. She had always said so, and the police had always believed so, which is why they initially charged him and not her. The proper question should have been, 'At what point did the police decide that it was before Frederick West came out of prison that little Charmaine was taken away?' To which the answer was, after his suicide.

Early on in the investigation there had been a statement from somebody who knew a girl at Cromwell Street called Charmaine, aged sixteen, and this had confused the police for a moment. It was Rosemary West who put them right, and told them that that must have been a lodger, as the last time she had seen the little Charmaine was when Rena had come to collect her. Mr Justice Mantell reminded the jury of this little-noticed fact, but resisted the implication that the defendant had, on that occasion at least, been helpful and truthful. In the defendant's favour he did allow the reflection that Anne Marie had lived at Cromwell Street for much of the time that remains were being buried there, even that murders were being committed there. 'If she was ignorant of the murders', he said, 'why should not Rosemary West also be ignorant?'

But then the arguments against the defendant began to stack up, with little allowance made for alternative interpretations. Picking out the detail that Anne Marie remembered her father had been wearing his work overalls when he had intercourse with her in the cellar, he said that 'she was unlikely to have made that up.' That was true, but tangential to the issue, for one did not contest that the intercourse had taken place, only that the defendant had been present at the time, a matter which would not have been affected by the detail of his overalls in any way. Secondly, he said that the defence had claimed Caroline Owens had exaggerated her evidence, but they did not actually contradict it. 'It deserves your very close consideration,' he said. 'Compare and contrast it with what Rosemary West said in the witness-box and what Frederick West gave as his account.' Again, it had not been contested that an assault had taken place, only that it had been dealt with by a Gloucester magistrate and was now much more elaborately painted than it had been at the time. As for the fine imposed in 1973, 'At the very lowest, members of the jury . . . it was a ludicrous sentence, was it not?'

Suddenly, stepping out of the narrative, Mr Justice Mantell turned to the question of the media corruption of witnesses, in what one anticipated to be a long disquisition and ruling upon its relevance or interference with due process. Surprisingly, he limited himself to two sentences. The jury would have to decide whether deals with the media compromised witnesses and rendered their evidence valueless. Or whether it was to be expected. 'It's a fact of life,' he said, 'it happens.' And that was all. The newspapermen present in court were much relieved by this, for it demonstrated once and for all that the judge was a man of the world. He was now echoing their language, for the usual justification for breaking the law by contempt of court was that 'in the real world' newspapers could not be expected to wait for the judicial process to tread its measured course before they got their information, as they were all in competition for 'exclusives'. It was a fact of life. It happened. So much for the precedence of law.

In commenting upon Frederick West's confession, the judge was firm. He told the jury, 'The question for you is whether or not you can rely on a single word Frederick

West said to the police or for that matter to anyone else.' Implied within this was the suggestion that when he said his wife had had nothing whatever to do with his crimes, he should not be believed. To push the matter home, he made reference to West's fanciful account of his relationship with Lucy Partington, and added, 'Why was it necessary to re-write the script? To write out the part played by Rosemary West.'

He would return to West's confession at intervals throughout his summing-up to underline its inconsistencies. Fred had told the police he had strangled Shirley Robinson about six months before his daughter Heather, whereas there were nine years separating the two crimes. He had once stated that, as far as he knew, Rosemary had never met Shirley, which was manifest nonsense. He had said Heather was involved as a drug dealer, whereas she was nine years old at the time this allegation related. So, Fred told absurd lies. It was one step further to bring the lies which Rosemary West told into parallel relief. How well did she know Shirley Robinson? The judge asked, 'Is her account fair, or just not true? Suppose you think Fred and Rose separately are not being truthful about the extent of Rose's awareness of Shirley. Then, by coincidence or otherwise, you have the same lie being told by two people being interviewed separately. What do you make of that?'

This was a just reflection, and a helpful guide to the jury's deliberations. That 'or otherwise' was nicely placed. There was nothing improper about it. But it was selective, and protected from misdirection by the introductory 'suppose you think that'. Mr Justice Mantell did not point out the occasions, far more numerous and surprising, when Fred and Rosemary, interviewed separately, told the same *truth* about a material event, such as their accounts of Heather's last days at Cromwell Street, corroborated by other witnesses, or their memories of Charmaine's wish to rejoin her mother Rena and the arrangements made to effect it, also widely corroborated. He did not ask the jury, 'What do you make of that?'

Moreover, when it suited the Crown's case to believe what Fred had said, the judge seemed to support it. He had told Dr MacMaster that Rosemary abused his daughters with vibrators and enjoyed cruelty, that she was burying people without his knowledge and that he did not know what bodies lay beneath the concrete. The judge reminded us that Dr MacMaster had received no payment from the press, implying that what Fred had told him was thereby rendered more significant and reliable, which was a classic *non sequitur* the jury could not be expected to rumble. As for the tainted evidence of Janet Leach, he pointed out that she had been expressly released from the confidentiality agreement in order to give evidence at this trial, but failed to mention that she had released herself from any undertaking long before, by entering into a contract with the Mirror Group five months before Frederick West committed suicide, and while she was presumably still bound by it. He did not allude to her reasons for nurturing Fred's friendship.

When, therefore, he warned the jury not to pay attention to her testimony, it was too late. 'You cannot take it as direct evidence against Rosemary West,' he said. 'If someone tells someone else that Rosemary West is up to her neck in this, that cannot be used by you against her. You must exclude from your mind anything that Fred said against Rose, other than on the four tapes you have heard and save with regard to the effect on your mind of his evidence [on these four tapes].' In other words, everything Fred said against Rosemary in gossip with Janet Leach was inadmissible. But it had already been admitted, heard, pondered, weighed and absorbed by the jury. To ask them to proceed on the basis that they had not taken it in was unrealistic.

He invited the jury to review Mrs West's taped interviews with him, turning the pages as he did so and pointing out the many obvious lies they contained, in particular concerning Shirley Robinson. In contrast, he reminded the jury that Fred had told Janet Leach he was at work on the day Shirley died, and that Rosemary had told him what happened when he came home. He said he was upset that Rosemary had taken the baby from where it was supposed to be. He did not remind the jury that Anne McFall's baby had also been taken from the womb when she was buried in a field two years before Frederick West had met Rosemary.

As for Rosemary's sobs and shock when she was told that her husband had confessed to murdering Heather, the prosecution claimed that this was an Oscar-winning performance, said Mr Justice Mantell. 'That is something on which a judge cannot help a jury. You were here. You heard the tapes. You saw her in the witness-box. It is for you to decide.'

As the summing-up progressed, the judge moved from occasional levity to the most sombre gravity. On the first day, for example, he interrupted himself to pounce upon junior Crown counsel. 'Mr Chubb,' he said, 'you haven't done anything for the last few minutes. Tell me, what page is the photograph I am looking for?' He then added, 'That's the meanest trick a judge can play. I know. I've had it done to me.' There were smiles all round, and a certain gratitude that Mr Justice Mantell should be so human as to rescue us from intense concentration on iniquity. But by the third day, his mood was severe. It was as if he sensed that relaxation might create an atmosphere of typical British tolerance and willingness to allow 'the benefit of the doubt' – one of our most civilized traits. By the last morning, Monday, 20 November, it seemed that he was anxious to dispel doubt. Having placed considerable weight upon the evidence of Caroline Owens, Anne Marie Davis and Miss A, in so far as they shed light on seven of the charges faced by Rosemary West ('their evidence shows why the victims were taped, and also shows that Rosemary West was one of those who did the taping'), he dealt with the issue of severance, upon which he had earlier promised to give the clearest possible direction, in a matter of minutes. This evidence, he said, was not available or relevant to the deaths of Charmaine, Shirley Robinson or Heather. There was no sufficient coincidence of circumstances between these three counts and the other seven. 'You must disregard the evidence of these three witnesses when you come to consider these three counts.'

So what else did they have? 'Rosemary West was present in the house when Shirley Robinson must have met her death', said the judge, 'because Elizabeth Brewer went out when she was there and came back to discover Shirley had vanished.' As for Heather, the defendant had antipathy against her as well as the opportunity for murder. And one had to consider her lies. 'Lying in itself is not evidence of guilt. One may lie out of panic, or confusion, or to avoid embarrassment. But if you're sure she lied for some other reason, consciousness of guilt for example, or to deflect enquiries and mislead the investigation, then it may go to prove guilt.' She lied about Heather. She lied to Mrs Gough. 'Members of the jury, she has lied to you. Is there no innocent explanation? Then it supports the prosecution case, depending on how you view it.'

This was a cardinal error. A judge must never tell the jury that the defendant is a liar. That is for the jury to decide. For once Mr Justice Mantell forgot his covering 'you may think that'.

The judge rose at 4.30 p.m. on 20 November. The jury returned verdicts of guilty on the three counts of Charmaine, Heather and Shirley Robinson late the next day, but they could not agree on the other seven. They spent a second night ensconced in an hotel with court ushers lying awake to ensure they did not consult except when all eleven were present. On Wednesday 22nd they filed back into court with two questions put by the foreman:

1) 'Is the total absence of direct evidence other than the presence of their remains linking a victim to 25 Cromwell Street an obstacle to bringing in a guilty verdict?'
2) 'Is the jury entitled to rely on a combination of the presence of the remains together with conclusions drawn from the evidence of other actions taken by the defendant with, for example, Caroline Owens, Miss A, etc?'

In reply, Mr Justice Mantell re-read that part of his summing-up which dealt with similar fact evidence presented by the prosecution. The answer was no, the absence of direct evidence did not constitute an obstacle, and yes, they could rely on similar fact evidence allied to the discovery of human remains.

The jury returned to their room. Richard Ferguson QC invited the judge to call them back in order that he might read the defence's submission, namely that to infer guilt on one matter by reference to guilt on another and different matter was too great a leap to make. This would restore the balance of the instruction. The judge declined so to do, and the jury returned twenty-three minutes later with guilty verdicts on all remaining counts.

The defendant was impassive in the dock. Mantell made his now-famous remark after passing sentence of life imprisonment – 'If attention is paid to what I think, you will never be released.' Below stairs, out of sight of press and public, Rosemary West wept. Her step-daughter Anne Marie collapsed in the public gallery and was led away helpfully by her *Daily Star* friends.

Outside, Kathryn Halliday marched before cameras to tell the world how pleased she was.

Four months later, on Monday, 18 March 1996, the prisoner made application before the Lord Chief Justice of England, Lord Taylor of Gosforth, sitting with Mr Justice Newman and Mr Justice Mitchell at the Royal

Courts of Justice in London, for leave to appeal against her conviction. Once again it was Richard Ferguson QC who spoke on her behalf, and Brian Leveson QC who responded for the Crown.

Ferguson submitted that there were seven separate grounds for appeal. The reader is already familiar with most of them, as they had been anticipated as long ago as the committal proceedings, so a summarized form of them here should suffice. Furthermore, although counsel spoke all day Monday and part of Tuesday morning, and Mr Leveson rose to his feet to reply on Tuesday, it might be more useful to interlace their remarks, appending Leveson's response to each application before going on to the next.

The first ground for appeal was *Abuse of Process*, which was itself divided into three sub-sections. First, that the delay of over twenty years in bringing charges made it impossible to mount a cogent defence; second, that documentary evidence was not available, and in particular the 1972 statement of Caroline Owens had gone missing; third, that publicity in advance of the trial militated against fairness. Ferguson concentrated on this last limb, pointing out that the adverse publicity which had reflected upon the applicant (Mrs West) personally made her the victim of sensational and prejudicial attention, and also implied that because she was the occupant of the house in which human remains were found then her possible innocence on charges of murder was simply not credible (the 'she must have known' argument). Press influence upon the proceedings had been, said Mr Ferguson, 'malign'.

Mr Leveson replied that publicity alone could never be enough to stop a trial, and that some, in a case such as this, was inevitable. He allowed that there had been other cases wherein the degree of judgement exercised by newspapers had subverted the course of justice, but this was not one of them. The two bouts of publicity, in March 1994 (following the arrest of Frederick West) and

January 1995 (following his suicide) had been forgotten by the time Rosemary West came to trial, and the only really prejudicial piece, when the *Daily Mail* falsely alleged a friendship between the applicant and Myra Hindley, was not relevant in the context of the trial and had been the subject of a warning by the judge.

The second ground for appeal advanced by Mr Ferguson was *press interference* with all major witnesses by means of financial inducement. The dangers were threefold: that there would be a temptation to exaggerate testimony to make it more lurid, that testimony was rehearsed with journalists, and that witnesses had a conscious or unconscious desire to fulfil their contracts with newspapers. Whereas when a witness makes a statement to the police, the contact between them is monitored and subject to record, contacts with journalists were not monitored in any way, and there were no means of knowing whether a witness was drawn to a particular conclusion by a journalist in order to make his account more newsworthy. (Mr Ferguson did not say so, but the fierce competition between newspapers makes it certain that each will try to make his 'exclusive' account more outrageous than the other, and the witness is a mere pawn in this exercise.) Also unlike police officers, a journalist can attend throughout the trial, may have contact with a witness during it, and could discuss evidence with the witness.

Mr Leveson countered with the fact that, apart from Janet Leach, the payment of witnesses was known before the trial and disclosed to the defence, and also that Caroline Owens, Anne Marie Davis and Miss A had made their statements to the police long before having any contact with the press, and in the case of the first two, before the discovery of human remains at Cromwell Street, when there could be no commercial value in what they had to say. Only Kathryn Halliday had entered into a contract before making an official statement, and only Janet Leach's duplicity came close to derailing the proceedings. All of the defence's summonses to news-paper editors dropped away; none was fought through to a conclusion. Mr Leveson did not address the problem of corruption of witnesses by having conversations with pressmen, except to hint that it was only guesswork on the part of Mr Ferguson.

Mrs West's next contention was that evidence of her *sexual proclivity* should not have been allowed by the trial judge. Disclosing that he had written in advance of the trial (on 12 September 1995) objecting to the proposed inclusion of such evidence, Mr Ferguson accepted some blame for a failure to object with sufficient vigour during the course of the trial, but wished to make up for that now. He listed a number of occasions when the only purpose of a line of questioning was to illustrate the lack of morals of the accused, and not in any way to address an issue which the jury would have to consider. For example, witnesses Stanniland and Evans had been there to admit to intimate relations with Mrs West, Gillian Britt to testify that she heard noises from the room in which Mrs West entertained male friends, Mrs Tonks to indicate that she had been told the videos at the house were 'the real McCoy', Mr Dobbs to admit to meeting the defendant for regular sexual intercourse. The judge had gone so far, he went on, as to encourage the admission of irrelevant evidence. Witness Mr Jones was asked about the occasion when he had seen two women semi-naked in the living-room at Cromwell Street. When he had finished, Mr Justice Mantell reminded Mr Leveson that he had not asked what they were doing together. In fact, said Ferguson, they had been using a cucumber, and the judge seemed to think that this should have been told to the jury. In the event, it wasn't, but Ferguson claimed the incident served to illustrate that when you have such a dearth of evidence and reliance on prejudice there was a heavy responsibility upon the judge to ensure that the trial did not degenerate into a display of the moral conduct of the defendant.

The Lord Chief Justice instructed Mr Leveson that he did not need to hear him on the matter of sexual proclivity.

The fourth ground for appeal was the weight given to *similar fact* evidence, a subject already much addressed in this book. Ferguson's contention was that the issue to which the similar fact evidence was directed was not identified with sufficient clarity by the judge. 'The jury should have been told its purpose', he said, 'and should have been warned of the purpose for which it could not be relied upon.' Its effect was to try the accused on her character rather than on the evidence, on the doubtful principle of giving a dog a bad name. Evidence which went to criminal propensity used, for that reason, not to be allowed. Nowadays, he said, it was sometimes allowed if it was highly probative, but still the jury should be brought into the process and told what was going on. This did not happen at the West trial.

Mr Ferguson gave examples of the way in which it might have happened. It could have been pointed out that there were as many dissimilarities to weigh as there were similarities. For instance, none of the four living witnesses (Anne Marie Davis, Caroline Owens, Kathryn Halliday, Miss A) was threatened with death. The judge omitted to mention this when summing up. They were all voluntarily at Cromwell Street, and one of them lived there, whereas the prosecution claimed that seven victims were abducted and taken there by force; that was another 'striking dissimilarity'. All four were known to the Wests, whereas the seven who were presumably hijacked were necessarily strangers, another dissimilarity. It was therefore incumbent upon the judge to warn the jury that evidence of propensity could not be relied upon in the light of such weak similarities with other 'facts'.

The Lord Chief Justice and Richard Ferguson had an altercation over the difference between 'identity' and 'identification', with Lord Taylor pointing out that there was no dispute over the identity of Rosemary West, and

Mr Ferguson claiming that there was every reason to argue about her identification as the perpetrator of the crimes (this was by way of analysing legal opinions relating to 'similar fact' evidence being allowed for purposes of identification, looked at in Chapter Two). Counsel maintained that such evidence should only be admitted 'if there was no reasonable explanation [to account for it] other than the inculpation of the accused, no possible innocent explanation. We submit that there is another reasonable explanation, namely that Frederick West committed these crimes. He murdered, raped, assaulted and harassed young women prior to meeting the applicant and continued to do so afterwards.'

Brian Leveson responded to this ground in some detail, and with considerable effect. This case, he said, was concerned with *participation,* and similar fact evidence was therefore adduced in order to demonstrate the participation of the accused in joint venture with her husband. The four living victims were all subjected to sustained sexual abuse, as were, according to forensic study of their remains, the girls found at Cromwell Street. Moreover, the four living witnesses and seven dead ones were united by the use of gags and bindings. It was accepted that Fred West was capable of accosting women alone, but that did not mean he could not also accost them in the company of his wife, and the gags were in this regard very significant. Of those women picked up by Fred West acting alone, 'none was ever bound, none was ever gagged, none was ever stripped', and so the presence of gags indicated the participation of Rosemary West. Mr Leveson reminded us also that the sexual affair West conducted with Anne Marie, away from his wife Rosemary, never involved any use of gags or bindings. Nor was there a gag of any kind found with the remains of Anne McFall, murdered two years before Fred met Rose. (There were other restraining devices, which he did not mention, and other similarities which pointed to the same person being responsible for this murder and for the murder of Shirley Robinson eleven years later.)

The fifth appeal against conviction was made on the grounds that three counts of murder (Charmaine, Heather, Shirley Robinson) should have been *severed* from the other seven and tried separately, since the similar fact evidence could not have applied to them and it was unrealistic to expect any jury to ignore dramatically prejudicial evidence when deliberating upon those three counts. 'No direction, however stringent, could eliminate the possibility of their minds being influenced,' said Mr Ferguson. Lord Taylor interrupted to point out that severance was a matter entirely for the discretion of the trial judge and his decision had to be accepted. Ferguson responded that there had been no proper exercise of discretion and Mr Justice Mantell had not divulged any judicial reasoning – he had merely decided.

The Lord Chief Justice did not invite any remarks from Mr Leveson on this ground of appeal.

The final two grounds were concerned with *directions given by the judge* and the *partiality of his summing-up*. They were, in the event, conflated into one. Mr Ferguson read out to the court the final paragraphs of this summing-up to demonstrate how it rehearsed a series of Crown arguments which he put to the jury, while neglecting to mention the defence arguments which might counter them. Furthermore, he recalled the two questions put to the court by the foreman of the jury on Wednesday, 22 November. They concerned the absence of direct evidence and the reliance upon circumstantial evidence. The answer to the first question was no, to the second yes, in both instances supported by reading out the Crown's contentions while ignoring the defence's, except to say that the jury had to be satisfied they could draw the inferences which the Crown invited them to draw.

Mr Leveson retorted that the very nature of the questions indicated that the jury well understood the defence argument, and quite properly sought a direction in law only. They had, after all, returned verdicts of guilty on the other three counts which did not rely upon similar fact evidence the day before, and were now turning their attention to the seven counts to which this evidence did apply. That showed they had been properly directed and knew what they had to do. They also knew that the burden of proof lay on the prosecution.

Richard Ferguson, for the applicant, was given one last chance to come back on this defining moment of the trial. The fact that the jury felt the need to ask such questions, he said, showed that they had still not grasped the significance of similar fact evidence and were still uncertain, even after a lengthy summing-up, how to approach it. Therefore the summing-up had been faulty and unclear.

The Lord Chief Justice then withdrew for fifteen minutes' consultation with his fellow judges Mitchell and Newman and returned to announce that leave to appeal was refused. His reasons were published in a detailed judgement released on 2 April.

Lord Taylor began with a review of the narrative of events, which the reader may be spared (it contained only minor inaccuracies). He lay specific emphasis upon the evidence of Mrs West's responsibility for the murder of Shirley Robinson, pointing out that she 'must have been in the house' at the material time and that she had nodded in agreement when Fred had given Elizabeth Brewer spurious reasons for Shirley's departure (that, had she stayed, she would have 'ripped Liz's knickers off'). The Lord Chief further accepted that the atmosphere in the house had been tense since Fred's taunting reference to making Shirley his next wife, and cited Fred's admission to Janet Leach that Rosemary had told him what had happened to Shirley. He did not refer to Fred's chronic unreliability in recognizing truth, nor to the damning signature of the removed foetus which allied the death of Shirley to that of Anne McFall eleven years earlier.

Turning to the specific grounds which Mrs West had lodged to appeal against her conviction, the justices first considered whether or not there had been an abuse of process, a) because the trial had come too long after the offences, b) because publicity had prejudiced it, c) because documentation had disappeared (namely, Caroline Owens' 1972 statement). The first contention was dismissed with this very plain eloquence: 'The logic of the defence argument must be that if a murderer can bury victims and thereby conceal them for long enough, he or she should be immune from prosecution when they are discovered.' That assumes that the murderer is the person accused; if it is somebody else, then the person accused cannot summon a proper defence twenty or more years after the event. The three judges were satisfied that the delay was caused by concealment of bodies 'by both husband and wife'.

On the matter of publicity, they accepted that it had been 'extensive and hostile', but thought such was unavoidable in a case such as this and did not preclude a fair trial. 'To hold otherwise would mean that if allegations of murder are sufficiently horrendous so as inevitably to shock the nation, the accused cannot be tried. That would be absurd.' So would it, but the contention was not that the allegations were horrifying, rather that the character of the accused had been widely broadcast to her detriment. The Lord Chief Justice and his colleagues quoted Mr Justice Lawton in *Regina v. Kray* (1953) to the effect that 'the drama of a trial almost always has the effect of excluding from recollection that which went before', as well as Lord Taylor's own 1993 ruling that 'the nature of a trial is to focus the jury's minds on the evidence put before them rather than on matters outside the courtroom.' Briefly then, the jury can be relied upon to ignore sensational publicity.

As for Caroline Owens' crucial but missing statement, the judges decided 'we do not consider that its absence ... was a matter of such moment as could possibly found an application for a stay on the proceedings.'

They also thought that the corruption of witnesses with newspaper money was, though serious in principle, of minimal import in the West case. 'We reached the conclusion that they [media contracts] did not in the circumstances of this particular case render the verdicts unsafe. That is not to say that we wish to condone the payment or promise of payment to witnesses in advance of a trial. Far from it. We believe that in some circumstances it could put justice at risk.' The Lord Chief Justice hinted that, had Janet Leach been unable to return from hospital to continue her evidence, the case may have collapsed. He was clearly close to anger, but contained it. He hoped the possible prohibition of such contracts would be reviewed, but 'it is not for us to answer those questions.' It was, by implication, for the politicians and legislators, and they had better get on with it.

Disentangling the complex issues knotted within the 'similar fact' principle, the justices held their attention very closely upon the reasons adduced for admitting this kind of evidence against Rosemary West. For the first time, they made the tiny but telling point that no human remains were found in any kind of container (as might have been expected had they been carried to Cromwell Street), and averred that there were 'compelling inferences' that death, mutilation and dismemberment had all occurred at the premises, as had the sexual abuse which had preceded them. 'Throughout the material period', said the Lord Chief Justice, 'the applicant was living at the premises with her husband and children. Five of the seven victims [for which similar fact evidence was called] were buried in the cellar to which the applicant had a key.' Moreover, she was 'an energetic and committed participator' in acts of sexual violence . . . 'certainly no less active than her husband', which was why the jury were entitled to hear evidence pointing to her participation in such acts. Mr Ferguson had claimed there were striking dissimilarities to which the court should pay equal attention. Lord Taylor said dissimilarities alone would be insufficient to exclude such evidence (i.e., that the four living victims knew the defendant, were voluntary visitors to Cromwell Street or lived there, and survived, contrary in each particular to the seven dead ones), because 'the true relevance of the similar fact evidence lay in what *had* happened to the witnesses rather than in what had *not* happened to them.' It 'illuminated the circumstances which preceded the deaths.'

Mr Ferguson had further objected to evidence of the sexual proclivities of Mrs West. Lord Taylor said it was 'so slight . . . in advancing the prosecution's case' that it could not have had much effect. Besides, he said, Mr Justice Mantell had carefully monitored how much of it they should hear. 'In no sense were the prosecution being given a free hand.' So much for the learned judge's invitation to Mr Leveson to reveal that the defendant and another woman had been employing a cucumber for sexual gratification, which, to his credit, Leveson resisted. The judge was right to show the jury the size of the dildo which the defendant was in the habit of using because the Crown's case alleged sadism.

On the matter of severance, whether the three counts to which similar fact evidence could not apply should be tried separately from the other seven counts, the Lord Chief agreed with the trial judge that such a procedure would have achieved the opposite to that intended, for the publicity attending the first trial would have made a second one impossible without prejudice. That, too, was not a valid ground for appeal.

Finally, the three judges considered whether or not, having correctly admitted similar fact evidence, the trial judge gave sufficient direction to the jury as to when and where it could and could not be held relevant. 'The jury could not have been in any doubt as to why the evidence had been called,' they said, as they had been given very clear directions and it would be mischievous to assume they defied them. 'We see nothing unfair or unbalanced in the course taken by the judge,' they continued, and 'in our minds there can have been no confusion in the minds of the jury.' To which one may well assent – they knew perfectly well by this time that they should convict.

The two questions which the jury foreman put to the judge, after they had returned guilty verdicts on the three counts which did not require attention to similar fact evidence, exercised the judges' interpretation as a final point. Mr Leveson had maintained that the questions demonstrated the jury knew exactly what they were doing; Mr Ferguson contended that if they had done they would not have needed to ask. Lord Chief Justice Taylor agreed with Leveson. 'The very careful wording by the jury of the two questions they posed shows that they were clearly and accurately focusing on the very issue on which they had to decide.'

Lord Taylor made concluding remarks which did not address so much the grounds for appeal, all of which he and his colleagues had refused, but widened the court's purpose to a consideration of the correctness of the verdict. In this he was, unconsciously perhaps, reflecting public opinion rather than guiding it. Having stated that the evidence showed Fred and Rosemary were in the habit of sexually and sadistically abusing young girls in the cellar (even on the Crown's evidence there was only one young girl thus treated in the cellar, namely Anne Marie, and that on only two occasions before her long sexual association with her father began), the Lord Chief said that the jury had had the advantage of seeing and hearing Rosemary West for themselves. He concluded: 'Clearly they rejected her evidence. We fully understand their doing so. The concept of all these murders and burials taking place at the applicant's home and concurrently grave sexual abuse of other young girls being committed by both husband and wife together, without the latter being party to the killings, is, in our view, clearly one the jury were entitled to reject.'[3]

Not only must she have known about it, but she must have done it.

Unless new evidence turns up in the years to come, that is the end of the road for Rosemary Pauline West.

13

Folie à Deux

So, did the jury get it right after all? Did their ordinary collective wisdom, their intuition, hunch or 'gut reaction' lead them to the truth of Rosemary West's guilt? If so, that is as it should be, for while counsel may present information to them, and the judge may advise them how to interpret that information, it is ultimately upon their good sense that we must all rely, and nobody can dictate in what way that attribute should be used. Lord Scarman gave the view that the interpretation of fact depended to some extent upon common sense, and that a jury was brought into the legal system in order to provide it.[1] Was it therefore obvious to all but the myopic or legally precise that Rosemary West was guilty as charged, that she was part of a joint venture with Frederick West to commit murder, seven times for sadistic pleasure and three times for convenience? Was she, after all, 'in it together' with her husband from the day they met?

That married couples may grow to resemble one another is a banal truism which nevertheless warrants remark. The pathology of relationships is still imperfectly understood and scarcely studied in any depth. One of the only two possible explanations for the grim alliance of the Wests, if such it was, is that Frederick West corrupted his young wife and invested her with his murderous impulses, changing her character and moulding it to suit his purposes. She correspondingly fell prey, through love, to a dangerously immature and emotionally warped man. (The other possibility, that two equally psychotic and diseased individuals met by chance and discovered their shared interest is statistically implausible, though it was the rock of the prosecution's case.) Carl Gustav Jung worried about the danger of mental contagion within a marriage, when one partner's personality may impose and intrude upon the other's, stifling his or her growth towards individual autonomy. He wrote about a 'participation mystique', wherein an unconscious association took place between two people intimately connected, producing harmful effects. Jung held that the individual should be able to develop into the sunlit summits of a unique personality, free from undue influence, and that some intimate connections may work disastrously against this with, in effect, one partner kidnapping the other's ego.[2] In common parlance, this contamination of one person by another is referred to, erroneously, as 'folie à deux'.

Strictly speaking, 'folie à deux' is limited to the transference of one person's delusion, usually of a persecutory kind, on to another person, who then adopts the delusion as his or her own and shares its intensity. It should not be applied to couples who murder together, unless the motive for the crime is delusional and shared, but it has been so applied in a number of cases that, for the sake of convenience, it may be used here, as long as one bears its origin in mind. The term was first coined by Lasègue and Falret in 1877; although other authorities came up with alternative descriptions, such as 'infectiousness of insanity' and 'insanity by contagion', it is the more catchy 'folie à deux' which has endured. For the purposes of this discussion, it might have been helpful had the term 'conjugal insanity' advanced by J. Rhein in 1922 survived, because that is essentially what the proponents of marital influence in murder are suggesting.

Folie à deux involves the transference of delusional ideas and/or abnormal behaviour from one person to another, or the communication of an 'insane intellectual conception' from one mind to another mind. The receiving mind must be weak, dependent and impressionable for

377

this peculiar communication to work. Put more technically, it is 'the transference of delusional ideas from a person psychically ill to another, psychically healthy, who then accepts the delusional system of the ill person and assimilates it into the content of his own consciousness.'[3] Applied in the present case, it would suppose that the psychotic Frederick West infected Rosemary West with his psychosis and made her as mentally deranged as he was.

Most writers on the subject agree that for the transference to work the relationship between the partners must be one of dominance and submission. The psychotic who induces behaviour must be domineering and the recipient who is induced must be submissive. Further, the person induced is usually intellectually and morally weaker than the primary agent (by which it is meant that the primary agent is morally stronger, not morally better, i.e., that he is able to impose his own moral structure upon the other), or that the secondary partner is neurotic and feebleminded. One study points out that the passive partner is influenced to accept and absorb the delusions of the instigator 'by sheer force of superiority of will' – a significant choice of words in the circumstances. This is the language of aggression and of the sadistic impulse.

In the majority of cases studied the relationship is one of two sisters close in age, and the most fascinating case histories concern the transference of delusions of fame or persecution from sister to sister. But the second largest group involves husbands and wives. In both groups there is evidence of some defect of personality, as might be expected, and emotional immaturity. In the secondary person, the one influenced, there must be 'an innate inherent receptivity to a psychosis that finds root in his inborn willingness to receive the suggested pattern.' This would seem to run counter to the premise of a diseased person contaminating a healthy one, with which we started, for if the person influenced is already an empty vessel waiting to be filled, then influence is hardly necessary; both partners in the folie à deux would be psychotic, but only one of them would have acted on the psychosis prior to their joining forces. This is precisely what the protagonists of Rosemary West's guilt maintained; essentially it repeats the idea that both Fred and Rosemary were mad before they ran into each other, so that Rosemary did not need much 'infecting'.

Clearly, when one sister passes her own pattern of delusion on to another, the heredity of both must play a part, making them equally susceptible to influence – it is just a matter of timing which one will succumb first. With husband and wife heredity can play no part, but delusions are easily transmitted within a partnership which is glued by an especially close interdependence, of the sort which prosecutors claimed had developed between Fred and Rosemary. It may be an interdependence in which the desire of the weaker partner to imitate the perceived strengths of the other is the route she adopts to earn his exclusive attention. On this reading, it would be important to Rosemary West that she be infected by Frederick West's bold, assertive, magical and myth-making personality; she sought contamination, wanted it, embraced it.

The influence can best flourish if there is in addition an atmosphere of intense secrecy, privacy within the marriage, the two turning inwards with suffocating exclusivity and wilfully denying the possibility of influence from without. This intimacy of association is, according to a more recent study, facilitated by 'an anchoritic attitude towards their fellow creatures: thus, they tend to isolate themselves not only from the community at large but even from their own neighbours.'⁴ The authors identify the same prevalence of dominance and submission that we have already indicated within a 'leader-follower' relationship, and further add that the non-psychotic partner will experience great shock and strain when first confronted with the 'psychotic affliction of the inducer'. This would seem to tally with Rosemary West's anguished flight to her mother at the beginning of

1971 when she told her 'you don't know what he's capable of', which could pinpoint her first discovery of Fred's condition. On the other hand, the suffocating secrecy of a folie à deux relationship does not fit easily with various testimonies that the Wests' marriage was characterized by quite uncommon openness and candour, and especially by Mrs Agius' statement of their admissions to her personally (although that is only one neighbour). Very pertinently, the study affirms that 'the delusions of one person will only be taken over by a second person when they provoke in the latter a repressed phantasy life of similar content.' Accordingly, even if Rosemary was contaminated by Fred's madness and absorbed it into her own personality, she was ready for it, a view which reiterates the 'empty vessel' theory adumbrated above and the notion that Rosemary welcomed the infection.

We shall have to look more closely at the personalities of these two people to determine whether or not they might fit the pattern of transferred psychosis, but first, it is instructive to cast a glance at some other cases wherein something like folie à deux clearly operated to see what comparisons, if any, can be advanced with the West case. There is no example better known in Britain than the so-called Moors Murderers, Ian Brady and Myra Hindley, whose slaughter of five children took place between the summer of 1963 and the autumn of 1965. What is interesting about them, in the light of the present discussion, is that Ian Brady was definitely psychotic before the crimes, and has remained so since (he currently resides in Ashworth Hospital in Liverpool), whereas Hindley was not so before, and is not so now. Brady, the illegitimate son of a Glasgow waitress, grew up in slums and was nurtured on petty crime. He took part in many burglaries and spent some time in a Borstal institution. At twenty-one he was an outcast and misfit, morose and withdrawn, fascinated by Nazism and the Marquis de Sade. Myra Hindley was an ordinary girl from an ordinary family in Manchester, very fond of animals and children, a Catholic convert and law-abiding young woman who had done no harm to anyone. At eighteen she went to work as a typist at the same firm where Brady was employed as a stock-clerk. With their encounter began a catastrophic love affair.

There is no doubt that, had she met and fallen in love with somebody else, Myra Hindley's subsequent history would have been vastly different. 'She was, at that moment, in a state of abeyance,' wrote Emlyn Williams. 'As unconscious as an empty goblet ready to be filled to the brim, whether the potion is to be harmless wine, or arsenic. If . . . she had grown to take pride in her position as the wife of a successful man, and had become determined to share in that success, she would have exercised every ounce of will-power to bring her character into line with his.' But it was the degenerate and diseased Brady who fascinated her. She did not know why at first. She thought him reserved. She longed for him to take notice of her. And then, 'she scents the dark.' Gradually she was drawn in to his mysterious, elusive, satanic world, not quite knowing why and where it would lead, but hypnotized by Brady's power, 'as impassive as the gods who arrange the direst mischief, and then watch it happen.' In her diary she wrote, 'He has a cold and I would love to mother him.' Williams precisely describes Myra as an 'hallucinated lover', echoing the very process of transference of delusion which must operate in folie à deux. She was terrified of losing him, because she recognized that he did not need her, could exist without her, was an impenetrable stranger. In order to penetrate, she must become him. She evolved into a 'platinum-rinsed robot' in thrall to his commands, the slave to his master. Williams delineates the nature of this peculiar relationship, intimate yet false, in this way: 'No married couple of their age, in the history of the world, have spent so much time together, for so long. If they were handcuffed to each other, they could not be more inseparable . . . Indivisible. Yet he, every day, is more on his own.'[5]

As a result, for a period of more than two years Hindley attempted to share Brady's madness, was infected by it, her moral sense stifled by it, her autonomy cancelled by it. She helped him find children to abuse and kill, helped him clear up the mess afterwards, was triumphant with him posing on their graves, but in the end she could not reach him. For his part, Brady now claims she was not so passive, but insisted on killing one of the victims herself, but since he is irretrievably insane his word must be treated with caution. She now accepts that she was bad, not mad, at the time, but we may be allowed to suggest that she was temporarily mad as well, for she had tried to capture his madness and hold it within her own breast. That is the meaning of 'folie à deux'.

Her own recollections support the thesis of pathological connection. She says that she became estranged from her friends as the relationship with Brady developed, for they were appalled that she let him walk all over her. It mattered to him that she should be his exclusive property. 'He had a powerful personality, a magnet-like charisma into which my own personality, my whole self, became almost totally subsumed,' she wrote, admitting to fatal flaws in her character 'that contributed to the disintegration of that which was good in me and resulted in my sinking into the depths of depravity.' Interestingly, for those who believe Frederick West killed himself to save his wife, Myra Hindley has revealed that at one point Brady planned to commit suicide with the glass of a jamjar, telling her that she could not be found guilty if she went on trial without him.[6]

We have already had cause to look at the case of Cameron Hooker, who kidnapped hitch-hiker Colleen Stan in 1977 and kept her as his slave in a box for a period of seven years, with the complicity of his wife Janice. Both women seem to have been infected by Hooker's madness; not only did they not resist him for a long time, but they came to accept the bizarre arrange-

382

ment he imposed upon them as attractive. Janice had hoped Colleen would remove some of the pressure on her to submit to her husband's weird desire for bondage and throttling games, and though she was at first sickened by Hooker's treatment of Colleen, she slowly grew used to it. So did Colleen, who was allowed to go out jogging, to shop, to accompany Janice to a dance, to telephone her parents, and made no attempt to escape. With her it was a case of brainwashing, as she was made by custom and attrition to believe she really was a slave and wanted to bear her master a baby; but with Janice Hooker it was more likely a case of adopted or transferred madness. As with most of these cases, the induced madness was temporary – Janice Hooker eventually recovered and turned her husband in, having formed a more healthy alliance of trust and friendship with Colleen herself. Cameron Hooker, the inducer, like Ian Brady, never did recover. He was sentenced to one hundred and four years' imprisonment. His wife was not charged. It appeared they had previously kidnapped another hitch-hiker who had died under Cameron Hooker's torture.

The trial of David and Catherine Birnie in Perth, Western Australia, on 3 March 1987, was over in thirty minutes. Having pleaded guilty, they were each sentenced to life imprisonment for the torture and murder of several girls. There was no question but that their crimes had been the result of 'joint venture' and that Catherine had participated fully in them, but since no evidence as to character or influence was required in support of a guilty plea, public knowledge of the dynamics of their relationship is sparse. A psychologist who examined Mrs Birnie after her arrest said that he had never seen anyone so emotionally dependent upon another person; the inference was that she became a criminal by falling in love with a man who had a criminal personality.

The most vivid example of folie à deux involving murder must be that which came to light in Sacramento,

California, in 1980 with the arrest of Gerald and Charlene Gallego. Gallego was the son of a murderer (his father had been executed for three murders in 1955) and with an early history which shows some resemblance to that of Frederick West. He had been sentenced to youth custody at the age of thirteen for having sexual relations with a girl of seven. He married first at the age of eighteen, and six more times before he was thirty-two. He committed incest with his daughter from the time she was eight years old, then sodomized her at fourteen and raped her girlfriend. He married Charlene in 1978 (illegally – he was not divorced from his previous wife). She had led a sheltered, ordinary life as the spoilt daughter of a businessman. There was no history of law-breaking or any harmful act in her childhood and adolescence, though she appears to have been highly sexed at college. She married and divorced twice before she encountered Gallego.

Immediately, Charlene was fascinated by Gallego's passion for violence during their sexual relations, and appreciated his desire for a perfect sex slave. She said she would help him find one. Over the next two years they abducted nine young women, whom Gallego raped in the back of his van before killing and burying them. One was bound with a nylon rope; another had sand in her windpipe, indicating that she had been alive at the time of burial.

Gerald Gallego was sentenced to death on 21 June 1983. Charlene was given sixteen years only, as the result of an agreement to testify against her 'husband'. This was an example of the widespread practice in the United States of 'plea-bargaining', whereby a deal is done with justice in order to secure a conviction by doctoring the evidence of a crucial witness. Charlene said that she had needed the emotional support of Gallego and had agreed to help him search for sex slaves in return for it, but as she was told what to say by the prosecutors, who would have had no evidence without her, her *post facto* version of events cannot be trusted. The case has been pored over by students of folie à deux ever since, for it can show not only that infection by a murderer of a non-murderous person is possible, but even, if you credit the theories, that a non-murderous person may overtake the inducer in intensity.

It has been claimed that the one who appears to be the dominant partner in public is not always so in the criminal activity, and that therefore Charlene was the real criminal and Gallego merely seduced by her into taking part. Gallego's lawyers have gone so far as to suggest that she committed the murders alone, without his help. No-one knows for sure, of course. A Sacramento detective is on record as having it both ways. 'Her style', he said, 'was to pull the strings subtly, behind the scenes. She would discover her man's weak points and use them to her advantage.' On the other hand, when it came to murdering, Gallego was the manipulative one. 'He knew exactly how to push the right buttons to make her obey him.'' All of this is guesswork, familiar in weight to anyone who listened to the trial of Rosemary West. Gallego's lawyers, unwilling to accept he could be the inducer in folie à deux, sought to transfer the blame on to Charlene. The prosecutors of Rosemary West did so because the guilty man was already dead and could not be punished. Neither wished to look at the histories of the two protagonists. Any examination of the past and characters of Gerald and Charlene Gallego must conclude that he was the perpetrator of the crimes; the only question is how far he was able to seduce Charlene into colluding with him, and to what extent she absorbed and assimilated his murderous personality, given that her own personality had been harmless before she knew him. Charlene's plea-bargain did not include the contention that she knew nothing about the murders, because, of course, she could not have testified against her husband had that been the case. However superficially the two cases may resemble one another, Rosemary West was in a different situation. She did not claim she had been swallowed by her husband's personality in a kind of folie à deux – she said she did not know that he had such a personality. Does the evidence tell us she is lying?

Following the arrest of Frederick West and the gradual revelation of his crimes, Rosemary West turned utterly and completely against him. It was from her solicitor Leo Goatley that she heard of his confessions, as they mounted day after day, and other facts about him which she had not known, and she had occasionally to go to the lavatory to deal with the shock. To his daughter Anne Marie on a visit in prison Fred said, 'I've told them here I want you down as my next of kin. Rose don't want me no more. She don't want to know.'[8] Shortly afterwards they appeared side by side at Gloucester Magistrates' Court. As she squeezed past him, Fred placed his hand lightly on her shoulder. She visibly shrank from his touch. He tried again as they were led away, reaching out towards her. A police officer intercepted and pushed his hand away as Rosemary stretched to avoid him.[9] He tried to send messages to her through Stephen, imploring her to respond, but she adamantly refused to send any message back. Her daughter Mae considered visiting him and decided against it because she might upset Rosemary by so doing. The division between husband and wife was by then absolute. It mirrored the two previous occasions when, as Rosemary would see it, Fred had got her into trouble and she had put her foot down. The first was the assault on Caroline Owens in 1972, after which she made him promise never to involve her in anything like that again, and kept the press cutting of their appearance in court (she claimed) as a reminder. The second was the 1992 child-abuse case and the break-up of her family, following which she told the police to destroy the sex videos and aids which they had removed from the house because she did not want them around the place any more; she also made it clear to Fred that never again would she accede to his orders to sleep with other men. Now, the discovery that her husband had all along been a murderer was so stark that she blotted him out. That, at least, was her contention, from which she did not waver. Thenceforth she referred to him as 'Fred West' – the name of a semi-stranger who inhabited the man to whom she had been married. Mae was so convinced of her mother's innocence that she delayed her sister Heather's funeral until after the trial, in order that Rosemary should be free to attend. It was not to be.

'It was quite rare to see both my parents together,' said Stephen West. That was because, apart from their frequent sexual coupling, they had little in common and nothing to say to one another. Even the sex was unsatisfactory, with West making his wife feel cheap and exhorting her to sleep with as many men as possible so that he could satisfy her by proxy, as it were (which is not to say that she was not herself abnormally oversexed). He required to penetrate her himself after she returned. When she was with clients, she made sure the children knew that they could shout and she would come running, and she tried to protect them from predators. Fred, on the other hand, did not think that discretion in front of the children was either necessary or normal, and would not think twice about making his daughters available to other men. She told her children that if by chance they answered a telephone call from a man who began to talk dirty, they were to hang up immediately. In contrast, Fred sprinkled his every conversation with smutty talk to such an extent that he became a figure of fun, a kind of *commedia dell'arte* buffoon, boasting about his attractiveness to women and his countless conquests, a man whom nobody ever believed for an instant. Rosemary told her children never to get into strange cars; Fred's van was equipped with mattress and sex aids. When Fred built a small pond in the back garden, Rosemary persuaded him to fill it in because she had read somewhere of a child having wandered into such a pond and drowned. And when she had listened to the summing-up of Mr Justice Mantell at her trial and seen the very real possibility of a future behind bars, she told her daughter not to feel she would have to organize herself to visit. 'You'll have to go on as if I'd died,' she said. 'Try to make a life.'[10]

(Incidentally, Mae never doubted her mother's innocence, and her integrity was confirmed by her father. 'Mae's certainly not going to lie anyway,' he told the police. 'Whatever Mae says will be the dead truth . . . Mae will tell you exactly what she knows and it will be the truth . . . there's nothing about Mae that's false . . . she's a very educated young lady.'[11] His confidence ricocheted when Mae made a ten-page statement the following day in which she said that her father had regularly touched her lewdly; tense and embarrassed, he was stung into silence.)

Yet more disparities between the Wests were obvious to all who knew them. The boyfriend of one of the lodgers said of Fred that 'he never lost his temper. He was always all over you, joking and jolly.'[12] Rose lost her temper frequently and easily, and would lash out punishingly. 'She did have eight kids and a husband like Dad,' said Mae, 'so it's not surprising she was so stressed.' She chastised her children where Fred was indifferent to them; she was emotional when he was cold; she was maternal when he was distant and unreachable; she was shocked when he was unmoved; most of all, she was domestic when he was satanic and depraved.

Was Rosemary West depraved also? Very possibly. Had the evidence in the 1992 case been heard and weighed, it is quite likely that her acquiescence in child abuse and sexual assault would have earned her a prison sentence. Nor should one shirk the additional possibility that she was more than an accessory in these offences, that she was a prime mover, and that she lied about her involvement out of shame and guilt. That, too, incidentally, would place another gulf between her and Frederick West, who would not understand what it meant to feel shame. The same may apply to the important matter of the assaults against Anne Marie, which tipped the balance of jury feeling against her in Winchester. If she participated to the extent that the witness claimed, then that, too, would be enough to merit a substantial prison term as well as all the public denigration which has befallen her. But it is very important to remember that the relationship between Frederick West and his daughter was of long duration and in deepest secrecy. Mrs West did not know that her own stepdaughter was her rival in sexual matters because Fred made certain that his encounters with Anne Marie took place when Rosemary was out of the way, or in his van, in derelict houses and in fields, and moreover he exhorted Anne Marie never to tell her. She said so herself, so the fact is not in dispute. On one occasion, she said, Rosemary West was present in the van when an assault took place, after mother and stepdaughter had spent the evening in a pub. Mrs West was ignorant of the countless other occasions of sexual congress between Fred and Anne Marie (as she had also been ignorant of his furtive intercourse with Caroline Owens, quickly accomplished in her absence from the room).

There is no identity of purpose in all this, no confluence of character, no evidence of a shared psychosis which regarded the murder of adolescent girls as an illusion of pleasure, no indication whatever of a folie à deux properly understood. If it was there, then the usual manifestations of it were entirely lacking. The allegation that Rosemary West was part of a joint venture to kill rests upon one voice, that of the discredited Janet Leach, assigned to sit in on police interviews with Frederick West and, by her own admission, prepared to turn the opportunity thus offered to profitable use. West told her that he had been lying during his confession to cover up for Rosemary who was the real murderer.

He also said that he had come home to his caravan one day to discover that his first wife Rena had killed his mistress Anne McFall! An imputation of shared or imposed psychosis requires rather more than this to sustain it. The only proven psychotic in this miserable and overwhelmingly sad affair was Frederick Walter Stephen West.

One may even go further and posit Mrs West as a long-term victim of her husband. In their seminal study of 'Compliant Victims of the Sexual Sadist', Hazelwood, Warren and Dietz trace the strategy by which the sadist cancels the will of his female partner in a series of careful stages. It certainly takes months, and could take years, to accomplish, by which time the woman has been reduced to an appendage. In some of the stages identified by the authors (though not in all) one may frankly recognize the developing relationship between the Wests.

To begin with, the sexual sadist has an uncanny knack of selecting a woman with such low self-esteem that his unsubtle attentions astonish and captivate her. One woman in the sample said that she succumbed to the seduction of the sadist because she could not believe that he found her attractive, a sentiment echoed in Rosemary's early letter to Fred when she wrote, 'It just seems queer that anyone should think so much of me', and in her school report a few years before, that she was 'rather unsure of herself'. The men were all initially charming, generous and considerate, cultivating genuine affection before moving on to the next step. Fred gave Rosemary presents and made her feel useful in looking after his daughters.

The sadist will then subject his partner to systematic and escalating abuse, coupled with the threat that she will lose him if she does not submit. The wives or girlfriends were habitually kept captive for various periods, up to three days, bound with adhesive tape, or suspended by the wrists, or whipped with leather belts. Some were strangled manually during sexual activity or penetrated by large objects. Others were forced to have sex with other men, to submit to rape by the husband's friends, or to engage in sexual acts with another woman kidnapped by the husband for the purpose. All this demonstrably accords with Fred West's practices and with Rosemary's assertion that he required her to be sexually available to his mates. The women interviewed also said that the degree of pain and humiliation they suffered enabled their men to become sufficiently aroused for vaginal intercourse, another characteristic displayed by Fred. Ultimately, the sadists appear to lose all interest in vaginal intercourse *per se*.

Nearly half of the women sampled had been forced to write and sign documents of slavery or servitude. So had Rosemary West. Readers will recall the signed declaration, 'I Rose will do exactly what I am told, without questions, without losing my temper, for a period of three months from the end of my next period, as I think I owe this to Fred', and the other, unquotable in its entirety, which began, 'I Rosemary West known as Fred's cow' offering her bodily orifices for him to use as he would. These were manifestly the writings of a degraded and reduced woman; both documents bore the signature of Fred West as a demonstration that he 'owned' her. Whether or not he owned her to the extent of forcing her complicity in murder was at the root of the prosecution's case, based though it was on surmise.

Some of the women studied also reported that their men had demanded they describe sexual acts to them in language which they dictated, as the sadist needed certain 'trigger' words to satisfy him. Rosemary likewise had to describe what had been done to her by the other men her husband sent her to. Many were filmed or photographed naked in demeaning positions, as was Rosemary.

Gradually, the compliant victim comes under the control of her partner in every aspect of her life, though it may not appear so to outsiders, and as the sadist develops the need to repeat his perversions beyond the marital home with non-compliant victims, he is sometimes able to enlist the assistance of his spouse in his criminal activities, despite the fact that she is not herself criminally minded. Then, indeed, he will have the perfect slave.[13] This is what happened in some of the cases listed above (Birnie, Gallego, Hooker, Brady/Hindley), and what might have happened in the peculiar relationship between Frederick and Rosemary West. But with the death of Frederick West and the Crown's determination to depict his surviving wife as equally monstrous, the dynamics of this relationship were never properly explored. Whether she helped him or was, as she claimed, ignorant of his criminal activity outside the marriage may never wholly be known.

Repetitive or addictive murderers do not invent themselves. Their crimes do not erupt suddenly from a void, but are the final stage in a long period of gradual disintegration of personality, presaged by smaller offences such as theft or arson, and, even earlier, by delinquency and sullen withdrawal. You do not become a murderer because somebody asks you to, but because you have murderous impulses which are no longer impeded by inhibition. The idea that a 'serial killer' emerges out of a discussion, as a decision taken to follow an example, is not psychologically tenable. Murderers do not develop in that way. There was nothing in Rosemary's past to indicate criminal tendencies, and there had not been time, when she was a teenager, for the development of any such propensity, had it existed, to have advanced far enough or fast enough to explode into murder.

There were no witnesses to the alleged crimes, no confession from the defendant, no cause of death had been established for any of the victims, no time or place of death could be accurately ascribed, and on six counts there was nothing to suggest the defendant had even met the girls she was alleged to have killed. The only sure evidence was that their remains had been unearthed from beneath the house in which she had lived with the man who had confessed to murder and had not once, in 151 police interviews, implicated his wife. After her arrest she had been placed in safe houses by the police, who had installed devices to monitor her every conversation for two months, and not once had she said anything to indicate any knowledge of the crimes whatever.

Justice is not to do with popularity. It is to do with ascertainable facts and reasonable conclusions which may be deduced from them.

It is a fact that Frederick West killed before he met his second wife, and in recognizably the same manner as he continued to kill after he met her. It is a fact that his dismemberment and disposal of bodies did not alter in manner and ferocity after he set up home with the adolescent Rosemary from what it had been before. It is a fact that he had a string of offences on his record. It is a fact that he was in prison from November 1970 to (at the latest) 24 June 1971. It is a fact that his stepdaughter Charmaine had a permit to visit him on June 15, and that she therefore died between that date and the end of July 1971. It is a fact that when she died she had been living with, as her parents, a man who was a murderer and a sixteen-year-old girl who was not. And yet from these facts the inference was drawn twenty-three years later that she had been killed not by the murderer but by the sixteen-year-old girl. It has been part of the purpose of this book to propose as a fact that Charmaine was murdered by Frederick West and no-one else.

It is a fact that West attempted to pick up young girls when he was driving alone, and sometimes succeeded, going so far as to assault them. This continued during his marriage to Rosemary and without her knowledge. It is a fact that he picked up one girl when Rosemary was in the car with him, a girl already known to them both, and that they were both fined for indecent assault upon this girl. It is a fact that she lived. From these facts inferences have been drawn to suggest that Rosemary West was in a car with her husband when the deceased young women whose remains were discovered beneath their house were

393

abducted. It has been part of the purpose of this book to suggest that such inferences were improper.

It is a fact that Frederick West, and Frederick West only, indicated to police officers where they should dig for human remains, and in every case his indication proved to be accurate.

It is a fact that Anne Marie West had a long sexual relationship with her father and brought some girls to 25 Cromwell Street. It is a fact that she detested her step-mother Rosemary. It is a fact that she was horribly abused by both of them, but especially by the father whom she worshipped. The inference that Rosemary West was therefore capable of murder was, I submit, unjustifiable.

It is a fact that at the material time, 25 Cromwell Street was brimming with children, lodgers and lodgers' friends, none of whom was accused of having knowledge of the crimes committed there.

Questions as to the secret personalities of addictive (or 'serial') murderers, their preferences for acting alone, their lack of emotional understanding or affective responses, their necrophilic character and habit cannot be matters of fact but only of interpretation, experience and deduction by comparison. They are, however, a lot more than conjecture.

There remains one blatant fact which defeated explanation or interpretation, and from which an obvious inference was not drawn. This relates to the mystery of the missing bones. We recall that it was agreed these bones can only have disappeared as the result of deliberate mutilation; they did not drop off or wash away. It was tacitly agreed, therefore, that they still existed as physical objects after mutilation. The Crown maintained that death and dismemberment both took place at 25 Cromwell Street, and in the case of Shirley and Heather this is probably true. Yet if one adds up the number of bones which are missing from the totality of human remains, the figure runs into hundreds. Some are small, but others are vertebrae and ribs, and one is a shoulder-blade. Together they would fill a large space. Where are they?*

If the Crown is right, and all these bones were removed at 25 Cromwell Street, then it is simply not credible that not a single one of them should have been found. Even allowing for a scrupulous desire to get rid of evidence, or merely to clean up properly, something of these hundreds of fragments would remain, would have been missed or passed over or got covered up somehow, to be discovered years later. Yet they weren't. Given that the police search of the premises was so thorough as to be faultless, it follows that whatever they did not find was not there to be found in the first place. Therefore the missing bones were never at Cromwell Street.

There is a reasonable inference to be drawn from this, namely that the victims of these crimes were murdered and dismembered elsewhere. West said so himself more than once, though I should not wish that to be sufficient to lift conjecture into fact. It is not a fact. But it is an extremely strong likelihood in view of the facts, and the moment one accepts the logic of it, the idea that Mrs West must have known what was happening under her own roof loses most of its force.

It may be unpopular to posit the injury done to Rosemary West, a woman of deep flaws and lamentable morals whose behaviour inflicted harm upon a number of people close to her, and whose greatest misfortune was to have been the wife of a psychotic. Her conviction

---

* Lynda Gough was missing 113 bones, Carol Cooper 49, Lucy Partington 72, Thérèse Siegenthaler 39, Shirley Hubbard 40, Juanita Mott 88, Shirley Robinson 77, Alison Chambers 96, Heather West 38, a total of 612 at 25 Cromwell Street alone. When Frederick West was shown photographs of these remains on 11 May 1994, he felt faint and was permitted to go out to the yard for some fresh air.

at Winchester Crown Court arose fron concocted evidence with regard to Charmaine and conjecture with regard to all the other victims. No more. But justice demands that even the wicked must be treated fairly and not be condemned by suspicion merely. In the case of this particular defendant, the presumption of innocence was largely ignored even in court, and utterly derided by the popular press, which scented a new source of gold.

Nevertheless, her case was thoroughly prepared by Leo Goatley and put with eloquence by Richard Ferguson and Sasha Wass, and her jury attended to it assiduously. That they should decide she was guilty as charged was their privilege.

I only say that there were grounds for a reasonable man to argue for an acquittal.

Postscriptum

When this book was first published, it was not possible to name other men who might have been connected with criminal activities at Cromwell Street without transgressing against two principles which the author had striven hard to uphold, namely to rely on evidence rather than suspicion, and not to besmirch the course of justice by untimely interference. Frederick West's brother, John West, was facing charges of rape committed at the premises and would eventually go to trial. He had, therefore, to remain largely absent from this narrative in order to respect his right to an unprejudiced hearing. In November 1996, however, John West committed suicide while his jury were deliberating the evidence against him, thus cheating the system in exactly the same way as his brother had done. He died untainted by a verdict.

The jury had heard testimony of his repeated sexual intercourse with two girls at Cromwell Street. One of them, his niece Anne Marie West, said that she had been made to submit over 300 times to 'Uncle John' over a period of years. It was inferred that he was part of the perverted masculine right of conquest which held sway in that house, and which involved other men besides the two West brothers. It is still possible that charges may be brought against one or more of these other individuals. In the meantime, any chance that John West might have thrown additional light on the murders to which Frederick West confessed has been removed. He left no explanation for his act of self-destruction. Whether he expected conviction or further allegations can only be surmised. Anne Marie, overwhelmed with grief at the effect of her evidence, maintained that everything she had said in the witness-box had been the truth.

It was further confirmed in other published accounts that Bill Letts, Mrs West's father, had been a frequent visitor to the house and had continued his incest with her until long after her marriage, presumably with Frederick West's connivance. Rosemary West was required only to do as she was told and submit. The extent of her debasement at the hands of the men in her life can scarcely bear imagining. Interestingly, Bill Letts died in 1979, after which the sequence of murders of girls who were strangers came to an end. The only murder after this date is Frederick West's impetuous killing of his daughter Heather eight years later.

Rosemary West appears to have kept every scrap of paper which was relevant to her life. It was this 'archive' in the attic which enabled the police to reconstruct her movements and her moods and, to some extent, provide ammunition for a case against her. The most damaging piece of paper was the cutting from a local newspaper in 1972, which reported her and her husband's guilty pleas to the sexual assault upon Caroline Owens and their total fine of £100 for it. Mrs West's explanation was that she kept this cutting as a warning to her husband that he must never again get her into such trouble and that she would hold him to his promise not to involve other people in his fantasies. The prosecution's case was that she kept the cutting to flaunt her success in 'getting away with it' and evading a sentence commensurate with the crime committed. The jury accepted the prosecution's version.

There is a glaring inconsistency here which deserved greater attention. The disappearance of Lucy Partington was given huge coverage in the *Gloucester Citizen* and *Gloucester Echo*. When Carol Ann Cooper and Shirley Hubbard were spirited off the streets, they, too, appeared in the press, with photographs and accounts of their last known movements. Mysteriously, not one of these press reports was cut out by Mrs West and added to her private hoard. Had she been party to their disappearance and death, and had she wanted to gloat, she would have had far more reason than in 1972, for the girls' disappearance remained unsolved at the time and for long afterward. One could hardly 'get away with it' more spectacularly than that. But she didn't gloat. She paid no more attention to the reports than would anyone else reading the papers and watching the local news. The only reason can be that she simply did not know that the disappearance of these poor young women had anything to do with her or with the house in which she lived.

In this circuitous manner, the very weight which the prosecution gave to the 1972 press cutting must ultimately swing round and count in Mrs West's favour.

Moreover, Rosemary made it known that she wanted to move out of Cromwell Street, but she could not persuade her husband to agree. He was adamant that he would never leave the house, and faced with such obduracy, she had to acquiesce, apart from a brief period when she took a flat alone in Stroud Road. She could not fathom why he was so attached to the place. He, of course, knew what was hidden beneath it.

More is now known of Rosemary West's utter rejection of her husband after the gradual revelation of his murderous career in February, 1994. She was desperate to learn what had really happened to her daughter Heather and beseeched people for information in the days following the shocking news that he had confessed to her murder. They never spoke again, and she scorned his attempts to look at her. The inquest into Frederick West's suicide on New Year's Day, 1995, made it clear that he had been preparing for several weeks. The meticulous stitching of a rope made from prison blankets and the concealment of layers of tape made to slot through the small air vent above the door of his cell indicated that this was no impulsive gesture, but the result of morose brooding over a long period. As he said to both his children and the police, he could never recover from Rosemary's bitter contempt; his suicide was the only escape from it.

One of the most tragic figures to survive this appalling tale is Anne Marie. Daughter and long-term mistress of Frederick West, used as a sexual object by her own uncle, bereaved by the deaths of her sister, her mother, and a friend, she has borne the responsibility of revelation with courage and a rare capacity for endurance under relentless pressure of publicity. She has, for the most part, been isolated. Perhaps she might now be permitted a quiet life in an unremarkable street of an unknown town. Yet Anne Marie could still, perhaps, throw some further light on the fetid secrets of Cromwell Street by way of an exploration of her relationship with her father. It is acknowledged that this relationship was for the most part concealed from Rosemary West and that Anne Marie and her father had occasion for covert, private conversation. It is also acknowledged in various statements to the police that Anne Marie was the first person within the family to suspect that Heather was 'under the patio'. How she came to this conclusion has never been properly explored.

Brian Masters
Castries, 1997

Notes

1. CHARMAINE

1. Stephen and Mae West, *Inside 25 Cromwell Street* (Peter Grose, 1995), p. 4.
2. Andrew O'Hagan, *The Missing* (Picador, 1995), p. 204.
3. 22 August 1964.
4. O'Hagan, *The Missing*, p. 216.
5. *ibid.*, p. 219.
6. Gloucestershire Constabulary, interview No 25, 3 March 1994, pp. 1057–8.
7. Interview No 133, 30 June 1994, p. 5808.
8. Stephen and Mae West, *Inside 25 Cromwell Street*, p. 188.
9. Winchester Crown Court, 30 October 1995.
10. Winchester Crown Court, 10 October 1995.
11. 30 October 1995.
12. Statement of John Graham Ritchie, 24 August 1995.
13. Winchester Crown Court, 5 October 1995.
14. 30 October 1995.
15. quoted from letters exchanged between Frederick and Rosemary West in March, April and May 1971.
16. Interview No 69, 21 March 1994, pp. 3130–1, 3139.
17. Interview, 4 March 1994, pp. 44–52.
18. Interview No 69, 21 March 1994, pp. 3130–1, 3139.
19. Interview No 138, 2 July 1994, pp. 5925, 5931.

20. Interview No 88, 30 March 1994, p. 4079.
21. Winchester Crown Court, 9 and 30 October 1995.
22. *Daily Telegraph*, 23 November 1995.
23. Stephen and Mae West, *Inside 25 Cromwell Street*, p. 7.
24. Interview No 53, 14 March 1994, p. 2413.
25. Interview No 83, 28 March 1994, p. 3833.
26. Stephen and Mae West, *Inside 25 Cromwell Street*, pp. 18, 21.

2. SIMILAR FACTS

1. Winchester Crown Court, 30 October 1995.
2. 10 October 1995.
3. Interview No 87, 29 March 1994, p. 4009.
4. *Gloucester Citizen*, 13 January 1973.
5. Dursley Magistrates' Court, 7 February 1995.
6. Interview, 28 March 1994.
7. John Sprack, *Emmins on Criminal Procedure* (Blackstone Press, 6th ed. 1995), p. 96.
8. *D.P.P. v. Kilbourne* (1973), A.C. 729, 756.
9. Exall (1866), in Richard May, *Criminal Evidence* (Sweet & Maxwell, 3rd ed., 1995), 1–06.
10. Lord Chancellor Viscount Sankey in *Maxwell v. D.P.P.* (1935), A.C. 309.
11. May, *Criminal Evidence*, 7–21, 7–22.
12. Lord Simon of Glaisdale, in *Regina v. Kilbourne* (1973), A.C. 729.
13. *The Law Times*, 10 February 1894, p. 780.
14. *D.P.P. v. Boardman*, House of Lords, 9 April–13 November 1974, A.C. 421–464.
15. *ibid.*, p. 460.
16. Stephen Tumim, *Great Legal Disasters* (Arthur Barker, 1983), pp. 5–11.
17. May, *Criminal Evidence*, pp. 6–28.
18. *Woolmington v. D.P.P.* (1935), p. 481.
19. May, *Criminal Evidence*, pp. 4–28.
20. Winchester Crown Court, 11 October 1995.

21. *Daily Telegraph*, 23 November 1995.
22. Winchester Crown Court, 20 October 1995.

3. AT HOME

1. Gloucestershire Area Child Protection Committee, *Key Questions Answered – Contacts between the Public Services and the West Family 1965–1994*, pp. 13–14.
2. O'Hagan, *The Missing*, p. 237.
3. Interview No 49.
4. Howard Sounes, *Fred and Rose* (Warner Books, 1995), p. 165.
5. Daisy Letts to Rosemary West, 16 July 1981.
6. Interview No 55, 14 March 1994, pp. 2500–2505.
7. Stephen and Mae West, *Inside 25 Cromwell Street*, pp. 29–31.
8. *ibid.*, p. 28.
9. Sounes, *Fred and Rose*, p. 211.
10. *ibid.*, p. 212.
11. Witness Linda Tonks, Winchester Crown Court, 17 October 1995.
12. Stephen and Mae West, *Inside 25 Cromwell Street*, p. 34.
13. Gloucestershire Area Child Protection Committee, *Key Questions*, p. 9.
14. Stephen and Mae West, *Inside 25 Cromwell Street*, p. 44.
15. Winchester Crown Court, 17 October 1995.
16. *ibid.*
17. Interview No 62, 18 March 1994, p. 2858.
18. Stephen and Mae West, *Inside 25 Cromwell Street*, p. 43.
19. Interview No 79.
20. Anne Marie West, *Out of the Shadows* (Simon & Schuster, 1995) p. 154.
21. Interview No 8, 26 February 1994, p. 269.
22. Winchester Crown Court, 30 October 1995.

23. Stephen and Mae West, *Inside 25 Cromwell Street*, p. 70.
24. Interview at Fromside Clinic, 16 June 1994.
25. Stephen and Mae West, *Inside 25 Cromwell Street*, p. 18.
26. Sounes, *Fred and Rose*, p. 110.
27. Gloucestershire Area Child Protection Committee, *Key Questions*, p. 12.
28. Gloucestershire Area Child Protection Committee, *Bridge Report*, p. 8.
29. Stephen and Mae West, *Inside 25 Cromwell Street*, pp. 57, 58, 63.
30. Sounes, *Fred and Rose*, p. 31.
31. Stephen and Mae West, *Inside 25 Cromwell Street*, pp. 13–15.
32. Anne Marie West, *Out of the Shadows*, p. 121.
33. Interviews No 45 and No 74.
34. Sounes, *Fred and Rose*, p. 335.
35. *ibid.*, p. 66.
36. private conversation.
37. Anne Marie West, *Out of the Shadows*, p. 85.
38. Stephen and Mae West, *Inside 25 Cromwell Street*, p. 82.

4. ANNE MARIE

1. Dursley Magistrates' Court, 9 February 1995.
2. Anne Marie West, *Out of the Shadows*, p. 115.
3. Gloucestershire Area Child Protection Committee, *Key Questions*, p. 13.
4. Stephen and Mae West, *Inside 25 Cromwell Street*, pp. 75–78.
5. Anne Marie West, *Out of the Shadows*, p. 21.
6. S. K. Weinberg, *Incest Behaviour* (Citadel, New York, 1955).
7. Narcyz Lukianowicz, 'Paternal Incest', in *British Journal of Psychiatry* (1972), vol. 120, p. 305.
8. Ingrid Cooper and Bruno Cormier, 'Inter-

Generational Transmission of Incest', in *Canadian Journal of Psychiatry* (1982), vol. 27, p. 231.

9. Cooper and Cormier, in *Principles and Practice of Forensic Psychiatry* (Bluglass & Bowden eds., Churchill Livingstone, 1990), p. 753.

10. Roland C. Summit, 'The Child Sexual Abuse Accommodation Syndrome', in *Child Abuse & Neglect*, vol. 7 (1983), p. 183.

11. Karin C. Meiselman, *Incest* (Jossey-Bass, San Francisco, Washington & London, 1978).

12. *Principles and Practice of Forensic Psychiatry*, p. 758.

13. Cooper and Cormier, 'Inter-Generational Transmission of Incest', p. 234.

14. see discussion in Lukianowicz, 'Paternal Incest'.

15. Erich Fromm, *The Anatomy of Human Destructiveness* (Penguin, 1977), pp. 477–483.

16. Herschel Prins, *Dangerous Behaviour, the Law, and Mental Disorder* (Tavistock, 1986), p. 180.

17. Robert Bluglass, 'Incest', in *British Journal of Hospital Medicine*, August 1972, p. 155.

18. Herschel Prins, *Dangerous Behaviour, the Law, and Mental Disorder*, pp. 170, 179.

19. Summit, 'The Child Sexual Abuse Accommodation Syndrome', p. 178.

20. *Principles and Practice of Forensic Psychiatry*, p. 751.

21. *ibid.*, pp. 750, 752.

22. *ibid.*, p. 760.

23. Lisa Swanson and Mary Kay Biaggio, 'Therapeutic Perspectives on Father–Daughter Incest', in *The American Journal of Psychiatry*, vol. 142:6, June 1985, pp. 668–9.

24. Stephen and Mae West, *Inside 25 Cromwell Street*, p. 100.

25. Swanson and Biaggio, *op. cit.*, p. 671, quoted from de Young, *The Sexual Victimization of Children*, 1982.

26. *Principles and Practice of Forensic Psychiatry*, p. 755.

27. Stephen and Mae West, *Inside 25 Cromwell Street*, p. 96.

28. *ibid.*, p. 98.

29. Summit, 'The Child Sexual Abuse Accommodation Syndrome', pp. 183–4.

30. Anne Marie West, *Out of the Shadows*, pp. 61, 84.

31. Summit, 'The Child Sexual Abuse Accommodation Syndrome', p. 185.

32. *ibid.*, p. 182.

33. C.H. Kempe, in Swanson and Biaggio, *op. cit.*, p. 670.

34. Summit, 'The Child Sexual Abuse Accommodation Syndrome', pp. 186, 188.

35. Sounes, *Fred and Rose*, p. 196.

36. see, for example, Lukianowicz, 'Paternal Incest', who only found three, one of whom was neurotic and another schizophrenic, and J.E. Hall Williams, 'The Neglect of Incest', in *Medicine, Science and the Law*, vol. 14, no 1 (1974).

37. Summit, 'The Child Sexual Abuse Accommodation Syndrome', p. 187.

38. Stephen and Mae West, *Inside 25 Cromwell Street*, pp. 81, 83.

39. *Principles and Practice of Forensic Psychiatry*, p. 752.

40. Kaufman, *op. cit.*, p. 270.

41. Swanson and Biaggio, 'Therapeutic Perspectives on Father–Daughter Incest', p. 670.

42. Winchester Crown Court, 18 October 1995.

43. Anne Marie West, *Out of the Shadows*, p. 70.

44. Kaufman, *op. cit.*, p. 276.

45. Fromm, *The Anatomy of Human Destructiveness*, p. 483.

46. Alexandra Artley, *Murder in the Heart* (Hamish Hamilton, 1993), Foreword and *passim*.

5. CONTROL

1. Fromm, *The Anatomy of Human Destructiveness*, p. 318.
2. D.M. Gresswell and C.R. Hollin, 'Multiple Murder', in *British Journal of Criminology*, vol. 34, no 1 (1994).
3. Roy Hazelwood, Janet Warren, Park Dietz, 'Compliant Victims of the Sexual Sadist', in *Australian Family Physician*, vol. 22, part IV (1993).
4. Colin Wilson and Donald Seaman, *The Serial Killers* (W. H. Allen, 1990), p. 237.
5. quoted in Herschel Prins, *Dangerous Behaviour, The Law, and Mental Disorder*, p. 149.
6. Fromm, *The Anatomy of Human Destructiveness*, p. 335.
7. Sigmund Freud, *Three Essays on the Theory of Sexuality* (1905).
8. Alexander Pope, *An Essay on Man*, Epistle 2, line 131.
9. J. Paul de River, *The Sexual Criminal* (Charles Thomas, Springfield, Ill., 1956), p. 3.
10. Fromm, *The Anatomy of Human Destructiveness*, p. 386.
11. de River, *The Sexual Criminal*, p. 11.
12. Robert P. Brittain, 'The Sadistic Murderer', in *Medicine, Science and the Law*, vol. 10, no 4 (1970), pp. 198–207.
13. Fromm, *The Anatomy of Human Destructiveness*, p. 388.
14. Anthony Storr, 'Sadomasochism', in *Principles and Practice of Forensic Psychiatry*, VIII.7, p. 714.
15. Wilson and Seaman, *The Serial Killers*, p. 225.
16. Stanley Milgram, *Obedience to Authority* (Harper & Rowe, 1974), pp. 3–10.
17. Anthony Storr, 'Sadomasochism', p. 714.
18. *Principles and Practice of Forensic Psychiatry*, p. 566.

19. Park Elliott Dietz and Barbara Evans, Pornographic Imagery and Prevalence of Paraphilia', in *American Journal of Psychiatry*, 139:11 (November 1982), p. 1494.
20. *ibid.*
21. Wilson and Seaman, *The Serial Killers*, pp. 94–203, 139–146.
22. Jack Levin and James Alan Fox, *Mass Murder* (Plenum, 1985), pp. 65–68.
23. Interview, 28 March 1994.
24. Sounes, *Fred and Rose*, p. 251.
25. see various examples in Hazelwood, Warren, Dietz, 'Compliant Victims of the Sexual Sadist'.
26. Interview No 27.
27. Breslow, Evans, Langley, 'On the Prevalence and Roles of Females in the Sadomasochistic Subculture: Report of an Empirical Study', in *Archives of Sexual Behaviour*, vol. 14, no 4 (1985) pp. 303–317.
28. Anthony Storr, *Human Aggression* (Allen Lane, 1968), Introduction.
29. Fromm, *The Anatomy of Human Destructiveness*, p. 294.
30. Michael Ignatieff, 'Torture's Dead Simplicity', in *New Statesman*, 20 September 1985.
31. Sidney Bloch, 'Interrogation and Torture', in *Principles and Practice of Forensic Psychiatry*, VII.15, p. 618.

6. SHIRLEY AND HEATHER

1. Anne Marie West, *Out of the Shadows*, pp. 179–180.
2. Winchester Crown Court, 31 October 1995.
3. dated 11 August 1980.
4. Interview No 9.
5. Sounes, *Fred and Rose*, p. 176.
6. *ibid.*, p. 177.

7. Winchester Crown Court, 13 October 1995.
8. Interviews No 11, 12, 13, pp. 351, 389, 441.
9. Interviews No 17 and 18.
10. Interview No 18, 1 March 1994, p. 687.
11. Interview No 15, 28 February 1994, pp. 545, 568.
12. Anne Marie West, *Out of the Shadows*, p. 180.
13. Winchester Crown Court, 31 October 1995.
14. Winchester Crown Court, 13 October 1995.
15. Winchester Crown Court, 5 October 1995.
16. Statement of 15 March 1994, referred to in Interview No 67.
17. Stephen and Mae West, *Inside 25 Cromwell Street*, p. 78.
18. Interview with Rosemary West, 24 February 1994, p. 16.
19. Stephen and Mae West, *Inside 25 Cromwell Street*, p. 80.
20. Winchester Crown Court, 31 October 1995.
21. Interview No 3, 25 February 1994.
22. Interview No 4, 25 February 1994, p. 161.
23. Interview No 59, 17 March 1994, pp. 2719–2720.
24. Winchester Crown Court, 31 October 1995.
25. 2 February 1989.
26. Stephen and Mae West, *Inside 25 Cromwell Street*, p. 88.
27. Interview No 2.
28. Interview No 2, 24 February 1994, p. 85.
29. transcript of interviews on 24 and 25 February 1994, provided by Gloucestershire Constabulary.
30. Interview No 3, 25 February 1994.
31. Interview No 5, 25 February 1994, p. 195; No 12, 27 February 1994, pp. 404–406.
32. Interview No 4, p. 159.
33. Interview No 5, p. 177.
34. *ibid.*, p. 190.
35. Interview with Rosemary West, 26 February 1994.
36. Sounes, *Fred and Rose*, pp. 82–84.
37. Interview No 107, 23 April 1994, p. 4919.

7. DESTRUCTION

1. M. Hirschfeld, *Sexual Anomalies* (Emerson Books, New York, 1956).
2. H. von Hentig, *Der Nekrotope Mensch*, quoted in Fromm, *The Anatomy of Human Destructiveness*, p. 437.
3. de River, *The Sexual Criminal*, p. 141.
4. Howard Sounes, *Fred and Rose*, p. 77.
5. *ibid.*, p. 178.
6. see David Pitcher's article in *Principles and Practice of Forensic Psychiatry*, VIII.3.
7. Stephen and Mae West, *Inside 25 Cromwell Street*, p. 129.
8. Interview No 79, 26 March 1994, p. 3626.
9. *ibid.*, p. 3622.
10. Interview No 52, 11 March 1994, pp. 2371–2.

8. ARREST

1. Sounes, *Fred and Rose*, p. 229.
2. Gloucestershire Area Child Protection Committee, *Bridge Report*, pp. 12, 21; *Key Questions*, p. 5; Frederick West Interview No 21; transcripts of Frederick West tapes, pp. 121–122; Anne Marie West, *Out of the Shadows*, p. 14; Stephen and Mae West, *Inside 25 Cromwell Street*, pp. 109–119; Sounes, *Fred and Rose*, pp. 227–237; Gloucestershire Constabulary, Media Information Packs.
3. Stephen and Mae West, *Inside 25 Cromwell Street*, p. 120.
4. *ibid.*, p. 123.
5. Frederick West, Interview No 21.
6. Interview No 1, 24 February 1994, p. 33.
7. Interview No 86, 29 March 1994, p. 3967.
8. *ibid.*, p. 3999.
9. Interview No 36, 6 March 1994, p. 1618.
10. *ibid.*, p. 1651.

11. Interview No 118, 5 May 1994, pp. 5275, 5278, 5280.
12. Interview No 132, 13 May 1994, pp. 5710, 5714, 5718.
13. *ibid.*, p. 5720, and Interview No 138, 2 July 1994, p. 5923.
14. *ibid.*
15. Winchester Crown Court, 31 October 1995.
16. Karl Berg, *The Sadist* (Acorn Press, 1938).
17. *The Times*, 19 December 1991.

9. COMMITTAL

1. Sprack, *Emmins on Criminal Procedure*, p. 27.
2. Tumim, *Great Legal Disasters*, p. 46.
3. all references to the committal proceedings at Dursley Magistrates' Court are taken from the author's handwritten notes made at the time, supplemented by reports made for the Press Association by Allan Smith, Brendan Berry and Sue Clough.
4. see May, *Criminal Evidence*, pp. 6–30.

10. TRIAL

1. Fromside Clinic Report, provided for the defence.
2. Banks [1916], 2 KB 621.

11. TRIAL (cont.)

1. Interview No 83, 28 March 1994.
2. Interview No 27, 4 March 1994, pp. 1127–8.

12. VERDICT

1. May, *Criminal Evidence*, 14–21.
2. *ibid.*, 14–20.
3. judgement on *Regina v. Rosemary Pauline West* before the Lord Chief Justice, Mr Justice Mitchell and Mr Justice Newman, 2 April 1996.

13. FOLIE A DEUX

1. in *Moloney* (1985).
2. Anthony Storr, *Jung* (Fontana, 1973), pp. 26–27.
3. Alexander Gralnick, 'Folie à Deux – the Psychosis of Association: a review of 103 cases and the entire English literature with case presentations', in *Psychiatric Quarterly*, vol. 16, pp. 230–263 (1942).
4. Kenneth Dewhurst and John Todd, 'The Psychosis of Association – Folie à Deux', in *The Journal of Nervous and Mental Disease*, vol. 124, pp. 451–459.
5. Emlyn Williams, *Beyond Belief* (Hamish Hamilton, 1967; Pan Books, 1968), pp. 127, 135, 137, 140, 142, 149, 178.
6. *Guardian*, 18 December 1995.
7. *Frontier Justice*, p. 167.
8. Anne Marie West, *Out of the Shadows*, p. 200.
9. Howard Sounes, *Fred and Rose*, pp. 272–273.
10. Stephen and Mae West, *Inside 25 Cromwell Street*, p. 180.
11. Interview No 56, 14 March 1994, pp. 2540, 2541, 2545.
12. *Daily Telegraph*, 23 November 1995.
13. Hazelwood, Warren, Dietz, 'Compliant Victims of the Sexual Sadist', pp. 97–101.

Index

429

THE JIGSAW MAN
The Remarkable Career of Britain's Foremost Criminal Psychologist
by Paul Britton

'Riveting . . . Everyone should read it'
Frances Fyfield, *Observer*

Forensic psychologist Paul Britton asks himself four questions when he is faced with a crime: what has happened; who is the victim; how was it done; and why? Only when he has the answers to these questions can he address the fifth: who is responsible?

Paul Britton has assisted the police in over a hundred cases and has an almost mythic status in the field of crime deduction. His achievements read as though from the pages of Conan Doyle or Agatha Christie. What he searches for at the scene of the crime are not fingerprints, fibres or bloodstains – he looks for the 'mind trace' left behind by those responsible: the psychological characteristics that can help the police to identify and understand the nature of the perpetrator.

The Jigsaw Man is not only a detective story involving some of the most high-profile cases of recent years, but also a journey of discovery into the darkest recesses of the human mind to confront the question, 'Where does crime come from?'

'Britton has done hugely important work that saves lives. He is fascinating. His book is compelling'
Sunday Times

'A unique insight into the criminal mind . . . fascinating'
The Sun

THE EVIL THAT MEN DO
From Saints to Serial Killers:
Penetrating the nature of good and evil
by Brian Masters

The contradictions within human nature are many. We can be good and kind as well as cruel and selfish. According to science we are prisoners of our genetic inheritance. Are our impulses therefore to some extent inescapable, compelling us to behave in a certain manner, irrespective of the guidelines imposed by civilisation? Or can we determine our individual patterns of behaviour? Do we really have a choice?

The Evil That Men Do is a penetrating investigation into the nature of good and evil and the different ways in which they can be manifested. Using a diverse multitude of examples, it examines an age-old yet intensely contemporary subject at a time when civilisation seems to be on the verge of meltdown. It is an incisive, thoughtful and provocative meditation on a fundamental human question.

'A welcome link in the chain of understanding: a work of ambition and complexity underpinned by an obvious desire to grasp the fundamental nature of ourselves'
John Stalker, *Sunday Times*

'His discussion of evil and good is calmly, even cooly detailed. It is not merely by his compassionate distancing that Masters' study manages to engage the reader; his research seems to have been exhaustive and copious. His range is impressive'
Times Literary Supplement